SECOND EDITION

Fundamentals of Deep Learning

*Designing Next-Generation Machine
Intelligence Algorithms*

*Nithin Buduma, Nikhil Buduma, and Joe Papa
with contributions by Nicholas Locascio*

Beijing · Boston · Farnham · Sebastopol · Tokyo

Fundamentals of Deep Learning

by Nithin Buduma, Nikhil Buduma, and Joe Papa

Published by O'Reilly Media, Inc., 1005 Gravenstein Highway North, Sebastopol, CA 95472.

O'Reilly books may be purchased for educational, business, or sales promotional use. Online editions are also available for most titles (*http://oreilly.com*). For more information, contact our corporate/institutional sales department: 800-998-9938 or *corporate@oreilly.com*.

Acquisitions Editor: Rebecca Novack
Development Editor: Melissa Potter
Production Editor: Katherine Tozer
Copyeditor: Sonia Saruba
Proofreader: Stephanie English

Indexer: Judith McConville
Interior Designer: David Futato
Cover Designer: Karen Montgomery
Illustrator: Kate Dullea

June 2017:   First Edition
May 2022:   Second Edition

Revision History for the Second Edition
2022-05-16:   First Release

See *http://oreilly.com/catalog/errata.csp?isbn=9781492082187* for release details.

978-1-492-08218-7

LSI

Table of Contents

Preface

With the reinvigoration of neural networks in the 2000s, deep learning has become an extremely active area of research that is paving the way for modern machine learning. This book uses exposition and examples to help you understand major concepts in this complicated field. Large companies such as Google, Microsoft, and Facebook have taken notice and are actively growing in-house deep learning teams. For the rest of us, deep learning is still a pretty complex and difficult subject to grasp. Research papers are filled to the brim with jargon, and scattered online tutorials do little to help build a strong intuition for why and how deep learning practitioners approach problems. Our goal is to bridge this gap.

In this second edition, we provide more rigorous background sections in mathematics with the aim of better equipping you for the material in the rest of the book. In addition, we have updated chapters in sequence analysis, computer vision, and reinforcement learning with deep dives into the latest advancements in the fields. And finally, we have added new chapters in the fields of generative modeling and interpretability to provide you with a broader view of the field of deep learning. We hope that these updates inspire you to practice deep learning on their own and apply their learnings to solve meaningful problems in the real world.

Prerequisites and Objectives

This book is aimed at an audience with a basic operating understanding of calculus and Python programming. In this latest edition, we provide extensive mathematical background chapters, specifically in linear algebra and probability, to prepare you for the material that lies ahead.

By the end of the book, we hope you will be left with an intuition for how to approach problems using deep learning, the historical context for modern deep learning approaches, and a familiarity with implementing deep learning algorithms using the PyTorch open source library.

How Is This Book Organized?

The first chapters of this book are dedicated to developing mathematical maturity via deep dives into linear algebra and probability, which are deeply embedded in the field of deep learning. The next several chapters discuss the structure of feed-forward neural networks, how to implement them in code, and how to train and evaluate them on real-world datasets. The rest of the book is dedicated to specific applications of deep learning and understanding the intuition behind the specialized learning techniques and neural network architectures developed for those applications. Although we cover advanced research in these latter sections, we hope to provide a breakdown of these techniques that is derived from first principles and digestible.

Conventions Used in This Book

The following typographical conventions are used in this book:

Italic
> Indicates new terms, URLs, email addresses, filenames, and file extensions.

`Constant width`
> Used for program listings, as well as within paragraphs to refer to program elements such as variable or function names, databases, data types, environment variables, statements, and keywords.

This element signifies a general note.

This element indicates a warning or caution.

Using Code Examples

Supplemental material (code examples, exercises, etc.) is available for download at *https://github.com/darksigma/Fundamentals-of-Deep-Learning-Book*.

If you have a technical question or a problem using the code examples, please email *bookquestions@oreilly.com*.

This book is here to help you get your job done. In general, if example code is offered with this book, you may use it in your programs and documentation. You do not need to contact us for permission unless you're reproducing a significant portion of the code. For example, writing a program that uses several chunks of code from this book does not require permission. Selling or distributing examples from O'Reilly books does require permission. Answering a question by citing this book and quoting example code does not require permission. Incorporating a significant amount of example code from this book into your product's documentation does require permission.

We appreciate, but do not require, attribution. An attribution usually includes the title, author, publisher, and ISBN. For example: *Fundamentals of Deep Learning* by Nithin Buduma, Nikhil Buduma, and Joe Papa (O'Reilly). Copyright 2022 Nithin Buduma and Mobile Insights Technology Group, LLC, 978-1-492-08218-7."

If you feel your use of code examples falls outside fair use or the permission given above, feel free to contact us at *permissions@oreilly.com*.

O'Reilly Online Learning

 For more than 40 years, *O'Reilly Media* has provided technology and business training, knowledge, and insight to help companies succeed.

Our unique network of experts and innovators share their knowledge and expertise through books, articles, and our online learning platform. O'Reilly's online learning platform gives you on-demand access to live training courses, in-depth learning paths, interactive coding environments, and a vast collection of text and video from O'Reilly and 200+ other publishers. For more information, visit *https://oreilly.com*.

How to Contact Us

Please address comments and questions concerning this book to the publisher:

O'Reilly Media, Inc.
1005 Gravenstein Highway North
Sebastopol, CA 95472
800-998-9938 (in the United States or Canada)
707-829-0515 (international or local)
707-829-0104 (fax)

We have a web page for this book, where we list errata, examples, and any additional information. You can access this page at *https://oreil.ly/fundamentals-of-deep-learning-2e*.

Email *bookquestions@oreilly.com* to comment or ask technical questions about this book.

For news and information about our books and courses, visit *https://oreilly.com*.

Find us on LinkedIn: *https://www.linkedin.com/company/oreilly-media*.

Follow us on Twitter: *https://twitter.com/oreillymedia*.

Watch us on YouTube: *https://www.youtube.com/oreillymedia*.

Acknowledgements

We'd like to thank several people who have been instrumental in the completion of this text. We'd like to start by acknowledging Mostafa Samir and Surya Bhupatiraju, who contributed heavily to the content of Chapters 7 and 8. We also appreciate the contributions of Mohamed (Hassan) Kane and Anish Athalye, who worked on early versions of the code examples in this book's GitHub repository.

Nithin and Nikhil

This book would not have been possible without the never-ending support and expertise of our editor, Shannon Cutt. We'd also like to appreciate the commentary provided by our reviewers, Isaac Hodes, David Andrzejewski, Aaron Schumacher, Vishwesh Ravi Shrimali, Manjeet Dahiya, Ankur Patel, and Suneeta Mall, who provided thoughtful, in-depth, and technical commentary on the original drafts of the text. Finally, we are thankful for all of the insight provided by our friends and family members, including Jeff Dean, Venkat Buduma, William, and Jack, as we finalized the manuscript of the text.

Joe

Updating the code for this book with PyTorch has been an enjoyable and exciting experience. No endeavor like this can be achieved by one person alone. First, I would like to thank the PyTorch community and its 2,100+ contributors for continuing to grow and improve PyTorch and its deep learning capabilities. It is because of you that we can demonstrate the concepts described in this book.

I am forever grateful to Rebecca Novack for bringing me into this project and for her confidence in me as an author. Many thanks to Melissa Potter and the O'Reilly production staff in making this updated version come to life.

For his encouragement and support, I'd like to thank Matt Kirk. He's been my rock through it all. Thank you for our countless chats full of ideas and resources.

Special thanks to my kids, Savannah, Caroline, George, and Forrest, for being patient and understanding when Daddy had to work. And, most of all, thank you to my wife, Emily, who has always supported my dreams throughout life. While I diligently wrote code, she cared for our newborn through sleepless nights while ensuring the "big" kids had their needs met too. Without her, my contributions to this project would not be possible.

## CHAPTER 1

Fundamentals of Linear Algebra for Deep Learning

In this chapter, we cover important prerequisite knowledge that will motivate our discussion of deep learning techniques in the main text and the optional sidebars at the end of select chapters. Deep learning has recently experienced a renaissance, both in academic research and in the industry. It has pushed the limits of machine learning by leaps and bounds, revolutionizing fields such as computer vision and natural language processing. However, it is important to remember that deep learning is, at its core, a culmination of achievements in fields such as calculus, linear algebra, and probability. Although there are deeper connections to other fields of mathematics, we focus on the three listed here to help us broaden our perspective before diving into deep learning. These fields are key to unlocking both the big picture of deep learning and the intricate subtleties that make it as exciting as it is. In this first chapter on background, we cover the fundamentals of linear algebra.

Data Structures and Operations

The most important data structure in linear algebra (whenever we reference linear algebra in this text, we refer to its applied variety) is arguably the *matrix*, a 2D array of numbers where each entry can be indexed via its row and column. Think of an Excel spreadsheet, where you have offers from Company X and Company Y as two rows, and the columns represent some characteristic of each offer, such as starting salary, bonus, or position, as shown in Table 1-1.

Table 1-1. Excel spreadsheet

	Company X	Company Y
Salary	$50,000	$40,000
Bonus	$5,000	$7,500
Position	Engineer	Data Scientist

The table format is especially suited to keep track of such data, where you can index by row and column to find, for example, Company X's starting position. Matrices, similarly, are a multipurpose tool to hold all kinds of data, where the data we work in this book is of numerical form. In deep learning, matrices are often used to represent both datasets and weights in a neural network. A dataset, for example, has many individual data points with any number of associated features. A lizard dataset might contain information on length, weight, speed, age, and other important attributes. We can represent this intuitively as a matrix or table, where each row represents an individual lizard, and each column represents a lizard feature, such as age. However, as opposed to Table 1-1, the matrix stores only the numbers and assumes that the user has kept track of which rows correspond to which data points, which columns correspond to which feature, and what the units are for each feature, as you can see in Figure 1-1.

	Length	Weight	Speed	Age
Gecko Grayson	0.5m	0.1kg	4kph	10 years
Komodo Ken	2.5m	50kg	15kph	20 years
Iguana Ian	0.4m	9kg	30kph	15 years

$$\longrightarrow \begin{bmatrix} 0.5 & 0.1 & 4 & 10 \\ 2.5 & 50 & 15 & 20 \\ 0.4 & 9 & 30 & 15 \end{bmatrix}$$

Figure 1-1. A comparison of tables and matrices

On the right side, we have a matrix, where it's assumed, for example, that the age of each lizard is in years, and Komodo Ken weighs a whopping 50 kilograms! But why even work with matrices when tables clearly give the user more information? Well, in linear algebra and even deep learning, operations such as multiplication and addition are done on the tabular data itself, but such operations can only be computed efficiently when the data is in solely numerical format.

Much of the work in linear algebra centers on the emergent properties of matrices, which are especially interesting when the matrix has certain base attributes, and operations on these data structures. *Vectors*, which can be seen as a subset type of matrices, are a 1D array of numbers. This data structure can be used to represent an individual data point or the weights in a linear regression, for example. We cover properties of matrices and vectors as well as operations on both.

Matrix Operations

Matrices can be added, subtracted, and multiplied—there is no division of matrices, but there exists a similar concept called *inversion*.

When indexing a matrix, we use a tuple, where the first index represents the row number and the second index represents the column number. To add two matrices A and B, one loops through each index *(i,j)* of the two matrices, sums the two entries at the current index, and places that result in the same index *(i,j)* of a new matrix C, as can be seen in Figure 1-2.

$$\begin{bmatrix} 1 & 0 & 5 \\ 2 & 4 & 7 \end{bmatrix} + \begin{bmatrix} 5 & 3 & 2 \\ 6 & 1 & 4 \end{bmatrix} = \begin{bmatrix} 1+5 & 0+3 & 5+2 \\ 2+6 & 4+1 & 7+4 \end{bmatrix} = \begin{bmatrix} 6 & 3 & 7 \\ 8 & 5 & 11 \end{bmatrix}$$

Figure 1-2. Matrix addition

This algorithm implies that we can't add two matrices of different shapes, since indices that exist in one matrix wouldn't exist in the other. It also implies that the final matrix C is of the same shape as A and B. In addition to adding matrices, we can multiply a matrix by a scalar. This involves simply taking the scalar and multiplying each of the entries of the matrix by it (the shape of the resultant matrix stays constant), as depicted in Figure 1-3.

$$2 * \begin{bmatrix} 1 & 0 & 5 \\ 2 & 4 & 7 \end{bmatrix} = \begin{bmatrix} 2*1 & 2*0 & 2*5 \\ 2*2 & 2*4 & 2*7 \end{bmatrix} = \begin{bmatrix} 2 & 0 & 10 \\ 4 & 8 & 14 \end{bmatrix}$$

Figure 1-3. Scalar-matrix multiplication

These two operations, addition of matrices and scalar-matrix multiplication, lead us directly to matrix subtraction, since computing $A - B$ is the same as computing the matrix addition $A + (-B)$, and computing $-B$ is the product of a scalar -1 and the matrix B.

Multiplying two matrices starts to get interesting. For reasons beyond the scope of this text (motivations in a more theoretical flavor of linear algebra where matrices represent linear transformations), we define the matrix product $A \cdot B$ as:

Equation 1-1. Matrix multiplication formula

$$(A \cdot B)_{i,j} = \Sigma_{k'=1}^{k} A_{i,k'} B_{k',j}$$

In simpler terms, this means that the value at the index *(i,j)* of $A \cdot B$ is the sum of the product of the entries in the *i*th row of A with those of the *j*th column of B. Figure 1-4 is an example of matrix multiplication.

$$\begin{bmatrix} 4 & 6 \\ 2 & 7 \end{bmatrix} \cdot \begin{bmatrix} 1 & 9 \\ 5 & 2 \end{bmatrix} = \begin{bmatrix} 4*1+6*5 & 4*9+6*2 \\ 2*1+7*5 & 2*9+7*2 \end{bmatrix} = \begin{bmatrix} 34 & 48 \\ 37 & 32 \end{bmatrix}$$

Figure 1-4. Matrix multiplication

It follows that the rows of A and the columns of B must have the same length, so two matrices can be multiplied only if the shapes align. We use the term *dimension* to formally represent what we have referred to so far as *shape*: i.e., A is of dimension *m* by *k*, meaning it has *m* rows and *k* columns, and B is of dimension *k* by *n*. If this weren't the case, the formula for matrix multiplication would give us an indexing error. The dimension of the product is *m* by *n*, signifying an entry for every pair of rows in A and columns in B. This is the computational way of thinking about matrix multiplication, and it doesn't lend itself well to theoretical interpretation. We'll call Equation 1-1 the *dot product interpretation of matrix multiplication*, which will make more sense after reading "Vector Operations" on page 6.

Note that matrix multiplication is not commutative, i.e., $A \cdot B \neq B \cdot A$. Of course, if we were to take a matrix A that is 2 by 3 and a matrix B that is 3 by 5, for example, by the rules of matrix multiplication, $B \cdot A$ doesn't exist. However, even if the product were defined due to both matrices being *square*, where square means that the matrix has an equal number of rows and columns, the two products will not be the same (this is an exercise for you to explore on your own). However, matrix multiplication is associative, i.e., $A \cdot (B + C) = A \cdot B + A \cdot C$.

Let's delve into matrix multiplication a bit further. After some algebraic manipulation, we can see that another way to formulate matrix multiplication is:

$$(A \cdot B)_{.,j} = A \cdot B_{.,j}$$

This states that the *j*th column of the product $A \cdot B$ is the matrix product of A and the *j*th column of B, a vector. We'll call this *column vector interpretation of matrix multiplication*, as can be seen in Figure 1-5.

$$\begin{bmatrix} 4 & 6 \\ 2 & 7 \end{bmatrix} \cdot \begin{bmatrix} 1 & 9 \\ 5 & 2 \end{bmatrix} = \begin{bmatrix} \begin{bmatrix} 4 & 6 \\ 2 & 7 \end{bmatrix} \cdot \begin{bmatrix} 1 \\ 5 \end{bmatrix} & \begin{bmatrix} 4 & 6 \\ 2 & 7 \end{bmatrix} \cdot \begin{bmatrix} 9 \\ 2 \end{bmatrix} \end{bmatrix}$$

$$= \begin{bmatrix} 4*1 + 6*5 & 4*9 + 6*2 \\ 2*1 + 7*5 & 2*9 + 7*2 \end{bmatrix}$$

$$= \begin{bmatrix} 34 & 48 \\ 37 & 32 \end{bmatrix}$$

Figure 1-5. Matrix multiplication: another view

In a later section, we cover matrix-vector multiplication and different ways to think about this computation, which leads to more exciting properties regarding matrices.

One of the most important matrices in linear algebra is the *identity matrix*, which is a square matrix with 1s along the main diagonal and 0s in every other entry. This matrix is usually denoted as *I*. When computing the product of *I* with any other matrix *A*, the result is always *A*—thus its name, the identity matrix. Try multiplying a few matrices of your choosing with the appropriate-sized identity matrix to see why this is the case.

As noted at the beginning of the section, there is no such division operation for matrices, but there is the concept of inversion. The inverse of matrix *A* is matrix *B*, such that *AB* = *BA* = *I*, the identity matrix (similar in idea to a number's reciprocal—when dividing by a number on both sides of an equation, we can also think of this operation as multiplying both sides by its reciprocal). If such a *B* exists, we denote it as A^{-1}. From this definition, we know that *A* must be, at the very least, a square matrix since we are able to multiply *A* on either side by the same matrix A^{-1}, as you can see in Figure 1-6. Matrix inversion is deeply tied to other properties of matrices that we will discuss soon, which are the backbone of fundamental data science techniques. These techniques influenced their more complex neural variants, which researchers still use to this day.

$$\begin{bmatrix} \frac{-5}{4} & \frac{3}{4} \\ \frac{3}{4} & \frac{-1}{4} \end{bmatrix} \begin{bmatrix} 1 & 3 \\ 3 & 5 \end{bmatrix} = \begin{bmatrix} 1 & 3 \\ 3 & 5 \end{bmatrix} \begin{bmatrix} \frac{-5}{4} & \frac{3}{4} \\ \frac{3}{4} & \frac{-1}{4} \end{bmatrix} = \begin{bmatrix} 1 & 0 \\ 0 & 1 \end{bmatrix}$$

Figure 1-6. Matrix inversion

When trying to solve an equation such as $Ax = b$ for x, we would multiply both sides on the left by A^{-1} to get $x = A^{-1}b$ if A is invertible. There exists another necessary condition for A to be invertible, which we'll discuss later.

Vector Operations

Vectors can be seen as a subset of matrices, so a lot of the operations follow from the properties of addition, subtraction, multiplication, and inversion. However, there is some vector-specific terminology we should cover. When a vector is of dimension $1 \times n$, we call this vector a *row vector*, and when the vector is of dimension $n \times 1$, we call it a *column vector*. When taking matrix product of a row vector and a column vector, we can see that the result is a single number—we call this operation the *dot product*. Figure 1-7 is an example of the dot product of two vectors.

$$\begin{bmatrix} 4 & 3 & 6 \end{bmatrix} \begin{bmatrix} 2 \\ 7 \\ 1 \end{bmatrix} = 4*2 + 3*7 + 6*1 = 35$$

Figure 1-7. Dot product

Now the reason for the name dot product interpretation of matrix multiplication might make more sense. Looking back at Equation 1-1, we see that every entry in the matrix product $(A \cdot B)_{i,j}$ is just the dot product of the corresponding row $A_{i,\,\cdot}$ and the corresponding column $B_{\cdot,\,j}$.

When the dot product of two vectors is 0, we term the two vectors to be *orthogonal*. Orthogonality is a generalization of perpendicularity to any dimension, even those far beyond the ones we can imagine. You can check in the 2D case, for example, that any two vectors are perpendicular if and only if (also termed *iff*) they have a dot product of 0.

When we instead take the matrix product of a column vector and a row vector, we see that the result is quite surprisingly a matrix! This is termed the *outer product*. Figure 1-8 is the outer product of the same two vectors from the dot product example, except their roles as row and column vectors have been reversed.

$$\begin{bmatrix} 2 \\ 7 \\ 1 \end{bmatrix} \begin{bmatrix} 4 & 3 & 6 \end{bmatrix} = \begin{bmatrix} 2*4 & 2*3 & 2*6 \\ 7*4 & 7*3 & 7*6 \\ 1*4 & 1*3 & 1*6 \end{bmatrix}$$

Figure 1-8. Outer product

Matrix-Vector Multiplication

When multiplying a matrix A and a vector v, we can again do this via the dot product interpretation of matrix multiplication, as described previously. However, if we instead manipulate the expression slightly, we'll see that another way to formulate this product is:

$$Av = \Sigma_j v_j A_{.,j}$$

Where each v_j is a constant to be multiplied with its corresponding column of A. Figure 1-9 is an example of this method in action.

$$
\begin{bmatrix} 4 & 6 \\ 2 & 7 \\ 5 & 8 \end{bmatrix} \cdot \begin{bmatrix} 1 \\ 5 \end{bmatrix} = 1 * \begin{bmatrix} 4 \\ 2 \\ 5 \end{bmatrix} + 5 * \begin{bmatrix} 6 \\ 7 \\ 8 \end{bmatrix}
$$

$$
= \begin{bmatrix} 34 \\ 37 \\ 45 \end{bmatrix}
$$

Figure 1-9. Matrix-vector multiplication

This section introduced matrix and vector operations, which are fundamental to understanding the inner workings of a neural network. In the next section, we will use our knowledge of matrix and vector operations to concretely define some matrix properties, which serve as the basis for important data science and deep learning techniques.

The Fundamental Spaces

In this section, we will formally discuss some important matrix properties and provide some background knowledge on key algorithms in deep learning, such as representation learning.

The Column Space

Consider the set of all possible vectors v and their products Av. We term this the *column space* of A, or *C(A)*. The term column space is used because *C(A)* represents all possible linear combinations of the columns of A, where a linear combination of vectors is a sum of constant scalings of each vector. The constant scaling for each column vector of *A* is determined by the choice of *v*, as we just saw in the previous section.

The column space is an example of a *vector space,* which is the space defined by a list of vectors and all possible linear combinations of this collection. Properties for formally defining a vector space pop up directly from this intuition. For example, if a set of vectors is a vector space, then the vector that arises from multiplying any vector in the space by a scalar must also be in the space. In addition, if we were to add any two vectors in the space, the result should still be in the space. In both of these operations, the vectors we start with are known to be in the vector space, and thus can be formulated as linear combinations of the original list. By performing scalar multiplication or addition on the vectors in question, we are just computing linear combinations of linear combinations, which are still linear combinations, as can be seen in Figure 1-10.

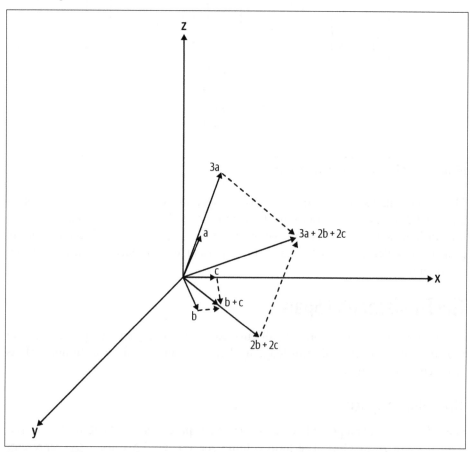

Figure 1-10. The sum, or linear combination, of the two linear combinations 3a and 2b + 2c is still a linear combination of the original vectors a, b, and c

We term these key properties of vector spaces *closed under scalar multiplication* and *closed under addition*. If a set of vectors doesn't always satisfy either of these properties, then the set clearly doesn't contain all possible linear combinations of the original list and is not a vector space.

An example of a vector space you're probably familiar with is $\mathbb{R}^3$, or the entire space defined by the *x-y-z* coordinate axis. The reason for the notation $\mathbb{R}^3$ is that each coordinate can take on any value in the reals, or $\mathbb{R}$, and there are three coordinates that uniquely define any such vector in this space. A collection of vectors that defines this space are the vectors (0,0,1),(0,1,0),(1,0,0), the unit vectors of each axis. Any vector *(a,b,c)* in the space can be written as $a*(1,0,0) + b*(0,1,0) + c*(0,0,1)$, a linear combination of the collection. In the other direction, any possible linear combination of the three vectors represents some vector *(a,b,c)* that lies in $\mathbb{R}^3$.

Often, there exist matrices A for which some columns are linear combinations of other columns. For example, imagine if in our lizard dataset from Figure 1-2, we had an additional feature for each lizard's weight, but instead in pounds. This is a clear redundancy in the data since this feature is completely determined by the feature for weight in kilograms. In other words, the new feature is a linear combination of the other features in the data—simply take the column for weight in kilograms, multiply it by 2.2, and sum it with all the other columns multiplied by zero to get the column for weight in pounds. Logically, if we were to remove these sorts of redundancies from *A,* then *C(A)* shouldn't change. One method to do this is to first create a list of all the original column vectors of *A,* where order is assigned arbitrarily. When iterating through the list, check to see if the current vector is a linear combination of all the vectors that precede it. If so, remove this vector from the list and continue. It's clear that the removed vector provided no additional information beyond the ones we've already seen.

The resulting list is called the *basis* of *C(A),* and the length of the basis is the *dimension* of *C(A)*. We say that the basis of any vector space *spans* the space, which means that all of the elements in the vector space can be formulated as a linear combination of basis vectors. In addition, the basis vectors are *linearly independent*, which means that none of the vectors can be written as a linear combination of the others, i.e., no redundancies. Going back to the example where we defined vector space, (0,0,1), (0,1,0),(1,0,0) would be a basis for the space $\mathbb{R}^3$, since no vector in the list is a linear combination of the others, and this list spans the entire space. And instead, the list (0,0,1),(0,1,0),(1,0,0),(2,5,1) spans the entire space, but is not linearly independent because (2,5,1) can be written as a linear combination of the first three vectors (we call such a list of vectors a *spanning list*, and of course the set of bases for a vector space is a subset of the set of spanning lists for the same space).

As we alluded to in the discussion of our lizard dataset, the basis of the column space, given each lizard feature is a column, is a concise representation of the information represented in the feature matrix. In the real world, where we often have thousands of features (e.g., each pixel in an image), achieving a concise representation of our data is quite desirable. Though this is a good start, identifying the clear redundancies in our data often isn't enough, as the randomness and complexity that exist in the real world tend to obscure these redundancies. Quantifying relationships between features can inform concise data representations, as we discuss at the end of this chapter and in Chapter 9 on representation learning.

The Null Space

Another key vector space is the *null space* of a matrix A, or N(A). This space consists of the vectors v such that $Av = 0$. We know that $v = 0$, the trivial solution, will always satisfy this property. If only the trivial solution is in the null space of a matrix, we call the space trivial. However, it is possible that there exist other solutions to this equation depending on the properties of A, or a nontrivial null space. For a vector v to satisfy $Av = 0$, v must be orthogonal to each of the rows of A, as shown in Figure 1-11.

$$\begin{bmatrix} 4 & 6 \\ 2 & 7 \\ 5 & 8 \end{bmatrix} \cdot \begin{bmatrix} x \\ y \end{bmatrix} = \begin{bmatrix} 0 \\ 0 \\ 0 \end{bmatrix}$$

$$\implies \begin{bmatrix} 4x + 6y = 0 \\ 2x + 7y = 0 \\ 5x + 8y = 0 \end{bmatrix}$$

Figure 1-11. The implication that the dot product between each row and the vector v must be equal to 0

Let's assume A is of dimension 2 by 3, for example. In our case, A's rows cannot span $\mathbb{R}^3$ due to A having only two rows (remember from our recent discussion that all bases have the same length, and all spanning lists are at least as long as all bases, so A's rows can be neither of these). At best, A's rows define a plane in the 3D coordinate system. The other two options are that the rows define a line or a point. The former occurs when A either has two nonzero rows, where one is a multiple of the other, or has one zero row and one nonzero row. The latter occurs when A has two zero rows, or in other words, is the zero matrix.

In the case where A's row space defines a plane (or even a line for that matter), all we'd need to do to find a vector in N(A) is:

1. Pick any vector v that doesn't lie in A's row space.

2. Find its projection v' onto the row space, where the projection of v is defined as the vector in the space closest to v. Geometrically, the projection looks as if we had dropped a line down from the tip of v perpendicular to the space, and connected a vector from the origin to that point on the space.

3. Compute $v - v'$, which is orthogonal to the row space and thus, each row vector.

Figure 1-12 depicts this.

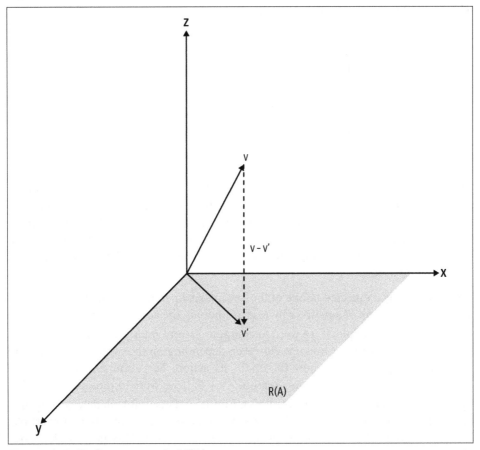

Figure 1-12. Finding a vector in N(A)

 Note that $v - v'$ is perpendicular to $R(A)$, the row space of A, since v' was formed by dropping a perpendicular to the plane down from its tip.

An important takeaway is that nontrivial solutions to $Av = 0$ exist when the rows of A do not span $\mathbb{R}^3$; more generally, if A is of dimension m by n, nontrivial solutions to $Av = 0$ exist when the row vectors do not span $\mathbb{R}^n$. The process is similar to that shown: pick a vector in $\mathbb{R}^n$ not in the row space, find its projection onto the row space, and subtract to get a vector in null space.

But we still must show that $N(A)$ itself is a vector space. We can easily see that any linear combination of nontrivial solutions to $Av = 0$ is still a solution. For example, given two nontrivial solutions v_1 and v_2 and their linear combination $c_1 v_1 + c_2 v_2$, where c_1 and c_2 are constants, we see that:

$$
\begin{aligned}
A(c_1 v_1 + c_2 v_2) & \\
= A(c_1 v_1) + A(c_2 v_2) & \\
= c_1 A v_1 + c_2 A v_2 & \\
= c_1 * 0 + c_2 * 0 & \\
= 0 &
\end{aligned}
$$

Where the first equality arises from the associativity of matrix multiplication and the second from the fact that c_1 and c_2 are constants. Note that this logic can be used for any number of nontrivial solutions, not just two. Thus, the null space is defined by some collection of vectors that can be boiled down to a basis, and contains all possible linear combinations of these vectors. These characteristics make the null space a vector space.

This is all deeply connected to one of the key matrix operations presented, the *matrix inverse*. We can think of a matrix's inverse as undoing the action of a matrix upon any other entity. For example, if we were to compute Av and multiply on the left by A^{-1}, we should be left with our initial v. However, depending on the properties of A, there can exist ambiguities as to how to "undo" its action. For example, let's say v was some nonzero vector, but for some reason, $Av = 0$. If we were to multiply on the left by A^{-1}, we'd be left with $v = 0$ instead of our initial v. This unfortunately goes against the properties of an inverse, and we declare that such a matrix is noninvertible, or *singular*. But why does this happen in the first place? This goes back to our observation about ambiguities. Because an inverse is supposed to undo the action of a matrix, if there are multiple initial vectors that map to the same vector via the matrix's action, trying to undo this action is impossible. Going back to our example, we know that nonzero vectors are mapped to 0 by A when A has a nontrivial null space. Thus, any matrix with a nontrivial null space is also singular.

Next, we will cover eigenvectors and eigenvalues, which puts all of the information we've learned so far into practice.

Eigenvectors and Eigenvalues

Matrices can act on vectors in many different ways. For most combinations of matrices and vectors, plotting the vector and its transformation doesn't provide us with any interesting patterns. However, for certain matrices and specific vectors for those matrices, the action of the matrix upon the vector gives us an informative and surprising result: the transformation is a scalar multiple of the original. We call these vectors *eigenvectors*, and the scalar multiple its corresponding *eigenvalue*. In this section, we discuss these very special vectors, relate back to the material presented in the previously, and begin the discussion connecting the theory of linear algebra with the practice of data science.

More formally, an eigenvector for a matrix A is a nonzero vector v such that $Av = cv$, where c is some constant (including zero, potentially), as shown in Figure 1-13.

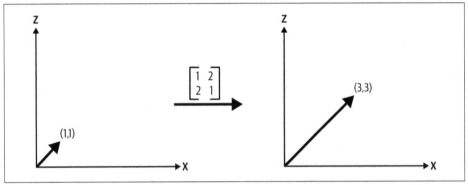

Figure 1-13. The vector (1,1) is an eigenvector of our matrix, with a corresponding eigenvalue of 3

Note that if we were to pick any random vector, such as (2,5), the transformation wouldn't look as meaningful as it does in Figure 1-13.

Of course, if A is a rectangular matrix, it's impossible for A to have any eigenvectors. The original vector and its transformation have different sizes, and thus transformation couldn't be a scalar multiple of the original. For this reason, we limit our discussion in this section to square matrices.

The simplest example is the identity matrix. Every nonzero vector is an eigenvector of the identity matrix since $Iv = v$ for all v, with each having an eigenvalue of

1. Oftentimes, however, the eigenvectors of a matrix won't be so obvious. How do we find these vectors and their corresponding eigenvalues? We know the conditions of any potential eigenvector; that is, if v is an eigenvector, it must satisfy $Av = cv$ for some scalar c:

$$Av = cv \Longleftrightarrow Av - cv = 0 \Longleftrightarrow (A - cI)v = 0$$

The implication here is that if $Av = cv$, then $A - cI$ must have a nontrivial null space. In the other direction, if we find a c such that $A - cI$ has a nontrivial null space, the nonzero vectors in the null space are eigenvectors of A. Of course, if A itself has a nontrivial null space, then all nonzero v in the null space satisfy the above implication when c is 0. More generally, however, we must find the c such that $A - cI$ has a nontrivial null space. As established previously, checking for a nontrivial null space is equivalent to testing for a matrix being singular. For reasons beyond the scope of this text, one way to test if $A - cI$ for some c is a singular matrix is to check whether its *determinant* is 0. We won't go into too much depth here, but we can think about the determinant as a function, or polynomial, that encodes properties of the matrix and results in a value of 0 iff the matrix is singular.

However, it would be inefficient, and frankly impossible, for us to test every possible c for a zero determinant. We can instead think of c as a variable in an equation and solve for it via the *characteristic polynomial,* which is the determinant of the matrix $A - cI$ set equal to 0. The roots of this polynomial give us the eigenvalues of A. To find their corresponding eigenvectors, we can plug each solution for c into $A - cI$ and then solve for the v that make(s) $(A - cI)v = 0$.

Calculating the determinant for any matrix of reasonable size is quite prohibitive in terms of computational cost. Although we won't delve further into this, algorithms today use a version of the QR algorithm (named after the QR matrix decomposition) to calculate the eigenvalues of a matrix. If you'd like to learn more about these and similar such algorithms, we highly recommend lecture notes or books on numerical linear algebra.

How does our study of eigenvalues and eigenvectors connect to that of data science? Principal component analysis, or PCA, is one of the most famous algorithms in data science, and it uses the eigenvectors and eigenvalues of a special matrix called the correlation matrix, which represents the quantifiable relationships between features alluded to earlier, to perform dimensionality reduction on the original data matrix. We will discuss correlation and related concepts in the next chapter on probability, and learn more about PCA in Chapter 8.

Summary

In this chapter, we investigated some of the basics of applied linear algebra. We learned about the key data structures and operations that rule both applied linear algebra and deep learning, and different ways to view these fundamental operations. For example, we learned that the dot product view of matrix multiplication was important from a computational lens, while the column vector approach led us into our discussion on the fundamental spaces quite naturally. We also got a peek at some of the surprising hidden properties of matrices, such as eigenvalues and eigenvectors, and how these properties are widely utilized in data science even to this day. In the next chapter, we will learn about the field of probability, which is often used in tandem with linear algebra to build complex, neural models used in the world.

## CHAPTER 2

Fundamentals of Probability

Probability is a field of mathematics that quantifies our uncertainty regarding events. For example, when rolling dice or flipping a coin, barring any irregularities in the dice or coin themselves, we are uncertain about the result to come. However, we can quantify our belief in each of the potential outcomes via probabilities. We say, for example, that on every coin toss the probability of the coin showing up heads is $\frac{1}{2}$. And on every dice roll, we say the probability of a die facing up with a five is $\frac{1}{6}$. These are the sorts of probabilities we talk about with ease in our daily lives, but how can we define and utilize them effectively? In this chapter we'll discuss the fundamentals of probability and how they connect to key concepts in deep learning.

Events and Probability

When running a trial such as rolling a dice or tossing a coin, we intuitively assign some belief to the trial's possible outcomes. In this section, we aim to formalize some of these concepts. In particular, we will begin by working in this *discrete* space, where discrete signifies a finite or countably infinite number of possibilities. Both rolling a dice and tossing a coin are in the discrete space—when rolling a fair dice there are six possible outcomes and when tossing a fair coin there are two. We term the entire set of possibilities for an experiment the *sample space*. For example, the numbers one through six would make up the sample space for rolling a fair dice. We can define *events* as subsets of the sample space. The event of rolling at least a three corresponds with the dice facing up any number in the subset of three, four, five, and six in the sample space defined previously. A set of probabilities that sum to one over all outcomes in the sample space is termed a *probability distribution* over that sample space, and these distributions will be the main focus of our discussion.

In general, we won't worry too much about where exactly these probabilities come from, as that requires a much more rigorous and thorough examination beyond the scope of this text. However, we will give some intuition about the different interpretations. At a high level, the *frequentist* view sees the probability of an outcome as arising from its frequency over a long-run experiment. In the case of fair dice, this view claims we can say the probability of any side of the dice showing up on a given roll is $\frac{1}{6}$, since performing a large number of rolls and counting up the occurrences of each side will give us an estimate that is roughly this fraction. As the number of rolls in the experiment grows, we see that this estimate gets closer and closer to the limit $\frac{1}{6}$, the outcome's probability.

On the other hand, the *Bayesian* view of probability is based more on quantifying our prior belief in hypotheses and how we update our beliefs in light of new data. For a fair dice, the Bayesian view would claim there is no prior information, both from the dice's structure and the rolling process, that would suggest any side of the dice as being more likely to turn up than any other side. Thus, we would say each outcome has probability $\frac{1}{6}$, our prior belief. The set of probabilities, in this case all being $\frac{1}{6}$, associated with each outcome is termed our *prior*. As we see new data, the Bayesian view gives us a methodology to update our prior accordingly, where we term this new belief our *posterior*. This Bayesian view is sometimes directly applied to neural network training, where we first assume that each weight in the network has some prior associated with it. As we train the network, we update the prior associated with each weight accordingly to better fit the data we see. At the end of the training, we are left with a posterior distribution associated with each weight.

We will assume throughout this chapter that the probabilities associated with any outcome have been determined via reasonable methods, and focus on how we can manipulate these probabilities for use in our analyses. We start with the four tenets of probability, specifically in the discrete space:

1. The sum of probabilities for all possible outcomes in a sample space must be equal to one. In other words, the probability distribution over the sample space must sum to one. This should make sense intuitively, since the set of all outcomes in the sample space must represent the entire set of possibilities. The probability distribution not summing to one would imply the existence of possibilities not accounted for, which is contradictory. Mathematically, we say that for any valid probability distribution, $\sum_o P(o) = 1$, where o represents an outcome.

2. Let E_1 be an event, and recall that we define an event as a subset of possible outcomes. We call E_1^c the *complement* of E_1, or all possible outcomes in the sample space that are not in E_1. The second tenet of probability is that $P(E_1) = 1 - P(E_1^c)$. This is just an application of the first tenet—if this were not true, it would clearly contradict the first tenet. In Figure 2-1, we see an example

of this, where S represents the entire space of outcomes, and the event and its complement together form the entirety of S.

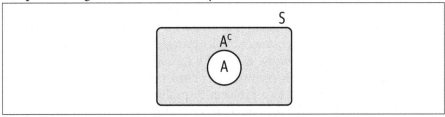

Figure 2-1. Event A and its complement interact to form the entire set of possibilities, S. The complement simply defines all the possibilities not originally in A.

3. Let E_1 and E_2 be two events, where E_1 is a subset (not necessarily strict) of E_2. The third tenet is that $P(E_1) \le P(E_2)$. This, again, shouldn't be too surprising—the second event has at least as many outcomes as the first event, and all the outcomes the first event has since the second is a superset of the first. If this tenet were not true, that would imply the existence of outcomes with negative probability, which is impossible from our definitions.

4. The fourth and last tenet of probability is the principle of inclusion and exclusion, which states that $P(A \cup B) = P(A) + P(B) - P(A \cap B)$. For those not familiar with this terminology, the $\cup$ denotes the *union* of the two events, a set operation that takes the two events and returns an event that contains all elements from the two original sets. The $\cap$, or *intersection*, is a set operation that returns an event that contains all elements belonging to both of the two original sets. The idea behind the equality presented is that by just naively summing the probabilities of A and B, we double-count the elements that belong to both sets. Thus, to accurately obtain the probability of the union, we must subtract the probability of the intersection. In Figure 2-2, we show two events and what their intersection would look like physically, while the union is all the outcomes in the combined area of the events.

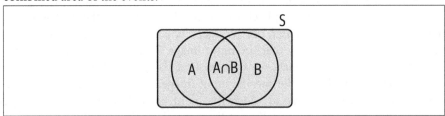

Figure 2-2. The middle sliver is the overlap between the two sets, containing all the outcomes that are in both sets. The union is all the events in the combined area of the two circles; if we were to add their probabilities naively, we would double-count all the outcomes in the middle sliver.

These tenets of probability find their way into everything that has to do with the field. For example, in deep learning, most of our problems fall into one of two categories: *regression* and *classification*. In the latter, we train a neural model that can predict the likelihood that the input belongs to one of a discrete number of classes. The famous MNIST digits dataset, for example, provides us with pictures of digits and associated numerical labels in the range of 0 through 9. Our objective is to build a *classifier* that can take in this picture and return the most likely label as its guess. This is naturally formulated as a problem in probability—the classifier produces a probability distribution over the sample space, 0 through 9, for any given input and its best guess is the digit that is assigned the highest probability. How does this relate to our tenets? Since the classifier is producing a probability distribution, it must follow the tenets. For example, the probabilities associated with each digit must sum to one—a quick back-of-the-envelope check to ensure the model isn't buggy. In the next section, we cover probabilities where we are initially given relevant information that affects our beliefs and how to use that information.

Conditional Probability

Knowing information often changes our beliefs, and by consequence, our probabilities. Going back to our classic dice example, we may roll the dice thinking that it's fair, while in reality there's a hidden weight at the dice's core, making it more likely to land up a number greater than three. As we roll the dice, we of course start to notice this pattern, and our belief regarding the dice's fairness starts to shift. This is at the core of conditional probability itself. Instead of thinking simply about $P(biased)$ or $P(fair)$, we have to think about probabilities like $P(biased|information)$ instead. This quantity, which we term a *conditional probability,* is spoken as "the probability the dice is biased *given* the information we've seen."

How do we think about such probabilities intuitively? For starters, we must imagine that we are now in a different universe than the one we started in. The new universe is one that incorporates the information we've seen since the start of the experiment, e.g., our past dice rolls. Going back to our MNIST example, the probability distribution that the trained neural net produces is actually a conditional probability distribution. The probability that the input image is zero, for example, can be seen as *P(0|input)*. In plain English, we want to find the probability of a zero given all of the pixels that make up the specific input image we fed into our neural net. Our new universe is the universe in which the input pixels have taken on this specific configuration of values. This is distinct from simply looking at *P(0)*, the probability of returning a zero, which we can think about in terms of prior belief. Without any knowledge of the input pixel configuration, we'd have no reason to believe that the possibility of returning a zero is any more or less likely than that of any other digit.

Sometimes, seeing certain information does not change our probabilities—we call this property *independence*. For example, Tom Brady may have thrown a touchdown pass after the third roll of our experiment, but incorporating that information into our new universe should (hopefully!) have no impact on the likelihood of the dice being biased. We state this independence property as *P(biased|Tom Brady throws a touchdown pass) = P(biased)*. Note that any two events E_1 and E_2 that satisfy this property are independent. Perhaps slightly more counterintuitively, if it happens to be the case that all of our dice rolls so far don't numerically change our prior belief regarding the dice's fairness (maybe the dice rolls so far have shown up evenly across one through six and our initial prior belief was that the dice was fair), we'd still say that these events are independent. Finally, note that independence is symmetric: if $P(E_1|E_2) = P(E_1)$, then it is also the case that $P(E_2|E_1) = P(E_2)$.

In the previous section, we introduced intersection and union notation. It turns out that we can break down the intersection operation into a product of probabilities. We have the following equality: $P(E_1 \cap E_2) = P(E_1|E_2) * P(E_2)$. Let's break down the intuition here. On the left side, we have the probability that both events E_1 and E_2 have occurred. On the right side, we have the same idea, but expressed slightly differently. In the universe where both events have occurred, one way to arrive in this universe is to first have E_2 occur, followed by E_1. Porting this intuition into mathematical terms, we must first find the probability that E_2 has occurred, followed by the probability that E_1 has occurred in the universe where E_2 has already occurred. How do we combine these two probabilities? Intuitively, it makes sense that we multiply them—we must have both events occur, the first unconditionally and the second in the universe where the first has already occurred. Note that the order of these events doesn't really matter, as both paths get us to the same universe. So, more completely, $P(E_1 \cap E_2) = P(E_1|E_2) * P(E_2) = P(E_2|E_1) * P(E_1)$.

However, some of these paths make much more physical sense than others. For example, if we think of E_1 as the event where someone contracts a disease, and E_2 as the event where the patient shows symptoms of the disease, the path in which the patient contracts the disease and then shows symptoms makes much more physical sense than the reverse.

In the case where the two events are independent, we have that $P(E_1 \cap E_2) = P(E_1|E_2) * P(E_2) = P(E_1) * P(E_2)$. Hopefully this makes some intuitive sense. In the independence scenario, the fact that E_2 has occurred doesn't affect the chances of E_1 occurring; i.e., incorporating this information into the new universe doesn't affect the probability of the next event. In the next section, we cover random variables, which are relevant summaries of events and also have their own probability distributions.

Random Variables

Once again, let's consider the coin flipping experiment. If we flip a coin some finite number of times, natural questions start to arise. How many heads did we encounter during our experiment? How many tails? How many tails until the first head? Every outcome in such an experiment has an answer to each of the listed questions. If we flip a coin say, five times, and we receive the sequence TTHHT, we have seen two heads, three tails, and two tails until the first head.

We can think of a *random variable* as a map, or a function, from the sample space to another space, such as the integers in Figure 2-3. Such a function would take as input the sequence TTHHT and output one of the three answers listed depending on the question we ask. The value that the random variable takes on would be the output associated with result of the experiment. Although random variables are deterministic in that they map a given input to a single output, they are not deterministic in that they also have a distribution associated with their output space. This is due to the inherent randomness in the experiment—depending on the probability of the input outcome, its corresponding output may be more or less likely than other outputs.

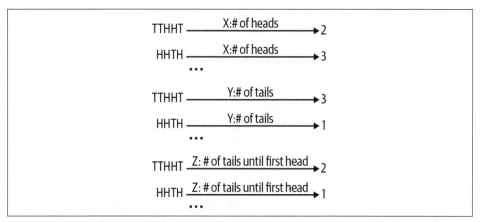

Figure 2-3. Random variables X, Y, and Z all act on the same sample space, but have varying outputs. It's important to keep in mind what you're measuring!

 Note that multiple inputs could map to the same output. For example, $X(HHH) = 3$ in addition to $X(HHTH)$ in Figure 2-3.

One easy way to begin is to just think of this map as an identity function—whatever we flip or roll, its map in the output space is exactly the same as the input. Encoding a heads as a one and a tails as a zero, we can define a random variable representing the coin flip as whether the coin came up heads, i.e., *C(1) = 1,* where *C* is our random variable. In the dice scenario, the mapped output is the same as whatever we rolled, i.e., *D(5) = 5,* where *D* is our random variable.

Why should we care about random variables and their distributions? It turns out they play a vital role in deep learning and machine learning as a whole. For example, in Chapter 4, we will cover the concept of *dropout*, a technique for mitigating overfitting in neural networks. The idea of a dropout layer is that, during training, it independently and at random masks every neuron in the previous layer with some probability. This prevents the network from becoming overly dependent on specific connections or subnetworks. We can think of every neuron in the previous layer as representing a coin flip-type experiment. The only difference is that we set the probability of this experiment, rather than a fair coin having the default probability $\frac{1}{2}$ of showing up either side. Each neuron has a random variable *X* associated with it, with input one if the dropout layer decides to mask it and zero otherwise. *X* is an identity function from the input space to the output space, i.e., *X(1) = 1* and *X(0) = 0.*

Random variables, in general, need not be the identity map. Most functions you can think of are valid methods of mapping the input space to an output space where the random variable is defined. For example, if the input space were every possible length *n* sequence of coin flips, the function could be to count the number of heads in the sequence and square it. Some random variables can even be expressed as functions of other random variables, or a function of a function, as we will cover later. If we again consider the input space of every possible length *n* sequence of coin flips, the random variable counting the number of heads in the input sequence is the same as counting whether each individual coin flip turned up heads and taking a sum of all of those values. In mathematical terms, we say $X = \Sigma_{i=1}^{n} C_i$, where *X* is the random variable representing the total number of heads, and C_i is the binary random variable associated with the *i*th coin flip. Back to the dropout example, we can think of the random variable representing the total number of masked-out neurons as the sum of binary random variables representing each neuron.

In the future, when we want to refer to the event where the random variable takes on a specific value *c* (the domain being the output space we've been referring to, e.g., the number of heads in a sequence of coin flips), we will write this concisely as *X = c.* We denote the probability that the random variable takes on a specific value as *P(X = c),* for example. The probability that the random variable takes on any given value in the output space is just the sum of the probabilities of the inputs that map to it. This should make some intuitive sense, as this is basically the fourth tenet of probability where the intersection between any two events is the empty set since all the events we start from are individual, distinct inputs. Note that *P(X)* itself is also a probability distribution that follows all the basic tenets of probability described in the first section. In the next section, we consider statistics regarding random variables.

Expectation

As we discussed, a random variable is a map from input space to output space, where inputs are generated according to some probability distribution. The random variable can be thought of as a relevant summary of the input, and can take on many forms depending on the question we ask. Sometimes, it's useful to understand statistics regarding the random variable. For example, if we flip a coin eight times, how many heads do we expect to see on average? And, of course, we don't see the average number of heads all the time—how much does the number of heads we see tend to vary? The first quantity is what we call the random variable's *expectation*, and the second is the random variable's *variance*.

For a random variable X, we denote its expectation as $\mathbb{E}[X]$. We can think of this as the average value that X takes on, weighted by the probability of each of those outcomes. Mathematically, this is written as $\mathbb{E}[X] = \Sigma_o o * P(X = o)$. Note that if all outcomes o are equally likely, we get a simple average of all the outcomes. It makes sense to use the probability of the outcome as a weighting, since some outcomes are more likely than others, and the average value we observe will be skewed toward such outcomes. For a single fair coin flip, the expected number of heads would be $\Sigma_{o \in \{0, 1\}} o * P(o) = 0 * 0.5 + 1 * 0.5 = 0.5$. In other words, we'd expect to see half of a head for any given fair coin flip. Of course, this makes no physical sense in that we could never possibly flip half of a head, but this gives you an idea of the proportions we'd expect to see over a long run experiment.

Returning to our example of length n sequences of coin flips, let's try to find the expected number of heads in such a sequence. We have $n + 1$ possible number of heads, and according to our formula, we'd need to find the probability of attaining each possible number to use as our weights. Mathematically, we'd need to compute $\Sigma_{x \in \{0, ..., n\}} x * P(X = x)$, where X is the random variable representing the total number of heads. However, as n gets larger and larger, performing this calculation starts to become more and more complicated.

Instead, let's denote X_i as the binary random variable for the ith coin flip and use the observation we made in the last section of being able to break up the total number of heads into a sum over heads/tails for all the individual coin flips. Since we know $X = X_1 + X_2 + ... + X_n$, we can also say that $\mathbb{E}[X] = \mathbb{E}[X_1 + X_2 + ... + X_n]$. How does making this substitution make our problem easier? We now introduce the concept of *linearity of expectation*, which states we can break up the right side into the sum $\mathbb{E}[X_1] + \mathbb{E}[X_2] + ... + \mathbb{E}[X_n]$. We know that the expected number of heads for each flip is 0.5, so the expected number of heads in a sequence of n flips is just $0.5 * n$. This is much simpler than going down the previous route, as this approach's difficulty does not scale with the number of flips.

Let's go over the simplification we made in a bit more detail. Mathematically, if we have any two independent random variables A and B:

$$\mathbb{E}[A + B] = \Sigma_{a,b}(a + b) * P(A = a, B = b)$$

$$= \Sigma_{a,b}(a + b) * P(A = a) * P(B = b)$$

$$= \Sigma_{a,b} a * P(A = a) * P(B = b) + b * P(A = a) * P(B = b)$$

$$= \Sigma_{a,b} a * P(A = a) * P(B = b) + \Sigma_{a,b} b * P(A = a) * P(B = b)$$

$$= \Sigma_a a * P(A = a)\Sigma_b P(B = b) + \Sigma_b b * P(B = b)\Sigma_a P(A = a)$$

$$= \Sigma_a a * P(A = a) + \Sigma_b b * P(B = b)$$

$$= \mathbb{E}[A] + \mathbb{E}[B]$$

 Note that we made the independence assumption we talked about earlier in the chapter here when we broke up the probability of the event $A = a$ and the event $B = b$ into a product of the two individual probabilities. The rest of the derivation doesn't require additional assumptions, so we recommend working through the algebra on your own. Although we won't show this for the dependent case, linearity of expectation also holds for dependent random variables.

Going back to the dropout example, the expectation of the total number of masked neurons can be broken up into a sum of expectations over each neuron. The expected number of masked neurons, similarly to the expected number of heads in a sequence of coin flips, is $p*n$, where p is the probability of being masked (and the expectation of each individual binary random variable representing a neuron) and n is the number of neurons.

As mentioned, we don't always see the expected number of occurrences of an event in every repetition of an experiment. In some cases, such as the expected number of heads in a single, fair coin flip from earlier, we never see it! Next, we will quantify the average deviation, or variance, from the expected value we see in repetitions of an experiment.

Variance

We define the variance, or Var(X), as $\mathbb{E}\left[(X - \mu)^2\right]$, where we let $\mu = \mathbb{E}[X]$. In plain English, this measure represents the average squared difference between the value X takes on and its expectation. Note that $(X - \mu)^2$ itself is also a random variable since it is a function of a function (X), which is still a function. Although we won't get into too much detail about why we use this formula in particular, we encourage you to think about why we don't use a formula such as $\mathbb{E}[X - \mu]$ instead. To obtain a slightly simpler form for the variance, we can perform the following simplification:

$$\mathbb{E}\left[(X - \mu)^2\right] = \mathbb{E}\left[X^2 - 2\mu X + \mu^2\right]$$

$$= \mathbb{E}\left[X^2\right] - \mathbb{E}[2\mu X] + \mathbb{E}\left[\mu^2\right]$$

$$= \mathbb{E}\left[X^2\right] - 2\mu\mathbb{E}[X] + \mu^2$$

$$= \mathbb{E}\left[X^2\right] - 2\mathbb{E}[X]^2 + \mathbb{E}[X]^2$$

$$= \mathbb{E}\left[X^2\right] - \mathbb{E}[X]^2$$

Let's take a moment to go through each of these steps. In the first step, we fully express the random variable as all of its component terms via classic binomial expansion. In the second step, we perform linearity of expectation to break out the component terms into their own, individual expectations. In the third step, we note that μ, or $\mathbb{E}[X]$, and its square are both constants and thus can be pulled out of the surrounding expectation. They are constants since they are not a function of the value X takes on and are instead evaluated using the entire domain (the set of values X can take on). Constants can be seen as random variables that can take on only one value, which is the constant itself. Thus, their expectations, or the average value the random variable takes on, is the constant itself since we always see the constant. The final steps are algebraic manipulations that bring us to the simplified result. Let's use this formula to find the variance of the binary random variable representing a single neuron under dropout, and p is the probability of the neuron being masked out:

$$\mathbb{E}\left[X^2\right] - \mathbb{E}[X]^2 = \Sigma_{x \in 0,1} x^2 * P(X = x) - \left(\Sigma_{x \in 0,1} x * P(X = x)\right)^2$$

$$= \Sigma_{x \in 0,1} x^2 * P(X = x) - p^2$$

$$= p - p^2$$

$$= p(1 - p)$$

These simplifications should make sense. We know from "Expectation" on page 24 that the expectation of the binary random variable representing a neuron is just p, and the rest is algebraic simplifications. We highly encourage you to work through these derivations on your own. As we start to think about the random variable representing the number of masked neurons in the entire layer, we naturally ask the question of whether there exists a similar linearity property for variance as there does for expectation. Unfortunately, the property does not hold in general:

$$Var(A + B) = \mathbb{E}\left[(A + B)^2\right] - \mathbb{E}[A + B]^2$$

$$= \mathbb{E}\left[A^2 + 2 * A * B + B^2\right] - (\mathbb{E}[A] + \mathbb{E}[B])^2$$

$$= \mathbb{E}\left[A^2\right] + 2\mathbb{E}[A * B] + \mathbb{E}\left[B^2\right] - \mathbb{E}[A]^2 - 2\mathbb{E}[A]\mathbb{E}[B] - \mathbb{E}[B]^2$$

$$= \mathbb{E}\left[A^2\right] - \mathbb{E}[A]^2 + \mathbb{E}\left[B^2\right] - \mathbb{E}[B]^2 + 2\mathbb{E}[A * B] - 2\mathbb{E}[A]\mathbb{E}[B]$$

$$= Var(A) + Var(B) + 2(\mathbb{E}[A * B] - \mathbb{E}[A]\mathbb{E}[B])$$

$$= Var(A) + Var(B) + 2Cov(A, B)$$

As we can see from the last line, the final term in the expression, which we call the *covariance* between the two random variables, ruins our hope for linearity. However, covariance is another key concept in probability—the intuition for covariance is that it measures the dependence between two random variables. As one random variable more completely determines the value of another random variable (think of A as the number of heads in a sequence of coin flips and B as the number of tails in the same sequence of coin flips), the magnitude of the covariance increases. Thus, it stands to reason that if A and B are independent random variables, the covariance between them should be zero, and linearity should hold in this special case. We highly encourage you to work through the math and show this on your own.

Back to the dropout example, the variance of the total number of masked neurons can be broken up into a sum of variances over each neuron, since each neuron is masked independently. The variance of the number of masked neurons is $p(1 - p)*n$, where $p(1 - p)$ is the variance for any given neuron and n is the number of neurons. Expectation and variance in dropout allow us to understand more deeply what we expect to see when applying such a layer in a deep neural network.

Bayes' Theorem

Returning to our discussion on conditional probability, we noted that the probability of intersection between two events could be written as a product of a conditional distribution and a distribution over a single event. Let's translate this into the language of random variables, now that we have introduced this new terminology. We denote A to be one random variable, and B to denote a second. Let a be a value that A can take on, and b be a value that B can take on. The analogy to the intersection operation for random variables is the *joint probability distribution $P(A=a,B=b)$*, which denotes the event where $A = a$ and $B = b$. We can think of $A = a$ and $B = b$ as individual events, and when we write $P(A = a, B = b)$, we are considering the probability that both events have occurred, i.e., their intersection $P(A = a \cap B = b)$. Note that we generally write the joint probability distribution as $P(A,B)$, since this encompasses all possible joint settings of the random variables A and B.

We mentioned earlier that intersection operations could be written as the product of a conditional distribution and a distribution over a single event. Rewriting this in the format for random variables, we have $P(A = a, B = b) = P(A = a|B = b)P(B = b)$. And more generally, considering all possible joint settings of the two random variables, we have $P(A,B) = P(A|B)P(B)$. We also discussed how there always exists a second way of writing this joint distribution as a product: $P(A = a, B = b) = P(B = b|A = a)P(A=a)$, and more generally, $P(A,B) = P(B|A)P(A)$. We noted that sometimes one of these paths makes more sense than the other. For example, in the case where symptoms are represented by A and disease is represented by B, the path in which B takes on a value b, and then A takes on a value a in that universe makes much more sense than the reverse since, biologically, people contract a disease first and only then show symptoms for that disease.

However, this doesn't mean that the reverse isn't useful. It is almost universally the case that people show up at a hospital with mild symptoms, and medical professionals must try to infer the most likely disease from these symptoms to effectively treat the underlying disease. *Bayes' Theorem* gives us a way of calculating the probability of a disease given the observed symptoms. Since the same joint probability distribution can be written in the two ways mentioned in the previous paragraph, we have the following equality:

$$P(B|A) = \frac{P(A|B)P(B)}{P(A)}$$

If B represents disease, while A represents symptoms, this gives us a method for computing the likelihood of any disease given the observed symptoms. Let's analyze the right side to see if the equality also makes intuitive sense. The likelihood of symptoms given the disease times the likelihood of the disease is just the joint distribution, which makes sense as the numerator here. The denominator is the likelihood of seeing those symptoms, which can also be expressed as a sum of the numerator over all possible diseases. This is an instance of a more general process called *marginalization*, or removing a subset of random variables from a joint distribution by summing over all possible configurations of the subset:

$$P(A) = \Sigma_b P(A, B = b)$$

In more concise terms, we have:

$$P\left(B = b_{query}\middle|A\right) = \frac{P\left(B = b_{query}, A\right)}{\Sigma_b P(B = b, A)}$$

Bayes' Theorem is a very valuable application of probability in the real world, especially in the case of disease prediction. Additionally, if we replace the random variable for symptoms with a random variable representing the result of a test for a specific disease, and the random variable over all diseases with a random variable over presence of the specific disease, we can infer the likelihood of actually having a specific disease given a positive test for it using Bayes' Theorem. This is a common problem in most hospitals, and is especially relevant to epidemiology given the outbreak of COVID-19.

Entropy, Cross Entropy, and KL Divergence

Probability distributions, by definition, give us a way of comparing the likelihoods of various possible events. However, even if we know the most likely event (or events) that is to occur, when running the experiment we are bound to see all sorts of events. In this section, we first consider the problem of defining a single metric that encapsulates all of the uncertainty within a probability distribution, which we will define as the distribution's *entropy*.

Let's set up the following scenario. I am a researcher who is running an experiment. The experiment could be something as simple as flipping a coin or rolling a dice. You are recording the results of the experiment. We are both in different rooms, but connected through a phone line. I run the experiment and receive a result, and communicate that result to you via the phone. You record that result in a notebook, where you pick some binary string representation of that result as what you write down. As a scribe, you are necessary in this situation—I may run hundreds of trials and my memory is limited, so I cannot remember the results of all of my trials.

For example, if I roll a dice and neither of us knows anything about the fairness of the dice, you could denote the outcome one as "0," two as "1," three as "10," four as "11," five as "100," and six as "101." Whenever I communicate a result of the experiment to you, you add that result's corresponding string representation to the end of the string consisting of all results so far. If I were to roll a one, followed by two twos, and finally a one, using the encoding scheme defined so far you would have written down "0110."

After all runs of the experiment have ended, I have a meeting with you and try to decipher this string "0110" into a sequence of outcomes for use in my research. However, as the researcher, I am puzzled by this string—does it represent a one, followed by two twos, and finally a one? Or does it represent a one, followed by a two, followed by a three? Or even a one, followed by a four, followed by a one? It seems that there are at least a few possible translations of this string into outcomes using the encoding scheme.

To prevent this situation from ever occurring again, we decide to enforce some limitations on the binary strings you can use to represent outcomes. We use what is called a *prefix code*, which disallows binary string representations of different outcomes from being prefixes of each other. It's not too difficult to see why this would result in a unique translation of string to outcomes. Let's say we have a binary string, some prefix of which we have been able to successfully decode into a series of outcomes. To decode the rest of the string, or the suffix, we must first find the next outcome in the series. When we find a prefix of this suffix that translates to an outcome, we already know that, by definition, there is no smaller prefix that translates to a valid outcome. We now have a larger prefix of the binary string that has been successfully translated to a series of outcomes. We then recursively use this logic until we have reached the end of the string.

Now that we have some guidelines on string representations for outcomes, we redo the original experiment with one as "0," two as "10," three as "110," four as "1110," five as "11110," and six as "111110." However, as noted earlier, I may carry out hundreds of trials, and as the scribe you probably want to limit the amount of writing you have to do. With no information about the dice, we can't do too much better than this. Assuming each outcome shows up with probability $\frac{1}{6}$, the expected number of letters you'd need to write down per trial is 3.5. We could get down to 3 if we set one as "000," two as "001," three as "010," four as "011," five as "100," and six as "101," for example.

But what if we knew information about the dice? For example, what if it were a weighted dice that showed up six almost all of the time? In that case, you probably want to assign a shorter binary string to six, for example "0" (instead of assigning "0" to one) so you can limit the expected amount of writing you have to do. It makes intuitive sense that, as the result of any single trial becomes more and more certain, the expected number of characters you'd need to write becomes lower by assigning the shortest binary strings to the most likely outcomes.

This raises the question: given a probability distribution over outcomes, what is the optimal encoding scheme, where optimal is defined as the fewest expected number of characters you'd need to write per trial? Although this whole situation may feel a bit contrived, it provides us with a slightly different lens through which we can understand the uncertainty within a probability distribution. As we noted, as the result of an experiment becomes more and more certain, the optimal encoding scheme would allow the scribe to write fewer and fewer characters in expectation per trial. For example, in the extreme case where we already knew beforehand that a six would always show up, the scribe wouldn't need to write anything down.

It turns out that, although we won't show it here, the best you can do is assign a binary string of length $\log_2 \frac{1}{p(x_i)}$ to each possible outcome x_i, where $p(x_i)$ is its probability. The expected string length of any given trial would then be:

$$\mathbb{E}_{p(x)}\left[\log_2 \frac{1}{p(x)} \right] = \Sigma_{x_i} p(x_i) \log_2 \frac{1}{p(x_i)}$$

$$= - \Sigma_{x_i} p(x_i) \log_2 p(x_i)$$

This expression is defined as the *entropy* of a probability distribution. In the case where we are completely certain of the final outcome (e.g., the dice always lands up six), we can evaluate the expression for entropy and see that we get a result of 0.

In the case where we are completely certain of the final outcome (e.g., the dice always lands up six), we can evaluate the expression for entropy and see that we get a result of 0. Additionally, the probability distribution that has the highest entropy is the one that places equal probability over all possible outcomes. This is because, for any given trial, we are no more certain that a particular outcome will appear as opposed to any other outcome. As a result, we cannot use the strategy of assigning a shorter string to any single outcome.

Now that we have defined entropy, we can discuss cross entropy, which provides us a way of measuring the distinctness of two distributions.

Equation 2-1. Cross entropy

$$CE(p||q) = \mathbb{E}_{p(x)}\left[\log_2 \frac{1}{q(x)} \right] = \Sigma_x p(x) \log_2 \frac{1}{q(x)} = - \Sigma_x p(x) \log_2 q(x)$$

Note that cross entropy has a $\log \frac{1}{q(x)}$ term, which can be interpreted as the optimal binary string length assigned to each outcome, assuming outcomes appear according to probability distribution $q(x)$. However, note that this is an expectation with respect to $p(x)$, so how do we interpret this entire expression? Well, we can understand the cross entropy to mean the expected string length for any trial given we have optimized for the encoding scheme for distribution $q(x)$ while, in reality, all of the outcomes are appearing according to the distribution $p(x)$. This can definitely happen in an experiment where we have only limited a priori information about the experiment, so we assume some distribution $q(x)$ to optimize our encoding scheme, but as we carry out trials, we learn more information that gets us closer to the true distribution $p(x)$.

The KL divergence takes this logic a bit further. If we take the cross entropy, which tells us the expected number of bits per trial given we have optimized our encoding for the incorrect distribution $q(x)$, and subtract from that the entropy, which tells us the expected number of bits per trial given we have optimized for the correct distribution $p(x)$, we get the expected number of extra bits required to represent a trial when using $q(x)$ compared to $p(x)$. Here is the expression for the KL divergence:

$$KL(p||q) = \mathbb{E}_{p(x)}\left[\log_2 \frac{1}{q(x)} - \log_2 \frac{1}{p(x)} \right] = \mathbb{E}_{p(x)}\left[\log_2 \frac{p(x)}{q(x)} \right]$$

At the unique global minimum $q(x) = p(x)$, the KL divergence is exactly zero. Why this is the unique minimum is a bit beyond the scope of this text, so we leave that as an exercise for you.

In practice, when trying to match the true distribution $p(x)$ with a learned distribution $q(x)$, KL divergence is often minimized as an objective function. Most models will actually minimize the cross entropy in place of the KL divergence, which is effectively the same optimization problem due to the KL being a difference between the cross entropy and the entropy of $p(x)$, where the entropy of $p(x)$ is a constant and has no dependence on the weights that parameterize $q(x)$. Thus, the gradient with respect to the weights that parameterize $q(x)$ when using either objective is the same.

One common example where cross-entropy/KL divergence is optimized is in the standard training of a neural network classifier. The neural network's objective is to learn a distribution over target classes such that, for any given example x_i, $p_\theta(y|x = x_i)$ matches the true distribution $p(y|x = x_i)$, which has all of its probability mass placed over the true label y_i and zero probability over all other classes. Minimizing the sum of cross entropies between the learned distribution and the true distribution over all examples is actually the exact same as minimizing the negative log likelihood of the data. Both are valid interpretations of how neural networks are trained, and lead to the same objective function. We encourage you to try writing out both expressions independently to see this.

Continuous Probability Distributions

So far, we have looked at probability distributions through the lens of discrete outcomes and events. However, as it turns out, probability distributions aren't just for sets of discrete outcomes like the CIFAR-10 target classes or the MNIST digits. We can define probability distributions over sample spaces of infinite size, such as all the real numbers. In this section, we will extend principles covered in the previous sections to the continuous realm.

In the continuous realm, probability distributions are often referred to as *probability density functions*, or PDFs. PDFs are nonnegative functions over a sample space, such as all the reals, that integrate to one. Recall from calculus that the integration of a function is the area of the region underneath the function, bounded by the x-axis. PDFs follow the basic tenets introduced in the first section, but instead of adding the probability of outcomes to get the probability of an event, we use integration. For example, say X is a continuous random variable that is defined over all the real numbers. If we'd like to know the probability of the event $P(X \leq 2)$, all we'd need to do is integrate the PDF of X from negative infinity to 2.

But how about the probability of any individual outcome, say $P(X = 2)$? Since we use integration to find probabilities in the continuous space, the probability of any individual outcome is actually zero due to the width of the region being infinitesimal. We instead use the term *likelihood* to distinguish between the probability of events and the value that the PDF evaluates to when we input a setting of X. Likelihoods are still valuable, as they tell us what individual outcomes we are most likely to see when performing an experiment over a continuous space. Going forward, when considering continuous probability distributions, we will only refer to events as having probability, rather than individual outcomes.

One famous example of a continuous probability distribution is the *uniform distribution* over some interval on the real line. Under the uniform distribution, the likelihood of each outcome is the same, meaning that no outcome is any more likely to appear than another. Thus, the uniform distribution looks like a rectangle, where the base of the rectangle is the interval constituting its domain, and the height, or the likelihood for each outcome, is the value that makes the area of the rectangle equal to one. Figure 2-4 shows the uniform distribution over the interval [0,0.5].

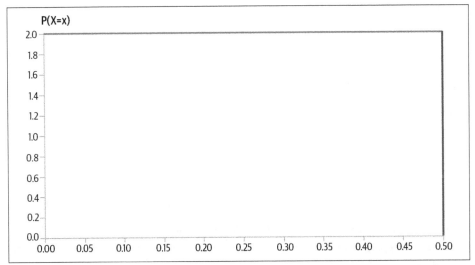

Figure 2-4. The uniform distribution has uniform height over its entire area, which shows that each value in the domain of the distribution has equal likelihood.

This example was chosen specifically to show a concrete difference between likelihoods and probabilities in the continuous realm. The height of the rectangle being

2 was no error—there is no constraint on the magnitude of the likelihood in continuous distributions, unlike probabilities, which must be less than or equal to 1.

Another famous example of a continuous probability distribution is the *Gaussian distribution,* which is one of the more common ways in which data presents itself in the real world. The Gaussian distribution is defined by two parameters: its mean μ and its standard deviation σ. The PDF of a Gaussian distribution is:

$$f(x; \mu, \sigma) = \frac{1}{\sigma\sqrt{2\pi}} e^{-\frac{1}{2}\left(\frac{x-\mu}{\sigma}\right)^2}$$

Why this function integrates to 1 over the real domain is beyond the scope of this chapter, but one important characteristic of a Gaussian distribution is that its mean is also its unique mode. In other words, the outcome with the highest likelihood is also, uniquely, the mean outcome. This is not the case for all distributions. For example, Figure 2-4 does not have this property. The graph of a standard Gaussian, which has mean zero and unit variance, is shown in Figure 2-5 (the PDF asymptotically reaches zero in the limit in both directions).

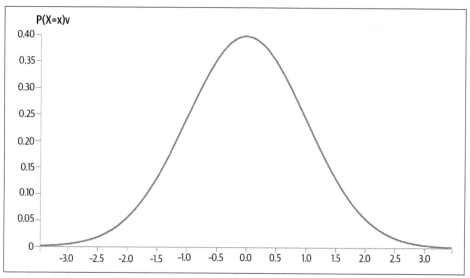

Figure 2-5. The Gaussian distribution has a bell shape, with highest likelihood in the center and dropping exponentially as the value in question gets farther and farther from the center.

Why is the Gaussian distribution so prevalent in real-world data? One reason for this is a theorem called the *Central Limit Theorem* (CLT). This theorem states that sums of independent random variables converge to a Gaussian distribution as the number of variables in the sum goes to infinity, even if each variable is not distributed as a Gaussian. One example is the number of masked neurons after a dropout layer is applied. As the number of neurons from the previous layer goes to infinity, the number of masked neurons (which is a sum of independent Bernoulli random variables, as discussed in "Random Variables" on page 22), when standardized correctly, is approximately distributed as a standard Gaussian distribution. We won't cover CLT in much depth here, but it has more recently been extended to weakly dependent variables under certain special conditions.

Many real-world datasets can be seen as approximately sums of many random variables. For example, the distribution of a disease prevalence within a given population, similarly to the number of masked neurons after applying dropout, is the sum of many Bernoulli random variables (where each person is a Bernoulli random variable that has a value of 1 if they have the disease and a value of 0 if they do not)—although likely dependent.

Continuous random variables are still functions, just as we defined discrete random variables. The only difference is that the range of this function is a continuous space. To compute the expectation and variance of a continuous random variable, all we need to do is replace our summations with integrations, as follows:

$$\mathbb{E}[X] = \int_x x * f(X = x)dx$$

$$Var(X) = \int_x (x - \mathbb{E}[X])^2 * f(X = x)dx$$

As an example, let's evaluate the expectation for our uniform random variable defined earlier. But first, confirm that it makes intuitive sense that the expectation should be 0.25, since the endpoints of the interval are 0 and 0.5 and all values in between are of equal likelihood. Now, let's evaluate the integral and see if the computation matches our intuition:

$$\int_0^{0.5} x * f(x)dx = \int_0^{0.5} 2xdx$$

$$= x^2 \big|_0^{0.5}$$

$$= 0.25$$

Where the superscript and the subscript of the | symbol represent the values at which we will evaluate the preceding function, which we will then difference to get the value of the integral. We see that the expectation comes out to the same value as our intuition, which is a great sanity check.

Bayes' Theorem also holds for continuous variables. The only major difference is when marginalizing out a subset of variables, you will need to integrate over the entire domain of the marginalized subset rather than taking a discrete sum over all possible configurations of the marginalized subset. Again, this is an example of extending the tenets of probability to the continuous space by replacing summations with integrations. Here is Bayes' Theorem for continuous probability distributions, following the notation from "Bayes' Theorem" on page 27:

$$P\left(B = b_{query}\,\big|\,A\right) = \frac{P\left(A\,\big|\,B = b_{query}\right)P\left(B = b_{query}\right)}{P(A)} = \frac{P\left(A\,\big|\,B = b_{query}\right)P\left(B = b_{query}\right)}{\int_b P(A, B = b)db}$$

And finally, we have our discussion on entropy, cross entropy, and KL divergence. All three of these extend nicely to the continuous space as well. We replace our summations with integrations and note that the properties introduced in the previous section still hold. For example, over a given domain, the distribution with the highest entropy is the uniform distribution, and the KL divergence between two distributions is zero if and only if the two distributions are the exact same. Here are the definitions in their continuous form, following Equation 2-1:

$$H(f(x)) = -\int_x f(x) \log_2 f(x) dx$$
$$KL(f(x)\,||\,g(x)) = \int_x f(x) \log_2 \frac{f(x)}{g(x)} dx$$
$$CE(f(x)\,||\,g(x)) = -\int_x f(x) \log_2 g(x) dx$$

Our extension of these concepts to the continuous space will come in handy in Chapter 10, where we model many distributions as Gaussians. Additionally, we use the KL divergence/cross-entropy terms as a regularization procedure on the complexity of one of our learned distributions. Since KL divergence is only zero when the query distribution matches the target distribution, setting the target distribution to a Gaussian forces the learned distribution to approximate a Gaussian.

Summary

In this chapter we covered the fundamentals of probability, first building the intuition behind the basics of probability distributions and then moving to relevant applications of probability, such as conditional probability, random variables, expectation, and variance. We saw the applications of probability in deep learning, such as how a neural net parametrizes a probability distribution during classification tasks, and how we can quantify the mathematical properties of dropout, a regularization technique in neural nets. Finally, we discussed measurements of uncertainty in probability distributions such as entropy, and generalized these concepts to the continuous realm.

Probability is a field that affects the choices in our everyday lives, and it's key to understand the meaning behind the numbers. Additionally, we hope that this introduction puts the rest of the book in perspective and allows you to more rigorously understand future concepts. In the next chapter, we will discuss the structure of neural networks, and the motivations behind their design.

## CHAPTER 3

The Neural Network

Building Intelligent Machines

The brain is the most incredible organ in the human body. It dictates the way we perceive every sight, sound, smell, taste, and touch. It enables us to store memories, experience emotions, and even dream. Without it, we would be primitive organisms, incapable of anything other than the simplest of reflexes. The brain is, inherently, what makes us intelligent.

The infant brain weighs only a single pound, but somehow it solves problems that even our biggest, most powerful supercomputers find impossible. Within a matter of months after birth, infants can recognize the faces of their parents, discern discrete objects from their backgrounds, and even tell voices apart. Within a year, they've already developed an intuition for natural physics, can track objects even when they become partially or completely blocked, and can associate sounds with specific meanings. And by early childhood, they have a sophisticated understanding of grammar and thousands of words in their vocabularies.[1]

For decades, we've dreamed of building intelligent machines with brains like ours—robotic assistants to clean our homes, cars that drive themselves, microscopes that automatically detect diseases. But building these artificially intelligent machines requires us to solve some of the most complex computational problems we have ever grappled with; problems that our brains can already solve in a manner of microseconds. To tackle these problems, we'll have to develop a radically different way of programming a computer using techniques largely developed over the past decade. This is an extremely active field of artificial computer intelligence often referred to as *deep learning*.

1 Kuhn, Deanna, et al. *Handbook of Child Psychology. Vol. 2, Cognition, Perception, and Language.* Wiley, 1998.

The Limits of Traditional Computer Programs

Why exactly are certain problems so difficult for computers to solve? Well, it turns out that traditional computer programs are designed to be very good at two things: (1) performing arithmetic really fast and (2) explicitly following a list of instructions. So if you want to do some heavy financial number crunching, you're in luck. Traditional computer programs can do the trick. But let's say we want to do something slightly more interesting, like write a program to automatically read someone's handwriting. Figure 3-1 will serve as a starting point.

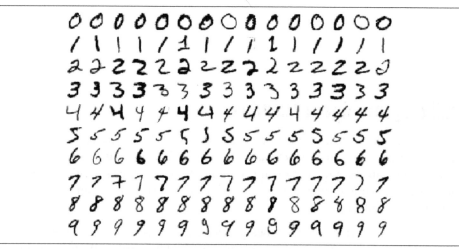

Figure 3-1. Image from MNIST handwritten digit dataset[2]

Although every digit in Figure 3-1 is written in a slightly different way, we can easily recognize every digit in the first row as a zero, every digit in the second row as a one, etc. Let's try to write a computer program to crack this task. What rules could we use to tell one digit from another?

Well, we can start simple! For example, we might state that we have a zero if our image has only a single, closed loop. All the examples in Figure 3-1 seem to fit this bill, but this isn't really a sufficient condition. What if someone doesn't perfectly close the loop on their zero? And, as in Figure 3-2, how do you distinguish a messy zero from a six?

---

2 Y. LeCun, L. Bottou, Y. Bengio, and P. Haffner. "Gradient-Based Learning Applied to Document Recognition." *Proceedings of the IEEE*, 86(11):2278-2324, November 1998.

Figure 3-2. A zero that's algorithmically difficult to distinguish from a six

You could potentially establish some sort of cutoff for the distance between the starting point of the loop and the ending point, but it's not exactly clear where we should be drawing the line. But this dilemma is only the beginning of our worries. How do we distinguish between threes and fives? Or between fours and nines? We can add more and more rules, or *features*, through careful observation and months of trial and error, but it's quite clear that this isn't going to be an easy process.

Many other classes of problems fall into this same category: object recognition, speech comprehension, automated translation, etc. We don't know what program to write because we don't know how it's done by our brains. And even if we did know how to do it, the program might be horrendously complicated.

The Mechanics of Machine Learning

To tackle these classes of problems, we'll have to use a different kind of approach. A lot of the things we learn in school growing up have much in common with traditional computer programs. We learn how to multiply numbers, solve equations, and take derivatives by internalizing a set of instructions. But the things we learn at an extremely early age, the things we find most natural, are learned by example, not by formula.

For instance, when we were two years old, our parents didn't teach us how to recognize a dog by measuring the shape of its nose or the contours of its body. We learned to recognize a dog by being shown multiple examples and being corrected when we made the wrong guess. When we were born, our brains provided us with a model that described how we would be able to see the world. As we grew up, that model would take in our sensory inputs and make a guess about what we were experiencing. If that guess was confirmed by our parents, our model would be reinforced. If our parents said we were wrong, we'd modify our model to incorporate this new information. Over our lifetime, our model becomes more and more accurate as we assimilate more and more examples. Obviously all of this happens subconsciously, but we can use this to our advantage.

Deep learning is a subset of a more general field of AI called *machine learning*, which is predicated on this idea of learning from example. In machine learning, instead of teaching a computer a massive list of rules to solve the problem, we give it a *model* with which it can evaluate examples, and a small set of instructions to modify the model when it makes a mistake. We expect that, over time, a well-suited model would be able to solve the problem extremely accurately.

Let's be a little bit more rigorous about what this means so we can formulate this idea mathematically. Let's define our model to be a function $h(\mathbf{x}, \theta)$. The input $\mathbf{x}$ is an example expressed in vector form. For example, if $\mathbf{x}$ were a grayscale image, the vector's components would be pixel intensities at each position, as shown in Figure 3-3.

Figure 3-3. The process of vectorizing an image for a machine learning algorithm

The input θ is a vector of the parameters that our model uses. Our machine learning program tries to perfect the values of these parameters as it is exposed to more and more examples. We'll see this in action and in more detail in Chapter 4.

To develop a more intuitive understanding for machine learning models, let's walk through a quick example. Let's say we wanted to determine how to predict exam performance based on the number of hours of sleep we get and the number of hours we study the previous day. We collect a lot of data, and for each data point $\mathbf{x} = [x_1 \ x_2]^T$, we record the number of hours of sleep we got (x_1), the number of hours we spent studying (x_2), and whether we performed above or below the class average. Our goal, then, might be to learn a model $h(\mathbf{x}, \theta)$ with parameter vector $\theta = [\theta_0 \ \theta_1 \ \theta_2]^T$ such that:

$$h(\mathbf{x}, \theta) = \begin{cases} -1 & \text{if } \mathbf{x}^T \cdot \begin{bmatrix} \theta_1 \\ \theta_2 \end{bmatrix} + \theta_0 < 0 \\ 1 & \text{if } \mathbf{x}^T \cdot \begin{bmatrix} \theta_1 \\ \theta_2 \end{bmatrix} + \theta_0 \geq 0 \end{cases}$$

So we guess that the blueprint for our model $h(\mathbf{x}, \theta)$ is as described (geometrically, this particular blueprint describes a linear classifier that divides the coordinate plane into two halves). Then, we want to learn a parameter vector θ such that our model makes the right predictions (-1 if we perform below average, and 1 otherwise) given an input example $\mathbf{x}$. This model is called a linear *perceptron*, and it's a model that's been used since the 1950s.[3] Let's assume our data is as shown in Figure 3-4.

---

3 Rosenblatt, Frank. "The perceptron: A Probabilistic Model for Information Storage and Organization in the Brain." *Psychological Review* 65.6 (1958): 386.

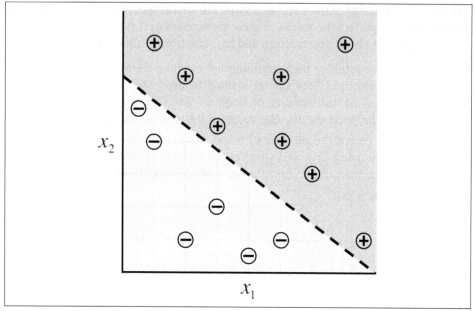

Figure 3-4. Sample data for our exam predictor algorithm and a potential classifier

Then it turns out that by selecting $\theta = [-24\ 3\ 4]^T$, our machine learning model makes the correct prediction on every data point:

$$h(\mathbf{x}, \theta) = \begin{cases} -1 & \text{if } 3x_1 + 4x_2 - 24 < 0 \\ 1 & \text{if } 3x_1 + 4x_2 - 24 \geq 0 \end{cases}$$

An optimal parameter vector θ positions the classifier so that we make as many correct predictions as possible. In most cases, there are many (or even infinitely many) possible choices for θ that are optimal. Fortunately for us, most of the time these alternatives are so close to one another that the difference is negligible. If this is not the case, we may want to collect more data to narrow our choice of θ.

While the setup seems reasonable, there are still some pretty significant questions that remain. First off, how do we even come up with an optimal value for the parameter vector θ in the first place? Solving this problem requires a technique commonly known as *optimization*. An optimizer aims to maximize the performance of a machine learning model by iteratively tweaking its parameters until the error is minimized. We'll begin to tackle this question of learning parameter vectors in more detail in Chapter 4, when we describe the process of *gradient descent*.[4] In later chapters, we'll try to find ways to make this process even more efficient.

Second, it's quite clear that this particular model (the linear perceptron model) is quite limited in the relationships it can learn. For example, the distributions of data shown in Figure 3-5 cannot be described well by a linear perceptron.

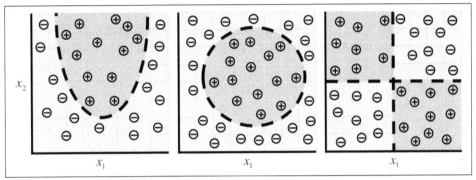

Figure 3-5. As our data takes on more complex forms, we need more complex models to describe them

But these situations are only the tip of the iceberg. As we move on to much more complex problems, such as object recognition and text analysis, our data becomes extremely high dimensional, and the relationships we want to capture become highly nonlinear. To accommodate this complexity, recent research in machine learning has attempted to build models that resemble the structures utilized by our brains. It's essentially this body of research, commonly referred to as *deep learning*, that has had spectacular success in tackling problems in computer vision and natural language processing. These algorithms not only far surpass other kinds of machine learning algorithms, but also rival (or even exceed) the accuracies achieved by humans.

The Neuron

The foundational unit of the human brain is the neuron. A tiny piece of the brain, about the size of grain of rice, contains over 10,000 neurons, each of which forms an average of 6,000 connections with other neurons.[5] It's this massive biological network that enables us to experience the world around us. Our goal in this section is to use this natural structure to build machine learning models that solve problems in an analogous way.

---

4 Bubeck, Sébastien. "Convex Optimization: Algorithms and Complexity." *Foundations and Trends® in Machine Learning*. 8.3-4 (2015): 231-357.

5 Restak, Richard M. and David Grubin. *The Secret Life of the Brain*. Joseph Henry Press, 2001.

At its core, the neuron is optimized to receive information from other neurons, process this information in a unique way, and send its result to other cells. This process is summarized in Figure 3-6. The neuron receives its inputs along antennae-like structures called *dendrites*. Each of these incoming connections is dynamically strengthened or weakened based on how often it is used (this is how we learn new concepts), and it's the strength of each connection that determines the contribution of the input to the neuron's output. After being weighted by the strength of their respective connections, the inputs are summed together in the *cell body*. This sum is then transformed into a new signal that's propagated along the cell's *axon* and sent off to other neurons.

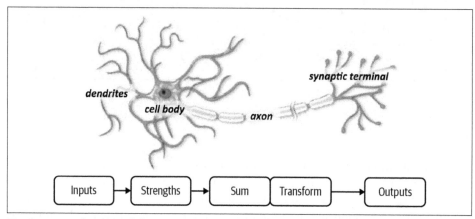

Figure 3-6. A functional description of a biological neuron's structure

We can translate this functional understanding of the neurons in our brain into an artificial model that we can represent on our computer. Such a model is described in Figure 3-7, leveraging the approach first pioneered in 1943 by Warren S. McCulloch and Walter H. Pitts.[6] Just as in biological neurons, our artificial neuron takes in some number of inputs, $x_1, x_2, ..., x_n$, each of which is multiplied by a specific weight, $w_1, w_2, ..., w_n$. These weighted inputs are, as before, summed to produce the *logit* of the neuron, $z = \sum_{i=0}^{n} w_i x_i$. In many cases, the logit also includes a *bias*, which is a constant (not shown in the figure). The logit is then passed through a function f to produce the output $y = f(z)$. This output can be transmitted to other neurons.

---

6 McCulloch, Warren S., and Walter Pitts. "A Logical Calculus of the Ideas Immanent in Nervous Activity." *The Bulletin of Mathematical Biophysics*. 5.4 (1943): 115-133.

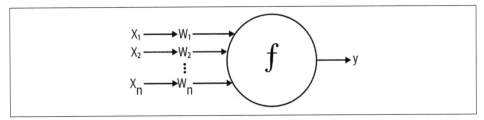

Figure 3-7. Schematic for a neuron in an artificial neural net

We'll conclude our mathematical discussion of the artificial neuron by re-expressing its functionality in vector form. Let's reformulate the inputs as a vector $\mathbf{x} = [x_1\ x_2\ \ldots\ x_n]$ and the weights of the neuron as $\mathbf{w} = [w_1\ w_2\ \ldots\ w_n]$. Then we can re-express the output of the neuron as $y = f(\mathbf{x} \cdot \mathbf{w} + b)$, where b is the bias term. We can compute the output by performing the dot product of the input and weight vectors, adding in the bias term to produce the logit, and then applying the transformation function. While this seems like a trivial reformulation, thinking about neurons as a series of vector manipulations will be crucial to how we implement them in software later in this book.

Expressing Linear Perceptrons as Neurons

In "The Mechanics of Machine Learning" on page 41, we talked about using machine learning models to capture the relationship between success on exams and time spent studying and sleeping. To tackle this problem, we constructed a linear perceptron classifier that divided the Cartesian coordinate plane into two halves:

$$h(\mathbf{x}, \theta) = \begin{cases} -1 & \text{if } 3x_1 + 4x_2 - 24 < 0 \\ 1 & \text{if } 3x_1 + 4x_2 - 24 \geq 0 \end{cases}$$

As shown in Figure 3-4, this is an optimal choice for θ because it correctly classifies every sample in our dataset. Here, we show that our model h is easily using a neuron. Consider the neuron depicted in Figure 3-8. The neuron has two inputs, a bias, and uses the function:

$$f(z) = \begin{cases} -1 & \text{if } z < 0 \\ 1 & \text{if } z \geq 0 \end{cases}$$

It's easy to show that our linear perceptron and the neuronal model are perfectly equivalent. And in general, it's quite simple to show that singular neurons are strictly more expressive than linear perceptrons. Every linear perceptron can be expressed as a single neuron, but single neurons can also express models that cannot be expressed by any linear perceptron.

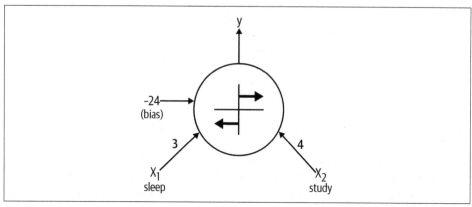

Figure 3-8. Expressing our exam performance perceptron as a neuron

Feed-Forward Neural Networks

Although single neurons are more powerful than linear perceptrons, they're not nearly expressive enough to solve complicated learning problems. There's a reason our brain is made of more than one neuron. For example, it is impossible for a single neuron to differentiate handwritten digits. So to tackle much more complicated tasks, we'll have to take our machine learning model even further.

The neurons in the human brain are organized in layers. In fact, the human cerebral cortex (the structure responsible for most of human intelligence) is made up of six layers.[7] Information flows from one layer to another until sensory input is converted into conceptual understanding. For example, the bottommost layer of the visual cortex receives raw visual data from the eyes. This information is processed by each layer and passed on to the next until, in the sixth layer, we conclude whether we are looking at a cat, or a soda can, or an airplane.

Borrowing from these concepts, we can construct an *artificial neural network*. A neural network comes about when we start hooking up neurons to each other, the input data, and to the output nodes, which correspond to the network's answer to a learning problem. Figure 3-9 demonstrates a simple example of an artificial neural network, similar to the architecture described in McCulloch and Pitt's work in 1943.

---

7 Mountcastle, Vernon B. "Modality and Topographic Properties of Single Neurons of Cat's Somatic Sensory Cortex." *Journal of Neurophysiology* 20.4 (1957): 408-434.

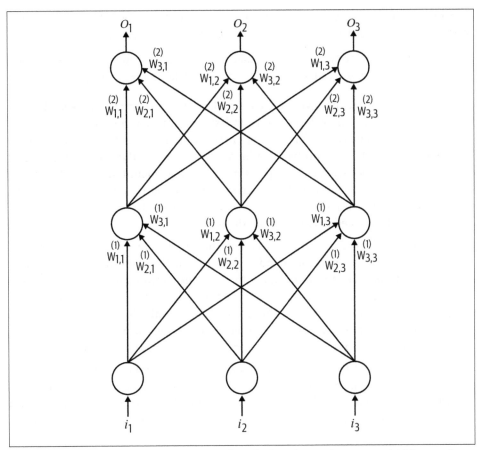

Figure 3-9. A feed-forward neural network with three layers (input, one hidden, and output) and three neurons per layer

The bottom layer of the network pulls in the input data. The top layer of neurons (output nodes) computes our final answer. The middle layer(s) of neurons are called the *hidden layers*, and we let $w_{i,j}^{(k)}$ be the weight of the connection between the ith neuron in the kth layer with the jth neuron in the $k + 1^{st}$ layer. These weights constitute our parameter vector, θ, and just as before, our ability to solve problems with neural networks depends on finding the optimal values to plug into θ.

We note that in this example, connections traverse only from a lower layer to a higher layer. There are no connections between neurons in the same layer, and there are no connections that transmit data from a higher layer to a lower layer. These neural networks are called *feed-forward* networks, and we start by discussing these networks because they are the simplest to analyze. We present this analysis (specifically, the process of selecting the optimal values for the weights) in Chapter 4. More complicated connectivities will be addressed in later chapters.

We'll discuss the major types of layers that are utilized in feed-forward neural networks, but before we proceed, here's a couple of important notes to keep in mind:

1. As we mentioned, the layers of neurons that lie sandwiched between the first layer of neurons (input layer) and the last layer of neurons (output layer) are called the hidden layers. This is where most of the magic is happening when the neural net tries to solve problems. Whereas (as in the handwritten digit example) we would previously have to spend a lot of time identifying useful features, the hidden layers automate this process for us. Oftentimes, taking a look at the activities of hidden layers can tell you a lot about the features the network has automatically learned to extract from the data.

2. Although in Figure 3-9 every layer has the same number of neurons, this is neither necessary nor recommended. More often than not, hidden layers have fewer neurons than the input layer to force the network to learn compressed representations of the original input. For example, while our eyes obtain raw pixel values from our surroundings, our brain thinks in terms of edges and contours. This is because the hidden layers of biological neurons in our brain, force us to come up with better representations for everything we perceive.

3. It is not required that every neuron has its output connected to the inputs of all neurons in the next layer. In fact, selecting which neurons to connect to which other neurons in the next layer is an art that comes from experience. We'll discuss this issue in more depth as we work through various examples of neural networks.

4. The inputs and outputs are *vectorized* representations. For example, you might imagine a neural network where the inputs are the individual pixel RGB values in an image represented as a vector (refer to Figure 3-3). The last layer might have two neurons that correspond to the answer to our problem: $[1, 0]$ if the image contains a dog, $[0, 1]$ if the image contains a cat, $[1, 1]$ if it contains both, and $[0, 0]$ if it contains neither.

We'll also observe that, similarly to our reformulation for the neuron, we can also mathematically express a neural network as a series of vector and matrix operations. Let's consider the input to the ith layer of the network to be a vector $\mathbf{x} = [x_1\ x_2\ ... \ x_n]$. We'd like to find the vector $\mathbf{y} = [y_1\ y_2\ ...\ y_m]$ produced by propagating the input through the neurons. We can express this as a simple matrix multiply if we construct a weight matrix $\mathbf{W}$ of size $n \times m$ and a bias vector of size m. In this matrix, each column corresponds to a neuron, where the jth element of the column corresponds to the weight of the connection pulling in the jth element of the input. In other words, $\mathbf{y} = f(\mathbf{W}^T\mathbf{x} + \mathbf{b})$, where the transformation function is applied to the vector element-wise. This reformulation will become all the more critical as we begin to implement these networks in software.

Linear Neurons and Their Limitations

Most neuron types are defined by the function f they apply to their logit z. Let's first consider layers of neurons that use a linear function in the form of $f(z) = az + b$. For example, a neuron that attempts to estimate a cost of a meal in a fast-food restaurant would use a linear neuron where $a = 1$ and $b = 0$. Using $f(z) = z$ and weights equal to the price of each item, the linear neuron in Figure 3-10 would take in some ordered triple of servings of burgers, fries, and sodas, and output the price of the combination.

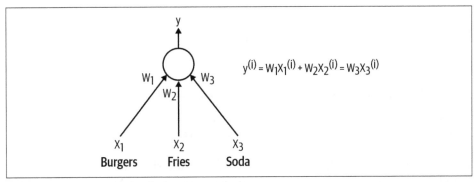

Figure 3-10. An example of a linear neuron

Linear neurons are easy to compute with, but they run into serious limitations. In fact, it can be shown that any feed-forward neural network consisting of only linear neurons can be expressed as a network with no hidden layers. This is problematic because, as we discussed, hidden layers are what enable us to learn important features from the input data. In other words, to learn complex relationships, we need to use neurons that employ some sort of nonlinearity.

Sigmoid, Tanh, and ReLU Neurons

Three major types of neurons are used in practice that introduce nonlinearities in their computations. The first of these is the *sigmoid neuron*, which uses the function:

$$f(z) = \frac{1}{1 + e^{-z}}$$

Intuitively, this means that when the logit is very small, the output of a logistic neuron is close to 0. When the logit is very large, the output of the logistic neuron is close to 1. In-between these two extremes, the neuron assumes an S-shape, as shown in Figure 3-11.

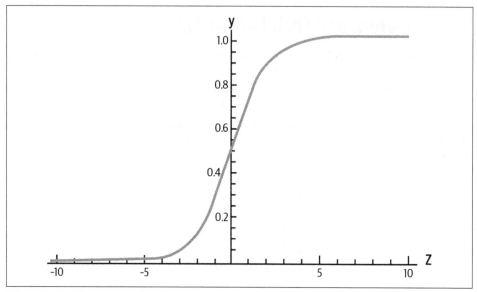

Figure 3-11. The output of a sigmoid neuron as z varies

Tanh neurons use a similar kind of S-shaped nonlinearity, but instead of ranging from 0 to 1, the output of tanh neurons ranges from −1 to 1. As you would expect, they use $f(z) = \tanh(z)$. The resulting relationship between the output y and the logit z is depicted in Figure 3-12. When S-shaped nonlinearities are used, the tanh neuron is often preferred over the sigmoid neuron because it is zero-centered.

A different kind of nonlinearity is used by the *Rectified Linear Unit (ReLU) neuron*. It uses the function $f(z) = \max(0, z)$, resulting in a characteristic hockey-stick-shaped response, as shown in Figure 3-13.

The ReLU has recently become the neuron of choice for many tasks (especially in computer vision) for a number of reasons, despite some drawbacks.[8] We'll discuss these reasons in Chapter 7, as well as strategies to combat the potential pitfalls.

---

8 Nair, Vinod, and Geoffrey E. Hinton. "Rectified Linear Units Improve Restricted Boltzmann Machines." *Proceedings of the 27th International Conference on Machine Learning* (ICML-10), 2010.

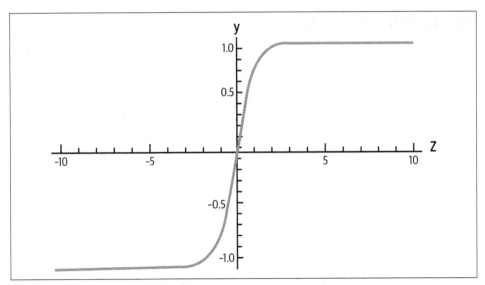

Figure 3-12. The output of a tanh neuron as z varies

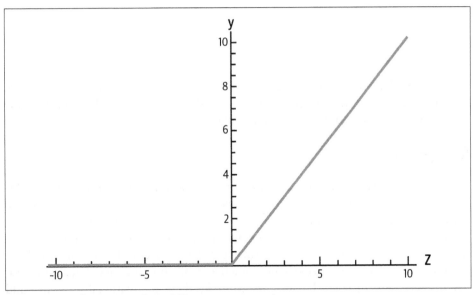

Figure 3-13. The output of a ReLU neuron as z varies

Softmax Output Layers

Oftentimes, we want our output vector to be a probability distribution over a set of mutually exclusive labels. For example, let's say we want to build a neural network to recognize handwritten digits from the MNIST dataset. Each label (0 through 9) is mutually exclusive, but it's unlikely that we will be able to recognize digits with 100% confidence. Using a probability distribution gives us a better idea of how confident we are in our predictions. As a result, the desired output vector is of the following form, where $\sum_{i=0}^{9} p_i = 1$:

$$\begin{bmatrix} p_0 & p_1 & p_2 & p_3 & \cdots & p_9 \end{bmatrix}$$

This is achieved by using a special output layer called a *softmax layer*. Unlike in other kinds of layers, the output of a neuron in a softmax layer depends on the outputs of all the other neurons in its layer. This is because we require the sum of all the outputs to be equal to 1. Letting z_i be the logit of the ith softmax neuron, we can achieve this normalization by setting its output to:

$$y_i = \frac{e^{z_i}}{\sum_j e^{z_j}}$$

A strong prediction would have a single entry in the vector close to 1, while the remaining entries would be close to 0. A weak prediction would have multiple possible labels that are more or less equally likely.

Summary

In this chapter, we've built a basic intuition for machine learning and neural networks. We've talked about the basic structure of a neuron, how feed-forward neural networks work, and the importance of nonlinearity in tackling complex learning problems. In the next chapter, we will begin to build the mathematical background necessary to train a neural network to solve problems. Specifically, we will talk about finding optimal parameter vectors, best practices while training neural networks, and major challenges. In later chapters, we will take these foundational ideas to build more specialized neural architectures.

## CHAPTER 4

Training Feed-Forward Neural Networks

The Fast-Food Problem

We're beginning to understand how we can tackle some interesting problems using deep learning, but one big question still remains: how exactly do we figure out what the parameter vectors (the weights for all of the connections in our neural network) should be? This is accomplished by a process commonly referred to as *training* (see Figure 4-1). During training, we show the neural net a large number of training examples and iteratively modify the weights to minimize the errors we make on the training examples. After enough examples, we expect that our neural network will be quite effective at solving the task it's been trained to do.

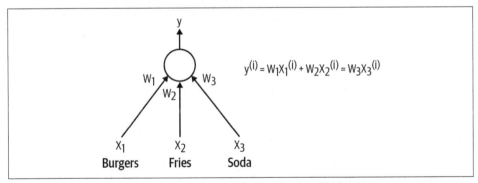

Figure 4-1. *This is the neuron we want to train for the fast-food problem*

Let's continue with an example from Chapter 3 involving a linear neuron: every single day, we purchase a restaurant meal consisting of burgers, fries, and sodas. We buy some number of servings for each item. We want to be able to predict how much a meal is going to cost us, but the items don't have price tags. The only thing the cashier will tell us is the total price of the meal. We want to train a single linear neuron to solve this problem. How do we do it?

One idea is to be intelligent about picking our training cases. For one meal we could buy only a single serving of burgers, for another we could buy only a single serving of fries, and then for our last meal we could buy a single serving of soda. In general, intelligently selecting training examples is a good idea. Lots of research shows that by engineering a clever training set, you can make your neural network a lot more effective. The issue with using this approach alone is that in real situations, it rarely ever gets you close to the solution. For example, there's no clear analog of this strategy in image recognition. It's just not a practical solution.

Instead, we try to motivate a solution that works well in general. Let's say we have a large set of training examples. Then we can calculate what the neural network will output on the ith training example using the simple formula in the diagram. We want to train the neuron so that we pick the most optimal weights possible—the weights that minimize the errors we make on the training examples. In this case, let's say we want to minimize the square error over all of the training examples that we encounter. More formally, if we know that $t^{(i)}$ is the true answer for the ith training example, and $y^{(i)}$ is the value computed by the neural network, we want to minimize the value of the error function E:

$$E = \tfrac{1}{2}\Sigma_i\left(t^{(i)} - y^{(i)}\right)^2$$

The squared error is zero when our model makes a perfectly correct prediction on every training example. Moreover, the closer E is to 0, the better our model is. As a result, our goal is to select our parameter vector θ (the values for all the weights in our model) such that E is as close to 0 as possible.

Now at this point you might be wondering why we need to bother ourselves with error functions when we can treat this problem as a system of equations. After all, we have a bunch of unknowns (weights) and we have a set of equations (one for each training example). That would automatically give us an error of 0, assuming that we have a consistent set of training examples.

That's a smart observation, but the insight unfortunately doesn't generalize well. Remember that although we're using a linear neuron here, linear neurons aren't used very much in practice because they're constrained in what they can learn. And the moment we start using nonlinear neurons like the sigmoidal, tanh, or ReLU neurons we talked about at the end of Chapter 3, we can no longer set up a system of linear equations. Clearly, we need a better strategy to tackle the training process.

Gradient Descent

Let's visualize how we might minimize the squared error over all of the training examples by simplifying the problem. Say our linear neuron has only two inputs (and thus only two weights, w_1 and w_2). Then we can imagine a 3D space where the horizontal dimensions correspond to the weights w_1 and w_2, and the vertical dimension corresponds to the value of the error function E. In this space, points in the horizontal plane correspond to different settings of the weights, and the height at those points corresponds to the incurred error. If we consider the errors we make over all possible weights, we get a surface in this 3D space, in particular, a quadratic bowl as shown in Figure 4-2.

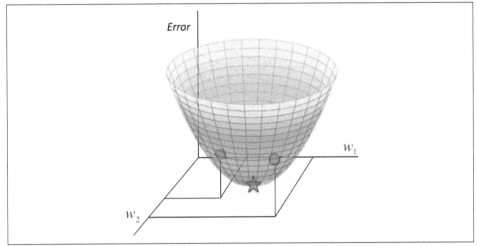

Figure 4-2. The quadratic error surface for a linear neuron

We can also conveniently visualize this surface as a set of elliptical contours, where the minimum error is at the center of the ellipses. In this setup, we are working in a 2D plane where the dimensions correspond to the two weights. Contours correspond to settings of w_1 and w_2 that evaluate to the same value of E. The closer the contours are to each other, the steeper the slope. In fact, it turns out that the direction of the steepest descent is always perpendicular to the contours. This direction is expressed as a vector known as the *gradient*.

Now we can develop a high-level strategy for how to find the values of the weights that minimizes the error function. Suppose we randomly initialize the weights of our network so we find ourselves somewhere on the horizontal plane. By evaluating the gradient at our current position, we can find the direction of steepest descent, and we can take a step in that direction. Then we'll find ourselves at a new position that's closer to the minimum than we were before. We can reevaluate the direction of steepest descent by taking the gradient at this new position and taking a step in this new direction. It's easy to see that, as shown in Figure 4-3, following this strategy will eventually get us to the point of minimum error. This algorithm is known as *gradient descent*, and we'll use it to tackle the problem of training individual neurons and the more general challenge of training entire networks.[1]

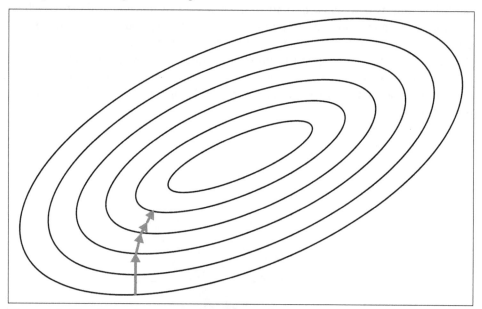

Figure 4-3. Visualizing the error surface as a set of contours

The Delta Rule and Learning Rates

Before we derive the exact algorithm for training our fast-food neuron, we have a quick note on *hyperparameters*. In addition to the weight parameters defined in our neural network, learning algorithms also require a couple of additional parameters to carry out the training process. One of these so-called hyperparameters is the *learning rate*.

In practice, at each step of moving perpendicular to the contour, we need to determine how far we want to walk before recalculating our new direction. This distance needs to depend on the steepness of the surface. Why? The closer we are to the minimum, the shorter we want to step forward. We know we are close to the minimum because the surface is a lot flatter, so we can use the steepness as an indicator of how close we are to the minimum. However, if our error surface is rather mellow, training can potentially take a large amount of time. As a result, we often multiply the

---

1 Rosenbloom, P. "The Method of Steepest Descent." *Proceedings of Symposia in Applied Mathematics.* Vol. 6. 1956.

gradient by a factor ϵ, the learning rate. Picking the learning rate is a hard problem (Figure 4-4). As we just discussed, if we pick a learning rate that's too small, we risk taking too long during the training process. But if we pick a learning rate that's too big, we'll mostly likely start diverging away from the minimum. In Chapter 5, we'll learn about various optimization techniques that utilize adaptive learning rates to automate the process of selecting learning rates.

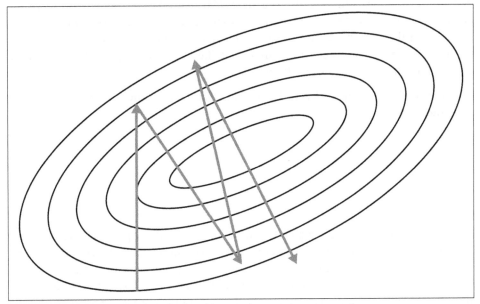

Figure 4-4. Convergence is difficult when our learning rate is too large

Now, we are finally ready to derive the *delta rule* for training our linear neuron. In order to calculate how to change each weight, we evaluate the gradient, which is essentially the partial derivative of the error function with respect to each of the weights. In other words, we want:

$$\Delta w_k = -\epsilon \frac{\partial E}{\partial w_k}$$

$$= -\epsilon \frac{\partial}{\partial w_k} \left(\frac{1}{2} \Sigma_i \left(t^{(i)} - y^{(i)} \right)^2 \right)$$

$$= \Sigma_i \epsilon \left(t^{(i)} - y^{(i)} \right) \frac{\partial y_i}{\partial w_k}$$

$$= \Sigma_i \epsilon x_k^{(i)} \left(t^{(i)} - y^{(i)} \right)$$

Applying this method of changing the weights at every iteration, we are finally able to utilize gradient descent.

Gradient Descent with Sigmoidal Neurons

In this section and the next, we will deal with training neurons and neural networks that utilize nonlinearities. We use the sigmoidal neuron as a model, and leave the derivations for other nonlinear neurons as an exercise for you. For simplicity, we assume that the neurons do not use a bias term, although our analysis easily extends to this case. We merely need to assume that the bias is a weight on an incoming connection whose input value is always one.

Let's recall the mechanism by which logistic neurons compute their output value from their inputs:

$$z = \Sigma_k w_k x_k$$

$$y = \frac{1}{1 + e^{-z}}$$

The neuron computes the weighted sum of its inputs, the logit z. It then feeds its logit into the input function to compute y, its final output. Fortunately for us, these functions have nice derivatives, which makes learning easy! For learning, we want to compute the gradient of the error function with respect to the weights. To do so, we start by taking the derivative of the logit with respect to the inputs and the weights:

$$\frac{\partial z}{\partial w_k} = x_k$$

$$\frac{\partial z}{\partial x_k} = w_k$$

Also, quite surprisingly, the derivative of the output with respect to the logit is quite simple if you express it in terms of the output:

$$\frac{dy}{dz} = \frac{e^{-z}}{\left(1 + e^{-z}\right)^2}$$

$$= \frac{1}{1 + e^{-z}} \frac{e^{-z}}{1 + e^{-z}}$$

$$= \frac{1}{1 + e^{-z}} \left(1 - \frac{1}{1 + e^{-z}}\right)$$

$$= y(1 - y)$$

We then use the chain rule to get the derivative of the output with respect to each weight:

$$\frac{\partial y}{\partial w_k} = \frac{dy}{dz}\frac{\partial z}{\partial w_k} = x_k y(1-y)$$

Putting all of this together, we can now compute the derivative of the error function with respect to each weight:

$$\frac{\partial E}{\partial w_k} = \Sigma_i \frac{\partial E}{\partial y^{(i)}}\frac{\partial y^{(i)}}{\partial w_k} = -\Sigma_i x_k^{(i)} y^{(i)}\left(1-y^{(i)}\right)\left(t^{(i)}-y^{(i)}\right)$$

Thus, the final rule for modifying the weights becomes:

$$\Delta w_k = \Sigma_i \epsilon x_k^{(i)} y^{(i)}\left(1-y^{(i)}\right)\left(t^{(i)}-y^{(i)}\right)$$

As you may notice, the new modification rule is just like the delta rule, except with extra multiplicative terms included to account for the logistic component of the sigmoidal neuron.

The Backpropagation Algorithm

Now we're finally ready to tackle the problem of training multilayer neural networks (instead of just single neurons). To accomplish this task, we'll use an approach known as *backpropagation*, pioneered by David E. Rumelhart, Geoffrey E. Hinton, and Ronald J. Williams in 1986.[2] So what's the idea behind backpropagation? We don't know what the hidden units ought to be doing, but what we can do is compute how fast the error changes as we change a hidden activity. From there, we can figure out how fast the error changes when we change the weight of an individual connection. Essentially, we'll be trying to find the path of steepest descent. The only catch is that we're going to be working in an extremely high-dimensional space. We start by calculating the error derivatives with respect to a single training example.

Each hidden unit can affect many output units. Thus, we'll have to combine many separate effects on the error in an informative way. Our strategy will be one of dynamic programming. Once we have the error derivatives for one layer of hidden units, we'll use them to compute the error derivatives for the activities of the layer below. And once we find the error derivatives for the activities of the hidden units, it's

---

2 Rumelhart, David E., Geoffrey E. Hinton, and Ronald J. Williams. "Learning Representations by Back-Propagating Errors." *Cognitive Modeling* 5.3 (1988): 1.

quite easy to get the error derivatives for the weights leading into a hidden unit. We'll redefine some notation for ease of discussion and refer to Figure 4-5.

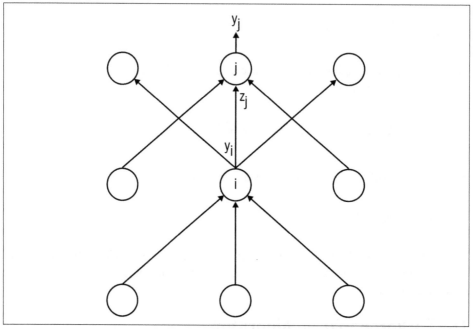

Figure 4-5. Reference diagram for the derivation of the backpropagation algorithm

The subscript we use will refer to the layer of the neuron. The symbol y will refer to the activity of a neuron, as usual. Similarly, the symbol z will refer to the logit of the neuron. We start by taking a look at the base case of the dynamic programming problem. Specifically, we calculate the error function derivatives at the output layer:

$$E = \tfrac{1}{2} \Sigma_{j \,\in\, output} \left(t_j - y_j \right)^2 \Rightarrow \frac{\partial E}{\partial y_j} = -\left(t_j - y_j \right)$$

Now we tackle the inductive step. Let's presume we have the error derivatives for layer j. We next aim to calculate the error derivatives for the layer below it, layer i. To do so, we must accumulate information about how the output of a neuron in layer i affects the logits of every neuron in layer j. This can be done as follows, using the fact that the partial derivative of the logit with respect to the incoming output data from the layer beneath is merely the weight of the connection w_{ij}:

$$\frac{\partial E}{\partial y_i} = \Sigma_j \frac{\partial E}{\partial z_j} \frac{dz_j}{dy_i} = \Sigma_j w_{ij} \frac{\partial E}{\partial z_j}$$

Furthermore, we observe the following:

$$\frac{\partial E}{\partial z_j} = \frac{\partial E}{\partial y_j}\frac{dy_j}{dz_j} = y_j\left(1 - y_j\right)\frac{\partial E}{\partial y_j}$$

Combining these two, we can finally express the error derivatives of layer i in terms of the error derivatives of layer j:

$$\frac{\partial E}{\partial y_i} = \Sigma_j w_{ij}y_j\left(1 - y_j\right)\frac{\partial E}{\partial y_j}$$

Once we've gone through the whole dynamic programming routine, having filled up the table appropriately with all of our partial derivatives (of the error function with respect to the hidden unit activities), we can then determine how the error changes with respect to the weights. This gives us a way to modify the weights after each training example:

$$\frac{\partial E}{\partial w_{ij}} = \frac{\partial z_j}{\partial w_{ij}}\frac{\partial E}{\partial z_j} = y_i y_j\left(1 - y_j\right)\frac{\partial E}{\partial y_j}$$

Finally, to complete the algorithm, just as before, we merely sum up the partial derivatives over all the training examples in our dataset. This gives us the following modification formula:

$$\Delta w_{ij} = -\Sigma_{k \in dataset}\epsilon y_i^{(k)}y_j^{(k)}\left(1 - y_j^{(k)}\right)\frac{\partial E^{(k)}}{\partial y_j^{(k)}}$$

This completes our description of the backpropagation algorithm.

Stochastic and Minibatch Gradient Descent

In the algorithms we described in "The Backpropagation Algorithm" on page 61, we used a version of gradient descent known as *batch gradient descent*. The idea behind batch gradient descent is that we use our entire dataset to compute the error surface and then follow the gradient to take the path of steepest descent. For a simple quadratic error surface, this works quite well. But in most cases, our error surface may be a lot more complicated. Let's consider the scenario in Figure 4-6.

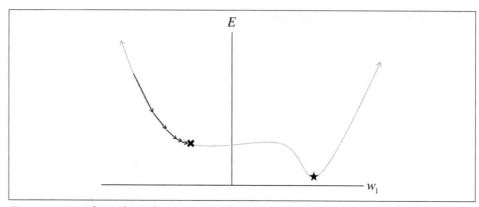

Figure 4-6. Batch gradient descent is sensitive to saddle points, which can lead to premature convergence

We have only a single weight, and we use random initialization and batch gradient descent to find its optimal setting. The error surface, however, has a flat region (also known as saddle point in high-dimensional spaces), and if we get unlucky, we might find ourselves getting stuck while performing gradient descent.

Another potential approach is *stochastic gradient descent* (SGD), where at each iteration, our error surface is estimated with respect to only a single example. This approach is illustrated by Figure 4-7, where instead of a single static error surface, our error surface is dynamic. As a result, descending on this stochastic surface significantly improves our ability to navigate flat regions.

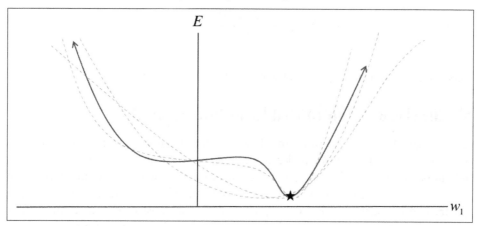

Figure 4-7. The stochastic error surface fluctuates with respect to the batch error surface, enabling saddle point avoidance

The major pitfall of SGD, however, is that looking at the error incurred one example at a time may not be a good enough approximation of the error surface. This, in turn, could potentially make gradient descent take a significant amount of time. One way to combat this problem is using *minibatch gradient descent*. In minibatch gradient descent, at every iteration we compute the error surface with respect to some subset of the total dataset (instead of just a single example). This subset is called a *minibatch*, and in addition to the learning rate, minibatch size is another hyperparameter. Minibatches strike a balance between the efficiency of batch gradient descent and the local-minima avoidance afforded by stochastic gradient descent. In the context of backpropagation, our weight update step becomes:

$$\Delta w_{ij} = -\Sigma_{k \in minibatch} \epsilon y_i^{(k)} y_j^{(k)} \left(1 - y_j^{(k)}\right) \frac{\partial E^{(k)}}{\partial y_j^{(k)}}$$

This is identical to what we derived in the previous section, but instead of summing over all the examples in the dataset, we sum over the examples in the current minibatch. For a more theoretical discussion of why SGD and minibatch gradient descent result in an unbiased estimate of the gradient over the total dataset, please refer to "Neural Net Learning Theory" on page 74.

Test Sets, Validation Sets, and Overfitting

One of the major issues with artificial neural networks is that the models are quite complicated. For example, let's consider a neural network that pulls data from an image from the MNIST database (28 × 28 pixels), feeds into two hidden layers with 30 neurons, and finally reaches a softmax layer of 10 neurons. The total number of parameters in the network is nearly 25,000. This can be quite problematic, and to understand why, let's consider a new toy example, illustrated in Figure 4-8.

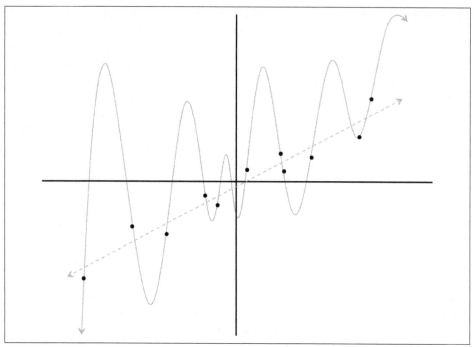

Figure 4-8. Two potential models that might describe our dataset: a linear model versus a degree 12 polynomial

We are given a bunch of data points on a flat plane, and our goal is to find a curve that best describes this dataset (i.e., will allow us to predict the *y* coordinate of a new point given its *x* coordinate). Using the data, we train two different models: a linear model and a degree 12 polynomial. Which curve should we trust? The line that gets almost no training example correct? Or the complicated curve that hits every single point in the dataset? At this point we might trust the linear fit because it seems much less contrived. But just to be sure, let's add more data to our dataset. The result is shown in Figure 4-9.

Now the verdict is clear: the linear model is not only better subjectively but also quantitatively (measured using the squared error metric). This leads to an interesting point about training and evaluating machine learning models. By building a very complex model, it's quite easy to perfectly fit our training dataset because we give our model enough degrees of freedom to contort itself to fit the observations in the training set. But when we evaluate such a complex model on new data, it performs poorly. In other words, the model does not *generalize* well. This is a phenomenon called *overfitting*, and it is one of the biggest challenges that a machine learning engineer must combat. This becomes an even more significant issue in deep learning, where our neural networks have large numbers of layers containing many neurons.

The number of connections in these models is astronomical, reaching the millions. As a result, overfitting is commonplace.

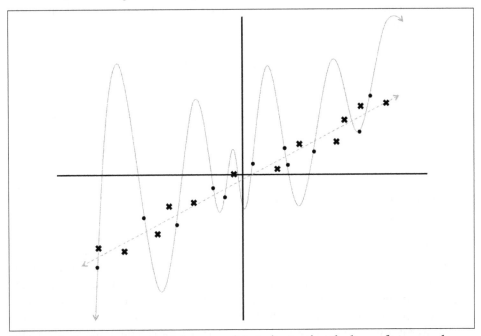

Figure 4-9. Evaluating our model on new data indicates that the linear fit is a much better model than the degree 12 polynomial

Let's see how this looks in the context of a neural network. Say we have a neural network with two inputs, a softmax output of size 2, and a hidden layer with 3, 6, or 20 neurons. We train these networks using minibatch gradient descent (batch size 10), and the results, visualized using ConvNetJS (*http://stanford.io/2pOdNhy*), are shown in Figure 4-10.

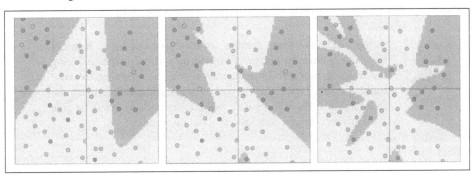

Figure 4-10. A visualization of neural networks with 3, 6, and 20 neurons (in that order) in their hidden layer

It's already quite apparent from these images that as the number of connections in our network increases, so does our propensity to overfit to the data. We can similarly see the phenomenon of overfitting as we make our neural networks deep. These results are shown in Figure 4-11.

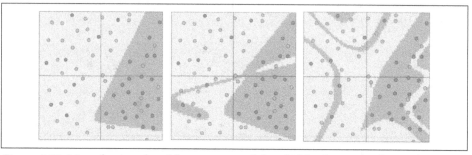

Figure 4-11. Neural networks with one, two, and four hidden layers (in that order) of three neurons each

This leads to three major observations. First, the machine learning engineer is always working with a direct trade-off between overfitting and model complexity. If the model isn't complex enough, it may not be powerful enough to capture all of the useful information necessary to solve a problem. However, if our model is very complex (especially if we have a limited amount of data at our disposal), we run the risk of overfitting. Deep learning takes the approach of solving complex problems with complex models and taking additional countermeasures to prevent overfitting. We'll see a lot of these measures in this and later chapters.

Second, it is misleading to evaluate a model using the data we used to train it. Using the example in Figure 4-8, this would falsely suggest that the degree 12 polynomial model is preferable to a linear fit. As a result, we almost never train our model on the entire dataset. Instead, we split up our data into a *training set* and a *test set* (Figure 4-12). This enables us to make a fair evaluation of our model by directly measuring how well it generalizes on new data it has not yet seen.

 In the real world, large datasets are hard to come by, so it might seem like a waste to not use all of the data at our disposal during the training process. Consequently, it may be tempting to reuse training data for testing or cut corners while compiling test data. Be forewarned: if the test set isn't well constructed, we won't be able draw any meaningful conclusions about our model.

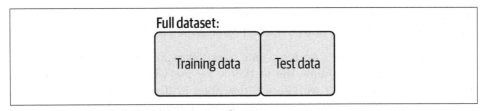

Figure 4-12. Nonoverlapping training and test sets

Third, it's quite likely that while we're training our data, there's a point in time when instead of learning useful features, we start overfitting to the training set. To avoid that, we want to be able to stop the training process as soon as we start overfitting to prevent poor generalization. To do this, we divide our training process into *epochs*. An epoch is a single iteration over the entire training set. If we have a training set of size d and we are doing minibatch gradient descent with batch size b, then an epoch would be equivalent to $\frac{d}{b}$ model updates. At the end of each epoch, we want to measure how well our model is generalizing. To do this, we use an additional *validation set*, which is shown in Figure 4-13.

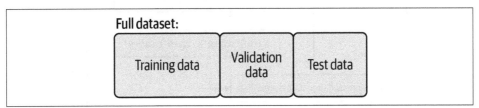

Figure 4-13. A validation set to prevent overfitting during the training process

At the end of an epoch, the validation set will tell us how the model does on data it has yet to see. If the accuracy on the training set continues to increase while the accuracy on the validation set stays the same (or decreases), it's a good sign that it's time to stop training because we're overfitting.

The validation set is also helpful as a proxy measure of accuracy during the process of *hyperparameter optimization*. We've covered several hyperparameters so far (learning rate, minibatch size, etc.), but we have yet to develop a framework for how to find the optimal values for these hyperparameters. One potential way to find the optimal setting of hyperparameters is by applying a *grid search*, where we pick a value for each hyperparameter from a finite set of options (e.g., $\epsilon \in \{0.001, 0.01, 0.1\}$, batch size $\in \{16, 64, 128\}, ...$), and train the model with every possible permutation of hyperparameter choices. We elect the combination of hyperparameters with the best performance on the validation set and report the accuracy of the model trained with the best combination on the test set.[3]

With this in mind, before we jump into describing the various ways to directly combat overfitting, let's outline the workflow we use when building and training deep learning models. The workflow is described in detail in Figure 4-14. It is a tad intricate, but it's critical to understand the pipeline to ensure that we're properly training our neural networks.

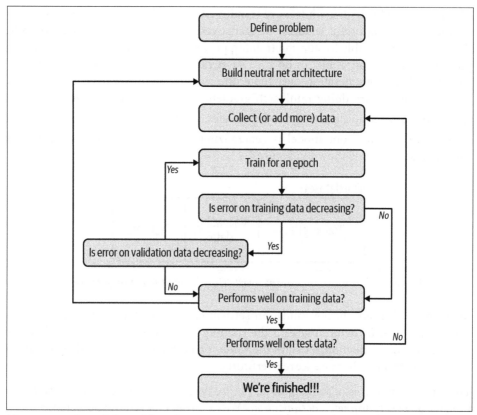

Figure 4-14. Detailed workflow for training and evaluating a deep learning model

First, we define our problem rigorously. This involves determining our inputs, the potential outputs, and the vectorized representations of both. For instance, let's say our goal was to train a deep learning model to identify cancer. Our input would be an RBG image, which can be represented as a vector of pixel values. Our output would be a probability distribution over three mutually exclusive possibilities: (1) normal,

---

3 Nelder, John A., and Roger Mead. "A Simplex Method for Function Minimization." *The Computer Journal* 7.4 (1965): 308-313.

(2) benign tumor (a cancer that has yet to metastasize), or (3) malignant tumor (a cancer that has already metastasized to other organs).

After we define our problem, we need to build a neural network architecture to solve it. Our input layer would have to be of appropriate size to accept the raw data from the image, and our output layer would have to be a softmax of size 3. We will also have to define the internal architecture of the network (number of hidden layers, the connectivities, etc.). We'll further discuss the architecture of image recognition models when we talk about convolutional neural networks in Chapter 6. At this point, we also want to collect a significant amount of data for training or modeling. This data would probably be in the form of uniformly sized pathological images that have been labeled by a medical expert. We shuffle and divide this data up into separate training, validation, and test sets.

Finally, we're ready to begin gradient descent. We train the model on our training set for an epoch at a time. At the end of each epoch, we ensure that our error on the training set and validation set is decreasing. When one of these stops improving, we terminate and make sure we're happy with the model's performance on the test data. If we're unsatisfied, we need to rethink our architecture or reconsider whether the data we collect has the information required to make the prediction we're interested in making. If our training set error stopped improving, we probably need to do a better job of capturing the important features in our data. If our validation set error stopped improving, we probably need to take measures to prevent overfitting.

If, however, we are happy with the performance of our model on the training data, then we can measure its performance on the test data, which the model has never seen before this point. If it is unsatisfactory, we need more data in our dataset because the test set seems to consist of example types that weren't well represented in the training set. Otherwise, we are finished!

Preventing Overfitting in Deep Neural Networks

Several techniques have been proposed to prevent overfitting during the training process. In this section, we'll discuss these techniques in detail.

One method of combatting overfitting is called *regularization*. Regularization modifies the objective function that we minimize by adding additional terms that penalize large weights. We change the objective function so that it becomes $Error + \lambda f(\theta)$, where $f(\theta)$ grows larger as the components of θ grow larger, and λ is the regularization strength (another hyperparameter). The value we choose for λ determines how much we want to protect against overfitting. A $\lambda = 0$ implies that we do not take any measures against the possibility of overfitting. If λ is too large, then our model will prioritize keeping θ as small as possible over trying to find the parameter values that perform well on our training set. As a result, choosing λ is a very important task and can require some trial and error.

The most common type of regularization in machine learning is *L2 regularization*.[4] It can be implemented by augmenting the error function with the squared magnitude of all weights in the neural network. In other words, for every weight w in the neural network, we add $\frac{1}{2}\lambda w^2$ to the error function. The L2 regularization has the intuitive interpretation of heavily penalizing peaky weight vectors and preferring diffuse weight vectors. This has the appealing property of encouraging the network to use all of its inputs a little rather than using only some of its inputs a lot. Of particular note is that during the gradient descent update, using the L2 regularization ultimately means that every weight is decayed linearly to zero. Because of this phenomenon, L2 regularization is also commonly referred to as *weight decay*.

We can visualize the effects of L2 regularization using ConvNetJS. Similar to Figures 2-10 and 2-11, we use a neural network with 2 inputs, a softmax output of size 2, and a hidden layer with 20 neurons. We train the networks using minibatch gradient descent (batch size 10) and regularization strengths of 0.01, 0.1, and 1. The results can be seen in Figure 4-15.

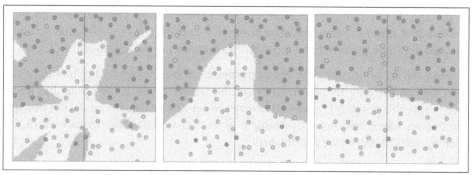

Figure 4-15. A visualization of neural networks trained with regularization strengths of 0.01, 0.1, and 1 (in that order)

Another common type of regularization is *L1 regularization*. Here, we add the term $\lambda|w|$ for every weight w in the neural network. The L1 regularization has the intriguing property that it leads the weight vectors to become sparse during optimization (i.e., close to exactly zero). Neurons with L1 regularization end up using only a small subset of their most important inputs and become quite resistant to noise in the inputs. In comparison, weight vectors from L2 regularization are usually diffuse, small numbers. L1 regularization is useful when you want to understand exactly

---

4 Tikhonov, Andrei Nikolaevich, and Vladlen Borisovich Glasko. "Use of the Regularization Method in Non-Linear Problems." *USSR Computational Mathematics and Mathematical Physics* 5.3 (1965): 93-107.

which features are contributing to a decision. If this level of feature analysis isn't necessary, we prefer to use L2 regularization because it empirically performs better.

Max norm constraints have a similar goal of attempting to restrict θ from becoming too large, but they do this more directly.[5] Max norm constraints enforce an absolute upper bound on the magnitude of the incoming weight vector for every neuron and use projected gradient descent to enforce the constraint. So any time a gradient descent step moves the incoming weight vector such that $\|w\|_2 > c$, we project the vector back onto the ball (centered at the origin) with radius c. Typical values of c are 3 and 4. One of the nice properties is that the parameter vector cannot grow out of control (even if the learning rates are too high) because the updates to the weights are always bounded.

Dropout is a different kind of method for preventing overfitting that has become one of the most favored methods of preventing overfitting in deep neural networks.[6] While training, dropout is implemented by only keeping a neuron active with some probability p (a hyperparameter), or setting it to zero otherwise. Intuitively, this forces the network to be accurate even in the absence of certain information. It prevents the network from becoming too dependent on any one neuron (or any small combination of neurons). Expressed more mathematically, it prevents overfitting by providing a way of approximately combining exponentially many different neural network architectures efficiently. The process of dropout is expressed in Figure 4-16.

Dropout is pretty intuitive, but there are some important intricacies to consider. First, we'd like the outputs of neurons during test time to be equivalent to their expected outputs at training time. We could fix this naively by scaling the output at test time. For example, if $p = 0.5$, neurons must halve their outputs at test time in order to have the same (expected) output they would have during training. This is easy to see because a neuron's output is set to 0 with probability $1 - p$. This means that if a neuron's output prior to dropout was x, then after dropout, the expected output would be $E[\text{output}] = px + (1 - p) \cdot 0 = px$. This naive implementation of dropout is undesirable, however, because it requires scaling of neuron outputs at test time. Test-time performance is extremely critical to model evaluation, so it's always preferable to use *inverted dropout*, where the scaling occurs at training time instead of at test time. In inverted dropout, any neuron whose activation hasn't been silenced has its output divided by p before the value is propagated to the next layer. With this fix, $E[\text{output}] = p \cdot \frac{x}{p} + (1 - p) \cdot 0 = x$, and we can avoid arbitrarily scaling neuronal output at test time.

---

5 Srebro, Nathan, Jason DM Rennie, and Tommi S. Jaakkola. "Maximum-Margin Matrix Factorization." *NIPS*, Vol. 17, 2004.

6 Srivastava, Nitish, et al. "Dropout: A Simple Way to Prevent Neural Networks from Overfitting." *Journal of Machine Learning Research* 15.1 (2014): 1929-1958.

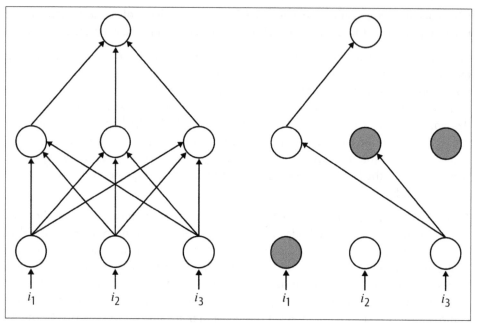

Figure 4-16. Dropout sets each neuron in the network as inactive with some random probability during each minibatch of training

Neural Net Learning Theory

Let's cover some of the theory underpinning SGD and minibatch gradient descent. We noted some of the empirical gains from SGD and minibatch gradient descent in this chapter. Here, we try to understand why it is even "OK," in theory, to use these learning algorithms as a substitute for the gradient update over the entire dataset, which can often be intractable with many training examples. The intractability arises from having to take the partial derivative with respect to every weight in the neural network for every training example in any given iteration, which is prohibitive for large datasets and neural networks of even moderate size.

Here, for simplicity, we will refer to X as the *data matrix*, which is a matrix of dimension n by d, where n refers to the number of inputs in the entire dataset and d refers to the number of features associated with any given input. In other words, each row of X corresponds to a single training example. In addition to X, we have y, a vector of labels, or desired outputs, associated with each input of the data matrix. As can be inferred, y is of dimension n by 1. We refer to $f(\,\cdot\,, \theta)$ as the function defined by the neural network, and θ as the weights (which we intend to learn through the training process) that parametrize it. Finally, we refer to $L(\widehat{y}, y)$ as the error, or loss, function when comparing the predicted output $\widehat{y}$ with the true output y.

Let's start with some basic assumptions. Where do X and y even come from? We assume that there is some underlying data-generating process from which X and y are produced. That is, there exists a joint distribution over inputs and labels $p(x, y)$ from which the dataset we observe has been randomly sampled. In classical learning theory, we would like our learned function, or neural network $f(\cdot, \theta)$, to minimize the objective:

$$E_{p(x, y)}[L(f(x, \theta), y)]$$

or the expected loss with respect to the true distribution $p(x, y)$. We term this objective the *population risk*. Why minimize the population risk? Intuitively, the more popular any given pairing of input datapoint $x^{(i)}$ and output label $y^{(i)}$ under the true distribution, the more we would like weight the output of $f(x^{(i)}, \theta)$ resembling $y^{(i)}$. $L(f(x^{(i)}, \theta), y^{(i)})$ quantifies how well (or in this case, equivalently, how poorly given L is an error function) the output of $f(x^{(i)}, \theta)$ resembles $y^{(i)}$. The optimal weight is simply $p(x^{(i)}, y^{(i)})$, which quantifies the popularity of the pairing. Putting this logic together over all possible pairings, we arrive at the population risk objective. Note that this logic holds regardless of whether x and y are discrete or continuous.

Unfortunately, we have no access to the true distribution. If we did, our problem would already be solved (more accurately, is instantly solved when y is discrete). The best we can do is approximate $p(x, y)$ with the data we see. We call this empirical distribution $p_D(x, y)$, which, in the limit of infinite data, converges to $p(x, y)$, making any gradient update based on the empirical distribution unbiased. The domain of the empirical distribution is our training set. Instead of minimizing the population risk, we minimize the *empirical risk* as a proxy:

$$E_{p_D(x, y)}[L(f(x; \theta), y)] = \frac{1}{n}\Sigma_{i=1}^{n} L(f(x^{(i)}; \theta), y^{(i)})$$

Now, we would like to find a set of weights θ, that minimize the empirical risk. We do that by taking the gradient of the objective with respect to θ:

$$\nabla_\theta E_{p_D(x, y)}[L(f(x; \theta), y)]$$

$$= \nabla_\theta \frac{1}{n}\Sigma_{i=1}^{n} L(f(x^{(i)}; \theta), y^{(i)})$$

$$= \frac{1}{n}\Sigma_{i=1}^{n} \nabla_\theta L(f(x^{(i)}; \theta), y^{(i)})$$

We now see that the newly introduced empirical risk minimization is the theoretical motivation for the gradient update over the entire dataset presented in "The Backpropagation Algorithm" on page 61. The only, subtle difference is the factor $\frac{1}{n}$, which is a constant that can be rolled into the learning rate. Extending the last equality, we have:

$$\frac{1}{n}\Sigma_{i=1}^{n} \nabla_{\theta} L\big(f\big(x^{(i)}; \theta\big), y^{(i)}\big) = E_{p_D(x,y)}[\nabla_{\theta} L(f(x; \theta), y)]$$

We can do something that uses almost the exact same logic, which allows us to use the empirical risk as a proxy for population risk: approximate the expectation with respect to the empirical distribution via sampling. Again, this is unbiased since we achieve the empirical distribution in the limit of infinite samples. The number of samples is left as a hyperparameter, where using a single sample has been popularly termed SGD; using a relatively small number of samples has been popularly termed minibatch gradient descent.

Summary

In this chapter, we've learned all of the basics involved in training feed-forward neural networks. We've talked about gradient descent, the backpropagation algorithm, as well as various methods we can use to prevent overfitting. In the next chapter, we'll put these lessons into practice when we use the PyTorch library to efficiently implement our first neural networks. Then in Chapter 6, we'll return to the problem of optimizing objective functions for training neural networks and design algorithms to significantly improve performance. These improvements will enable us to process much more data, which means we'll be able to build more comprehensive models.

## CHAPTER 5

Implementing Neural Networks in PyTorch

Introduction to PyTorch

In this chapter, you will learn the basics of PyTorch, one of the most popular deep learning frameworks in use today. PyTorch was introduced by Facebook's AI Research Lab in 2016 and gained users rapidly, both in industry and in research, through the following years. One reason for PyTorch's widespread adoption was its intuitive, Pythonic feel, which fit naturally into the preexisting workstreams and coding paradigms followed by deep learning practitioners.

In particular, this chapter will discuss the data structures utilized by PyTorch, how to define neural models in PyTorch, and how to connect data with models for training and testing. Finally, we implement a practical example in PyTorch—a classifier for the MNIST digits dataset, complete with code for training and testing the classifier.

Installing PyTorch

Installing a CPU-compatible version of PyTorch is relatively simple. The PyTorch docs recommend using conda, a package management system. Within conda, you can create multiple environments, where an environment is a context that encapsulates all of your package installs. Access to a package does not transfer across environments—this allows the user to have a clean separation between different contexts by downloading packages within individual environments. We recommend that you create a conda environment for deep learning purposes that you can switch into whenever necessary. We refer you to the conda docs for guidance on how to download conda and further notes on environments.

Once you have installed conda, created your deep learning environment, and switched into it, the PyTorch docs recommend running the following code from your command line to download a CPU-compatible version of PyTorch on macOS:

```
conda install pytorch torchvision torchaudio -c pytorch
```

Note that with this install come torchvision and torchaudio, which are specialized packages for working with image data and audio data, respectively. If you are on a Linux system, the docs recommend running the following code from your command line:

```
conda install pytorch torchvision torchaudio cpuonly -c pytorch
```

Now, you can navigate to a Python shell (still in your deep learning environment), and the following command should run with no issues:

```
import torch
```

It is important to get this command running with no errors in your Python shell before moving on to running the code in the following sections, as they all require the ability to import the PyTorch package.

PyTorch Tensors

Tensors are the primary data structure by which PyTorch stores and manipulates numerical information. Tensors can be seen as a generalization of arrays and matrices, which we covered in detail in our introduction to linear algebra in Chapter 1. Specifically, tensors, as a generalization of 2D matrices and 1D arrays, can store multidimensional data such as batches of three-channel images. Note that this requires 4D data storage, since each image is 3D (including the channel dimension), and a fourth dimension that is required to index each individual image. Tensors can even represent dimensionalities beyond the 4D space, although the usage of such tensors in practice is uncommon.

In PyTorch, tensors are utilized universally. They are used to represent the inputs to models, the weight layers within the models themselves, and the outputs of models. The standard linear algebra operations of transposition, addition, multiplication, inversion, etc., can all be run on tensors.

Tensor Init

How do we initialize tensors? We can initialize a tensor from a variety of data types. Some examples are Python lists and Python numerical primitives:

```
arr = [1,2]
tensor = torch.tensor(arr)
val = 2.0
tensor = torch.tensor(val)
```

Tensors can also be initialized from NumPy arrays, allowing PyTorch to be integrated easily into existing data science and machine learning workflows:

```
import numpy as np
np_arr = np.array([1,2])
x_t = torch.from_numpy(np_arr)
```

Additionally, tensors can be formed via some common PyTorch API endpoints:

```
zeros_t = torch.zeros((2,3)) # Returns 2x3 tensor of zeros
ones_t = torch.ones((2,3)) # Returns 2x3 tensor of ones
rand_t = torch.randn((2,3)) # Returns 2x3 tensor of random numbers
```

Tensor Attributes

In the examples we just saw, we passed a tuple as the argument to each function call. The number of indices in the tuple is the dimensionality of the tensor to be created, while the number at each index represents the desired size of that particular dimension. To access the dimensionality of a tensor, we can call its shape attribute:

```
zeros_t.shape # Returns torch.Size([2, 3])
```

Calling the shape attribute on any of the previous examples should return the same tuple as the input argument, assuming the tensor has not been significantly modified in-between.

What are some other attributes of tensors? In addition to dimension, tensors also store information on the type of data being stored: floating point, complex, integer, and boolean. There exist subtypes within each of these categories, but we won't go into the differences between each subtype here. It's also important to note that a tensor cannot contain a mix and match of various data types—all data within a single tensor must be of the same data type. To access the data type of a tensor, we can call its dtype attribute:

```
x_t = torch.tensor(2.0)
x_t.dtype # Returns torch.float32
```

Additionally, although we haven't shown this yet, we can set the data type of a tensor during initialization. Extending one of our previous examples:

```
arr = [1,2]
x_t = torch.tensor(arr, dtype=torch.float32)
```

In addition to the data type and shape of a tensor, we can also learn the device on which the tensor is allocated. These devices include the famous CPU, which is standard with any computer and is the default storage for any tensor, and the GPU, or graphics processing unit, which is a specialized data processing unit often used in the image space. GPUs massively speed up many common tensor operations such as multiplication via parallel processing over hundreds of small, specialized cores, thus making them immensely useful for most deep learning applications. To access the tensor device, we can call its device attribute:

```
x_t.device # Returns device(type='cpu') by default
```

Similarly to data type, we can set the device of a tensor upon initialization:

```
# PyTorch will use GPU if it's available
device = 'cuda' if torch.cuda.is_available() else 'cpu'
arr = [1,2]
x_t = torch.tensor(arr, dtype=torch.float32, device=device)
```

This is a common approach to checking whether a GPU is available via code and using a GPU if it is available. If the GPU is not available, it will use a CPU without error.

If you have defined a tensor with a certain set of attributes and would like to modify these attributes, you can use the to function:

```
x_t = x_t.to(device, dtype=torch.int)
```

And finally, as we'll cover in "Gradients in PyTorch" on page 83, PyTorch tensors can be initialized with the argument requires_grad, which when set to True, stores the tensor's gradient in an attribute called grad.

Tensor Operations

The PyTorch API provides us with many possible tensor operations, ranging from tensor arithmetic to tensor indexing. In this section we will cover some of the more useful tensor operations—ones that you will likely use often in your deep learning applications.

One of the most basic operations is multiplying a tensor by some scalar c. This can be achieved via the code:

```
c = 10
x_t = x_t*c
```

This results in an element-wise product of the scalar with the entries of the tensor. Another one of the most basic tensor operations is tensor addition and subtraction. To do this, we can simply add tensors via +. Subtraction follows directly from being able to do addition and multiplying the second tensor by the scalar −1:

```
x1_t = torch.zeros((1,2))
x2_t = torch.ones((1,2))
x1_t + x2_t
# returns tensor([[1., 1.]])
```

The result is an element-wise sum of the two tensors. This can be seen as a direct generalization of matrix addition for any dimensionality. Note that this direct generalization implicitly assumes the same constraint we discussed for matrix addition a while ago: that the two tensors being summed are of the same dimension. PyTorch, similarly, will accept any two broadcastable inputs with no issues, where broadcasting is a procedure by which the two inputs are resolved to a common shape, and broadcastable refers to whether it is even possible for the two inputs to be resolved to a common shape. If the two tensors are already of the same shape, no broadcasting is necessary. We refer you to the PyTorch documentation (*https://oreil.ly/rHEdO*) for more information on how the API determines if the two inputs are broadcastable, and how broadcasting is performed in such cases.

Tensor multiplication is another useful operation to become familiar with. Tensor multiplication works the same as matrix and vector multiplication when the dimensionality of each tensor is less than or equal to 2. However, tensor multiplication also works on tensors of arbitrarily high dimensionality, given the two tensors are compatible. We can think of tensor multiplication in high dimensions as batched matrix multiplications: imagine we have two tensors, the first is of shape (2,1,2) and the second is of shape (2,2,2). We can further represent the first tensor as a length-two list of 1×2 matrices, while the second is a length-two list of 2×2 matrices. Their product is a length-two list, where index i of the product is the matrix product of index i of the first tensor and index i of the second tensor, as shown in Figure 5-1.

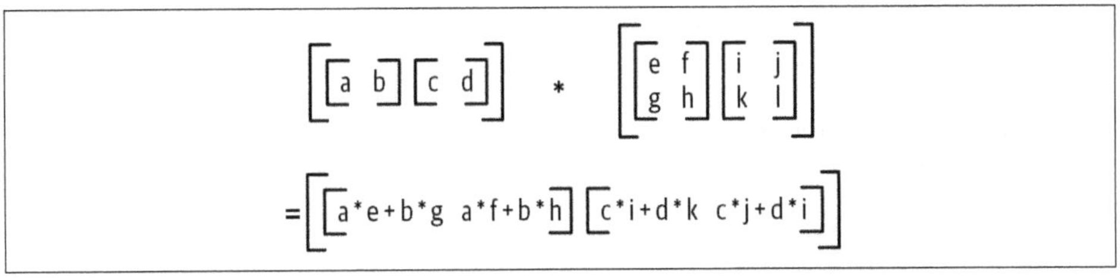

Figure 5-1. To help visualize the general tensor multiplication method, this figure shows the matrix multiplication that occurs before restacking.

Restacking the resultant list into a 3D tensor, we see that the product is of shape (2,1,2). Now, we can generalize this to four dimensions, where instead of imagining we have a list of matrices, we represent each 4D tensor as a grid of matrices and the *(i,j)*-th index of the product is the matrix product of the *(i,j)*-th indices of the two 4D input tensors. We represent this mathematically:

$$P_{i,j,x,z} = \Sigma_y A_{i,j,x,y} {}^* B_{i,j,y,z}$$

This procedure is generalizable to any dimensionality, assuming that the two input tensors follow the constraints of matrix multiplication. As with tensor addition, there are exceptions that involve broadcasting, though we won't cover those in detail here.

We refer you to the PyTorch documentation for detailed information on broadcasting. To multiply two tensors in PyTorch, you can use the torch matmul function:

```
x1_t = torch.tensor([[1,2],[3,4]])
x2_t = torch.tensor([[1,2,3],[4,5,6]])
torch.matmul(x1_t, x2_t) # Returns tensor([[9,12,15],[19,26,33]])
```

In addition to arithmetic operations on tensors, we can also index and slice tensors. If you have prior experience with NumPy, you'll notice that PyTorch indexing is very similar and is based on linear algebra fundamentals. If you have a 3D tensor, you can access the value at position (i,j,k) via the following code:

```
i,j,k = 0,1,1
x3_t = torch.tensor([[[3,7,9],[2,4,5]],[[8,6,2],[3,9,1]]])
print(x3_t)
# out:
# tensor([[[3, 7, 9],
#          [2, 4, 5]],
#         [[8, 6, 2],
#          [3, 9, 1]]])

x3_t[i,j,k]
# out:
# tensor(4)
```

To access larger slices of the tensor, say the matrix at position 0 in a 3D tensor, you can use the following code:

```
x3_t[0] # Returns the matrix at position 0 in tensor
x3_t[0,:,:] # Also returns the matrix at position 0 in tensor!
# out:
# tensor([[3, 7, 9],
#         [2, 4, 1]])
```

where the two lines of code are interpreted to be equivalent by the PyTorch API. This is because using a single indexer, such as x3_t[0], implicitly assumes that the user would like to access all indices (i,j,k) that satisfy the condition $i = 0$ (i.e., the top matrix in the stack of matrices that is the original 3D tensor). Usage of the : symbol makes this implicit assumption clear by telling PyTorch directly that the user would not like to subset the data at that dimension. We can also use the : symbol to subset the data, for example:

```
x3_t[0,1:3,:]
# returns tensor([[2, 4, 5]])
```

where the last line of code is interpreted as: find all indices (i,j,k) such that $i = 0$, $j \geq 1$, and $j < 3$ (: follows the standard Python list indexing convention of being inclusive at the start of the defined range and exclusive at the end). In plain English, we want to access the second and third rows of the top matrix in the stack of matrices that is the original 3D tensor. Note that this usage of : is consistent with standard Python list indexing.

In addition to accessing indices or slices of a tensor, we can also set those indices and slices to new values. In the single index case, this is as simple as:

```
x3_t[0,1,2] = 1

# out:
# tensor([[[3, 7, 9],
#          [2, 4, 1]],

#         [[8, 6, 2],
#          [3, 9, 1]]])
```

To set larger slices of the tensor, the most straightforward way is to define a tensor that is of the same dimensionality as the slice, and use the following code:

```
x_t = torch.randn(2,3,4)
sub_tensor = torch.randn(2,4)
x_t[0,1:3,:] = sub_tensor
```

Additionally, via broadcasting, we can do things like:

```
x_t[0,1:3,:] = 1
sub_tensor = torch.randn(1,4)
x_t[0,1:3,:] = sub_tensor
```

The first line sets the entirety of those two rows to 1, and the second sets both rows of the slice to the single row passed in as sub_tensor. In the next section, we will show how to compute the gradients of a function in PyTorch, and how to access the values of those gradients.

Gradients in PyTorch

Just as a recap, let's recall derivatives and partial derivatives from calculus. The partial derivative of a function, which could be as simple as a polynomial function of a few variables to something as complex as a neural network, with respect to one of the function's inputs represents the rate of change of the output of the function as that input's value changes slightly. So, large magnitude derivatives indicate that the output is very volatile with small changes in the input (think $f(x) = x^{10}$ when x is of moderate size), while small magnitude derivatives indicate that the output is relatively stable with small changes in the input (think $f(x) = \frac{x}{10}$). If the function takes in more than one input, the gradient is the vector that is composed of all of these partial derivatives:

$$f(x, y, z) = x^2 + y^2 + z^2$$

$$\frac{\partial f}{\partial x} = \nabla_x f(x, y, z) = 2x$$

$$\nabla f = [2x \ 2y \ 2z]$$

Continuing from this example, how would we represent this in PyTorch? We can use the following code:

```
x = torch.tensor(2.0, requires_grad=True)
y = torch.tensor(3.0, requires_grad=True)
z = torch.tensor(1.5, requires_grad=True)
f = x**2+y**2+z**2
f.backward()
x.grad, y.grad, z.grad
# out:
# (tensor(4.), tensor(6.), tensor(3.))
```

The call to `backward()` computes the partial derivative of the output f with respect to each of the input variables. We should expect the values for `x.grad`, `y.grad`, and `z.grad` to be 4.0, 6.0, and 3.0, respectively. In the case of neural networks, we can represent the neural network as $f(x, \theta)$, where f is the neural network, x is some vector representing the input, and θ is the parameters of f. Instead of computing the gradient of the output of f with respect to x as done in the previous example, we compute the gradient of the loss of the output of f with respect to θ. Adjusting θ via the gradient will eventually lead to a setting of θ that results in a small loss for the training data and one that hopefully generalizes to data that f hasn't seen before. In the next section, we will introduce the building blocks of neural networks.

The PyTorch nn Module

The PyTorch nn module provides all of the baseline functionality necessary for defining, training, and testing a model. To import the nn module, all you need to do is run the following line of code:

```
import torch.nn as nn
```

In this section, we will cover some of the most common uses of the nn module. For example, to initialize a weight matrix needed for a feed-forward neural network, you can use the following code:

```
in_dim, out_dim = 256, 10
vec = torch.randn(256)
layer = nn.Linear(in_dim, out_dim, bias=True)
out = layer(vec)
```

This defines a single layer with bias in a feed-forward neural network, which is a matrix of weights that takes as input a vector of dimension 256 and outputs a vector of dimension 10. The last line of code demonstrates how we can easily apply this layer to an input vector and store the output in a new tensor. If we wanted to do the same thing using only our knowledge from prior sections, we would need to manually define a weight matrix W and bias vector b via torch.tensor and explicitly compute:

```
W = torch.rand(10,256)
b = torch.zeros(10,1)
out = torch.matmul(W, vec) + b
```

The nn module's Linear layer allows us to abstract away these manual operations so we can write clean, concise code.

A feed-forward neural network can be thought of as simply a composition of such layers, for example:

```
in_dim, feature_dim, out_dim = 784, 256, 10
vec = torch.randn(784)
layer1 = nn.Linear(in_dim, feature_dim, bias=True)
layer2 = nn.Linear(feature_dim, out_dim, bias=True)
out = layer2(layer1(vec))
```

This code represents a neural network that is the function composition `layer2(layer1(vec))`, or mathematically: $W_2(W_1 * x + b_1) + b_2$. To represent more complex, nonlinear functions, the nn module additionally provides nonlinearities such as ReLU, which can be accessed via nn.ReLU, and tanh, which can be accessed via nn.Tanh. These nonlinearities are applied in between layers, as follows:

```
relu = nn.ReLU()
out  = layer2(relu(layer1(vec)))
```

We've gone over almost everything necessary to define a model in PyTorch. The last thing to cover is the nn.Module class—the base class from which all neural networks are subclassed in PyTorch.

The nn.Module class has one important method that your specific model's subclass will override. This method is the forward method, and it defines how the layers initialized in your model's constructor interact with the input to generate the model's output. Here is an example of some code that can be used to encapsulate the simple two-layer neural network we just defined:

```
class BaseClassifier(nn.Module):
  def __init__(self, in_dim, feature_dim, out_dim):
    super(BaseClassifier, self).__init__()
    self.layer1 = nn.Linear(in_dim, feature_dim, bias=True)
    self.layer2 = nn.Linear(feature_dim, out_dim, bias=True)
    self.relu = nn.ReLU()

  def forward(self, x):
    x = self.layer1(x)
    x = self.relu(x)
    out = self.layer2(x)
    return out
```

We've written our first neural network in PyTorch! `BaseClassifier` is a bug-free model class that can be instantiated after defining `in_dim`, `feature_dim`, and `out_dim`. The constructor takes in these three variables as arguments in the constructor, which makes the model flexible in terms of layer size. This is the sort of model that can be used effectively as a first-pass classifier for datasets such as MNIST, as we will demonstrate in "Building the MNIST Classifier in PyTorch" on page 89. To generate the output of a model on some input, we can use the model as follows:

```
no_examples = 10
in_dim, feature_dim, out_dim = 784, 256, 10
x = torch.randn((no_examples, in_dim))
classifier = BaseClassifier(in_dim, feature_dim, out_dim)
out = classifier(x)
```

Note that we implicitly call the forward function when using the classifier model as a function in the final line. Comparing this to the initial approach of manually defining each layer's parameters as a torch tensor and computing the output via `matmul` operations, this is a much more clean, modular, and reusable approach to defining neural networks.

In addition to being able to define the model, instantiate it, and run data through it, we must be able to train and test the model. To train (and test) the model, we need a loss metric to evaluate the model. During training, once we calculate this loss metric, we can use our knowledge from the previous section and call `backward()` on the computed loss. This will store the gradient in each parameter p's `grad` attribute. Since we have defined a classifier model, we can use the cross-entropy `loss` metric from PyTorch nn:

```
loss = nn.CrossEntropyLoss()
target = torch.tensor([0,3,2,8,2,9,3,7,1,6])
computed_loss = loss(out, target)
computed_loss.backward()
```

In the preceding code, `target` is a tensor of shape (`no_examples`), and each index represents the ground truth class of the input corresponding with that index. Now that we've computed the gradient of the loss of the minibatch of examples with respect to all of the parameters in the classifier, we can perform the gradient descent step. When defining a neural network as a subclass of `nn.Module`, we can access all of its parameters via the `parameters()` function—another convenience provided by the PyTorch API. To view the shape of each parameter in the neural network, you can run the code:

```
for p in classifier.parameters():
  print(p.shape)

# out:
# torch.Size([256, 784])
# torch.Size([256])
```

```
# torch.Size([10, 256])
# torch.Size([10])
```

As we can see, the first layer has 256 × 784 weights and a bias vector of length 256. The last layer has 10 × 256 weights and a bias vector of length 10.

During gradient descent, we need to adjust the parameters based on their gradients. We could do this manually, but PyTorch has abstracted away this functionality into the `torch.optim` module. This module provides functionality for determining the optimizer, which may be more complex than classic gradient descent, and updating the parameters of the model. You can define the optimizer as follows:

```
from torch import optim

lr = 1e-3
optimizer = optim.SGD(classifier.parameters(), lr=lr)
```

This code creates an optimizer that will update the parameters of the classifier via SGD at the end of each minibatch. To actually perform this update, you can use the following code:

```
optimizer.step() # Updates parameters via SGD
optimizer.zero_grad() # Zeroes out gradients between minibatches
```

In the simple case of a feed-forward network as defined in `BaseClassifier`, the testing mode of such a network is the same as the training mode—we can just call `classifier(test_x)` on any minibatch in the test set to evaluate the model. However, as we'll discuss later, this is not true for all neural architectures.

This code works for a single minibatch—performing training over the entire dataset would require manually shuffling the dataset at each epoch and splitting the dataset into minibatches that can be iterated through. Thankfully, PyTorch has also abstracted this process out into what are called PyTorch datasets and dataloaders. In the next section, we will cover these modules in detail.

PyTorch Datasets and Dataloaders

The PyTorch `Dataset` is a base class that can be used to access your specific data. In practice, you would subclass the `Dataset` class by overriding two important methods: `__len__()` and `__getitem__()`. The first method, as you can probably tell from its name, refers to the length of the dataset—i.e., the number of examples that the model will be trained or tested on. If we think of the dataset as a list of examples, the second method takes as input an index and returns the example at that index. Each example consists of both the data point (e.g., image) and label (e.g., value from 0 to 9 in the case of MNIST). Here is some example code for a dataset:

```
import os
from PIL import Image
```

```
from torchvision import transforms

class ImageDataset(Dataset):
    def __init__(self, img_dir, label_file):
        super(ImageDataset, self).__init__()
        self.img_dir = img_dir
        self.labels = torch.tensor(np.load(label_file, allow_pickle=True))
        self.transforms = transforms.ToTensor()

    def __getitem__(self, idx):
        img_pth = os.path.join(self.img_dir, "img_{}.jpg".format(idx))
        img = Image.open(img_pth)
        img = self.transforms(img).flatten()
        label = self.labels[idx]
        return {"data":img, "label":label}

    def __len__(self):
        return len(self.labels)
```

In this example, we assume that the directory containing our dataset consists of images that follow the naming convention *img-idx.png*, where *idx* refers to the index of the image. Additionally, we assume that our ground-truth labels are stored in a saved NumPy array, which can be loaded and indexed using *idx* to find each image's corresponding label.

The DataLoader class in PyTorch takes as input a dataset instantiation, and abstracts away all of the heavy lifting required to load in the dataset by the minibatch and shuffle the dataset between epochs. Although we won't go behind the scenes in too much depth, the DataLoader class does make use of Python's multiprocessing built-in module to efficiently load minibatches in parallel. Here is some example code that puts everything together:

```
train_dataset = ImageDataset(img_dir='./data/train/',
                             label_file='./data/train/labels.npy')

train_loader = DataLoader(train_dataset,
                          batch_size=4,
                          shuffle=True)
```

To iterate through these dataloaders, use the following code as a template:

```
for minibatch in train_loader:
    data, labels = minibatch['data'], minibatch['label']
    print(data)
    print(labels)
```

The data returned is a tensor of shape (64,784) and the labels returned are of shape (64,). As you can tell, the dataloader also does the work of stacking all of the examples into a single tensor that can simply be run through the network:

```
for minibatch in train_loader:
    data, labels = minibatch['data'], minibatch['label']
    out = classifier(data) # to be completed in the next section!
```

where out is of shape (64,10) in the case of MNIST. In the next section, we will put together all of our learnings to build a neural architecture that can be trained and tested on the MNIST dataset, provide code samples for training and testing the model by building off of work in this section, and show example training and testing loss curves.

Building the MNIST Classifier in PyTorch

It's time to build an MNIST classifier in PyTorch. For the most part, we can reuse a lot of the code presented and explained earlier:

```
import matplotlib.pyplot as plt
import torch
from torch import optim
import torch.nn as nn
from torch.utils.data import Dataset, DataLoader
from torchvision.datasets import MNIST
from torchvision.transforms import ToTensor

class BaseClassifier(nn.Module):
    def __init__(self, in_dim, feature_dim, out_dim):
        super(BaseClassifier, self).__init__()
        self.classifier = nn.Sequential(
            nn.Linear(in_dim, feature_dim, bias=True),
            nn.ReLU(),
            nn.Linear(feature_dim, out_dim, bias=True)
        )

    def forward(self, x):
        return self.classifier(x)

# Load in MNIST dataset from PyTorch
train_dataset = MNIST(".", train=True,
                      download=True, transform=ToTensor())
test_dataset = MNIST(".", train=False,
                     download=True, transform=ToTensor())
train_loader = DataLoader(train_dataset,
                          batch_size=64, shuffle=True)
test_loader = DataLoader(test_dataset,
                         batch_size=64, shuffle=False)
```

Note that, by default, the minibatch tensors and model parameters are on CPU, so there was no need to call the to function on each of these to change the device. Also, the MNIST dataset provided by PyTorch unfortunately does not come with a validation set, so we'll do our best to use insights solely from the training loss curve to inform our final hyperparameter decision for the test set:

```python
# Instantiate model, optimizer, and hyperparameter(s)
in_dim, feature_dim, out_dim = 784, 256, 10
lr=1e-3
loss_fn = nn.CrossEntropyLoss()
epochs=40
classifier = BaseClassifier(in_dim, feature_dim, out_dim)
optimizer = optim.SGD(classifier.parameters(), lr=lr)

def train(classifier=classifier,
          optimizer=optimizer,
          epochs=epochs,
          loss_fn=loss_fn):

  classifier.train()
  loss_lt = []
  for epoch in range(epochs):
    running_loss = 0.0
    for minibatch in train_loader:
      data, target = minibatch
      data = data.flatten(start_dim=1)
      out = classifier(data)
      computed_loss = loss_fn(out, target)
      computed_loss.backward()
      optimizer.step()
      optimizer.zero_grad()
      # Keep track of sum of loss of each minibatch
      running_loss += computed_loss.item()
    loss_lt.append(running_loss/len(train_loader))
    print("Epoch: {} train loss: {}".format(epoch+1,
          running_loss/len(train_loader)))

  plt.plot([i for i in range(1,epochs+1)], loss_lt)
  plt.xlabel("Epoch")
  plt.ylabel("Training Loss")
  plt.title(
      "MNIST Training Loss: optimizer {}, lr {}".format("SGD", lr))
  plt.show()

  # Save state to file as checkpoint
  torch.save(classifier.state_dict(), 'mnist.pt')

def test(classifier=classifier,
         loss_fn = loss_fn):
  classifier.eval()
  accuracy = 0.0
  computed_loss = 0.0

  with torch.no_grad():
      for data, target in test_loader:
          data = data.flatten(start_dim=1)
          out = classifier(data)
          _, preds = out.max(dim=1)
```

```
# Get loss and accuracy
computed_loss += loss_fn(out, target)
accuracy += torch.sum(preds==target)

print("Test loss: {}, test accuracy: {}".format(
    computed_loss.item()/(len(test_loader)*64),
    accuracy*100.0/(len(test_loader)*64)))
```

Additionally, note that we call `classifier.train()` and `classifier.eval()` at the beginning of the training and test functions, respectively. The calls to these functions communicate to the PyTorch backend whether the model is in training mode or inference mode. You might be wondering why we need to call `classifier.train()` and `classifier.eval()` if there is no difference between the behavior of the neural network at train and test time. Although this is true in our first-pass example, the training and testing modes for other neural architectures are not necessarily the same. For example, if dropout layers are added to the model architecture, the dropout layers need to be ignored during the testing phase. We add in the calls to `train()` and `eval()` here since it is generally considered good practice to do so.

As a first step, we need to set some starting hyperparameters for model training. We start with a slightly conservative learning rate in `1e-4` and inspect the training loss curve and testing accuracy after 40 epochs, or iterations through the entire dataset. Figure 5-2 shows a graph of the training loss curve through the epochs.

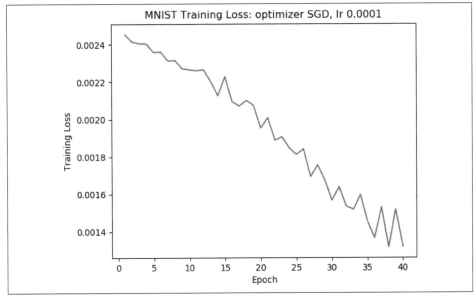

Figure 5-2. We see signs of underfitting as the model performance on the training set is failing to level out, meaning we have not yet settled into a local optimum

We can see that this loss curve is not particularly close to leveling out near the end of training, which we'd hope to start seeing for a model training at a sufficient learning rate. And although we don't have a validation set to confirm our suspicions, we have strong reason to suspect that a higher learning rate would help. After setting the learning rate to a slightly more aggressive 1e-3, we observe a training loss curve that is much more in line with what we'd hope to see (Figure 5-3).

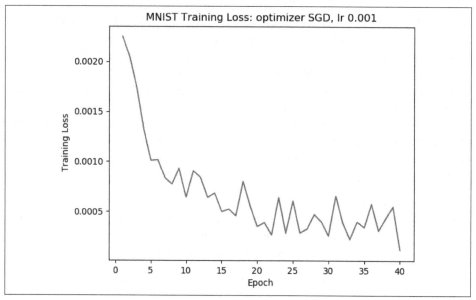

Figure 5-3. This leveling out of the loss curve is more like what we'd expect to see with an appropriate learning rate for the problem

The loss curve starts to level out only near the end of training. This trend indicates that the model is likely in the sweet spot between underfitting to the training data, like our previous attempt, and overfitting to the training data. Evaluating the trained model at 40 epochs on the test set achieves an accuracy of 91%! Although this is nowhere close to the top performers on MNIST today, which primarily use convolutional neural classifiers, it is a great start. We recommend you try some extensions to the code, such as increasing the number of hidden layers and substituting in a more sophisticated optimizer.

Summary

In this chapter, we covered the basics of PyTorch and its functionality. Specifically, we learned the concept of tensors in PyTorch, and how these tensors store numerical information. Additionally, we learned how to manipulate tensors via tensor operations, access the data within a tensor, and set a few important attributes. We also discussed gradients in PyTorch and how they can be stored within a tensor. We built our first neural network via standard nn functionality in the the PyTorch nn module section. Comparing the nn-based approach with an approach that used PyTorch tensors solely out of the box showed much of the effective abstraction that the nn module provides, lending to its ease of use. And finally, we put all of our learnings together in the final section, where we trained and tested an MNIST digits feed-forward neural classifier to 91% accuracy on the PyTorch-provided test set. Although we covered much of the fundamentals and have equipped you with the knowledge you need to get your hands dirty, we have only scratched the surface of all that the PyTorch API has to offer—we encourage you to explore further and improve upon the models we built in this section. We recommend that you visit the PyTorch documentation to learn more and build your own neural nets, including trying other architectures, on a variety of online datasets, such as the CIFAR-10 image recognition datasets. In the next section, we will cover neural network implementation, one of the other most popular deep learning frameworks in use today.

## CHAPTER 6

Beyond Gradient Descent

The Challenges with Gradient Descent

The fundamental ideas behind neural networks have existed for decades, but it wasn't until recently that neural network-based learning models have become mainstream. Our fascination with neural networks has everything to do with their expressiveness, a quality we've unlocked by creating networks with many layers. As we have discussed in previous chapters, deep neural networks are able to crack problems that were previously deemed intractable. Training deep neural networks end to end, however, is fraught with difficult challenges that took many technological innovations to unravel, including massive labeled datasets (ImageNet, CIFAR-10, etc.), better hardware in the form of GPU acceleration, and several algorithmic discoveries.

For several years, researchers resorted to layer-wise greedy pretraining to grapple with the complex error surfaces presented by deep learning models.[1] These time-intensive strategies would try to find more accurate initializations for the model's parameters one layer at a time before using minibatch gradient descent to converge to the optimal parameter settings. More recently, however, breakthroughs in optimization methods have enabled us to train models directly in an end-to-end fashion.

In this chapter, we will discuss several of these breakthroughs. The next couple of sections will focus primarily on local minima and whether they pose hurdles for successfully training deep models. Then we will further explore the nonconvex error surfaces induced by deep models, why vanilla minibatch gradient descent falls short, and how modern nonconvex optimizers overcome these pitfalls.

---

1 Bengio, Yoshua, et al. "Greedy Layer-Wise Training of Deep Networks." *Advances in Neural Information Processing Systems* 19 (2007): 153.

Local Minima in the Error Surfaces of Deep Networks

The primary challenge in optimizing deep learning models is that we are forced to use minimal local information to infer the global structure of the error surface. This is difficult because there is usually very little correspondence between local and global structure. Take the following analogy as an example.

Let's assume you're an insect on the continental United States. You're dropped randomly on the map, and your goal is to find the lowest point on this surface. How do you do it? If all you can observe is your immediate surroundings, this seems like an intractable problem. If the surface of the US were bowl-shaped (or mathematically speaking, convex) and we were smart about our learning rate, we could use the gradient descent algorithm to eventually find the bottom of the bowl. But the surface of the US is extremely complex, that is to say, is a nonconvex surface, which means that even if we find a valley (a local minimum), we have no idea if it's the lowest valley on the map (the global minimum). In Chapter 4, we talked about how a minibatch version of gradient descent can help navigate a troublesome error surface when there are spurious regions of magnitude zero gradients. But as we can see in Figure 6-1, even a stochastic error surface won't save us from a deep local minimum.

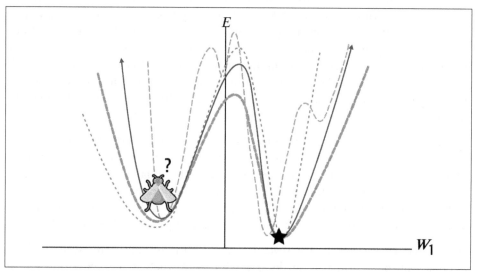

Figure 6-1. Minibatch gradient descent may aid in escaping shallow local minima, but often fails when dealing with deep local minima, as shown

Now comes the critical question. Theoretically, local minima pose a significant issue. But in practice, how common are local minima in the error surfaces of deep networks? And in which scenarios are they actually problematic for training? In the following two sections, we'll pick apart common misconceptions about local minima.

Model Identifiability

The first source of local minima is tied to a concept commonly referred to as *model identifiability*. One observation about deep neural networks is that their error surfaces are guaranteed to have a large—and in some cases, an infinite—number of local minima. There are two major reasons this observation is true.

The first is that within a layer of a fully connected feed-forward neural network, any rearrangement of neurons will still give you the same final output at the end of the network. We illustrate this using a simple three-neuron layer in Figure 6-2. As a result, within a layer with n neurons, there are $n!$ ways to rearrange parameters. And for a deep network with l layers, each with n neurons, we have a total of $n!^l$ equivalent configurations.

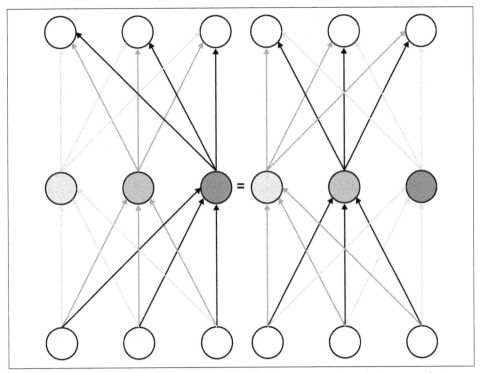

Figure 6-2. Rearranging neurons in a layer of a neural network results in equivalent configurations due to symmetry

In addition to the symmetries of neuron rearrangements, nonidentifiability is present in other forms in certain kinds of neural networks. For example, there is an infinite number of equivalent configurations that for an individual ReLU neuron result in equivalent networks. Because an ReLU uses a piecewise linear function, we are free to multiply all of the incoming weights by any nonzero constant k while scaling all of the outgoing weights by $\frac{1}{k}$ without changing the behavior of the network. We leave the justification for this statement as an exercise for you.

Ultimately, however, local minima that arise because of the nonidentifiability of deep neural networks are not inherently problematic. This is because all nonidentifiable configurations behave in an indistinguishable fashion no matter what input values they are fed. This means they will achieve the same error on the training, validation, and testing datasets. In other words, all of these models will have learned equally from the training data and will have identical behavior during generalization to unseen examples.

Instead, local minima are only problematic when they are *spurious*. A spurious local minimum corresponds to a configuration of weights in a neural network that incurs a higher error than the configuration at the global minimum. If these kinds of local minima are common, we quickly run into significant problems while using gradient-based optimization methods because we can take only local structure into account.

How Pesky Are Spurious Local Minima in Deep Networks?

For many years, deep learning practitioners blamed all of their troubles in training deep networks on spurious local minima, albeit with little evidence. Today, it remains an open question whether spurious local minima with a high error rate relative to the global minimum are common in practical deep networks. However, many recent studies seem to indicate that most local minima have error rates and generalization characteristics that are very similar to global minima.

One way we might try to naively tackle this problem is by plotting the value of the error function over time as we train a deep neural network. This strategy, however, doesn't give us enough information about the error surface because it is difficult to tell whether the error surface is "bumpy," or whether we merely have a difficult time figuring out which direction we should be moving in.

To more effectively analyze this problem, Goodfellow et al. (a team of researchers collaborating between Google and Stanford) published a paper in 2014 that attempted to separate these two potential confounding factors.[2] Instead of analyzing the error function over time, they cleverly investigated what happens on the error surface between a randomly initialized parameter vector and a successful final solution by using linear interpolation. So, given a randomly initialized parameter vector θ_i and

---

2 Goodfellow, Ian J., Oriol Vinyals, and Andrew M. Saxe. "Qualitatively characterizing neural network optimization problems." *arXiv preprint arXiv*:1412.6544 (2014).

---

stochastic gradient descent (SGD) solution θ_f, we aim to compute the error function at every point along the linear interpolation $\theta_\alpha = \alpha \cdot \theta_f + (1 - \alpha) \cdot \theta_i$.

They wanted to investigate whether local minima would hinder our gradient-based search method even if we knew which direction to move in. They showed that for a wide variety of practical networks with different types of neurons, the direct path between a randomly initialized point in the parameter space and a stochastic gradient descent solution isn't plagued with troublesome local minima.

We can even demonstrate this ourselves using the feed-forward ReLU network we built in Chapter 5. Using a checkpoint file that we saved while training our original feed-forward network, we can reinstantiate the model using load_state_dict and torch.load:

```
# Load checkpoint from SGD training
IN_DIM, FEATURE_DIM, OUT_DIM = 784, 256, 10
model = Net(IN_DIM, FEATURE_DIM, OUT_DIM)

model.load_state_dict(torch.load('mnist.pt'))
```

In PyTorch, we cannot access a model's parameters directly since the model.parame ters() method returns a generator that provides only a *copy* of the parameters. To modify a model's parameters, we use torch.load to read the state dictionary containing the parameter values from the file, and then use load_state_dict to set the model's parameters with these values.

Instead of using torch.load to load the state dictionary from a file, we can also access the state dictionary from a model itself using the state_dict method:

```
import copy

# Access parameters with state_dict
opt_state_dict = copy.deepcopy(model.state_dict())

for param_tensor in opt_state_dict:
    print(param_tensor, "\t",
          opt_state_dict[param_tensor].size())

# outputs:
# classifier.1.weight    torch.Size([256, 784])
# classifier.1.bias      torch.Size([256])
# classifier.3.weight    torch.Size([256, 256])
# classifier.3.bias      torch.Size([256])
# classifier.5.weight    torch.Size([10, 256])
# classifier.5.bias      torch.Size([10])
```

Note that we need to use the copy.deepcopy method to copy a dictionary with its values. Just setting opt_state_dict = model.state_dict() would result in a shallow copy, and `opt_state_dict` would be changed when we load our model with interpolated parameters later.

Next, we instantiate a new model with randomly initialized parameters and save those parameters as `rand_state_dict`:

```
# Create randomly initialized network
model_rand = Net(IN_DIM, FEATURE_DIM, OUT_DIM)
rand_state_dict = copy.deepcopy(model_rand.state_dict())
```

With these two networks appropriately initialized, we can now construct the linear interpolation using the mixing parameters `alpha` and `beta`:

```
# Create a new state_dict for interpolated parameters
test_model = Net(IN_DIM, FEATURE_DIM, OUT_DIM)
test_state_dict = copy.deepcopy(test_model.state_dict())

alpha = 0.2
beta = 1.0 - alpha
for p in opt_state_dict:
    test_state_dict[p] = (opt_state_dict[p] * beta +
                          rand_state_dict[p] * alpha)
```

Next, we will compute the average loss over the entire test dataset using the model with the interpolated parameters. For convenience, let's create a function for inference:

```
def inference(testloader, model, loss_fn):
  running_loss = 0.0
  with torch.no_grad():
    for inputs, labels in testloader:
      outputs = model(inputs)
      loss = loss_fn(outputs, labels)
      running_loss += loss
  running_loss /= len(testloader)
  return running_loss
```

Finally, we can vary the value of `alpha` to understand how the error surface changes as we traverse the line between the randomly initialized point and the final SGD solution:

```
results = []
for alpha in torch.arange(-2, 2, 0.05):
  beta = 1.0 - alpha

  # Compute interpolated parameters
  for p in opt_state_dict:
    test_state_dict[p] = (opt_state_dict[p] * beta +
                          rand_state_dict[p] * alpha)

  # Load interpolated parameters into test model
  model.load_state_dict(test_state_dict)
```

```
# Compute loss given interpolated parameters
loss = inference(trainloader, model, loss_fn)
results.append(loss.item())
```

This creates Figure 6-3, which we can inspect ourselves. In fact, if we run this experiment over and over again, we find that there are no truly troublesome local minima that would get us stuck. It seems that the true struggle of gradient descent isn't the existence of troublesome local minima, but instead is that we have a tough time finding the appropriate direction to move in. We'll return to this thought a little later.

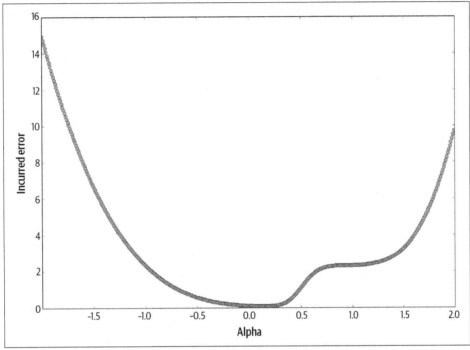

Figure 6-3. The cost function of a three-layer feed-forward network as we linearly interpolate on the line connecting a randomly initialized parameter vector and an SGD solution

Flat Regions in the Error Surface

Although it seems that our analysis is devoid of troublesome local minimum, we do notice a peculiar flat region where the gradient approaches zero when we get to approximately alpha=1. This point is not a local minima, so it is unlikely to get us completely stuck, but it seems like the zero gradient might slow down learning if we are unlucky enough to encounter it.

More generally, given an arbitrary function, a point at which the gradient is the zero vector is called a *critical point*. Critical points come in various flavors. We've already talked about local minima. It's also not hard to imagine their counterparts, the *local maxima*, which don't really pose much of an issue for SGD. But then there are these strange critical points that lie somewhere in between. These "flat" regions that are potentially pesky but not necessarily deadly are called *saddle points*. It turns out that as our function has more and more dimensions (i.e., we have more and more parameters in our model), saddle points are exponentially more likely than local minima. Let's try to intuit why.

For a 1D cost function, a critical point can take one of three forms, as shown in Figure 6-4. Loosely, let's assume each of these three configurations is equally likely. This means that given a random critical point in a random 1D function, it has one-third probability of being a local minimum. This means that if we have a total of k critical points, we can expect to have a total of $\frac{k}{3}$ local minima.

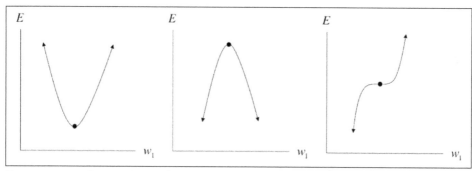

Figure 6-4. Analyzing a critical point along a single dimension

We can also extend this to higher dimensional functions. Consider a cost function operating in a d-dimensional space. Let's take an arbitrary critical point. It turns out that figuring out if this point is a local minimum, local maximum, or a saddle point is a little bit trickier than in the one-dimensional case. Consider the error surface in Figure 6-5. Depending on how you slice the surface (from A to B or from C to D), the critical point looks like either a minimum or a maximum. In reality, it's neither. It's a more complex type of saddle point.

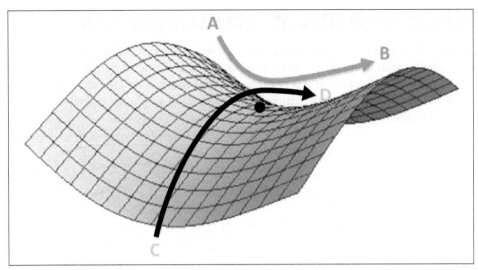

Figure 6-5. A saddle point over a 2D error surface

In general, in a d-dimensional parameter space, we can slice through a critical point on d different axes. A critical point can be a local minimum only if it appears as a local minimum in every single one of the d 1D subspaces. Using the fact that a critical point can come in one of three different flavors in a one-dimensional subspace, we realize that the probability that a random critical point is in a random function is $\frac{1}{3^d}$. This means that a random function with k critical points has an expected number of $\frac{k}{3^d}$ local minima. In other words, as the dimensionality of our parameter space increases, local minima become exponentially more rare. A more rigorous treatment of this topic is outside the scope of this book, but was explored more extensively by Dauphin et al. in 2014.[3]

So what does this mean for optimizing deep learning models? For stochastic gradient descent, it's still unclear. It seems like these flat segments of the error surface are pesky but ultimately don't prevent stochastic gradient descent from converging to a good answer. However, it does pose serious problems for methods that attempt to directly solve for a point where the gradient is zero. This has been a major hindrance to the usefulness of certain second-order optimization methods for deep learning models, which we will discuss later.

---

3 Dauphin, Yann N., et al. "Identifying and attacking the saddle point problem in high-dimensional non-convex optimization." *Advances in Neural Information Processing Systems*. 2014.

When the Gradient Points in the Wrong Direction

Upon analyzing the error surfaces of deep networks, it seems like the most critical challenge to optimizing deep networks is finding the correct trajectory to move in. It's no surprise, however, that this is a major challenge when we look at what happens to the error surface around a local minimum. As an example, we consider an error surface defined over a 2D parameter space, as shown in Figure 6-6.

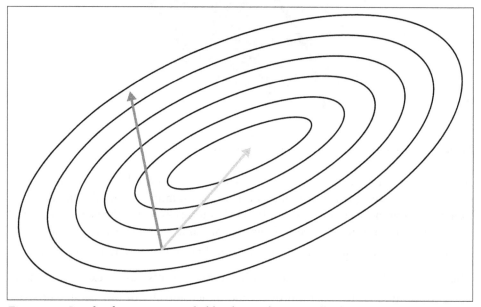

Figure 6-6. Local information encoded by the gradient usually does not corroborate the global structure of the error surface

Revisiting the contour diagrams we explored in Chapter 4, notice that the gradient isn't usually a very good indicator of the good trajectory. Specifically, only when the contours are perfectly circular does the gradient always point in the direction of the local minimum. However, if the contours are extremely elliptical (as is usually the case for the error surfaces of deep networks), the gradient can be as inaccurate as 90 degrees away from the correct direction.

We extend this analysis to an arbitrary number of dimensions using some mathematical formalism. For every weight w_i in the parameter space, the gradient computes the value of $\frac{\partial E}{\partial w_i}$, or how the value of the error changes as we change the value of w_i.

Taken together over all weights in the parameter space, the gradient gives us the direction of steepest descent. The general problem with taking a significant step in this direction, however, is that the gradient could be changing under our feet as we move! We demonstrate this simple fact in Figure 6-7. Going back to the 2D example,

---

if our contours are perfectly circular and we take a big step in the direction of the steepest descent, the gradient doesn't change direction as we move. However, this is not the case for highly elliptical contours.

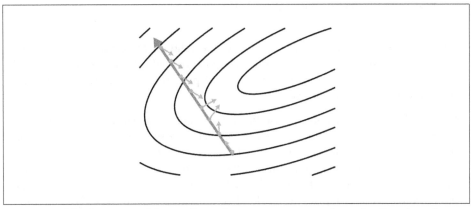

Figure 6-7. The direction of the gradient changes as we move along the direction of steepest descent, as determined from a starting point; the gradient vectors are normalized to identical length to emphasize the change in direction of the gradient vector

More generally, we can quantify how the gradient changes under our feet as we move in a certain direction by computing second derivatives. Specifically, we want to measure $\frac{\partial(\partial E / \partial w_j)}{\partial w_i}$, which tells us how the gradient component for w_j changes as we change the value of w_i. We can compile this information into a special matrix known as the *Hessian matrix* (**H**). And when describing an error surface where the gradient changes underneath our feet as we move in the direction of steepest descent, this matrix is said to be *ill-conditioned*.

Hessian Limits Optimization

Certain properties of the Hessian matrix (specifically that it is real and symmetric) allow us to efficiently determine the second derivative (which approximates the curvature of a surface) as we move in a specific direction. Specifically, if we have a unit vector $\boldsymbol{d}$, the second derivative in that direction is given by $\boldsymbol{d^H d}$. We can now use a second-order approximation via Taylor series to understand what happens to the error function as we step from the current parameter vector $\mathbf{x}^{(i)}$ to a new parameter vector $\mathbf{x}$ along gradient vector $\mathbf{g}$ evaluated at $\mathbf{x}^{(i)}$:

$$E(\mathbf{x}) \approx E\big(\mathbf{x}^{(i)}\big) + \big(\mathbf{x} - \mathbf{x}^{(i)}\big)^{\top} \mathbf{g} + \tfrac{1}{2}\big(\mathbf{x} - \mathbf{x}^{(i)}\big)^{\top} \mathbf{H}\big(\mathbf{x} - \mathbf{x}^{(i)}\big)$$

If we go further to state that we will be moving ϵ units in the opposite direction of the gradient, we can simplify our expression even more:

$$E\left(\mathbf{x}^{(i)} - \epsilon \mathbf{g}\right) \approx E\left(\mathbf{x}^{(i)}\right) - \epsilon \mathbf{g}^\top \mathbf{g} + \frac{1}{2}\epsilon^2 \mathbf{g}^\top \mathbf{H}\mathbf{g}$$

This expression consists of three terms: (1) the value of the error function at the original parameter vector, (2) the improvement in error afforded by the magnitude of the gradient, and (3) a correction term that incorporates the curvature of the surface as represented by the Hessian matrix.

In general, we should be able to use this information to design better optimization algorithms. For instance, we can even naively take the second-order approximation of the error function to determine the learning rate at each step that maximizes the reduction in the error function. It turns out, however, that computing the Hessian matrix exactly is a difficult task. In the next several sections, we'll describe optimization breakthroughs that tackle ill-conditioning without directly computing the Hessian matrix.

Momentum-Based Optimization

Fundamentally, the problem of an ill-conditioned Hessian matrix manifests itself in the form of gradients that fluctuate wildly. As a result, one popular mechanism for dealing with ill-conditioning bypasses the computation of the Hessian, and instead, focuses on how to cancel out these fluctuations over the duration of training.

One way to think about how we might tackle this problem is by investigating how a ball rolls down a hilly surface. Driven by gravity, the ball eventually settles into a minimum on the surface, but for some reason, it doesn't suffer from the wild fluctuations and divergences that happen during gradient descent. Why is this the case? Unlike in stochastic gradient descent (which uses only the gradient), there are two major components that determine how a ball rolls down an error surface. The first, which we already model in SGD as the gradient, is what we commonly refer to as acceleration. But acceleration does not single-handedly determine the ball's movements. Instead, its motion is more directly determined by its velocity. Acceleration indirectly changes the ball's position only by modifying its velocity.

Velocity-driven motion is desirable because it counteracts the effects of a wildly fluctuating gradient by smoothing the ball's trajectory over its history. Velocity serves as a form of memory, and this allows us to more effectively accumulate movement in the direction of the minimum while canceling out oscillating accelerations in orthogonal directions. Our goal, then, is to somehow generate an analog for velocity in our optimization algorithm. We can do this by keeping track of an *exponentially weighted decay* of past gradients. The premise is simple: every update is computed by combining the update in the last iteration with the current gradient. Concretely, we compute the change in the parameter vector as follows:

$$\mathbf{v}_i = m\mathbf{v}_{i-1} - \epsilon\mathbf{g}_i$$
$$\theta_i = \theta_{i-1} + \mathbf{v}_i$$

We use the momentum hyperparameter m to determine what fraction of the previous velocity to retain in the new update, and add this "memory" of past gradients to our current gradient. This approach is commonly referred to as *momentum*.[4] Because the momentum term increases the step size we take, using momentum may require a reduced learning rate compared to vanilla stochastic gradient descent.

To better visualize how momentum works, we'll explore a toy example. Specifically, we'll investigate how momentum affects updates during a *random walk*. A random walk is a succession of randomly chosen steps. In our example, we'll imagine a particle on a line that, at every time interval, randomly picks a step size between –10 and 10 and takes a moves in that direction. This is simply expressed as:

```
rand_walk = [torch.randint(-10, 10, (1,1)) for x in range(100)]
```

We'll then simulate what happens when we use a slight modification of momentum (i.e., the standard exponentially weighted moving average algorithm) to smooth our choice of step at every time interval. Again, we can concisely express this as:

```
momentum = 0.1
momentum_rand_walk = \
    [torch.randint(-10, 10, (1,1)) for x in range(100)]

for i in range(1, len(rand_walk) - 1):
  prev = momentum_rand_walk[i-1]
  rand_choice = torch.randint(-10, 10, (1,1)).item()
  new_step = momentum * prev + (1 - momentum) * rand_choice
  momentum_rand_walk[i] = new_step
```

The results, as we vary the momentum from 0 to 1, are quite staggering. Momentum significantly reduces the volatility of updates. The larger the momentum, the less responsive we are to new updates (e.g., a large inaccuracy on the first estimation of trajectory propagates for a significant period of time). We summarize the results of our toy experiment in Figure 6-8.

---

4 Polyak, Boris T. "Some methods of speeding up the convergence of iteration methods." *USSR Computational Mathematics and Mathematical Physics* 4.5 (1964): 1-17.

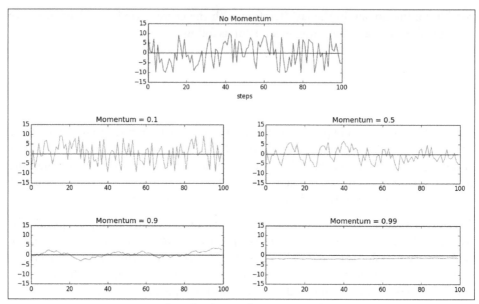

Figure 6-8. Momentum smooths volatility in the step sizes during a random walk using an exponentially weighted moving average

To investigate how momentum actually affects the training of feed-forward neural networks, we can retrain our trusty MNIST feed-forward network with a PyTorch momentum optimizer. In this case, we can get away with using the same learning rate (0.01) with a typical momentum of 0.9:

```
optimizer = optim.SGD(model.parameters(),
                      lr = 0.01,
                      momentum = 0.9)
optimizer.step()
```

Notice that when we create a PyTorch optimizer, we need to pass in `model.param eters()`. The resulting speedup is staggering. We display how the cost function changes over time by comparing the visualizations in Figure 6-9. The figure demonstrates that to achieve a cost of 0.1 without momentum (right) requires nearly 18,000 steps (minibatches), whereas with momentum (left), we require just over 2,000.

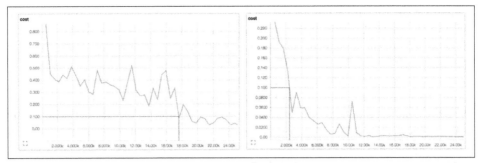

Figure 6-9. Comparing training a feed-forward network with (right) and without (left) momentum demonstrates a massive decrease in training time

Recently, more work has explored how the classical momentum technique can be improved. Sutskever et al. in 2013 proposed an alternative called Nesterov momentum, which computes the gradient on the error surface at $\theta + \mathbf{v}_{i-1}$ during the velocity update instead of at θ.[5] This subtle difference seems to allow Nesterov momentum to change its velocity in a more responsive way. It's been shown that this method has clear benefits in batch gradient descent (convergence guarantees and the ability to use a higher momentum for a given learning rate as compared to classical momentum), but it's not entirely clear whether this is true for the more stochastic minibatch gradient descent used in most deep learning optimization approaches.

Nerestov momentum is supported in PyTorch out-of-the-box by setting the `nesterov` argument:

```
optimizer = optim.SGD(model.parameters(),
                      lr = 0.01,
                      momentum = 0.9,
                      nesterov = True)
```

A Brief View of Second-Order Methods

As we discussed, computing the Hessian is a computationally difficult task, and momentum afforded us significant speedup without having to worry about it altogether. Several second-order methods, however, have been researched over the past several years that attempt to approximate the Hessian directly. For completeness, we give a broad overview of these methods, but a detailed treatment is beyond the scope of this text.

The first is *conjugate gradient descent*, which arises out of attempting to improve on a naive method of steepest descent. In steepest descent, we compute the direction

---

5 Sutskever, Ilya, et al. "On the importance of initialization and momentum in deep learning." *ICML* (3) 28 (2013): 1139-1147.

of the gradient and then line search to find the minimum along that direction. We jump to the minimum and then recompute the gradient to determine the direction of the next line search. It turns out that this method ends up zigzagging a significant amount, as shown in Figure 6-10, because each time we move in the direction of steepest descent, we undo a little bit of progress in another direction. A remedy to this problem is moving in a *conjugate direction* relative to the previous choice instead of the direction of steepest descent. The conjugate direction is chosen by using an indirect approximation of the Hessian to linearly combine the gradient and our previous direction. With a slight modification, this method generalizes to the nonconvex error surfaces we find in deep networks.[6]

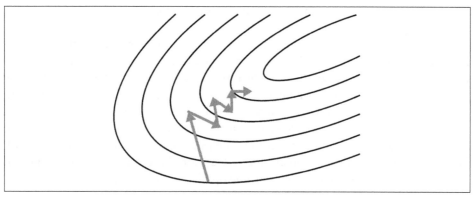

Figure 6-10. The method of steepest descent often zigzags; conjugate descent attempts to remedy this issue

An alternative optimization algorithm known as the *Broyden–Fletcher–Goldfarb–Shanno* (BFGS) algorithm attempts to compute the inverse of the Hessian matrix iteratively and use the inverse Hessian to more effectively optimize the parameter vector.[7] In its original form, BFGS has a significant memory footprint, but recent work has produced a more memory-efficient version known as *L-BFGS*.[8]

In general, while these methods hold some promise, second-order methods are still an area of active research and are unpopular among practitioners. PyTorch does, however, support L-BFGS as well as other second-order methods, such as Averaged Stochastic Gradient Descent, for your own experimentation.

6 Møller, Martin Fodslette. "A Scaled Conjugate Gradient Algorithm for Fast Supervised Learning." *Neural Networks* 6.4 (1993): 525-533.

7 Broyden, C. G. "A New Method of Solving Nonlinear Simultaneous Equations." *The Computer Journal* 12.1 (1969): 94-99.

8 Bonnans, Joseph-Frédéric, et al. *Numerical Optimization: Theoretical and Practical Aspects*. Springer Science & Business Media, 2006.

Learning Rate Adaptation

As we have discussed previously, another major challenge for training deep networks is appropriately selecting the learning rate. Choosing the correct learning rate has long been one of the most troublesome aspects of training deep networks because it has a major impact on a network's performance. A learning rate that is too small doesn't learn quickly enough, but a learning rate that is too large may have difficulty converging as we approach a local minimum or region that is ill-conditioned.

One of the major breakthroughs in modern deep network optimization was the advent of learning rate adaption. The basic concept behind learning rate adaptation is that the optimal learning rate is appropriately modified over the span of learning to achieve good convergence properties. Over the next several sections, we'll discuss AdaGrad, RMSProp, and Adam, three of the most popular adaptive learning rate algorithms.

AdaGrad—Accumulating Historical Gradients

The first algorithm we'll discuss is AdaGrad, which attempts to adapt the global learning rate over time using an accumulation of the historical gradients, first proposed by Duchi et al. in 2011.[9] Specifically, we keep track of a learning rate for each parameter. This learning rate is inversely scaled with respect to the square root of the sum of the squares (root mean square) of all the parameter's historical gradients.

We can express this mathematically. We initialize a gradient accumulation vector $\mathbf{r}_0 = \mathbf{0}$. At every step, we accumulate the square of all the gradient parameters as follows (where the $\odot$ operation is element-wise tensor multiplication):

$$\mathbf{r}_i = \mathbf{r}_{i-1} + \mathbf{g}_i \odot \mathbf{g}_i$$

Then we compute the update as usual, except our global learning rate ϵ is divided by the square root of the gradient accumulation vector:

$$\theta_i = \theta_{i-1} - \frac{\epsilon}{\delta \oplus \sqrt{\mathbf{r}_i}} \odot \mathbf{g}$$

Note that we add a tiny number δ ($\sim 10^{-7}$) to the denominator to prevent division by zero. Also, the division and addition operations are broadcast to the size of the gradient accumulation vector and applied element-wise. In PyTorch, a built-in optimizer allows for easily utilizing AdaGrad as a learning algorithm:

---

9 Duchi, John, Elad Hazan, and Yoram Singer. "Adaptive Subgradient Methods for Online Learning and Stochastic Optimization." *Journal of Machine Learning Research* 12.Jul (2011): 2121-2159.

```
optimizer = optim.Adagrad(model.parameters(),
                          lr = 0.01,
                          weight_decay = 0,
                          initial_accumulator_value = 0)
```

The only hitch is that in PyTorch, the δ and initial gradient accumulation vector are rolled together into the initial_accumulator_value argument.

On a functional level, this update mechanism means that the parameters with the largest gradients experience a rapid decrease in their learning rates, while parameters with smaller gradients observe only a small decrease in their learning rates. The ultimate effect is that AdaGrad forces more progress in the more gently sloped directions on the error surface, which can help overcome ill-conditioned surfaces. This results in some good theoretical properties, but in practice, training deep learning models with AdaGrad can be somewhat problematic. Empirically, AdaGrad has a tendency to cause a premature drop in learning rate, and as a result doesn't work particularly well for some deep models. In the next section, we'll describe RMSProp, which attempts to remedy this shortcoming.

RMSProp—Exponentially Weighted Moving Average of Gradients

While AdaGrad works well for simple convex functions, it isn't designed to navigate the complex error surfaces of deep networks. Flat regions may force AdaGrad to decrease the learning rate before it reaches a minimum. The conclusion is that simply using a naive accumulation of gradients isn't sufficient.

Our solution is to bring back a concept we introduced earlier while discussing momentum to dampen fluctuations in the gradient. Compared to naive accumulation, exponentially weighted moving averages also enables us to "toss out" measurements that we made a long time ago. More specifically, our update to the gradient accumulation vector is now as follows:

$$\mathbf{r}_i = \rho \mathbf{r}_{i-1} + (1 - \rho)\mathbf{g}_i \odot \mathbf{g}_i$$

The decay factor ρ determines how long we keep old gradients. The smaller the decay factor, the shorter the effective window. Plugging this modification into AdaGrad gives rise to the RMSProp learning algorithm, first proposed by Geoffrey Hinton.[10]

---

10 Tieleman, Tijmen, and Geoffrey Hinton. "Lecture 6.5-rmsprop: Divide the Gradient by a Running Average of Its Recent Magnitude." *COURSERA: Neural Networks for Machine Learning* 4.2 (2012).

In PyTorch, we can instantiate the RMSProp optimizer with the following code. Note that in this case, unlike in AdaGrad, we pass in δ separately as the `epsilon` argument to the constructor:

```
optimizer = optim.RMSprop(model.parameters(),
                          lr = 0.01,
                          alpha = 0.99,
                          eps = 1e-8,
                          weight_decay = 0,
                          momentum = 0)
```

As the template suggests, we can utilize RMSProp with momentum (specifically Nerestov momentum). Overall, RMSProp has been shown to be a highly effective optimizer for deep neural networks, and is a default choice for many seasoned practitioners.

Adam—Combining Momentum and RMSProp

Before concluding our discussion of modern optimizers, we discuss one final algorithm—Adam.[11] Spiritually, we can think about Adam as a variant combination of RMSProp and momentum.

The basic idea is as follows. We want to keep track of an exponentially weighted moving average of the gradient (essentially the concept of velocity in classical momentum), which we can express as follows:

$$\mathbf{m}_i = \beta_1 \mathbf{m}_{i-1} + (1 - \beta_1)\mathbf{g}_i$$

This is our approximation of what we call the *first moment* of the gradient, or $\mathbb{E}[\mathbf{g}_i]$. And similarly to RMSProp, we can maintain an exponentially weighted moving average of the historical gradients. This is our estimation of what we call the *second moment* of the gradient, or $\mathbb{E}[\mathbf{g}_i \odot \mathbf{g}_i]$:

$$\mathbf{v}_i = \beta_2 \mathbf{v}_{i-1} + (1 - \beta_2)\mathbf{g}_i \odot \mathbf{g}_i$$

However, it turns out these estimations are biased relative to the real moments because we start off by initializing both vectors to the zero vector. In order to remedy this bias, we derive a correction factor for both estimations. Here, we describe the derivation for the estimation of the second moment. The derivation for the first moment, which is analogous to the derivation here, is left as an exercise for you.

---

11 Kingma, Diederik, and Jimmy Ba. "Adam: A Method for Stochastic Optimization." *arXiv preprint arXiv*:1412.6980 (2014).

We begin by expressing the estimation of the second moment in terms of all past gradients. This is done by simply expanding the recurrence relationship:

$$\mathbf{v}_i = \beta_2 \mathbf{v}_{i-1} + (1 - \beta_2)\mathbf{g}_i \odot \mathbf{g}_i$$
$$\mathbf{v}_i = \beta_2^{i-1}(1 - \beta_2)\mathbf{g}_1 \odot \mathbf{g}_1 + \beta_2^{i-2}(1 - \beta_2)\mathbf{g}_2 \odot \mathbf{g}_2 + \dots + (1 - \beta_2)\mathbf{g}_i \odot \mathbf{g}_i$$
$$\mathbf{v}_i = (1 - \beta_2)\Sigma_{k=1}^{i} \beta^{i-k}\mathbf{g}_k \odot \mathbf{g}_k$$

We can then take the expected value of both sides to determine how our estimation $\mathbb{E}[\mathbf{v}_i]$ compares to the real value of $\mathbb{E}[\mathbf{g}_i \odot \mathbf{g}_i]$:

$$\mathbb{E}[\mathbf{v}_i] = \mathbb{E}\left[(1 - \beta_2)\Sigma_{k=1}^{i} \beta^{i-k}\mathbf{g}_k \odot \mathbf{g}_k\right]$$

We can also assume that $\mathbb{E}[\mathbf{g}_k \odot \mathbf{g}_k] \approx \mathbb{E}[\mathbf{g}_i \approx \mathbf{g}_i]$ because even if the second moment of the gradient has changed since a historical value, β_2 should be chosen so that the old second moments of the gradients are essentially decayed out of relevancy. As a result, we can make the following simplification:

$$\mathbb{E}[\mathbf{v}_i] \approx \mathbb{E}[\mathbf{g}_i \odot \mathbf{g}_i](1 - \beta_2)\Sigma_{k=1}^{i} \beta^{i-k}$$
$$\mathbb{E}[\mathbf{v}_i] \approx \mathbb{E}[\mathbf{g}_i \odot \mathbf{g}_i](1 - \beta_2^i)$$

Note that we make the final simplification using the elementary algebraic identity $1 - x^n = (1 - x)(1 + x + \dots + x^{n-1})$. The results of this derivation and the analogous derivation for the first moment are the following correction schemes to account for the initialization bias:

$$\tilde{\mathbf{m}}_i = \frac{m_i}{1 - \beta_1^i}$$

$$\tilde{\mathbf{v}}_i = \frac{\tilde{\mathbf{v}}_i}{1 - \beta_2^i}$$

We can then use these corrected moments to update the parameter vector, resulting in the final Adam update:

$$\theta_i = \theta_{i-1} - \frac{\epsilon}{\delta \oplus \sqrt{\tilde{\mathbf{v}}_i}}\tilde{\mathbf{m}}_i$$

Recently, Adam has gained popularity because of its corrective measures against the zero initialization bias (a weakness of RMSProp) and its ability to combine the core concepts behind RMSProp with momentum more effectively. PyTorch exposes the Adam optimizer through the following constructor:

```
optimizer = optim.Adam(model.parameters(),
                       lr = 0.001,
                       betas = (0.9, 0.999),
                       eps = 1e-08,
                       weight_decay = 0,
                       amsgrad = False)
```

The default hyperparameter settings for Adam for PyTorch generally perform quite well, but Adam is also generally robust to choices in hyperparameters. The only exception is that the learning rate may need to be modified in certain cases from the default value of 0.001.

The Philosophy Behind Optimizer Selection

In this chapter, we've discussed several strategies that are used to make navigating the complex error surfaces of deep networks more tractable. These strategies have culminated in several optimization algorithms, each with its own benefits and short-comings.

While it would be awfully nice to know when to use which algorithm, there is very little consensus among expert practitioners. Currently, the most popular algorithms are minibatch gradient descent, minibatch gradient with momentum, RMSProp, RMSProp with momentum, Adam, and AdaDelta (which we haven't discussed here, but is also supported by PyTorch). We encourage you to experiment with these optimization algorithms on the feed-forward network model we built.

One important point, however, is that for most deep learning practitioners, the best way to push the cutting edge of deep learning is not by building more advanced optimizers. Instead, the vast majority of breakthroughs in deep learning over the past several decades have been obtained by discovering architectures that are easier to train instead of trying to wrangle with nasty error surfaces. We'll begin focusing on how to leverage architecture to more effectively train neural networks in the rest of this book.

Summary

In this chapter, we discussed several challenges that arise when trying to train deep networks with complex error surfaces. We discussed how while the challenges of spurious local minima are likely exaggerated, saddle points and ill-conditioning do pose a serious threat to the success of vanilla minibatch gradient descent. We described how momentum can be used to overcome ill-conditioning, and briefly discussed recent research in second-order methods to approximate the Hessian matrix. We also described the evolution of adaptive learning rate optimizers, which tune the learning rate during the training process for better convergence.

Next, we'll begin tackling the larger issue of network architecture and design. We'll explore computer vision and how we might design deep networks that learn effectively from complex images.

## CHAPTER 7

Convolutional Neural Networks

Neurons in Human Vision

The human sense of vision is unbelievably advanced. Within fractions of seconds, we can identify objects within our field of view, without thought or hesitation. Not only can we name objects we are looking at, we can also perceive their depth, perfectly distinguish their contours, and separate the objects from their backgrounds. Somehow our eyes take in raw voxels of color data, but our brain transforms that information into more meaningful primitives—lines, curves, and shapes—that might indicate, for example, that we're looking at a house cat.[1]

Foundational to the human sense of vision is the neuron. Specialized neurons are responsible for capturing light information in the human eye.[2] This light information is then preprocessed, transported to the visual cortex of the brain, and then finally analyzed to completion. Neurons are single-handedly responsible for all of these functions. As a result, intuitively, it would make a lot of sense to extend our neural network models to build better computer vision systems. In this chapter, we will use our understanding of human vision to build effective deep learning models for image problems. But before we jump in, let's take a look at more traditional approaches to image analysis and why they fall short.

---

1 Hubel, David H., and Torsten N. Wiesel. "Receptive Fields and Functional Architecture of Monkey Striate Cortex." *The Journal of Physiology* 195.1 (1968): 215-243.

2 Cohen, Adolph I. "Rods and Cones." *Physiology of Photoreceptor Organs*. Springer Berlin Heidelberg, 1972. 63-110.

The Shortcomings of Feature Selection

Let's begin by considering a simple computer vision problem. I give you a randomly selected image, such as the one in Figure 7-1. Your task is to tell me if there is a human face in this picture. This is exactly the problem that Paul Viola and Michael Jones tackled in their seminal paper published in 2001.[3]

Figure 7-1. A hypothetical face-recognition algorithm should detect a face in this photograph of former US President Barack Obama

For a human like you or me, this task is completely trivial. For a computer, however, this is a difficult problem. How do we teach a computer that an image contains a face? We could try to train a traditional machine learning algorithm (like the one we described in Chapter 3) by giving it the raw pixel values of the image and hoping it can find an appropriate classifier. Turns out this doesn't work well at all because the signal-to-noise ratio is much too low for any useful learning to occur. We need an alternative.

The compromise that was eventually reached was essentially a trade-off between the traditional computer program, where the human defined all of the logic, and a pure

---

3 Viola, Paul, and Michael Jones. "Rapid Object Detection using a Boosted Cascade of Simple Features." Computer Vision and Pattern Recognition, 2001. CVPR 2001. *Proceedings of the 2001 IEEE Computer Society Conference* on. Vol. 1. IEEE, 2001.

machine learning approach, where the computer did all of the heavy lifting. In this compromise, a human would choose the features (perhaps hundreds or thousands) that they believed were important in making a classification decision. In doing so, the human would be producing a lower-dimensional representation of the same learning problem. The machine learning algorithm would then use these new *feature vectors* to make classification decisions. Because the *feature extraction* process improves the signal-to-noise ratio (assuming the appropriate features are picked), this approach had quite a bit of success compared to the state-of-the-art at the time.

Viola and Jones had the insight that faces had certain patterns of light and dark patches that they could exploit. For example, there is a difference in light intensity between the eye region and the upper cheeks. There is also a difference in light intensity between the nose bridge and the two eyes on either side. These detectors are shown in Figure 7-2.

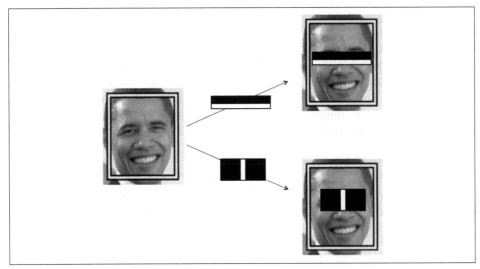

Figure 7-2. Viola-Jones intensity detectors

By themselves, each of these features is not very effective at identifying a face. But when used together (through a classic machine learning algorithm known as boosting, described in the original manuscript (*https://oreil.ly/UAgvR*)), their combined effectiveness drastically increases. On a dataset of 130 images and 507 faces, the algorithm achieves a 91.4% detection rate with 50 false positives. The performance was unparalleled at the time, but there are fundamental limitations of the algorithm. If a face is partially covered with shade, the light intensity comparisons no longer work. Moreover, if the algorithm is looking at a face on a crumpled flier or the face of a cartoon character, it would most likely fail.

The problem is the algorithm hasn't really learned that much about what it means to "see" a face. Beyond differences in light intensity, our brain uses a vast number of visual cues to realize that our field of view contains a human face, including contours, relative positioning of facial features, and color. And even if there are slight discrepancies in one of our visual cues (for example, if parts of the face are blocked from view or if shade modifies light intensities), our visual cortex can still reliably identify faces.

To use traditional machine learning techniques to teach a computer to "see," we need to provide our program with a lot more features to make accurate decisions. Before the advent of deep learning, huge teams of computer vision researchers would take years to debate about the usefulness of different features. As the recognition problems became more and more intricate, researchers had a difficult time coping with the increase in complexity.

To illustrate the power of deep learning, consider the ImageNet challenge, one of the most prestigious benchmarks in computer vision (sometimes even referred to as the Olympics of computer vision).[4] Every year, researchers attempt to classify images into one of 200 possible classes given a training dataset of approximately 450,000 images. The algorithm is given five guesses to get the right answer before it moves onto the next image in the test dataset. The goal of the competition is to push the state-of-the-art in computer vision to rival the accuracy of human vision itself (approximately 95% to 96%).

In 2011, the winner of the ImageNet benchmark had an error rate of 25.7%, making a mistake on one out of every four images.[5] Definitely a huge improvement over random guessing, but not good enough for any sort of commercial application. Then in 2012, Alex Krizhevsky from Geoffrey Hinton's lab at the University of Toronto did the unthinkable. Pioneering a deep learning architecture known as a *convolutional neural network* for the first time on a challenge of this size and complexity, he blew the competition out of the water. The runner-up in the competition scored a commendable 26.1% error rate. But AlexNet, over the course of just a few months of work, completely crushed 50 years of traditional computer vision research with an error rate of approximately 16%.[6] It would be no understatement to say that AlexNet single-handedly put deep learning on the map for computer vision and completely revolutionized the field.

---

4 Deng, Jia, et al. "ImageNet: A Large-Scale Hierarchical Image Database." *Computer Vision and Pattern Recognition*, 2009. CVPR 2009. IEEE Conference. IEEE, 2009.

5 Perronnin, Florent, Jorge Sénchez, and Yan Liu Xerox. "Large-Scale Image Categorization with Explicit Data Embedding." *Computer Vision and Pattern Recognition* (CVPR), 2010 IEEE Conference. IEEE, 2010.

6 Krizhevsky, Alex, Ilya Sutskever, and Geoffrey E. Hinton. "ImageNet Classification with Deep Convolutional Neural Networks." *Advances in Neural Information Processing Systems*. 2012.

Vanilla Deep Neural Networks Don't Scale

The fundamental goal in applying deep learning to computer vision is to remove the cumbersome, and ultimately limiting, feature selection process. As we discussed in Chapter 3, deep neural networks are perfect for this process because each layer of a neural network is responsible for learning and building up features to represent the input data that it receives. A naive approach might be for us to use a vanilla deep neural network using the network layer primitive we designed in Chapter 5 for the MNIST dataset to achieve the image classification task.

If we attempt to tackle the image classification problem in this way, however, we'll quickly face a pretty daunting challenge, visually demonstrated in Figure 7-3. In MNIST, our images were only 28 × 28 pixels and were black and white. As a result, a neuron in a fully connected hidden layer would have 784 incoming weights. This seems pretty tractable for the MNIST task, and our vanilla neural net performed quite well. This technique, however, does not scale well as our images grow larger. For example, for a full-color 200 × 200 pixel image, our input layer would have 200 × 200 × 3 = 120,000 weights. And we're going to want to have lots of these neurons over multiple layers, so these parameters add up quite quickly. Clearly, this full connectivity is not only wasteful, but also means that we're much more likely to overfit to the training dataset.

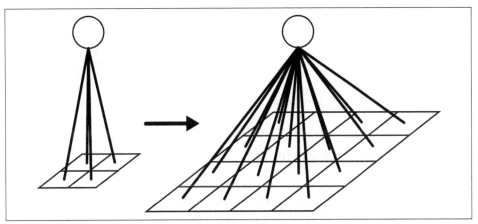

Figure 7-3. The density of connections between layers increases intractably as the size of the image increases

The convolutional network takes advantage of the fact that we're analyzing images, and sensibly constrains the architecture of the deep network so that we drastically reduce the number of parameters in our model. Inspired by how human vision works, layers of a convolutional network have neurons arranged in three dimensions, so layers have a width, height, and depth, as shown in Figure 7-4.[7]

As we'll see, the neurons in a convolutional layer are connected to only a small, local region of the preceding layer, so we avoid the wastefulness of fully connected neurons. A convolutional layer's function can be expressed simply: it processes a three-dimensional volume of information to produce a new three-dimensional volume of information. We'll take a closer look at how this works in the next section.

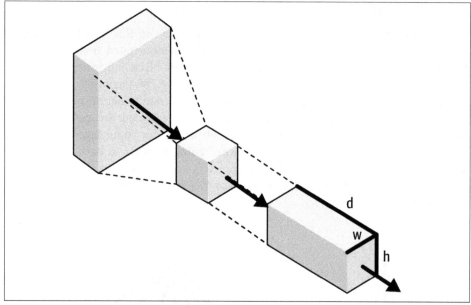

Figure 7-4. Convolutional layers arrange neurons in three dimensions, so layers have width, height, and depth

Filters and Feature Maps

In order to motivate the primitives of the convolutional layer, let's build an intuition for how the human brain pieces together raw visual information into an understanding of the world around us. One of the most influential studies in this space came from David Hubel and Torsten Wiesel, who discovered that parts of the visual cortex are responsible for detecting edges. In 1959, they inserted electrodes into the brain of a cat and projected black-and-white patterns on the screen. They found that some

---

7 LeCun, Yann, et al. "Handwritten Digit Recognition with a Back-Propagation Network." *Advances in Neural Information Processing Systems.* 1990.

neurons fired only when there were vertical lines, others when there were horizontal lines, and still others when the lines were at particular angles.[8]

Further work determined that the visual cortex was organized in layers. Each layer is responsible for building on the features detected in the previous layers—from lines, to contours, to shapes, to entire objects. Furthermore, within a layer of the visual cortex, the same feature detectors were replicated over the whole area in order to detect features in all parts of an image. These ideas significantly impacted the design of convolutional neural nets.

The first concept that arose was that of a *filter*, and it turns out that here, Viola and Jones were actually pretty close. A filter is essentially a feature detector, and to understand how it works, let's consider the toy image in Figure 7-5.

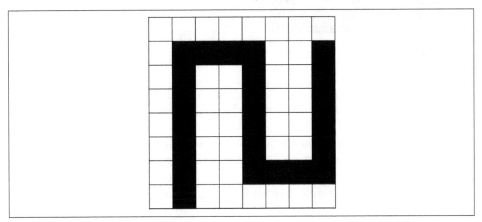

Figure 7-5. We'll analyze this simple black-and-white image as a toy example

Let's say that we want to detect vertical and horizontal lines in the image. One approach would be to use an appropriate feature detector, as shown in Figure 7-6. For example, to detect vertical lines, we would use the feature detector on the top, slide it across the entirety of the image, and at every step check if we have a match. We keep track of our answers in the matrix in the top right. If there's a match, we shade the appropriate box black. If there isn't, we leave it white. This result is our *feature map*, and it indicates where we've found the feature we're looking for in the original image. We can do the same for the horizontal line detector (bottom), resulting in the feature map in the bottom-right corner.

---

8 Hubel, David H., and Torsten N. Wiesel. "Receptive Fields of Single Neurones in the Cat's Striate Cortex." *The Journal of Physiology* 148.3 (1959): 574-591.

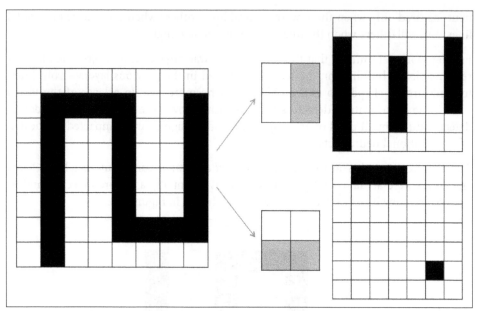

Figure 7-6. Applying filters that detect vertical and horizontal lines on our toy example

This operation is called a convolution. We take a filter and we multiply it over the entire area of an input image. Using the following scheme, let's try to express this operation as neurons in a network. In this scheme, layers of neurons in a feed-forward neural net represent either the original image or a feature map. Filters represent combinations of connections (one such combination is highlighted in Figure 7-7) that get replicated across the entirety of the input. In Figure 7-7, connections of the same color are restricted to always have the same weight. We can achieve this by initializing all the connections in a group with identical weights and by always averaging the weight updates of a group before applying them at the end of each iteration of backpropagation. The output layer is the feature map generated by this filter. A neuron in the feature map is activated if the filter contributing to its activity detected an appropriate feature at the corresponding position in the previous layer.

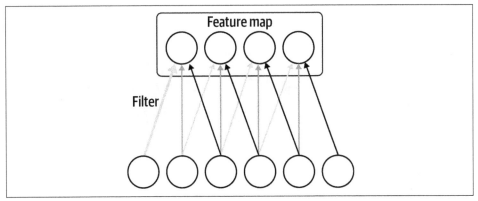

Figure 7-7. Representing filters and feature maps as neurons in a convolutional layer

Let's denote the kth feature map in layer m as m^k. Moreover, let's denote the corresponding filter by the values of its weights W. Then, assuming the neurons in the feature map have bias b^k (note that the bias is kept identical for all of the neurons in a feature map), we can mathematically express the feature map as follows:

$$m^k_{ij} = f\left((W * x)_{ij} + b^k\right)$$

This mathematical description is simple and succinct, but it doesn't completely describe filters as they are used in convolutional neural networks. Specifically, filters don't just operate on a single feature map. They operate on the entire volume of feature maps that have been generated at a particular layer. For example, consider a situation in which we would like to detect a face at a particular layer of a convolutional net. And we have accumulated three feature maps, one for eyes, one for noses, and one for mouths. We know that a particular location contains a face if the corresponding locations in the primitive feature maps contain the appropriate features (two eyes, a nose, and a mouth). In other words, to make decisions about the existence of a face, we must combine evidence over multiple feature maps. This is equally necessary for an input image that is of full color. These images have pixels represented as RGB values, so we require three slices in the input volume (one slice for each color). As a result, feature maps must be able to operate over volumes, not just areas. This is shown in Figure 7-8. Each cell in the input volume is a neuron. A local portion is multiplied with a filter (corresponding to weights in the convolutional layer) to produce a neuron in a filter map in the following volumetric layer of neurons.

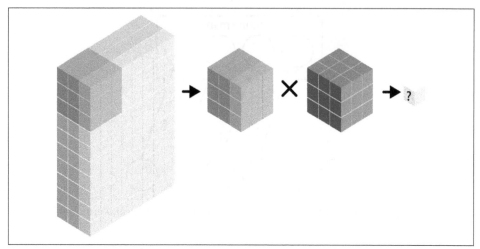

Figure 7-8. A full-color RGB image as a volume and applying a volumetric convolutional filter

As we discussed in the previous section, a convolutional layer (which consists of a set of filters) converts one volume of values into another volume of values. The depth of the filter corresponds to the depth of the input volume. This is so that the filter can combine information from all the features that have been learned. The depth of the output volume of a convolutional layer is equivalent to the number of filters in that layer, because each filter produces its own slice. We visualize these relationships in Figure 7-9.

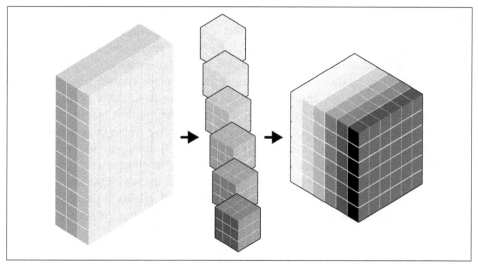

Figure 7-9. A three-dimensional visualization of a convolutional layer, where each filter corresponds to a slice in the resulting output volume

In the next section, we will use these concepts and fill in some of the gaps to create a full description of a convolutional layer.

Full Description of the Convolutional Layer

Let's use the concepts we've developed so far to complete the description of the convolutional layer. First, a convolutional layer takes in an input volume. This input volume has the following characteristics:

- Its width w_{in}
- Its height h_{in}
- Its depth d_{in}
- Its zero padding p

This volume is processed by a total of k filters, which represent the weights and connections in the convolutional network. These filters have a number of hyperparameters, which are described as follows:

- Their spatial extent e, which is equal to the filter's height and width.
- Their stride s, or the distance between consecutive applications of the filter on the input volume. If we use a stride of 1, we get the full convolution described in the previous section. We illustrate this in Figure 7-10.
- The bias b (a parameter learned like the values in the filter), which is added to each component of the convolution.

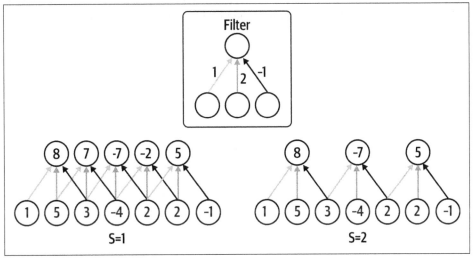

Figure 7-10. A filter's stride hyperparameter

This results in an output volume with the following characteristics:

- Its function f, which is applied to the incoming logit of each neuron in the output volume to determine its final value

- Its width $w_{out} = \left\lceil \dfrac{w_{in} - e + 2p}{s} \right\rceil + 1$

- Its height $h_{out} = \left\lceil \dfrac{h_{in} - e + 2p}{s} \right\rceil + 1$

- Its depth $d_{out} = k$

The mth "depth slice" of the output volume, where $1 \leq m \leq k$, corresponds to the function f applied to the sum of the mth filter convoluted over the input volume and the bias b^m. Moreover, this means that per filter, we have $d_{in}e^2$ parameters. In total, that means the layer has $kd_{in}e^2$ parameters and k biases. To demonstrate this in action, we provide an example of a convolutional layer in Figures 7-11 and 7-12 with a $5 \times 5 \times 3$ input volume with zero padding $p = 1$. We'll use two $3 \times 3 \times 3$ filters (spatial extent) with a stride $s = 2$. We'll use a linear function to produce the output volume, which will be of size $3 \times 3 \times 2$. We apply the first convolutional filter to the upper-leftmost 3×3 piece of the input volume to generate the upper-leftmost entry of the first depth slice.

Generally, it's wise to keep filter sizes small (size 3×3 or 5×5). Less commonly, larger sizes are used (7×7) but only in the first convolutional layer. Having more small filters is an easy way to achieve high representational power while also incurring a smaller number of parameters. It's also suggested to use a stride of 1 to capture all useful information in the feature maps, and a zero padding that keeps the output volume's height and width equivalent to the input volume's height and width.

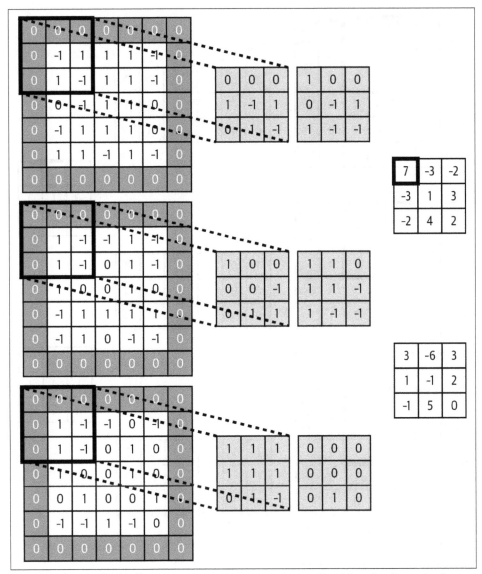

Figure 7-11. A convolutional layer with an input volume of width 5, height 5, depth 3, zero padding 1, and 2 filters (with spatial extent 3 and applied with a stride of 2) results in an output volume of 3 × 3 × 2

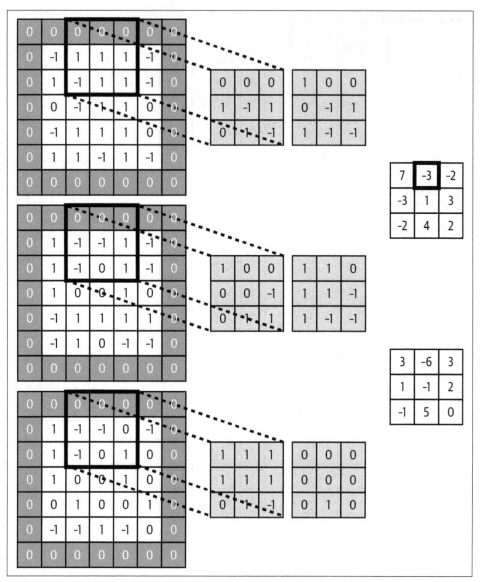

Figure 7-12. Using the same setup as Figure 7-11, we generate the next value in the first depth slice of the output volume

PyTorch provides us with a convenient operation to easily perform a 2D convolution on a minibatch of input volumes:

```
import torch.nn as nn

layer = nn.Conv2d(in_channels = 3,
                  out_channels = 64,
```

```
        kernel_size = (5, 5),
        stride = 2,
        padding = 1
        )
```

Here, in_channels represents the depth, d_{in}, or number of input planes. For color images, the number of input channels often equals three, representing the RGB channels. The nn.Conv2d layer will accept as an input a four-dimensional tensor of size, $b_{in} * d_{in} * h_{in} * w_{in}$, where b_{in} is the number of examples in our minibatch.

The out_channels argument represents the number of output planes or feature maps. The kernel_size argument determines the filter size or *spatial extent, e,* while the stride and padding arguments determine the stride size, s, and zero padding size, p, respectively. Note that you can pass in equal dimension settings with a single value as shown here with stride and padding.

Max Pooling

To aggressively reduce dimensionality of feature maps and sharpen the located features, we sometimes insert a *max pooling* layer (*https://oreil.ly/HOYaa*) after a convolutional layer. The essential idea behind max pooling is to break up each feature map into equally sized tiles. Then we create a condensed feature map. Specifically, we create a cell for each tile, compute the maximum value in the tile, and propagate this maximum value into the corresponding cell of the condensed feature map. This process is illustrated in Figure 7-13.

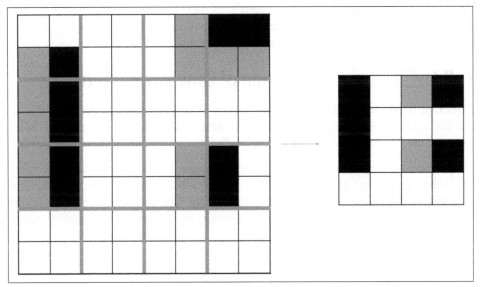

Figure 7-13. Max pooling significantly reduces parameters as we move up the network

More rigorously, we can describe a pooling layer with two parameters:

- Its spatial extent e
- Its stride s

It's important to note that only two major variations of the pooling layer are used. The first is the nonoverlapping pooling layer with $e = 2, s = 2$. The second is the overlapping pooling layer with $e = 3, s = 2$. The resulting dimensions of each feature map are as follows:

- Its width $w_{out} = \left\lceil \frac{w_{in} - e}{s} \right\rceil + 1$
- Its height $h_{out} = \left\lceil \frac{h_{in} - e}{s} \right\rceil + 1$

One interesting property of max pooling is that it is *locally invariant*. This means that even if the inputs shift around a little bit, the output of the max pooling layer stays constant. This has important implications for visual algorithms. Local invariance is a useful property if we care more about whether some feature is present than exactly where it is. However, enforcing large amounts of local invariance can destroy our network's ability to carry important information. As a result, we usually keep the spatial extent of our pooling layers quite small.

Some recent work along this line has come out of the University of Warwick from Graham,[9] who proposes a concept called *fractional max pooling*. In fractional max pooling, a pseudorandom number generator is used to generate tilings with noninteger lengths for pooling. Here, fractional max pooling functions as a strong regularizer, helping prevent overfitting in convolutional networks.

Full Architectural Description of Convolution Networks

Now that we've described the building blocks of convolutional networks, we start putting them together. Figure 7-14 depicts several architectures that might be of practical use.

One theme we notice as we build deeper networks is that we reduce the number of pooling layers and instead stack multiple convolutional layers in tandem. This is generally helpful because pooling operations are inherently destructive. Stacking several convolutional layers before each pooling layer allows us to achieve richer representations.

---

9 Graham, Benjamin. "Fractional Max-Pooling." *arXiv Preprint arXiv*:1412.6071 (2014).

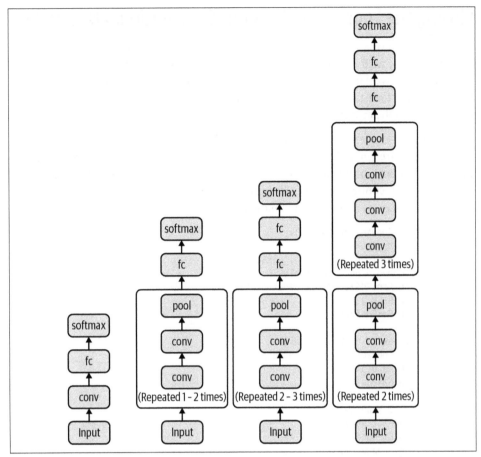

Figure 7-14. Various convolutional network architectures of various complexities

As a practical note, deep convolutional networks can take up a significant amount of space, and most casual practitioners are usually bottlenecked by the memory capacity on their GPU. The VGGNet architecture, for example, takes approximately 90 MB of memory on the forward pass per image, and more than 180 MB of memory on the backward pass to update the parameters.[10] Many deep networks make a compromise by using strides and spatial extents in the first convolutional layer that reduce the amount of information that needs to be propagated up the network.

---

10 Simonyan, Karen, and Andrew Zisserman. "Very Deep Convolutional Networks for Large-Scale Image Recognition." *arXiv Preprint arXiv*:1409.1556 (2014).

Closing the Loop on MNIST with Convolutional Networks

Now that we have a better understanding of how to build networks that effectively analyze images, we'll revisit the MNIST challenge we've tackled over the past several chapters. Here, we'll use a convolutional network to learn how to recognize handwritten digits. Our feed-forward network was able to achieve a 98.2% accuracy. Our goal will be to push the envelope on this result.

To tackle this challenge, we'll build a convolutional network with a pretty standard architecture (modeled after the second network in Figure 7-14): two convolutional/ReLU/maxpooling stacks, followed by a fully connected layer with dropout and a terminal fully connected layer. Building the network is easy in PyTorch using the built-in nn classes, as shown in the following code:

```
class MNISTConvNet(nn.Module):
  def __init__(self):
    super(MNISTConvNet, self).__init__()
    self.conv1 = nn.Sequential(
        nn.Conv2d(1, 32, 5, padding='same'),
        nn.ReLU(),
        nn.MaxPool2d(2)
    )
    self.conv2 = nn.Sequential(
        nn.Conv2d(32, 64, 5, padding='same'),
        nn.ReLU(),
        nn.MaxPool2d(2)
    )
    self.fc1 = nn.Sequential(
        nn.Flatten(),
        nn.Linear(7*7*64, 1024),
        nn.Dropout(0.5),
        nn.Linear(1024, 10)
    )

  def forward(self, x):
    x = self.conv1(x)
    x = self.conv2(x)
    return self.fc1(x)
```

The __init__ method generates two Conv2d/ReLU/MaxPool blocks followed by a block containing two fully connected layers. The convolutional layers are created with a particular shape. By default, the stride is set to be 1, while the padding is set to same to keep the width and height constant between input and output tensors. By default, each nn.Conv2d constructor automatically initializes the weights.

The max pooling layers consist of nonoverlapping windows of size k. The default, as recommended, is k=2, and we'll use this default in our MNIST convolutional network.

The forward method defines how our layers and blocks are connected together to perform the forward pass or inference.

The code here is quite easy to follow. The input is expected to be a tensor of size $N \times 1 \times 28 \times 28$, where N is the number of examples in a minibatch, 28 is the width and height of each image, and 1 is the depth (because the images are black and white; if the images were in RGB color, the depth would instead be 3 to represent each color map).

The first block, conv1, builds a convolutional layer with 32 filters that have spatial extent 5. This results in taking an input volume of depth 1 and emitting an output tensor of depth 32. This is then passed through a max pooling layer that compresses the information. The second block, conv2, then builds a second convolutional layer with 64 filters, again with spatial extent 5, taking an input tensor of depth 32 and emitting an output tensor of depth 64. This, again, is passed through a max pooling layer to compress information.

We then prepare to pass the output of the max pooling layer into a fully connected layer. To do this, we flatten the tensor. We can do this by computing the full size of each "subtensor" in the minibatch. We have 64 filters, which corresponds to the depth of 64. We now have to determine the height and width after passing through two max pooling layers. Using the formulas we found in the previous section, it's easy to confirm that each feature map has a height and width of 7. Confirming this is left as an exercise for you.

We use a fully connected layer to compress the flattened representation into a hidden state of size 1,024. We use a dropout probability in this layer of 0.5 during training and 1 during model evaluation (standard procedure for employing dropout). Finally, we send this hidden state into a output layer with 10 bins (the softmax is, as usual, performed in the loss constructor for better performance).

Finally, we train our network using the Adam optimizer. After several epochs over the dataset, we achieve an accuracy of 99.4%, which isn't state-of-the-art (approximately 99.7 to 99.8%), but is respectable:

```
lr = 1e-4
num_epochs = 40

model = MNISTConvNet()
loss_fn = nn.CrossEntropyLoss()
optimizer = optim.SGD(model.parameters(), lr=lr)

for epochs in range(num_epochs):
  running_loss = 0.0
  num_correct = 0
  for inputs, labels in trainloader:
    optimizer.zero_grad()
    outputs = model(inputs)
```

```
        loss = loss_fn(outputs, labels)
        loss.backward()
        running_loss += loss.item()
        optimizer.step()
        _, idx = outputs.max(dim=1)
        num_correct += (idx == labels).sum().item()
    print('Loss: {} Accuracy: {}'.format(running_loss/len(trainloader),
        num_correct/len(trainloader)))
```

Image Preprocessing Pipelines Enable More Robust Models

So far we've been dealing with rather tame datasets. Why is MNIST a tame dataset? Well, fundamentally, MNIST has already been preprocessed so that all the images in the dataset resemble each other. The handwritten digits are perfectly cropped in just the same way; there are no color aberrations because MNIST is black and white; and so on. Natural images, however, are an entirely different beast.

Natural images are messy, and as a result, there are a number of preprocessing operations that we can utilize in order to make training slightly easier. Fortunately, PyTorch offers a package called Torchvision that includes many commonly used transforms for image processing. One technique that is supported out of the box in PyTorch is image whitening. The basic idea behind whitening is to zero-center every pixel in an image by subtracting out the mean of the dataset and normalizing to unit 1 variance. This helps us correct for potential differences in dynamic range between images. In PyTorch, we can achieve this using the `Normalize` transform:

```
from torchvision import transforms

transform = transforms.Normalize(mean = (0.1307,),
                                  std = (0.3081,)
                                  )
```

The magic numbers for `mean`, 0.1307, and `std`, 0.3081, were computed over the entire MNIST dataset, and this technique is called dataset normalization. We can also expand our dataset artificially by randomly cropping the image, flipping the image, modifying saturation, modifying brightness, etc:

```
transform = transforms.Compose([
    transforms.RandomCrop(224),
    transforms.RandomHorizontalFlip(),
    transforms.ColorJitter(brightness=0,
                           contrast=0,
                           saturation=0,
                           hue=0),
    transforms.ToTensor(),
    transforms.Normalize(mean = (0.1307,),
                         std = (0.3081,)
                         )
])
```

Here, we use the Compose transform to create a sequence of transforms from a list. After applying random cropping, flipping, and color adjustments, we convert the image data to a PyTorch tensor and normalize the data. PyTorch models require the data to be in tensor format, and these last two steps are common practice in using PyTorch for deep learning.

Applying these transformations helps us build networks that are robust to the different kinds of variations that are present in natural images, and make predictions with high fidelity in spite of potential distortions.

Accelerating Training with Batch Normalization

In 2015, researchers from Google devised an exciting way to even further accelerate the training of feed-forward and convolutional neural networks using a technique called *batch normalization*.[11] We can think of the intuition behind batch normalization like a tower of blocks, as shown in Figure 7-15.

When a tower of blocks is stacked together neatly, the structure is stable. However, if we randomly shift the blocks, we could force the tower into configurations that are increasingly unstable. Eventually the tower falls apart.

A similar phenomenon can happen during the training of neural networks. Imagine a two-layer neural network. In the process of training the weights of the network, the output distribution of the neurons in the bottom layer begins to shift. The result of the changing distribution of outputs from the bottom layer means that the top layer not only has to learn how to make the appropriate predictions, but it also needs to somehow modify itself to accommodate the shifts in incoming distribution. This significantly slows down training, and the magnitude of the problem compounds the more layers we have in our networks.

---

11 S. Ioffe, C. Szegedy. "Batch Normalization: Accelerating Deep Network Training by Reducing Internal Covariate Shift." *arXiv Preprint arXiv*:1502.03167. 2015.

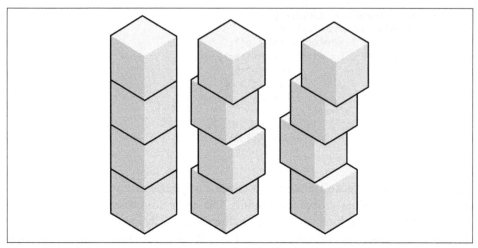

Figure 7-15. Batch normalization reduces shifts in the distribution of inputs of layers

Normalization of image inputs helps out the training process by making it more robust to variations. Batch normalization takes this a step further by normalizing inputs to every layer in our neural network. Specifically, we modify the architecture of our network to include operations that:

1. Grab the vector of logits incoming to a layer before they pass through the nonlinearity.

2. Normalize each component of the vector of logits across all examples of the minibatch by subtracting the mean and dividing by the standard deviation (we keep track of the moments using an exponentially weighted moving average).

3. Given normalized inputs $\hat{\mathbf{x}}$, use an affine transform to restore representational power with two vectors of (trainable) parameters: $\gamma\hat{\mathbf{x}} + \beta$.

PyTorch provides a `BatchNorm2d` class to perform batch normalization for a convolutional layer:

```
layer = nn.BatchNorm2d(num_features=32,
                       eps=1e-05,
                       momentum=0.1,
                       affine = True,
                       track_running_stats = True)
```

Here, the `num_features` argument represents the depth, or number of channels, of the inputs to the batch normalization layer. Hence, batch normalization is performed over the channel dimension, computing the mean and variance of each minibatch of 2D channels. The `num_features` is the only required argument. All other arguments are set to their defaults.

The `BatchNorm2d` layer performs the following `affine` transformation:

$$y = \frac{x - E[x]}{\sqrt{Var[x] + \epsilon}} * \gamma + \beta$$

The parameters γ and β are learnable parameters and will be trained during the training process if `affine = True`. Otherwise, the mean is subtracted from the inputs and divided by standard deviation to be normalized. The ϵ argument is only used for mathematical stability.

When `track_running_stats = True`, this layer will keep track of the running mean and variance for use in evaluation mode. The running mean and variance are updated using the `momentum` value.

We can also express batch normalization for nonconvolutional feed-forward layers by using the `BatchNorm1d` constructor. Here, we set only `num_features = 32` and use the defaults for other arguments:

```
layer = nn.BatchNorm1d(num_features=32)
```

In addition to speeding up training by preventing significant shifts in the distribution of inputs to each layer, batch normalization also allows us to significantly increase the learning rate. Moreover, batch normalization acts as a regularizer and removes the need for dropout and (when used) L2 regularization. Although we don't leverage it here, the authors also claim that batch regularization largely removes the need for photometric distortions, and we can expose the network to more "real" images during the training process. In the next section, we will motivate and discuss a variant of normalization across the feature axis, rather than the batch.

Group Normalization for Memory Constrained Learning Tasks

Various forms of normalization in image processing have been studied and utilized in the last decade. The most famous of these is batch normalization. Just to recap from the previous section, this technique computes the channel-wise mean and variance of the output of each convolutional layer, normalizes each channel using the computed statistics, and then feeds the normalized output to the next convolutional layer. Thus, any given channel in the normalized output will have the same mean and variance (zero and one, respectively) across batches. In practice, the model will also learn a mean parameter β and a standard deviation parameter γ, which are then applied to the normalized output such that it has mean β and standard deviation γ before being fed into the subsequent layer. This process is used to reduce the shift in distribution of any given channel from one batch to the next. Note that this is only a reduction of the shift and not a complete removal of it, since the channel distribution might still look completely different from one batch to the next even though they have the same mean and variance. In theory, and as has been observed empirically, reducing this internal covariate shift stabilizes training and results in strong performance gains.

However, in cases where the batch size is large, the channel-wise mean and variance computations lead to large memory costs. Additionally, the size of the batch itself is very important for batch normalization, as smaller batch sizes degrade performance significantly due to noisy mean and variance estimates. To avoid the issues that come with computations along the batch dimension, *group normalization* was introduced.[12] Instead of performing a normalization along the batch dimension, group normalization is performed along the channel dimension and is thus unaffected by the aforementioned issues. Group normalization predefines a number of groups of channels and, for each instance, computes the mean μ and variance σ for each group of channels in each instance of the batch. Each set of computed β and γ parameters is used to normalize the set of entries from which they were computed. Additionally, similarly to batch normalization, an offset/mean parameter β and a scale/standard deviation parameter γ are separately learned for each entry set.

This is similar to another popular technique known as *layer normalization*, which is effectively batch normalization but across the full length of the channel dimension rather than the full length of the batch dimension. Note that layer normalization is also just a special case of group normalization, where the number of groups of channels is set to one. Figure 7-16 compares batch normalization with group normalization and layer normalization. The blocked-off section in each cube demonstrates the dimension along which normalization occurs and the group of entries that are normalized together. Note that we condense the standard 4D representation into 3D for visualization purposes.

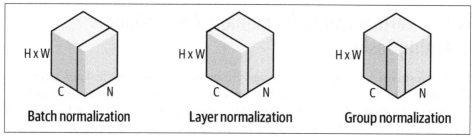

Figure 7-16. Comparison of batch normalization, layer normalization, and group normalization

---

12 Wu et. al. "Group Normalization." 2018. *https://arxiv.org/abs/1803.08494.*

You may be wondering why techniques like group normalization and layer normalization are even effective. After all, it seems as though batch normalization is only useful due to forcing each feature (or channels in our case) to have the same mean and variance. For some insight, the initial paper on layer normalization states that the reason for normalizing the features for each instance separately is that "changes in the output of one layer will tend to cause highly correlated changes in the summed input to the next layer." In summary, the neurons that make up every subsequent layer in the feed-forward network will see the same statistics from one training example to the next with layer normalization.

Furthermore, why group normalization over layer normalization? In Wu et al., the idea behind using group normalization is that it is less restrictive than layer normalization—a different distribution can be learned for each group of features, signifying the ability to learn potentially different levels of contribution and importance for different groups.

Now that we have sufficiently covered group normalization as a concept, its connection to prior work, and motivation for using group normalization in practice, we can now dive into some PyTorch code for implementing group normalization.

PyTorch provides a `torch.nn.GroupNorm` class to create group normalization layers:

```
layer = nn.GroupNorm(num_groups=1,
                     num_channels=32)
```

We need to specify only the number of groups and number of channels. Now that we've developed an enhanced toolkit for analyzing natural images with convolutional networks, we'll build a classifier for tackling the CIFAR-10 challenge.

Building a Convolutional Network for CIFAR-10

The CIFAR-10 challenge consists of 32×32 color images that belong to one of 10 possible classes.[13] This is a surprisingly hard challenge because it can be difficult for even a human to figure out what is in a picture. An example is shown in Figure 7-17.

---

13 Krizhevsky, Alex, and Geoffrey Hinton. "Learning Multiple Layers of Features from Tiny Images." University of Toronto (2009).

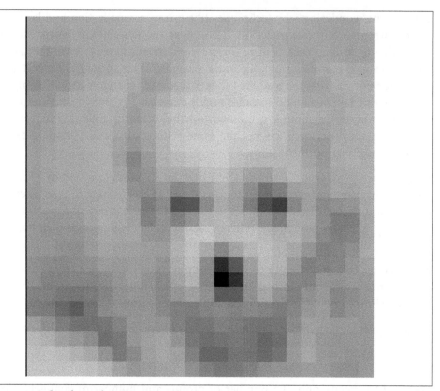

Figure 7-17. A dog from the CIFAR-10 dataset

In this section, we'll build networks both with and without batch normalization as a basis of comparison. We increase the learning rate by 10-fold for the batch normalization network to take full advantage of its benefits. We'll display code for only the batch normalization network here because building the vanilla convolutional network is similar.

We distort random 24 × 24 crops of the input images to feed into our network for training. We use the example code provided by Google to do this. We'll jump right into the network architecture. To start, let's take a look at how we integrate batch normalization into the convolutional and fully connected layers. As expected, batch normalization happens to the logits before they're fed into a nonlinearity:

```python
class Net(nn.Module):
    def __init__(self):
        super(Net, self).__init__()
        self.block1 = nn.Sequential(
            nn.Conv2d(1, 32, 3, 1),
            nn.BatchNorm2d(32),
            nn.ReLU(inplace=True),
            nn.Conv2d(32, 64, 3, 1),
            nn.BatchNorm2d(64),
            nn.ReLU(inplace=True),
            nn.MaxPool2d(2),
            nn.Dropout(0.25),
        )
        self.block2 = nn.Sequential(
            nn.Flatten(),
            nn.Linear(9216, 128),
            nn.BatchNorm1d(128),
            nn.ReLU(inplace=True),
            nn.Dropout(0.5),
            nn.Linear(128,10),
            nn.BatchNorm1d(10)
        )

    def forward(self, x):
        x = self.block1(x)
        return self.block2(x)
```

Finally, we use the Adam optimizer to train our convolutional networks. After some amount of time training, our networks are able to achieve an impressive 92.3% accuracy on the CIFAR-10 task without batch normalization and 96.7% accuracy with batch normalization. This result actually matches (and potentially exceeds) current state-of-the-art research on this task. In the next section, we'll take a closer look at learning and visualize how our networks perform.

Visualizing Learning in Convolutional Networks

On a high level, the simplest thing that we can do to visualize training is plot the cost function and validation errors over time as training progresses. We can clearly demonstrate the benefits of batch normalization by comparing the rates of convergence between our two networks. Plots taken in the middle of the training process are shown in Figure 7-18.

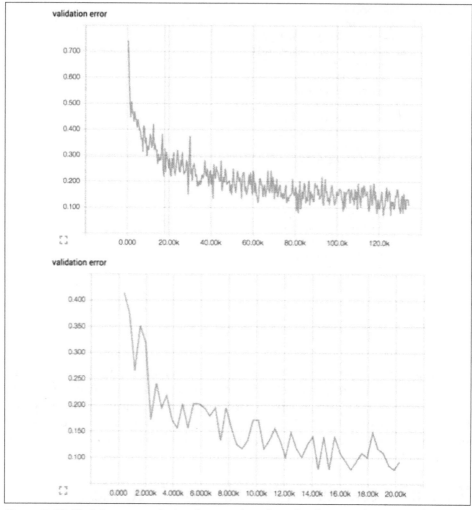

Figure 7-18. Training a convolutional network without batch normalization (left) versus with batch normalization (right)

Without batch normalization, cracking the 90% accuracy threshold requires over 80,000 minibatches. On the other hand, with batch normalization, crossing the same threshold requires only slightly over 14,000 minibatches.

We can also inspect the filters that our convolutional network learns in order to understand what the network finds important to its classification decisions. Convolutional layers learn hierarchical representations, so we'd hope that the first convolutional layer learns basic features (edges, simple curves, etc.), and the second convolutional layer will learn more complex features. Unfortunately, the second convolutional layer is difficult to interpret even if we decided to visualize it, so we only include the first layer filters in Figure 7-19.

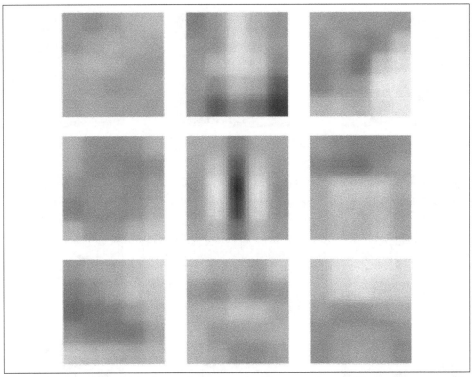

Figure 7-19. A subset of the learned filters in the first convolutional layer of our network

We can make out a number of interesting features in our filters: vertical, horizontal, and diagonal edges, in addition to small dots or splotches of one color surrounded by another. We can be confident that our network is learning relevant features because the filters are not just noise.

We can also try to visualize how our network has learned to cluster various kinds of images pictorially. To illustrate this, we take a large network that has been trained on the ImageNet challenge and then grab the hidden state of the fully connected layer just before the softmax for each image. We then take this high-dimensional representation for each image and use an algorithm known as *t-Distributed Stochastic Neighbor Embedding*, or *t-SNE*, to compress it to a 2D representation that we can visualize.[14] We don't cover the details of t-SNE here, but there are a number of publicly available software tools that will do it for us, including the script (*https://*

---

14 Maaten, Laurens van der, and Geoffrey Hinton. "Visualizing Data Using t-SNE." *Journal of Machine Learning Research* 9. Nov (2008): 2579-2605.

oreil.ly/7NA1K). We visualize the embeddings in Figure 7-20, and the results are quite spectacular.

Figure 7-20. The t-SNE embedding (center) surrounded by zoomed-in subsegments of the embedding (periphery)[15]

At first, on a high level, it seems that images that are similarly colored are closer together. This is interesting, but what's even more striking is when we zoom into parts of the visualization, we realize that it's more than just color. We realize that all pictures of boats are in one place, all pictures of humans are in another place, and all pictures of butterflies are in yet another location in the visualization. Quite clearly, convolutional networks have spectacular learning capabilities.

---

15 Image credit: Andrej Karpathy. *http://cs.stanford.edu/people/karpathy/cnnembed.*

Residual Learning and Skip Connections for Very Deep Networks

We have made great progress in the field of computer vision over the past decade, and in this section we introduce one of the more recent advancements. Earlier, we discussed AlexNet, which was a breakthrough in neural methods applied to image classification. Since then, researchers have pushed toward deeper and deeper architectures in the hope of solving image classification. However, since AlexNet's breakthrough, at least a few reputable studies tended to see *decreases* in training accuracy when naively stacking layers as compared to their shallower counterparts.

It's particularly interesting that the problem isn't even overfitting (as is suggested by a low training accuracy and a high validation accuracy), which would be understandable for a network with such a large number of parameters. Additionally, we can easily construct a deep network by ourselves that has the exact same performance as its shallow counterpart: take the trained shallow network layers and simply stack layers that perform the identity operation. The fact that we do worse via a specialized optimization algorithm compared to our naive construction is quite astounding. The problem is that training stalls for some inexplicable reason, settling in a local minimum that we can't get out of. Unfortunately, the theoretical justification for this is still a bit hazy.

In 2015, He et al.[16] introduced the ResNet34 architecture, a deep architecture that surpassed all of its peers in major image classification competitions. With a version that consisted of over 30 trainable layers, He et al. redefined how we train deep computer vision architectures. In particular, their contribution was the introduction of what we now call *skip connections*, which add the feature vector obtained from a layer to the feature vector obtained one or two layers after the current layer. More precisely, let's say we are midway through the network so far and our original input x has been converted to some intermediate representation x'. The skip connection would take x' and add it to the result of the next layer, $F(x')$, before passing the representation on to the following layer G. So instead of seeing $F(x')$, G sees $F(x') + x'$. Note that the skip connection does not need to add the current representation to the result of F. As represented in Figure 7-21, we could also add x' to the result of G, so the next layer H sees $G(F(x')) + x'$ instead of just $G(F(x'))$.

---

16 He et. al. "Deep Residual Learning for Image Recognition." *arXiv Preprint arXiv*:1512.03385. 2015.

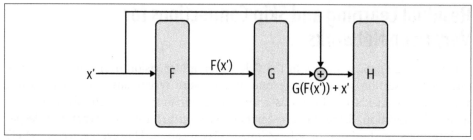

Figure 7-21. The skip connection here skips F and G, summing the input to F with the output of G, which comprises the input to H

These skip connections are just the identity operation, so they add no additional parameters to train. Additionally, since the skip connection is the identity operation, it must be the case that x' and $G(F(x'))$, in the example where the skip connection skips two layers, must be the same dimension. If this were not the case, we would not be able to add the two feature vectors. This does place a constraint on the network architecture, but we hope to construct a deep network anyway, and this approach lends itself well to such networks since we wouldn't want the dimensionality to decrease too rapidly (recall the discussion on padding).

It's natural to ask why skip connections work so well. After all, it does seem like a pretty simple modification to the plain deep network architecture. Let's think back to the original motivation: through experimentation, researchers had noticed a degradation in performance as networks got deeper and deeper. However, it must be the case that deeper networks are able to perform at least as well as their shallower counterparts, since we can construct a naive solution where the additional layers are the identity mapping. It's also important to note that the representations learned by shallower counterparts such as AlexNet are quite good, as they achieved state-of-the-art performance just a couple of years prior. If we make the assumption that representations at downstream layers in deep networks are only going to be slightly different from one layer to the next, which is reasonable due to the fact that shallower networks still can learn very good representations, it would instead make sense to optimize the difference between representations (which should be close to zero for all weights) rather than attempt to achieve something close to the identity operation, which is a very specific and imbalanced weight setting.

That's where residual connections come in. The downstream layers of the neural network, such as F and G, are learning precisely this difference between representations and then adding the difference back to the incoming representation x' to achieve an only slightly different representation $G(F(x')) + x'$. This is in contrast with the traditional feed-forward neural network paradigm, which would attempt to learn a weight setting that is approximately close to identity for *F* and *G*, which seems like a much harder problem. In the next section, we will put our knowledge together to build a residual network.

Building a Residual Network with Superhuman Vision

In the previous section, we discussed residual connections and how they allow for improved gradient flow through deep neural networks. In this section, we will replicate the implementation of a neural network with residual connections, specifically the ResNet34 architecture from He et al.'s original.

PyTorch's Torchvision library provides constructors for many commonly used resnets. We can use it to create a ResNet34 model:

```
from torchvision.models import resnet34

model = resnet34()
```

Let's see how `resnet34` creates a residual network.

Most versions of residual networks consist of the following structure:

- Convolutional block (CONV->BN->ReLU->MAXPOOL)
- Four residual layers
- A classifier block with average pooling and a linear layer

Each residual layer consists of one or more residual blocks. For example, the layers *F* and *G* from Figure 7-21 form a residual block. Here is the PyTorch code for a simplified implementation of a residual block for ResNet34:

```
class ResidualBlock(nn.Module):
    def __init__(self, in_layers, out_layers, downsample=None):
        super(ResidualBlock, self).__init__()
        self.conv1 = nn.Conv2d(in_layers, out_layers,
                               kernel_size=3, stride=1, padding=1)
        self.bn1 = nn.BatchNorm2d(out_layers)
        self.conv2 = nn.Conv2d(out_layers, out_layers,
                               kernel_size=3, stride=1, padding=1)
        self.bn2 = nn.BatchNorm2d(out_layers)
        self.downsample = downsample
        self.relu = nn.ReLU(inplace=True)

    def forward(self, inp):
        # Residual block
        out = self.conv1(inp)
        out = self.bn1(out)
        out = self.relu(out)
        out = self.conv2(out)
        out = self.bn2(out)
```

```
if self.downsample:
    inp = self.downsample(inp)

# Shortcut connection
out += inp
return out
```

Similarly to the previous section, each residual block in the ResNet34 architecture consists of two convolutional layers. The downsample argument allows for an optional downsampler function. The purpose of downsampling is to match the dimensions of the input with the output of the residual block, if the two are of different dimensions.

The following is an example of a downsampler that matches the number of channels of the input to that of the output of the residual block. Note that this downsampler does not change the size of each feature map given the kernel_size is 1 and the stride is also only 1, and affects the dimensions only by increasing the number of feature maps from 64 to 128:

```
downsample = nn.Sequential(
    nn.Conv2d(64, 128, kernel_size=1, stride=1, bias=False),
    nn.BatchNorm2d(128)
)
```

The number of residual blocks for each of the four residual layers in ResNet34 is defined as [3, 4, 6, 3], respectively. The ResNet34 architecture is named this way because it has 33 convolutional layers and 1 fully connected layer at the end, which serves as the predictor portion of the network. The 33 convolutional layers are arranged in four sections that have 3, 4, 6, and 3 residual blocks, in that order. To get to the total of 33, there is a single convolutional layer at the beginning that operates on the original image input, which is assumed to have 3 channels.

The following PyTorch code initializes each of these components, closely modeled after the official PyTorch implementation of the various versions presented in the original paper. The first component, up to the max pool, operates on the original input, and each of the following components requires downsampling only between components. This is because, within each component, the input and output of each ResidualBlock are of the same dimension. Although we won't show it explicitly in this section, the combination of a kernel_size of 3, stride of 1, and padding of 1 ensures that the size of each feature map stays constant from beginning to end. Additionally, given the number of feature maps stays constant within each component, all dimensions end up remaining the same:

```
class ResNet34(nn.Module):
    def __init__(self):
        super(ResNet34, self).__init__()

        self.conv1 = nn.Sequential(
```

```
        nn.Conv2d(3, 64, kernel_size=7,
                    stride=2, padding=3, bias=False),
        nn.BatchNorm2d(64),
        nn.ReLU(),
        nn.MaxPool2d(kernel_size=3,
                        stride=2, padding=1)
)

# Note that each ResidualBlock has 2 conv layers
# 3 blocks in a row, 6 conv layers
self.comp1 = nn.Sequential(
    ResidualBlock(64, 64),
    ResidualBlock(64, 64),
    ResidualBlock(64, 64)
)

# 4 blocks in a row, 8 conv layers
downsample1 = nn.Sequential(
    nn.Conv2d(64, 128, kernel_size=1,
            stride=1, bias=False),
    nn.BatchNorm2d(128)
)
self.comp2 = nn.Sequential(
    ResidualBlock(64, 128, downsample=downsample1),
    ResidualBlock(128, 128),
    ResidualBlock(128, 128),
    ResidualBlock(128, 128)
)

# 6 blocks in a row, 12 conv layers
downsample2 = nn.Sequential(
    nn.Conv2d(128, 256, kernel_size=1, stride=1, bias=False),
    nn.BatchNorm2d(256)
)
self.comp3 = nn.Sequential(
    ResidualBlock(128, 256, downsample=downsample2),
    ResidualBlock(256, 256),
    ResidualBlock(256, 256),
    ResidualBlock(256, 256),
    ResidualBlock(256, 256),
    ResidualBlock(256, 256),
)

# 3 blocks in a row, 6 conv layers
downsample3 = nn.Sequential(
    nn.Conv2d(256, 512, kernel_size=1, stride=1, bias=False),
    nn.BatchNorm2d(512)
)
self.comp4 = nn.Sequential(
    ResidualBlock(256, 512, downsample=downsample3),
    ResidualBlock(512, 512),
    ResidualBlock(512, 512)
```

```
    )
    self.avgpool = nn.AdaptiveAvgPool2d((1, 1))
    # ImageNet classifier: 1000 classes
    self.fc = nn.Linear(512, 1000)

def forward(self, inp):
    out = self.conv1(inp)

    out = self.comp1(out)
    out = self.comp2(out)
    out = self.comp3(out)
    out = self.comp4(out)

    out = self.avgpool(out)
    out = torch.flatten(out, 1)
    out = self.fc(out)

    return out
```

In the next section, we will present some of the latest advancements in computer vision regarding neural style transfer.

Leveraging Convolutional Filters to Replicate Artistic Styles

Over the past couple of years, we've also developed algorithms that leverage convolutional networks in much more creative ways. One of these algorithms is called *neural style*.[17] The goal of neural style is to be able to take an arbitrary photograph and render it as if it were painted in the style of a famous artist. This seems like a daunting task, and it's not exactly clear how we might approach this problem if we didn't have a convolutional network. However, it turns out that clever manipulation of convolutional filters can produce spectacular results on this problem.

Let's take a pretrained convolutional network. We're dealing with three images. The first two are the source of content p and the source of style a. The third image is the generated image x. Our goal is to derive an error function that we can backpropagate that, when minimized, will perfectly combine the content of the desired photograph and the style of the desired artwork.

We start with content first. If a layer in the network has k_l filters, then it produces a total of k_l feature maps. Let's call the size of each feature map m_l, the height times the width of the feature map. This means that the activations in all the feature maps of this layer can be stored in a matrix $F^{(l)}$ of size $k_l \times m_l$. We can also represent all the

---

17 Gatys, Leon A., Alexander S. Ecker, and Matthias Bethge. "A Neural Algorithm of Artistic Style." *arXiv Preprint arXiv*:1508.06576 (2015).

---

activations of the photograph in a matrix $\boldsymbol{P}^{(l)}$ and all the activations of the generated image in the matrix $\boldsymbol{X}^{(l)}$. We use the `relu4_2` of the original VGGNet:

$$E_{\text{content}}(\boldsymbol{p}, \boldsymbol{x}) = \Sigma_{ij}(\boldsymbol{P}_{ij}^{(l)} - \boldsymbol{X}_{ij}^{(l)})^2$$

Now we can try tackling style. To do this we construct a matrix known as the *Gram matrix*, which represents correlations between feature maps in a given layer. The correlations represent the texture and feel that is common among all features, irrespective of which features we're looking at. Constructing the Gram matrix, which is of size $k_l \times k_l$, for a given image, is done as follows:

$$\mathbf{G}^{(l)}{}_{ij} = \Sigma_{c=0}{}^{m_l} \mathbf{F}^{(l)}{}_{ic} \mathbf{F}^{(l)}{}_{jc}$$

We can compute the Gram matrices for both the artwork in matrix $\boldsymbol{A}^{(l)}$ and the generated image in $\mathbf{G}^{(l)}$. We can then represent the error function as:

$$E_{style}(\mathbf{a}, \mathbf{x}) = \frac{1}{4k_l^2 m_l^2} \Sigma_{l=1}^{L} \Sigma_{ij} \frac{1}{L}\left(A_{ij}^{(l)} - G_{ij}^{(l)}\right)^2$$

Here, we weight each squared difference equally (dividing by the number of layers we want to include in our style reconstruction). Specifically, we use the `relu1_1`, `relu2_1`, `relu3_1`, `relu4_1`, and `relu5_1` layers of the original VGGNet. We omit a full discussion of the TensorFlow code for brevity, but the results, as shown in Figure 7-22, are again quite spectacular. We mix a photograph of the iconic MIT dome and Leonid Afremov's *Rain Princess*.

Figure 7-22. The result of mixing the Rain Princess with a photograph of the MIT dome[18]

Learning Convolutional Filters for Other Problem Domains

Although our examples in this chapter focus on image recognition, there are several other problem domains in which convolutional networks are useful. A natural extension of image analysis is video analysis. In fact, using five-dimensional tensors (including time as a dimension) and applying three-dimensional convolutions is an easy way to extend the convolutional paradigm to video.[19] Convolutional filters have also been successfully used to analyze audiograms.[20] In these applications, a convolutional network slides over an audiogram input to predict phonemes on the other side.

Less intuitively, convolutional networks have also found some use in natural language processing. We'll see some examples of this in later chapters. More exotic uses of convolutional networks include teaching algorithms to play board games, and analyzing biological molecules for drug discovery. We'll also discuss both of these examples in later chapters of this book.

---

18 Image credit: Anish Athalye.

19 Karpathy, Andrej, et al. "Large-scale Video Classification with Convolutional Neural Networks." *Proceedings of the IEEE Conference on Computer Vision and Pattern Recognition.* 2014.

20 Abdel-Hamid, Ossama, et al. "Applying Convolutional Neural Networks Concepts to Hybrid NN-HMM Model for Speech Recognition." IEEE International Conference on Acoustics, Speech, and Signal Processing (ICASSP), Kyoto, 2012, pp. 4277-4280.

Summary

In this chapter, we learned how to build neural networks that analyze images. We developed the concept of a convolution, and leveraged this idea to create tractable networks that can analyze both simple and more complex natural images. We built several of these convolutional networks in TensorFlow and leveraged various image processing pipelines and batch normalization to make training our networks faster and more robust. Finally, we visualized the learning of convolutional networks and explored other interesting applications of the technology.

Images were easy to analyze because we were able to come up with effective ways to represent them as tensors. In other situations (e.g., natural language), it's less clear how one might represent our input data as tensors. To tackle this problem as a stepping stone to new deep learning models, we'll develop some key concepts in vector embeddings and representation learning in the next chapter.

## CHAPTER 8

Embedding and Representation Learning

Learning Lower-Dimensional Representations

In the previous chapter, we motivated the convolutional architecture using a simple argument. The larger our input vector, the larger our model. Large models with lots of parameters are expressive, but they're also increasingly data hungry. This means that without sufficiently large volumes of training data, we will likely overfit. Convolutional architectures help us cope with the curse of dimensionality by reducing the number of parameters in our models without necessarily diminishing expressiveness.

Regardless, convolutional networks still require large amounts of labeled training data. And for many problems, labeled data is scarce and expensive to generate. Our goal in this chapter will be to develop effective learning models in situations where labeled data is scarce, but wild, unlabeled data is plentiful. We'll approach this problem by learning *embeddings*, or low-dimensional representations, in an unsupervised fashion. Because these unsupervised models allow us to offload all of the heavy lifting of automated feature selection, we can use the generated embeddings to solve learning problems using smaller models that require less data. This process is summarized in Figure 8-1.

In the process of developing algorithms that learn good embeddings, we'll also explore other applications of learning lower-dimensional representations, such as visualization and semantic hashing. We'll start by considering situations where all of the important information is already contained within the original input vector itself. In this case, learning embeddings is equivalent to developing an effective compression algorithm.

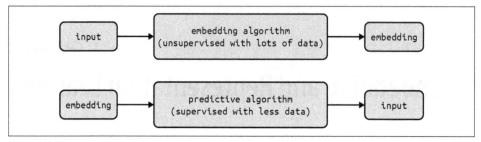

Figure 8-1. Using embeddings to automate feature selection in the face of scarce labeled data

In the next section, we'll introduce *principal component analysis* (PCA), a classic method for dimensionality reduction. In subsequent sections, we'll explore more powerful neural methods for learning compressive embeddings.

Principal Component Analysis

The basic concept behind PCA is to find a set of axes that communicates the most information about our dataset. More specifically, if we have d-dimensional data, we'd like to find a new set of $m < d$ dimensions that conserves as much valuable information from the original dataset as possible. For simplicity, let's choose $d = 2, m = 1$. Assuming that variance corresponds to information, we can perform this transformation through an iterative process. First, we find a unit vector along which the dataset has maximum variance. Because this direction contains the most information, we select this direction as our first axis. Then from the set of vectors orthogonal to this first choice, we pick a new unit vector along which the dataset has maximum variance. This is our second axis.

We continue this process until we have found a total of d new vectors that represent new axes. We project our data onto this new set of axes. We then decide a good value for m and toss out all but the first m axes (the principal components, which store the most information). The result is shown in Figure 8-2.

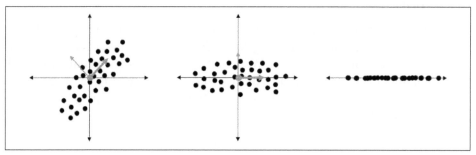

Figure 8-2. An illustration of PCA for dimensionality reduction to capture the dimension with the most information (as proxied by variance)

For the mathematically inclined, we can view this operation as a projection onto the vector space spanned by the top m eigenvectors of the dataset's correlation matrix, which is equivalent to the dataset's covariance matrix when the dataset has been z-score normalized (zero-mean and unit-variance per input dimension). Let us represent the dataset as a matrix $\mathbf{X}$ with dimensions $n \times d$ (i.e., n inputs of d dimensions). We'd like to create an embedding matrix $\mathbf{T}$ with dimensions $n \times m$. We can compute the matrix using the relationship $\mathbf{T} = \mathbf{X}$, where each column of $\mathbf{W}$ corresponds to an eigenvector of the matrix $\frac{1}{n}\mathbf{X}^{\mathsf{T}}\mathbf{X}$. Those with linear algebra background or core data science experience may be seeing a striking parallel between PCA and the singular value decomposition (SVD), which we cover in more depth in "Theory: PCA and SVD" on page 187.

While PCA has been used for decades for dimensionality reduction, it spectacularly fails to capture important relationships that are piecewise linear or nonlinear. Take, for instance, the example illustrated in Figure 8-3.

The example shows data points selected at random from two concentric circles. We hope that PCA will transform this dataset so that we can pick a single new axis that allows us to easily separate the dots. Unfortunately for us, there is no linear direction that contains more information here than another (we have equal variance in all directions). Instead, as human beings, we notice that information is being encoded in a nonlinear way, in terms of how far points are from the origin. With this information in mind, we notice that the polar transformation (expressing points as their distance from the origin, as the new horizontal axis, and their angle bearing from the original x-axis, as the new vertical axis) does just the trick.

Figure 8-3 highlights the shortcomings of an approach like PCA in capturing important relationships in complex datasets. Because most of the datasets we are likely to encounter in the wild (images, text, etc.) are characterized by nonlinear relationships, we must develop a theory that will perform nonlinear dimensionality reduction. Deep learning practitioners have closed this gap using neural models, which we'll cover in the next section.

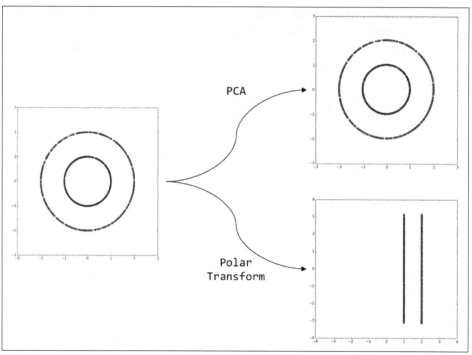

Figure 8-3. A situation in which PCA fails to optimally transform the data for dimensionality reduction

Motivating the Autoencoder Architecture

When we talked about feed-forward networks, we discussed how each layer learned progressively more relevant representations of the input. In fact, in Chapter 7, we took the output of the final convolutional layer and used that as a lower-dimensional representation of the input image. Putting aside the fact that we want to generate these low-dimensional representations in an unsupervised fashion, there are fundamental problems with these approaches in general. Specifically, while the selected layer does contain information from the input, the network has been trained to pay attention to the aspects of the input that are critical to solving the task at hand. As a result, there's a significant amount of information loss with respect to elements of the input that may be important for other classification tasks, but potentially less important than the one immediately at hand.

However, the fundamental intuition here still applies. We define a new network architecture that we call the *autoencoder*. We first take the input and compress it into a low-dimensional vector. This part of the network is called the *encoder* because it is responsible for producing the low-dimensional embedding or *code*. The second part of the network, instead of mapping the embedding to an arbitrary label as we would in a feed-forward network, tries to invert the computation of the first half of the network and reconstruct the original input. This piece is known as the *decoder*. The overall architecture is illustrated in Figure 8-4.

Figure 8-4. The autoencoder architecture attempts to construct a high-dimensional input into a low-dimensional embedding and then uses that low-dimensional embedding to reconstruct the input

To demonstrate the surprising effectiveness of autoencoders, we'll build and visualize the autoencoder architecture in Figure 8-4. Specifically, we will highlight its superior ability to separate MNIST digits as compared to PCA.

Implementing an Autoencoder in PyTorch

The seminal paper "Reducing the Dimensionality of Data with Neural Networks," which describes the autoencoder, was written by Hinton and Salakhutdinov in 2006.[1] Their hypothesis was that the nonlinear complexities afforded by a neural model would allow them to capture structure that linear methods, such as PCA, would miss. To demonstrate this point, they ran an experiment on MNIST using both an autoencoder and PCA to reduce the dataset into 2D data points. In this section, we will recreate their experimental setup to validate this hypothesis and further explore the architecture and properties of feed-forward autoencoders.

The setup shown in Figure 8-5 is built with the same principle, but the 2D embedding is now treated as the input, and the network attempts to reconstruct the original image. Because we are essentially applying an inverse operation, we architect the decoder network so that the autoencoder has the shape of an hourglass. The output of the decoder network is a 784-dimensional vector that can be reconstructed into a 28 × 28 image:

```
class Decoder(nn.Module):
    def __init__(self, n_in, n_hidden_1, n_hidden_2, n_hidden_3, n_out):
        super(Decoder, self).__init__()
        self.layer1 = nn.Sequential(
            nn.Linear(n_in, n_hidden_1, bias=True),
            nn.BatchNorm1d(n_hidden_1),
            nn.Sigmoid())
        self.layer2 = nn.Sequential(
```

---

1 Hinton, Geoffrey E., and Ruslan R. Salakhutdinov. "Reducing the Dimensionality of Data with Neural Networks." *Science* 313.5786 (2006): 504-507.

```
        nn.Linear(n_hidden_1, n_hidden_2, bias=True),
        nn.BatchNorm1d(n_hidden_2),
        nn.Sigmoid())
    self.layer3 = nn.Sequential(
        nn.Linear(n_hidden_2, n_hidden_3, bias=True),
        nn.BatchNorm1d(n_hidden_3),
        nn.Sigmoid())
    n_size = math.floor(math.sqrt(n_out))
    self.layer4 = nn.Sequential(
        nn.Linear(n_hidden_3, n_out, bias=True),
        nn.BatchNorm1d(n_out),
        nn.Sigmoid(),
        nn.Unflatten(1, torch.Size([1, n_size,n_size])))

def forward(self, x):
    x = self.layer1(x)
    x = self.layer2(x)
    x = self.layer3(x)
    return self.layer4(x)
```

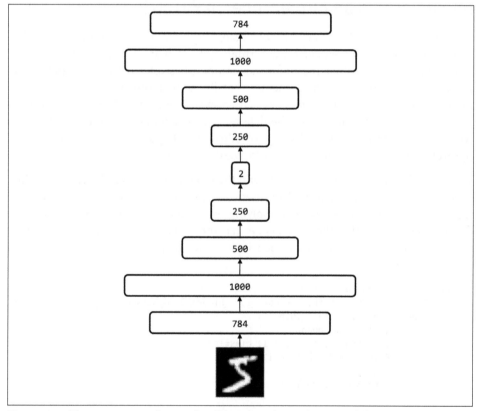

Figure 8-5. The experimental setup for dimensionality reduction of the MNIST dataset employed by Hinton and Salakhutdinov, 2006

In order to accelerate training, we'll reuse the batch normalization strategy we employed in Chapter 7. Also, because we'd like to visualize the results, we'll avoid introducing sharp transitions in our neurons. In this example, we'll use sigmoidal neurons instead of our usual ReLU neurons:

```
decoder = Decoder(2,250,500,1000,784)
```

Finally, we need to construct a measure (or objective function) that describes how well our model functions. Specifically, we want to measure how close the reconstruction is to the original image. We can measure this simply by computing the distance between the original 784-dimensional input and the reconstructed 784-dimensional output. More specifically, given an input vector I and a reconstruction O, we'd like to minimize the value of $\| I - O \| = \sqrt{\Sigma_i (I_i - O_i)^2}$, also known as the L2 norm of the difference between the two vectors. We average this function over the whole minibatch to generate our final objective function. Finally, we'll train the network using the Adam optimizer, logging a scalar summary of the error incurred at every minibatch using `torch.utils.tensorboard.SummaryWriter`. In PyTorch, we can concisely express the loss and training operations as follows:

```
loss_fn = nn.MSELoss()
optimizer = optim.Adam(decoder.parameters(),
                       lr = 0.001,
                       betas=(0.9,0.999),
                       eps=1e-08)

trainset = datasets.MNIST('.',
                          train=True,
                          transform=transforms.ToTensor(),
                          download=True)
trainloader = DataLoader(trainset,
                         batch_size=32,
                         shuffle=True)
# Training Loop
NUM_EPOCHS = 5
for epoch in range(NUM_EPOCHS):
  for input, labels in trainloader:
    optimizer.zero_grad()
    code = encoder(input)
    output = decoder(code)
    #print(input.shape, output.shape)
    loss = loss_fn(output, input)
    optimizer.step()
  print(f"Epoch: {epoch} Loss: {loss}")
```

Finally, we'll need a method to evaluate the generalizability of our model. As usual, we'll use a validation dataset and compute the same L2 norm measurement for model evaluation. In addition, we'll collect image summaries so that we can compare both the input images and the reconstructions:

```
i = 0
with torch.no_grad():
  for images, labels in trainloader:
    if i == 3:
      break
    grid = utils.make_grid(images)
    plt.figure()
    plt.imshow(grid.permute(1,2,0))

    code = encoder(images)
    output = decoder(code)

    grid = utils.make_grid(output)
    plt.figure()
    plt.imshow(grid.permute(1,2,0))
    i += 1
```

We can visualize the model graph, the training and validation costs, and the image summaries using TensorBoard. Simply run the following command:

```
$ tensorboard --logdir ~/path/to/mnist_autoencoder_hidden=2_logs
```

Then navigate your browser to *http://localhost:6006/*. The results of the "Graph" tab are shown in Figure 8-6.

Thanks to how we've namespaced the components of our model graph, our model is nicely organized. We can easily click through the components and delve deeper, tracing how data flows up through the various layers of the encoder and through the decoder, how the optimizer reads the output of our training module, and how gradients in turn affect all of the components of the model.

We also visualize both the training (after each minibatch) and validation costs (after each epoch), closely monitoring the curves for potential overfitting. The TensorBoard visualizations of the costs over the span of training are shown in Figure 8-7. As we would expect for a successful model, both the training and validation curves decrease until they flatten off asymptotically. After approximately 200 epochs, we attain a validation cost of 4.78. While the curves look promising, it's difficult, upon first glance, to understand whether we've reached a plateau at a "good" cost, or whether our model is still doing a poor job of reconstructing the original inputs.

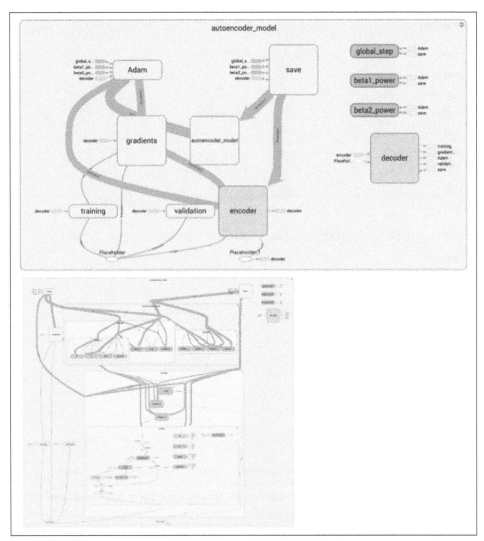

Figure 8-6. TensorBoard allows us to neatly view the high-level components and data flow of our computation graph (top) and also click through to more closely inspect the data flows of individual subcomponents (bottom)

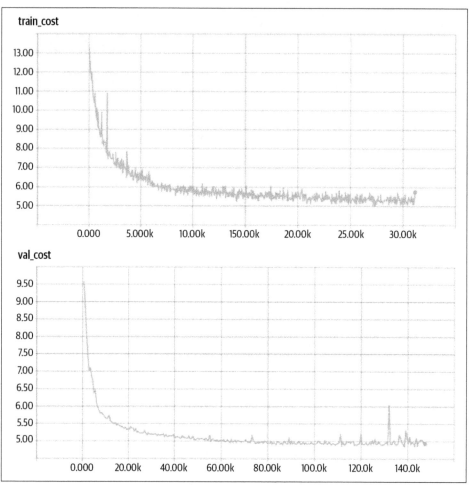

Figure 8-7. The cost incurred on the training set (logged after each minibatch) and on the validation set (logged after each epoch)

To get a sense of what that means, let's explore the MNIST dataset. We pick an arbitrary image of a 1 from the dataset and call it *X*. In Figure 8-8, we compare the image to all other images in the dataset. Specifically, for each digit class, we compute the average of the L2 costs, comparing *X* to each instance of the digit class. As a visual aid, we also include the average of all of the instances for each digit class.

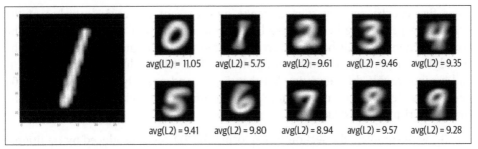

Figure 8-8. The image of the 1 on the left is compared to all of the other digits in the MNIST dataset; each digit class is represented visually with the average of all of its members and labeled with the average of the L2 costs, comparing the 1 on the left with all of the class members

On average, X is 5.75 units away from other 1s in MNIST. In terms of L2 distance, the non-1 digits closest to the X are the 7s (8.94 units) and the digits farthest are the 0s (11.05 units). Given these measurements, it's quite apparent that with an average cost of 4.78, our autoencoder is producing high-quality reconstructions.

Because we are collecting image summaries, we can confirm this hypothesis directly by inspecting the input images and reconstructions directly. The reconstructions for three randomly chosen samples from the test set are shown in Figure 8-9.

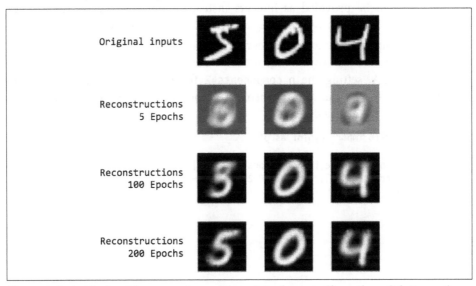

Figure 8-9. A side-by-side comparison of the original inputs (from the validation set) and reconstructions after 5, 100, and 200 epochs of training

After five epochs, we can start to make out some of the critical strokes of the original image that are being picked by the autoencoder, but for the most part, the reconstructions are still hazy mixtures of closely related digits. By 100 epochs, the 0 and 4 are reconstructed with strong strokes, but it looks like the autoencoder is still having trouble differentiating between 5s, 3s, and possibly 8s. However, by 200 epochs, it's clear that even this more difficult ambiguity is clarified, and all of the digits are crisply reconstructed.

Finally, we'll complete the section by exploring the 2D codes produced by traditional PCA and autoencoders. We'll want to show that autoencoders produce better visualizations. In particular, we'll want to show that autoencoders do a much better job of visually separating instances of different digit classes than PCA. We'll start by quickly covering the code we use to produce 2D PCA codes:

```
from sklearn import decomposition
import input_data


mnist = input_data.read_data_sets("data/", one_hot=False)
pca = decomposition.PCA(n_components=2)
pca.fit(mnist.train.images)
pca_codes = pca.transform(mnist.test.images)
```

We first pull up the MNIST dataset. We've set the flag one_hot=False because we'd like the labels to be provided as integers instead of one-hot vectors (as a quick reminder, a one-hot vector representing an MNIST label would be a vector of size 10 with the ith component set to one to represent digit i and the rest of the components set to zero). We use the commonly used machine learning library *scikit-learn* to perform the PCA, setting the n_components=2 flat so that scikit-learn knows to generate 2D codes. We can also reconstruct the original images from the 2D codes and visualize the reconstructions:

```
from matplotlib import pyplot as plt

pca_recon = pca.inverse_transform(pca_codes[:1])
plt.imshow(pca_recon[0].reshape((28,28)), cmap=plt.cm.gray)
plt.show()
```

The code snippet shows how to visualize the first image in the test dataset, but we can easily modify the code to visualize any arbitrary subset of the dataset. Comparing the PCA reconstructions to the autoencoder reconstructions in Figure 8-10, it's quite clear that the autoencoder vastly outperforms PCA with 2D codes. In fact, the PCA's performance is somewhat reminiscent of the autoencoder only five epochs into training. It has trouble distinguishing 5s from 3s and 8s, 0s from 8s, and 4s from 9s. Repeating the same experiment with 30-dimensional codes provides significant improvement to the PCA reconstructions, but they are still significantly worse than the 30-dimensional autoencoder.

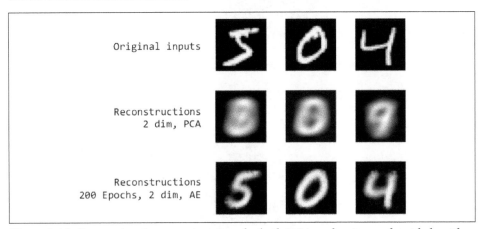

Figure 8-10. Comparing the reconstructions by both PCA and autoencoder side by side

Now, to complete the experiment, we must load up a saved PyTorch model, retrieve the 2D codes, and plot both the PCA and autoencoder codes. We're careful to rebuild the PyTorch graph exactly how we set it up during training. We pass the path to the model checkpoint we saved during training as a command-line argument to the script. Finally, we use a custom plotting function to generate a legend and appropriately color data points of different digit classes.

In the resulting visualization in Figure 8-11, it is extremely difficult to make out separable clusters in the 2D PCA codes; the autoencoder has clearly done a spectacular job at clustering codes of different digit classes. This means that a simple machine learning model is going to be able to much more effectively classify data points consisting of autoencoder embeddings as compared to PCA embeddings.

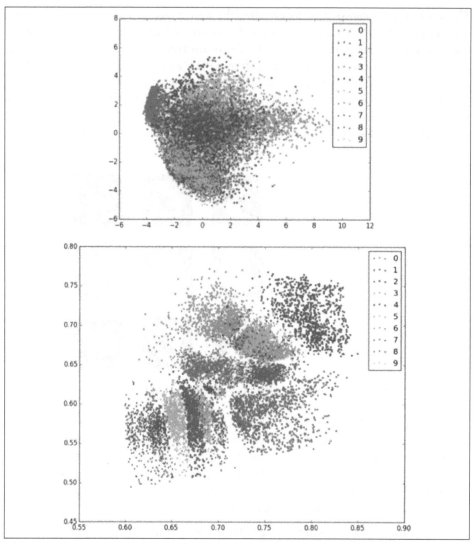

Figure 8-11. 2D embeddings produced by PCA (top) and by an autoencoder (bottom)

In this section, we successfully set up and trained a feed-forward autoencoder and demonstrated that the resulting embeddings were superior to PCA, a classical dimensionality reduction method. In the next section, we'll explore a concept known as denoising, which acts as a form of regularization by making our embeddings more robust.

Denoising to Force Robust Representations

Denoising improves the ability of the autoencoder to generate embeddings that are resistant to noise. The human ability for perception is surprisingly resistant to noise. Take Figure 8-12, for example. Despite the fact that I've corrupted half of the pixels in each image, you still have no problem making out the digit. In fact, even easily confused digits (like the 2 and the 7) are still distinguishable.

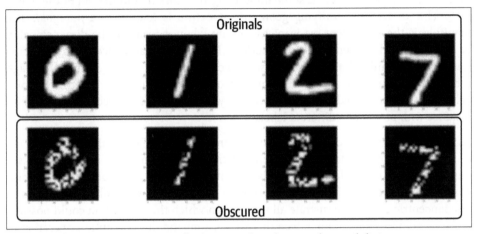

Figure 8-12. Human perception allows us to identify even obscured digits

One way to look at this phenomenon is probabilistically. Even if we're exposed to a random sampling of pixels from an image, if we have enough information, our brain is still capable of concluding the ground truth of what the pixels represent with maximal probability. Our mind is able to, quite literally, fill in the blanks to draw a conclusion. Even though only a corrupted version of a digit hits our retina, our brain is still able to reproduce the set of activations (i.e., the code or embedding) that we normally would use to represent the image of that digit. This is a property we might hope to enforce in our embedding algorithm, and it was first explored by Vincent et al. in 2008, when they introduced the *denoising autoencoder*.[2]

The basic principles behind denoising are quite simple. We corrupt some fixed percentage of the pixels in the input image by setting them to zero. Given an original input X, let's call the corrupted version $C(X)$. The denoising autoencoder is identical to the vanilla autoencoder except for one detail: the input to the encoder network is the corrupted $C(X)$ instead of X. In other words, the autoencoder is forced to learn a code for each input that is resistant to the corruption mechanism and is able

---

2 Vincent, Pascal, et al. "Extracting and Composing Robust Features with Denoising Autoencoders." *Proceedings of the 25th International Conference on Machine Learning.* ACM, 2008.

to interpolate through the missing information to recreate the original, uncorrupted image.

We can also think about this process more geometrically. Let's say we had a 2D dataset with various labels. Let's take all of the data points in a particular category (i.e., with some fixed label), and call this subset of data points S. While any arbitrary sampling of points could end up taking any form while visualized, we presume that for real-life categories, there is some underlying structure that unifies all of the points in S. This underlying, unifying geometric structure is known as a *manifold*. The manifold is the shape that we want to capture when we reduce the dimensionality of our data; and as Bengio et al. described in 2013, our autoencoder is implicitly learning this manifold as it learns how to reconstruct data after pushing it through a bottleneck (the code layer).[3] The autoencoder must figure out whether a point belongs to one manifold or another when trying to generate a reconstruction of an instance with potentially different labels.

As an illustration, let's consider the scenario in Figure 8-13, where the points in S are a simple low-dimensional manifold (a solid circle in the diagram). In part A, we see our data points in S (black xs) and the manifold that best describes them. We also observe an approximation of our corruption operation. Specifically, the arrow and nonconcentric circle demonstrate all the ways in which the corruption could possibly move or modify a data point. Given that we are applying this corruption operation to every data point (i.e., along the entire manifold), this corruption operation artificially expands the dataset to not only include the manifold but also all of the points in space around the manifold, up to a maximum margin of error. This margin is demonstrated by the dashed circles in A, and the dataset expansion is illustrated by the x's in part B. Finally the autoencoder is forced to learn to collapse all of the data points in this space back to the manifold. In other words, by learning which aspects of a data point are generalizable, broad strokes, and which aspects are "noise," the denoising autoencoder learns to approximate the underlying manifold of S.

---

3 Bengio, Yoshua, et al. "Generalized Denoising Auto-Encoders as Generative Models." *Advances in Neural Information Processing Systems*. 2013.

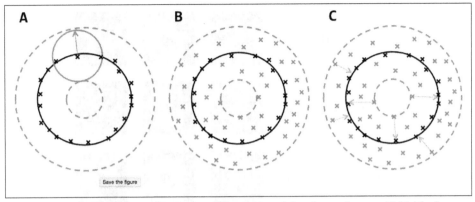

Figure 8-13. The denoising objective enables our model to learn the manifold (dark circle) by learning to map corrupted data (light x's in B and C) to uncorrupted data (dark x's) by minimizing the error (arrows in C) between their representations

With the philosophical motivations of denoising in mind, we can now make a small modification to our autoencoder script to build a denoising autoencoder:

```
def corrupt_input(x):
    corrupting_matrix = 2.0*torch.rand_like(x)

    return x * corrupting_matrix

# x = mnist data image of shape 28*28=784
x = torch.rand((28,28))
corrupt = 1.0 # set to 1.0 to corrupt input
c_x = (corrupt_input(x) * corrupt) + (x * (1 - corrupt))
```

This code snippet corrupts the input if the corrupt variable is equal to 1, and it refrains from corrupting the input if the corrupt variable is equal to 0. After making this modification, we can rerun our autoencoder, resulting in the reconstructions shown in Figure 8-14. It's quite apparent that the denoising autoencoder has faithfully replicated our incredible human ability to fill in the missing pixels.

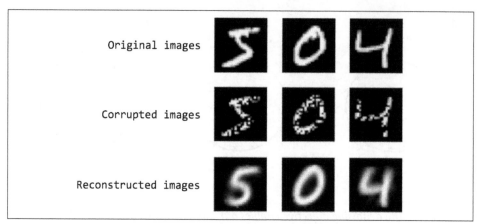

Figure 8-14. We apply a corruption operation to the dataset and train a denoising autoencoder to reconstruct the original, uncorrupted images

Sparsity in Autoencoders

One of the most difficult aspects of deep learning is a problem known as *interpretability*. Interpretability is a property of a machine learning model that measures how easy it is to inspect and explain its process and/or output. Deep models are generally difficult to interpret because of the nonlinearities and massive numbers of parameters that make up a model. While deep models are generally more accurate, a lack of interpretability often hinders their adoption in highly valuable, but highly risky, applications. For example, if a machine learning model is predicting that a patient has or does not have cancer, the doctor will likely want an explanation to confirm the model's conclusion.

We can address one aspect of interpretability by exploring the characteristics of the output of an autoencoder. In general, an autoencoder's representations are dense, and this has implications with respect to how the representation changes as we make coherent modifications to the input. Consider the situation in Figure 8-15.

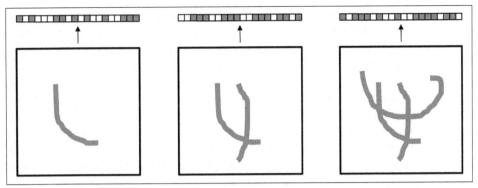

Figure 8-15. The activations of a dense representation combine and overlay information from multiple features in ways that are difficult to interpret

The autoencoder produces a *dense* representation, that is, the representation of the original image is highly compressed. Because we have only so many dimensions to work with in the representation, the activations of the representation combine information from multiple features in ways that are extremely difficult to disentangle. The result is that as we add components or remove components, the output representation changes in unexpected ways. It's virtually impossible to interpret how and why the representation is generated in the way it is.

The ideal outcome for us is if we can build a representation where there is a 1-to-1 correspondence, or close to a 1-to-1 correspondence, between high-level features and individual components in the code. When we are able to achieve this, we get very close to the system described in Figure 8-16, which shows how the representation changes as we add and remove components. The representation is the sum of the individual strokes in the image. With the right combination of space and sparsity, a representation is more interpretable.

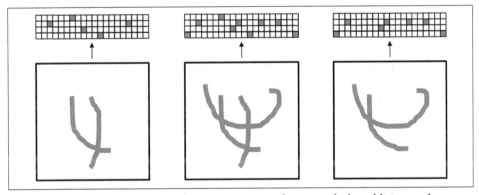

Figure 8-16. How activations in the representation change with the addition and removal of strokes

While this is the ideal outcome, we'll have to think through what mechanisms we can leverage to enable this interpretability in the representation. The issue here is clearly the bottlenecked capacity of the code layer; but unfortunately, increasing the capacity of the code layer alone is not sufficient. In the medium case, while we can increase the size of the code layer, there is no mechanism that prevents each individual feature picked up by the autoencoder from affecting a large fraction of the components with smaller magnitudes. In the more extreme case, where the features that are picked up are more complex and therefore more bountiful, the capacity of the code layer may be even larger than the dimensionality of the input. In this case, the code layer has so much capacity that the model could quite literally perform a "copy" operation where the code layer learns no useful representation.

What we really want is to force the autoencoder to utilize as few components of the representation vector as possible, while still effectively reconstructing the input. This is similar to the rationale behind using regularization to prevent overfitting in simple neural networks, as we discussed in Chapter 4, except we want as many components to be zero (or extremely close to zero) as possible. As in Chapter 4, we'll achieve this by modifying the objective function with a sparsity penalty, which increases the cost of any representation that has a large number of nonzero components:

$$E_{\text{Sparse}} = E + \beta \cdot \text{SparsityPenalty}$$

The value of β determines how strongly we favor sparsity at the expense of generating better reconstructions. For the mathematically inclined, you would do this by treating the values of each of the components of every representation as the outcome of a random variable with an unknown mean. We would then employ a measure of divergence comparing the distribution of observations of this random variable (the values of each component) and the distribution of a random variable whose mean is known to be 0. A measure that is often used to this end is the Kullback-Leibler (often referred to as KL) divergence. Further discussion on sparsity in autoencoders is beyond the scope of this text, but they are covered by Ranzato et al. (2007[4] and 2008[5]). More recently, the theoretical properties and empirical effectiveness of introducing an intermediate function before the code layer that zeroes out all but k of the maximum activations in the representation were investigated by Makhzani and Frey (2014).[6] These *k-Sparse autoencoders* were shown to be just as effective as other mechanisms

---

4 Ranzato, Marc'Aurelio, et al. "Efficient Learning of Sparse Representations with an Energy-Based Model." *Proceedings of the 19th International Conference on Neural Information Processing Systems.* MIT Press, 2006.

5 Ranzato, Marc'Aurelio, and Martin Szummer. "Semi-supervised Learning of Compact Document Representations with Deep Networks." *Proceedings of the 25th International Conference on Machine Learning.* ACM, 2008.

6 Makhzani, Alireza, and Brendan Frey. "k-Sparse Autoencoders." *arXiv preprint arXiv:1312.5663 (2013).*

of sparsity despite being shockingly simple to implement and understand (as well as computationally more efficient).

This concludes our discussion of autoencoders. We've explored how we can use autoencoders to find strong representations of data points by summarizing their content. This mechanism of dimensionality reduction works well when the independent data points are rich and contain all of the relevant information pertaining to their structure in their original representation. In the next section, we'll explore strategies that we can use when the main source of information is in the context of the data point instead of the data point itself.

When Context Is More Informative than the Input Vector

So far, we've mostly focused on the concept of dimensionality reduction. In dimensionality reduction, we generally have rich inputs that contain lots of noise on top of the core, structural information that we care about. In these situations, we want to extract this underlying information while ignoring the variations and noise that are extraneous to this fundamental understanding of the data.

In other situations, we have input representations that say very little at all about the content that we are trying to capture. In these situations, our goal is not to extract information but rather to gather information from context to build useful representations. All of this probably sounds too abstract to be useful at this point, so let's concretize these ideas with a real example.

Building models for language is a tricky business. The first problem we have to overcome when building language models is finding a good way to represent individual words. At first glance, it's not entirely clear how one builds a good representation. Let's start with the naive approach, considering Figure 8-17.

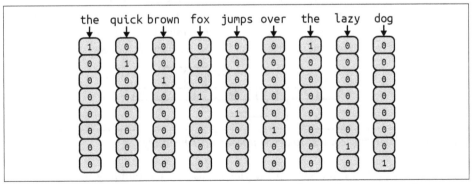

Figure 8-17. Generating one-hot vector representations for words using a simple document

---

If a document has a vocabulary V with $|V|$ words, we can represent the words with one-hot vectors. We have $|V|$-dimensional representation vectors, and we associate each unique word with an index in this vector. To represent unique word w_i, we set the ith component of the vector to be 1, and zero out all of the other components.

However, this representation scheme seems rather arbitrary. This vectorization does not make similar words into similar vectors. This is problematic, because we'd like our models to know that the words "jump" and "leap" have similar meanings. Similarly, we'd like our models to know when words are verbs or nouns or prepositions. The naive one-hot encoding of words to vectors does not capture any of these characteristics. To address this challenge, we'll need to find some way of discovering these relationships and encoding this information into a vector.

It turns out that one way to discover relationships between words is by analyzing their surrounding context. For example, synonyms such as "jump" and "leap" can be used interchangeably in their respective contexts. In addition, both words generally appear when a subject is performing the action over a direct object. We use this principle all the time when we run across new vocabulary while reading. For example, if we read the sentence "The warmonger argued with the crowd," we can immediately draw conclusions about the word "warmonger" even if we don't already know the dictionary definition. In this context, "warmonger" precedes a word we know to be a verb, which makes it likely that "warmonger" is a noun and the subject of this sentence. Also, the "warmonger" is "arguing," which might imply that a "warmonger" is generally a combative or argumentative individual. Overall, as illustrated in Figure 8-18, by analyzing the context (i.e., a fixed window of words surrounding a target word), we can quickly surmise the meaning of the word.

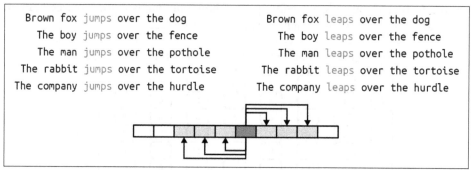

Figure 8-18. Analyzing context to determine a word's meaning

It turns out we can use the same principles we used when building the autoencoder to build a network that builds strong, distributed representations. Two strategies are shown in Figure 8-19. One possible method (shown in A) passes the target through an encoder network to create an embedding. Then we have a decoder network take this embedding; but instead of trying to reconstruct the original input as we did with the autoencoder, the decoder attempts to construct a word from the context. The second possible method (shown in B) does exactly the reverse: the encoder takes a word from the context as input, producing the target.

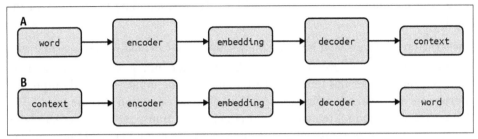

Figure 8-19. General architectures for designing encoders and decoders that generate embeddings by mapping words to their respective contexts (A) or vice versa (B)

In the next section, we'll describe how we use this strategy (along with some slight modifications for performance) to produce word embeddings in practice.

The Word2Vec Framework

Word2Vec, a framework for generating word embeddings, was pioneered by Mikolov et al. The original paper detailed two strategies for generating embeddings, similar to the two strategies for encoding context we discussed in the previous section.

The first flavor of Word2Vec that Mikolov et al. introduced was the *Continuous Bag of Words* (CBOW) model.[7] This model is much like strategy B from Figure 8-19. The CBOW model used the encoder to create an embedding from the full context (treated as one input) and predict the target word. It turns out this strategy works best for smaller datasets, an attribute that is further discussed in the original paper.

The second flavor of Word2Vec is the *Skip-Gram model*, introduced by Mikolov et al.[8] The Skip-Gram model does the inverse of CBOW, taking the target word as an input, and then attempting to predict one of the words in the context. Let's walk through a toy example to explore what the dataset for a Skip-Gram model looks like.

Consider the sentence "the boy went to the bank." If we broke this sentence down into a sequence of (context, target) pairs, we would obtain [(([the, went], boy), ([boy, to], went), ([went, the], to), ([to, bank], the)]. Taking this a step further, we have to split each (context, target) pair into (input, output) pairs where the input is the target and

---

7 Mikolov, Tomas, et al. "Distributed Representations of Words and Phrases and their Compositionality." *Advances in Neural Information Processing Systems.* 2013.

8 Tomas Mikolov, Kai Chen, Greg Corrado, and Jeffrey Dean. "Efficient Estimation of Word Representations in Vector Space." *ICLR Workshop*, 2013.

the output is one of the words from the context. From the first pair ([the, went], boy), we would generate the two pairs (boy, the) and (boy, went). We continue to apply this operation to every (context, target) pair to build our dataset. Finally, we replace each word with its unique index $i \in \{0, 1, ..., |V| - 1\}$ corresponding to its index in the vocabulary.

The structure of the encoder is surprisingly simple. It is essentially a lookup table with $|V|$ rows, where the ith row is the embedding corresponding to the ith vocabulary word. All the encoder has to do is take the index of the input word and output the appropriate row in the lookup table. This an efficient operation because on a GPU, this operation can be represented as a product of the transpose of the lookup table and the one-hot vector representing the input word. We can implement this simply in PyTorch with the following PyTorch function:

```
emb = nn.Embedding(10, 100)
x = torch.tensor([0])
out = emb(x)
```

Where out is the embedding matrix, and x is a tensor of indices we want to look up. For information on optional parameters, we refer you to the PyTorch API documentation (*https://oreil.ly/NaQWV*).

The decoder is slightly trickier because we make some modifications for performance. The naive way to construct the decoder would be to attempt to reconstruct the one-hot encoding vector for the output, which we could implement with a run-of-the-mill feed-forward layer coupled with a softmax. The only concern is that it's inefficient because we have to produce a probability distribution over the whole vocabulary space.

To reduce the number of parameters, Mikolov et al. used a strategy for implementing the decoder known as noise-contrastive estimation (NCE). The strategy is illustrated in Figure 8-20. A binary logistic regression compares the embedding of the target with the embedding of a context word and randomly sampled noncontext words. We construct a loss function describing how effectively the embeddings enable identification of words in the context of the target versus words outside the context of the target.

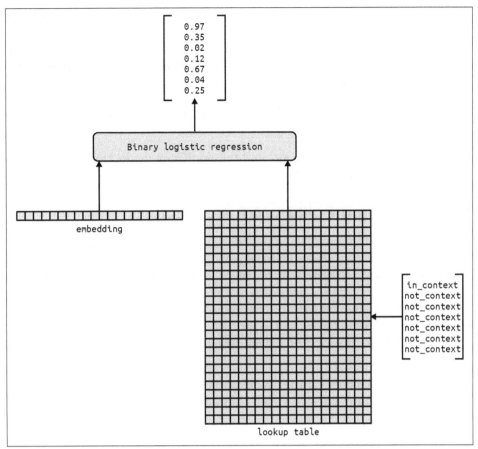

Figure 8-20. The NCE strategy

The NCE strategy uses the lookup table to find the embedding for the output, as well as embeddings for random selections from the vocabulary that are not in the context of the input. We then employ a binary logistic regression model that, one at a time, takes the input embedding and the embedding of the output or random selection, and then outputs a value between 0 to 1 corresponding to the probability that the comparison embedding represents a vocabulary word present in the input's context. We then take the sum of the probabilities corresponding to the noncontext comparisons and subtract the probability corresponding to the context comparison. This value is the objective function that we want to minimize (in the optimal scenario where the model has perfect performance, the value will be –1).

An example of implementing NCE in PyTorch can be found on GitHub (*https:// oreil.ly/lH2ip*).

While Word2Vec is admittedly not a deep machine learning model, we discuss it here for many reasons. First, it thematically represents a strategy (finding embeddings using context) that generalizes to many deep learning models. When we learn about models for sequence analysis in Chapter 9, we'll see this strategy employed for generating skip-thought vectors to embed sentences. Moreover, when we start building more and more models for language starting in Chapter 9, we'll find that using Word2Vec embeddings instead of one-hot vectors to represent words will yield far superior results.

Now that we understand how to architect the Skip-Gram model and its importance, we can start implementing it in PyTorch.

Implementing the Skip-Gram Architecture

To build the dataset for our Skip-Gram model, we'll utilize a modified version of the PyTorch Word2Vec data reader in `input_word_data.py`. We'll start off by setting a couple of important parameters for training and regularly inspecting our model. Of particular note, we employ a minibatch size of 32 examples and train for 5 epochs (full passes through the dataset). We'll use embeddings of size 128. We'll use a context window of five words to the left and to the right of each target word, and sample four context words from this window. Finally, we'll use 64 randomly chosen noncontext words for NCE.

Implementing the embedding layer is not particularly complicated. We merely have to initialize the lookup table with a matrix of values:

```
vocab_size = 500
emb_vector_len = 128

embedding = nn.Embedding(num_embeddings = vocab_size,
                         embedding_dim = emb_vector_len)
```

PyTorch does not currently have a built-in NCE loss function. However, there are some implementations on the internet. One example is the *info-nce-pytorch* library:

```
pip install info-nce-pytorch
```

We utilize `InfoNCE` to compute the NCE cost for each training example, and then compile all of the results in the minibatch into a single measurement:

```
loss = InfoNCE()
batch_size, embedding_size = 32, 128
query = embedding(outputs)
positive_key = embedding(targets)
output = loss(query, positive_key)
```

Now that we have our objective function expressed as a mean of the NCE costs, we set up the training as usual. Here, we follow in the footsteps of Mikolov et al. and employ stochastic gradient descent with a learning rate of 0.1:

```
optimizer = optim.SGD(embedding.parameters(),
                      lr = 0.1)
def train(inputs, targets, embedding):
  optimizer.zero_grad()
  input_emb = embedding(inputs)
  target_emb = embedding(targets)
  loss = loss_fn(input_emb, target_emb)
  loss.backward()
  optimizer.step()
  return loss
```

We also inspect the model regularly using a validation function, which normalizes the embeddings in the lookup table and uses cosine similarity to compute distances for a set of validation words from all other words in the vocabulary:

```
cosine_similarity = nn.CosineSimilarity()

def evaluate(inputs, targets, embedding):
  with torch.no_grad():
    input_emb = embedding(inputs)
    target_emb = embedding(targets)
    norm = torch.sum(input_emb, dim=1)
    normalized = input_emb/norm
    score = cosine_similarity(normalized, target_emb)
    return normalized, score
```

Putting all of these components together, we're finally ready to run the Skip-Gram model. We skim over this portion of the code because it is very similar to how we constructed models in the past. The only difference is the additional code during the inspection step. We randomly select 20 validation words out of the 500 most common words in our vocabulary of 10,000 words. For each of these words, we use the cosine similarity function we built to find the nearest neighbors:

```
n_epochs=1
for epoch in range(n_epochs):
  # Train
  running_loss = 0.0
  for inputs, targets in trainloader:
    loss = train(inputs, targets)
    running_loss += loss.item()

  writer.add_scalar('Train Loss',
                    running_loss/len(trainloader), epoch)
  #Validate
  running_score = 0.0
  for inputs, targets in valloader:
    _, score = evaluate(inputs, targets)
    running_score += score
```

```
writer.add_scalar('Val Score',
                  running_score/len(valloader), epoch)
```

The code starts to run, and we can begin to see how the model evolves over time. At the beginning, the model does a poor job of embedding (as is apparent from the inspection step). However, by the time training completes, the model has clearly found representations that effectively capture the meanings of individual words:

```
ancient: egyptian, cultures, mythology, civilization, etruscan,
greek, classical, preserved

however: but, argued, necessarily, suggest, certainly, nor,
believe, believed

type: typical, kind, subset, form, combination, single,
description, meant

white: yellow, black, red, blue, colors, grey, bright, dark

system: operating, systems, unix, component, variant, versions,
version, essentially

energy: kinetic, amount, heat, gravitational, nucleus,
radiation, particles, transfer

world: ii, tournament, match, greatest, war, ever, championship,
cold

y: z, x, n, p, f, variable, mathrm, sum,

line: lines, ball, straight, circle, facing, edge, goal, yards,

among: amongst, prominent, most, while, famous, particularly,
argue, many

image: png, jpg, width, images, gallery, aloe, gif, angel

kingdom: states, turkey, britain, nations, islands, namely,
ireland, rest

long: short, narrow, thousand, just, extended, span, length,
shorter

through: into, passing, behind, capture, across, when, apart,
goal

i: you, t, know, really, me, want, myself, we

source: essential, implementation, important, software, content,
genetic, alcohol, application
```

```
because: thus, while, possibility, consequently, furthermore,
but, certainly, moral

eight: six, seven, five, nine, one, four, three, b

french: spanish, jacques, pierre, dutch, italian, du, english,
belgian

written: translated, inspired, poetry, alphabet, hebrew,
letters, words, read
```

While not perfect, there are some strikingly meaningful clusters captured here. Numbers, countries, and cultures are clustered close together. The pronoun "I" is clustered with other pronouns. The word "world" is interestingly close to both "championship" and "war." And the word "written" is found to be similar to "translated," "poetry," "alphabet," "letters," and "words."

Finally, we conclude this section by visualizing our word embeddings in Figure 8-21. To display our 128-dimensional embeddings in 2D space, we'll use a visualization method known as t-SNE. If you'll recall, we also used t-SNE in Chapter 7 to visualize the relationships between images in ImageNet. Using t-SNE is quite simple, as it has a built-in function in the commonly used machine learning library scikit-learn.

We can construct the visualization using the following code:

```
tsne = TSNE(perplexity=30, n_components=2, init='pca',
            n_iter=5000)
plot_embeddings = np.asfarray(final_embeddings[:plot_num,:],
                             dtype='float')
low_dim_embs = tsne.fit_transform(plot_embeddings)
labels = [reverse_dictionary[i] for i in xrange(plot_only)]
data.plot_with_labels(low_dim_embs, labels)
```

In Figure 8-21, we notice that similar concepts are closer together than disparate concepts, indicating that our embeddings encode meaningful information about the functions and definitions of individual words.

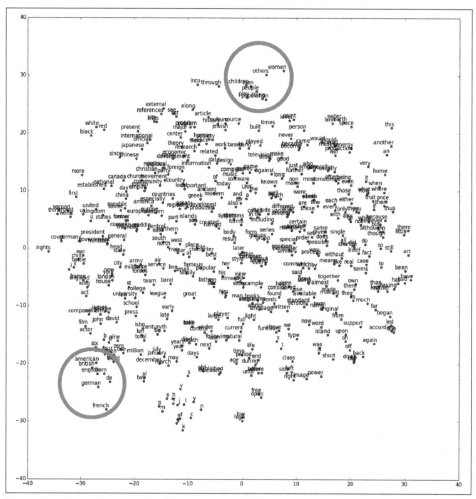

Figure 8-21. Skip-Gram embeddings using t-SNE

For a more detailed exploration of the properties of word embeddings and interesting patterns (verb tenses, countries and capitals, analogy completion, etc.), we refer you to the original Mikolov et al. paper.

Theory: PCA and SVD

Those who have taken any form of applied linear algebra are probably familiar with the SVD, one of the most important matrix factorizations in all of linear algebra. For those uninitiated with the SVD, I will first explain the key concepts behind it (assuming some prior linear algebra knowledge) before jumping into its relationship with PCA.

The SVD states that any matrix M with dimension m by n can be factorized into the form $U\Sigma V^\mathsf{T}$ (where T represents the transpose operation) with U of dimension m by m, Σ of dimension m by n, and V of dimension n by n. The matrices U and V are both orthogonal matrices. Orthogonal matrices are square matrices made up of orthonormal column vectors. An important fact about orthogonal matrices is that their transposes are also orthogonal matrices, so V^T in the decomposition is still orthogonal. In addition, the transpose of an orthogonal matrix is its inverse, so we have $U^\mathsf{T}U = UU^\mathsf{T} = I_m$ and $V^\mathsf{T}V = VV^\mathsf{T} = I_n$. Σ is a rectangular diagonal matrix with only nonnegative entries along its diagonal, which are termed the *singular values* of the M. Although the SVD itself is not unique, the singular values of a matrix are. If we inspect the product Σx, where x is any random vector, we note that Σ simply acts as a scaling factor for each dimension of x due to Σ being a diagonal matrix (and when rectangular diagonal, either adds dimensions with value 0 when tall or removes dimensions when wide).

Another important and potentially more nonobvious property of orthogonal matrices is that they preserve the length, or L2 norm, of any vector they are multiplied by (this is left as an exercise for you). Orthogonal matrices can change only a vector's orientation, and thus, we characterize the action of an orthogonal matrix upon a vector as a rotation. We call norms such as the L2 norm *rotationally invariant* for this reason. One famous example of an orthogonal matrix you're already familiar with is the identity matrix I—this matrix maps any vector to itself, so we can think of it as a rotation of 0.

To understand the SVD more intuitively, let's imagine the matrix-vector product Mx decomposed as $U\Sigma V^\mathsf{T}x$. Based on our discussion so far, we can see that the action of the matrix M upon x can be decomposed into a rotation, followed by a scaling, followed by another rotation.

Now that we have an intuitive understanding of SVD, let's connect it back to the PCA algorithm presented in the main text. Let's assume we have a data matrix X, which is of dimension d by n, where d represents the number of features per datapoint and n represents the number of datapoints. Again, we assume for simplicity that the rows of X have been z-score normalized. The PCA algorithm can be reduced to taking the eigendecomposition of the correlation matrix $\frac{1}{n}XX^\mathsf{T}$, which we will represent as PDP^T. The matrix of eigenvalues D is a diagonal matrix, while the matrix P is a matrix of the corresponding eigenvectors as columns. Generally, the eigendecomposition of a matrix looks like PDP^{-1}, but here the correlation matrix is symmetric so the eigenvectors are orthogonal (we leave this as an exercise for you). Thus, we can represent P as an orthogonal matrix once the eigenvectors are normalized to unit length, at which point the inverse and transpose are equal.

Instead of working with the correlation matrix, let's instead work with the data matrix first and then move to the correlation matrix. We first represent X as $U\Sigma V^\mathsf{T}$. Now, we express the correlation matrix in terms of components of the SVD:

$$\frac{1}{n}XX^\mathsf{T} = \frac{1}{n}U\Sigma V^\mathsf{T} V\Sigma^\mathsf{T} U^\mathsf{T}$$

$$= \frac{1}{n}U\Sigma^2 U^\mathsf{T}$$

We already see the obvious parallels to the correlation matrix's eigendecomposition: U is orthogonal, and the square of the singular value matrix is also a diagonal matrix (this matrix is just the diagonal matrix of the squares of all the singular values). One can show that U's columns, also termed the *left singular vectors*, are the eigenvectors of the correlation matrix. Imagine multiplying $\frac{1}{n}U\Sigma^2 U^\mathsf{T}$ by Ue_i, where e_i is a vector of all zeroes except for a one at the index corresponding to any single column (Ue_i is the ith column of U). In practice, it is actually ideal to use the SVD of the data matrix rather than take the eigendecomposition of the correlation matrix due to precision issues when calculating the correlation matrix, which is a product of two potentially very large matrices.

Summary

In this chapter, we explored various methods in representation learning. We learned about how we can perform effective dimensionality reduction using autoencoders. We also learned about denoising and sparsity, which augment autoencoders with useful properties. After discussing autoencoders, we shifted our attention to representation learning when context of an input is more informative than the input itself. We learned how to generate embeddings for English words using the Skip-Gram model, which will prove useful as we explore deep learning models for understanding language. In the next chapter, we will build on this tangent to analyze language and other sequences using deep learning.

## CHAPTER 9

Models for Sequence Analysis

Surya Bhupatiraju

Analyzing Variable-Length Inputs

Up until now, we've worked only with data with fixed sizes: images from MNIST, CIFAR-10, and ImageNet. These models are incredibly powerful, but there are many situations in which fixed-length models are insufficient. The vast majority of interactions in our daily lives require a deep understanding of sequences—whether it's reading the morning newspaper, making a bowl of cereal, listening to the radio, watching a presentation, or deciding to execute a trade on the stock market. To adapt to variable-length inputs, we'll have to be a little bit more clever about how we approach designing deep learning models.

Figure 9-1 illustrates how our feed-forward neural networks break when analyzing sequences. If the sequence is the same size as the input layer, the model can perform as expected. It's even possible to deal with smaller inputs by padding zeros to the end of the input until it's the appropriate length. However, the moment the input exceeds the size of the input layer, naively using the feed-forward network no longer works.

Feed-forward networks thrive on fixed input size problems. Zero padding can address the handling of smaller inputs, but when naively utilized, these models break when inputs exceed the fixed input size.

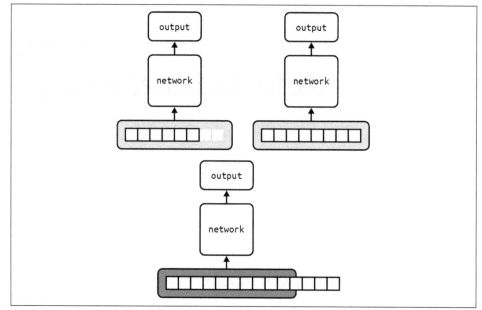

Figure 9-1. Broken feed-forward network

Not all hope is lost, however. In the next couple of sections, we'll explore several strategies we can leverage to "hack" feed-forward networks to handle sequences. Later in the chapter, we'll analyze the limitations of these hacks and discuss new architectures to address them. We will conclude the chapter by discussing some of the most advanced architectures explored to date to tackle some of the most difficult challenges in replicating human-level logical reasoning and cognition over sequences.

Tackling seq2seq with Neural N-Grams

In this section, we'll begin exploring a feed-forward neural network architecture that can process a body of text and produce a sequence of part-of-speech (POS) tags. In other words, we want to appropriately label each word in the input text as a noun, verb, preposition, and so on. An example of this is shown in Figure 9-2. While it's not the same complexity as building an AI that can answer questions after reading a story, it's a solid first step toward developing an algorithm that can understand the meaning of how words are used in a sentence. This problem is also interesting because it is an instance of a class of problems known as *seq2seq*, where the goal is to transform an input sequence into a corresponding output sequence. Other famous seq2seq problems include translating text between languages (which we will tackle later in this chapter), text summarization, and transcribing speech to text.

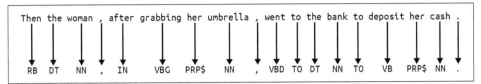

Figure 9-2. An example of an accurate POS parse of an English sentence

As we discussed, it's not obvious how we might take a body of text all at once to predict the full sequence of POS tags. Instead, we leverage a trick that is akin to the way we developed distributed vector representations of words in the previous chapter. The key observation is this: *it is not necessary to take into account long-term dependencies to predict the POS of any given word.*

The implication of this observation is that instead of using the whole sequence to predict all of the POS tags simultaneously, we can predict each POS tag one at a time by using a fixed-length subsequence. In particular, we utilize the subsequence starting from the word of interest and extending *n* words into the past. This *neural n-gram strategy* is depicted in Figure 9-3.

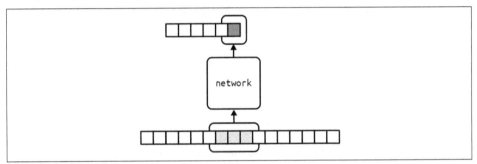

Figure 9-3. Using a feed-forward network to perform seq2seq when we can ignore long-term dependencies

Specifically, when we predict the POS tag for the ith word in the input, we use the the $i-n+1^{st}, i-n+2^{nd}, ..., i^{th}$ words as the input. We'll refer to this subsequence as the *context window*. In order to process the entire text, we'll start by positioning the network at the beginning of the text. We'll then proceed to move the network's context window one word at a time, predicting the POS tag of the rightmost word, until we reach the end of the input.

Leveraging the word embedding strategy from last chapter, we'll also use condensed representations of the words instead of one-hot vectors. This will allow us to reduce the number of parameters in our model and make learning faster.

Implementing a Part-of-Speech Tagger

Now that we have a strong understanding of the POS network architecture, we can dive into the implementation. On a high level, the network consists of an input layer that leverages a three-gram context window. We'll use word embeddings that are 300-dimensional, resulting in a context window of size 900. The feed-forward network will have two hidden layers of size 512 neurons and 256 neurons, respectively. Then, the output layer will be a softmax calculating the probability distribution of the POS tag output over a space of 44 possible tags. As usual, we'll use the Adam optimizer with our default hyperparameter settings, train for a total of 1,000 epochs, and leverage batch-normalization for regularization.

The actual network is extremely similar to networks we've implemented in the past. Rather, the tricky part of building the POS tagger is in preparing the dataset. We'll leverage pretrained word embeddings generated from Google News (*https://oreil.ly/Rsu9A*). It includes vectors for 3 million words and phrases and was trained on roughly 100 billion words. We can use the `gensim` Python package to read the dataset. Google Colab already has `gensim` preinstalled. If you are using another machine, you can use `pip` to install the package. You will also need to download the Google News data file:

```
$ pip install gensim
$ wget https://s3.amazonaws.com/dl4j-distribution/
  GoogleNews-vectors-negative300.bin.gz -O googlenews.bin.gz
```

We can subsequently load these vectors into memory using the following command:

```
from gensim.models import KeyedVectors

model = KeyedVectors.load_word2vec_format('./googlenews.bin.gz',
                                          binary=True)
```

The issue with this operation, however, is that it's incredibly slow (it can take up to an hour, depending on the specs of your machine). To avoid loading the full dataset into memory every single time we run our program, especially while debugging code or experimenting with different hyperparameters, we cache the relevant subset of the vectors to disk using a lightweight database known as LevelDB (*http://leveldb.org*). To build the appropriate Python bindings (which allow us to interact with a LevelDB instance from Python), we simply use the following command:

```
$ pip install leveldb
```

As we mentioned, the `gensim` model contains three million words, which is larger than our dataset. For the sake of efficiency, we'll selectively cache word vectors for words in our dataset and discard everything else. To figure out which words we'd like to cache, let's download the POS dataset from the CoNLL-2000 task (*https://oreil.ly/8qJeZ*).

```
$ wget http://www.cnts.ua.ac.be/conll2000/chunking/train.txt.gz
  -O - | gunzip |
  cut -f1,2 -d" " > pos.train.txt

$ wget http://www.cnts.ua.ac.be/conll2000/chunking/test.txt.gz
  -O - | gunzip |
  cut -f1,2 -d " " > pos.test.txt
```

The dataset consists of contiguous text that is formatted as a sequence of rows, where the first element is a word and the second element is the corresponding part of speech. Here are the first several lines of the training dataset:

```
Confidence NN
in IN
the DT
pound NN
is VBZ
widely RB
expected VBN
to TO
take VB
another DT
sharp JJ
dive NN
if IN
trade NN
figures NNS
for IN
September NNP
, ,
due JJ
for IN
release NN
tomorrow NN
...
```

To match the formatting of the dataset to the gensim model, we'll have to do some preprocessing. For example, the model replaces digits with '#' characters, combines separate words into entities where appropriate (e.g., considering "New_York" as a single token instead of two separate words), and utilizes underscores where the raw data uses dashes. We preprocess the dataset to conform to this model schema with the following code (analogous code is used to process the training data):

```
def create_pos_dataset(filein, fileout):
    dataset = []
    with open(filein) as f:
        dataset_raw = f.readlines()
        dataset_raw = [e.split() for e in dataset_raw
                          if len(e.split()) > 0]

    counter = 0
    while counter < len(dataset_raw):
```

```
    pair = dataset_raw[counter]
    if counter < len(dataset_raw) - 1:
      next_pair = dataset_raw[counter + 1]
      if (pair[0] + "_" + next_pair[0] in model) and \
      (pair[1] == next_pair[1]):
        dataset.append([pair[0] + "_" + next_pair[0], pair[1]])
        counter += 2
        continue

    word = re.sub("\d", "#", pair[0])
    word = re.sub("-", "_", word)

    if word in model:
      dataset.append([word, pair[1]])
      counter += 1
      continue

    if "_" in word:
      subwords = word.split("_")
      for subword in subwords:
        if not (subword.isspace() or len(subword) == 0):
          dataset.append([subword, pair[1]])
      counter += 1
      continue

    dataset.append([word, pair[1]])
    counter += 1

  with open(fileout, 'w') as processed_file:
    for item in dataset:
      processed_file.write("%s\n" % (item[0] + " " + item[1]))

  return dataset

train_pos_dataset = create_pos_dataset('./pos.train.txt',
                                        './pos.train.processed.txt')
test_pos_dataset = create_pos_dataset('./pos.test.txt',
                                        './pos.test.processed.txt')
```

Now that we've appropriately processed the datasets for use, we can load the words in LevelDB. If the word or phrase is present in the gensim model, we can cache that in the LevelDB instance. If not, we randomly select a vector to represent to the token, and cache it so that we remember to use the same vector in case we encounter it again:

```
import leveldb
db = leveldb.LevelDB("./word2vecdb")

counter = 0
dataset_vocab = {}
tags_to_index = {}
index_to_tags = {}
```

```
index = 0
for pair in train_pos_dataset + test_pos_dataset:
  if pair[0] not in dataset_vocab:
    dataset_vocab[pair[0]] = index
    index += 1
  if pair[1] not in tags_to_index:
    tags_to_index[pair[1]] = counter
    index_to_tags[counter] = pair[1]
    counter += 1

nonmodel_cache = {}

counter = 1
total = len(dataset_vocab.keys())
for word in dataset_vocab:

  if word in model:
    db.Put(bytes(word,'utf-8'), model[word])
  elif word in nonmodel_cache:
    db.Put(bytes(word,'utf-8'), nonmodel_cache[word])
  else:
    #print(word)
    nonmodel_cache[word] = np.random.uniform(-0.25,
                                             0.25,
                                             300).astype(np.float32)
    db.Put(bytes(word,'utf-8'), nonmodel_cache[word])
  counter += 1
```

After running the script for the first time, we can just load our data straight from the database if it already exists:

```
db = leveldb.LevelDB("./word2vecdb")

x = db.Get(bytes('Confidence','utf-8'))
print(np.frombuffer(x,dtype='float32').shape)
# out: (300,)
```

Next, we build dataset objects for both training and test datasets, which we can use to generate minibatches for training and testing purposes. Building the dataset object requires access to the LevelDB db, the dataset, a dictionary tags_to_index that maps POS tags to indices in the output vector, and a boolean flat get_all that determines whether getting the minibatch should retrieve the full set by default:

```
from torch.utils.data import Dataset
from torch.utils.data import DataLoader

class NgramPOSDataset(Dataset):
  def __init__(self, db, dataset, tags_to_index, n_grams):
    super(NgramPOSDataset, self).__init__()
    self.db = db
    self.dataset = dataset
    self.tags_to_index = tags_to_index
```

```
        self.n_grams = n_grams

    def __getitem__(self, index):
      ngram_vector = np.array([])

      for ngram_index in range(index, index + self.n_grams):
        word, _ = self.dataset[ngram_index]
        vector_bytes = self.db.Get(bytes(word, 'utf-8'))
        vector = np.frombuffer(vector_bytes, dtype='float32')
        ngram_vector = np.append(ngram_vector, vector)

        _, tag = self.dataset[index + int(np.floor(self.n_grams/2))]
        label = self.tags_to_index[tag]
      return torch.tensor(ngram_vector, dtype=torch.float32), label

    def __len__(self):
      return (len(self.dataset) - self.n_grams + 1)

  trainset = NgramPOSDataset(db, train_pos_dataset, tags_to_index, 3)
  trainloader = DataLoader(trainset, batch_size=4, shuffle=True)
```

Finally, we design our feed-forward network similarly to our approaches in previous chapters. We omit a discussion of the code and refer to the file *Ch09_01_POS_Tagger.ipynb* in the book's repository (*https://github.com/darksigma/Fundamentals-of-Deep-Learning-Book*).

Every epoch, we manually inspect the model by parsing the sentence: "The woman, after grabbing her umbrella, went to the bank to deposit her cash." Within 100 epochs of training, the algorithm achieves over 96% accuracy and nearly perfectly parses the validation sentence (it makes the understandable mistake of confusing the possessive pronoun and personal pronoun tags for the first appearance of the word "her"). We'll conclude this by including the visualizations of our model's performance using TensorBoard in Figure 9-4.

The POS tagging model was a great exercise, but it was mostly rinsing and repeating concepts we've learned in previous chapters. In the rest of the chapter, we'll start to think about much more complicated sequence-related learning tasks. To tackle these more difficult problems, we'll need to broach brand-new concepts, develop new architectures, and start to explore the cutting edge of modern deep learning research. We'll start by tackling the problem of dependency parsing next.

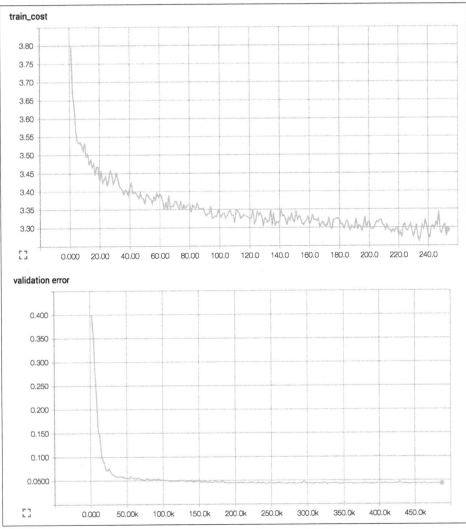

Figure 9-4. TensorBoard visualization of our feed-forward POS tagging model

Dependency Parsing and SyntaxNet

The framework we used to solve the POS tagging task was rather simple. Sometimes we need to be much more creative about how we tackle seq2seq problems, especially as the complexity of the problem increases. In this section, we'll explore strategies that employ creative data structures to tackle difficult seq2seq problems. As an illustrative example, we'll explore the problem of dependency parsing.

The idea behind building a dependency parse tree is to map the relationships between words in a sentence. Take, for example, the dependency in Figure 9-5. The words "I" and "taxi" are children of the word "took," specifically as the subject and direct object of the verb, respectively.

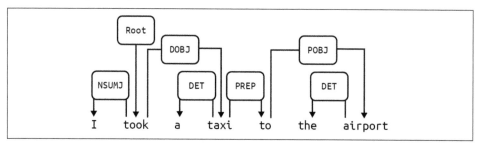

Figure 9-5. An example of a dependency parse, which generates a tree of relationships between words in a sentence

One way to express a tree as a sequence is by linearizing it. Let's consider the examples in Figure 9-6. Essentially, if you have a graph with a root R, and children A (connected by edge r_a), B (connected by edge r_b), and C (connected by edge r_c), we can linearize the representation as (R, r_a, A, r_b, B, r_c, C). We can even represent more complex graphs. Let's assume, for example, that node B actually has two more children named D (connected by edge b_d) and E (connected by edge b_e). We can represent this new graph as (R, r_a, A, r_b, [B, b_d, D, b_e, E], r_c, C).

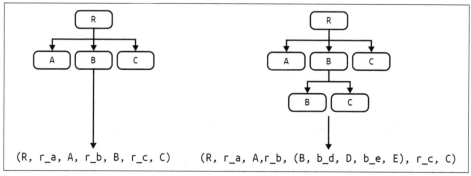

Figure 9-6. We linearize two example trees: the diagrams omit edge labels for the sake of visual clarity

Using this paradigm, we can take our example dependency parse and linearize it, as shown in Figure 9-7.

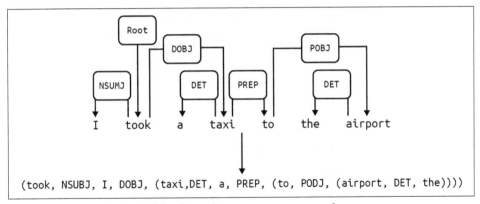

Figure 9-7. Linearization of the dependency parse tree example

One interpretation of this seq2seq problem would be to read the input sentence and produce a sequence of tokens as an output that represents the linearization of the input's dependency parse. It's not particularly clear, however, how we might port our strategy from the previous section, where there was a clear one-to-one mapping between words and their POS tags. Moreover, we could easily make decisions about a POS tag by looking at the nearby context. For dependency parsing, there's no clear relationship between how words are ordered in the sentence and how tokens in the linearization are ordered. It also seems like dependency parsing tasks us with identifying edges that may span a significantly large number of words. Therefore, at first glance, it seems like this setup directly violates our assumption that we need not take into account any long-term dependencies.

To make the problem more approachable, we instead reconsider the dependency parsing task as finding a sequence of valid "actions" that generates the correct dependency parse. This technique, known as the *arc-standard* system, was first described by Nivre in 2004 and later leveraged in a neural context by Chen and Manning in 2014.[1] In the arc-standard system, we start by putting the first two words of the sentence in the stack and maintaining the remaining words in the buffer, as shown in Figure 9-8.

---

1 Nivre, Joakim. "Incrementality in Deterministic Dependency Parsing." *Proceedings of the Workshop on Incremental Parsing: Bringing Engineering and Cognition Together.* Association for Computational Linguistics, 2004; Chen, Danqi, and Christopher D. Manning. "A Fast and Accurate Dependency Parser Using Neural Networks." *EMNLP.* 2014.

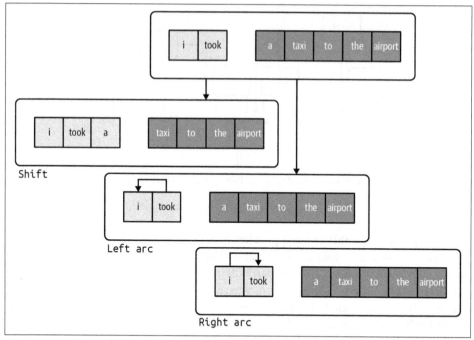

Figure 9-8. Three options in the arc-standard system: shift a word from the buffer to the stack, draw an arc from the right element to the left element (left arc), or draw an arc from the left element to the right element (right arc)

At any step, we can take one of three possible classes of actions:

Shift
>   Move a word from the buffer to the front of the stack.

Left arc
>   Combine the two elements at the front of the stack into a single unit where the root of the rightmost element is the parent node and the root of leftmost element is the child node.

Right arc
>   Combine the two elements at the front of the stack into a single unit where the root of the left element is the parent node, and the root of right element is the child node.

We note that while there is only one way to perform a shift, the arc actions can be of many flavors, each differentiated by the dependency label assigned to the arc that is generated. That being said, we'll simplify our discussions and illustrations in this section by considering each decision as a choice among three actions (rather than tens of actions).

We terminate this process when the buffer is empty and the stack has one element in it (which represents the full dependency parse). To illustrate this process in its entirety, we illustrate a sequence of actions that generates the dependency parse for our example input sentence in Figure 9-9.

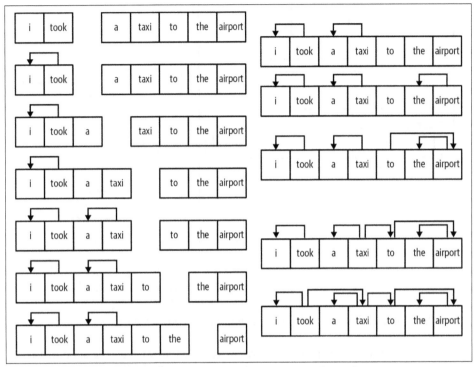

Figure 9-9. A sequence of actions that results in the correct dependency parse; we omit labels

It's not too difficult to reformulate this decision-making framework as a learning problem. At every step, we take the current configuration, and we vectorize the configuration by extracting a large number of features that describe the configuration (words in specific locations of the stack/buffer, specific children of the words in these locations, part of speech tags, etc.). During train time, we can feed this vector into a feed-forward network and compare its prediction of the next action to take to a gold-standard decision made by a human linguist. To use this model in the wild, we can take the action that the network recommends, apply it to the configuration, and use this new configuration as the starting point for the next step (feature extraction, action prediction, and action application). This process is shown in Figure 9-10.

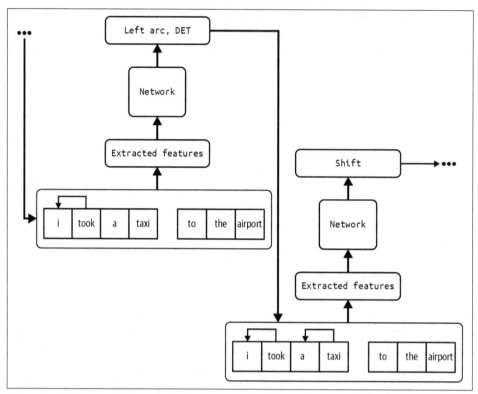

Figure 9-10. A neural framework for arc-standard dependency parsing

Taken together, these ideas form the core for Google's SyntaxNet, the state-of-the-art open source implementation for dependency parsing. Delving into the nitty-gritty aspects of implementation is beyond the scope of this text, but we refer you to the open source repository (*https://oreil.ly/UT1ga*), which contains an implementation of Parsey McParseface, the most accurate publicly reported English language parser as of the publication of this text.

Beam Search and Global Normalization

In the previous section, we described a naive strategy for deploying SyntaxNet in practice. The strategy was purely *greedy*; that is, we selected prediction with the highest probability without being concerned that we might potentially paint ourselves into a corner by making an early mistake. In the POS example, making an incorrect prediction was largely inconsequential. This is because each prediction could be considered a purely independent subproblem (the results of a given prediction do not affect the inputs of the next step).

This assumption no longer holds in SyntaxNet, because our prediction at step n affects the input we use at step $n + 1$. This implies that any mistake we make will influence all later decisions. Moreover, there's no good way of "going backward" and fixing mistakes when they become apparent.

Garden path sentences are an extreme case of where this is important. Consider the following sentence: "The complex houses married and single soldiers and their families." The first glance pass-through is confusing. Most people interpret "complex" as an adjective "houses" as a noun, and "married" as a past tense verb. This makes little semantic sense though, and starts to break down as the rest of the sentence is read. Instead, we realize that "complex" is a noun (as in a military complex) and that "houses" is a verb. In other words, the sentence implies that the military complex contains soldiers (who may be single or married) and their families. A *greedy* version of SyntaxNet would fail to correct the early parse mistake of considering "complex" as an adjective describing the "houses," and therefore would fail on the full version of the sentence.

To remedy this shortcoming, we use a strategy known as *beam search*, illustrated in Figure 9-11. We generally leverage beam searches in situations like SyntaxNet, where the output of our network at a particular step influences the inputs used in future steps. The basic idea behind beam search is that instead of greedily selecting the most probable prediction at each step, we maintain a *beam* of the most likely hypothesis (up to a fixed *beam size b*) for the sequence of the first k actions and their associated probabilities. Beam searching can be broken up into two major phases: expansion and pruning.

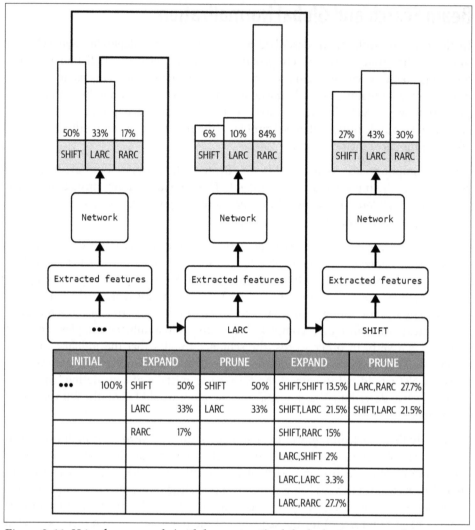

INITIAL		EXPAND		PRUNE		EXPAND		PRUNE	
•••	100%	SHIFT	50%	SHIFT	50%	SHIFT,SHIFT 13.5%		LARC,RARC 27.7%	
		LARC	33%	LARC	33%	SHIFT,LARC 21.5%		SHIFT,LARC 21.5%	
		RARC	17%			SHIFT,RARC 15%			
						LARC,SHIFT 2%			
						LARC,LARC 3.3%			
						LARC,RARC 27.7%			

Figure 9-11. Using beam search (with beam size 2) while deploying a trained SyntaxNet model

During the *expansion* step, we take each hypothesis and consider it as a possible input to SyntaxNet. Assume SyntaxNet produces a probability distribution over a space of $|A|$ total actions. We then compute the probability of each of the $b|A|$ possible hypotheses for the sequence of the first $k + 1$ actions. Then, during the *pruning* step, we keep only the b hypothesis out of the $b|A|$ total options with the largest probabilities. As Figure 9-11 illustrates, beam searching enables SyntaxNet to correct incorrect predictions post facto by entertaining less probable hypotheses early that might turn out to be more fruitful later in the sentence. In fact, digging deeper into the illustrated example, a greedy approach would have suggested that the correct sequence of moves would have been a shift followed by a left arc. In reality, the best (highest probability) option would have been to use a left arc followed by a right arc. Beam searching with beam size 2 surfaces this result.

The full open source version takes this a full step further and attempts to bring the concept of beam searching to the process of training the network. As Andor et al. described in 2016,[2] this process of *global normalization* provides both strong theoretical guarantees and clear performance gains relative to *local normalization* in practice. In a locally normalized network, our network is tasked with selecting the best action given a configuration. The network outputs a score that is normalized using a softmax layer. This is meant to model a probability distribution over all possible actions, provided the actions performed thus far. Our loss function attempts to force the probability distribution to the ideal output (i.e., probability 1 for the correct action and 0 for all other actions). The cross-entropy loss does a spectacular job of ensuring this for us.

In a globally normalized network, our interpretation of the scores is slightly different. Instead of putting the scores through a softmax to generate a per-action probability distribution, we instead add up all the scores for a hypothesis action sequence. One way of ensuring that we select the correct hypothesis sequence is by computing this sum over all possible hypotheses and then applying a softmax layer to generate a probability distribution. We could theoretically use the same cross-entropy loss function as we used in the locally normalized network. The problem with this strategy, however, is that there is an intractably large number of possible hypothesis sequences. Even considering an average sentence length of 10 and a conservative total number of 15 possible actions—1 shift and 7 labels for each of the left and right arcs—this corresponds to 1,000,000,000,000,000 possible hypotheses.

To make this problem tractable, as shown in Figure 9-12, we apply a beam search, with a fixed beam size, until we either (1) reach the end of the sentence, or (2) the correct sequence of actions is no longer contained on the beam. We then construct a loss function that tries to push the "gold standard" action sequence (highlighted in blue) as high as possible on the beam by maximizing its score relative to the other hypotheses. While we won't dive into the details of how we might construct this loss function here, we refer you to the original paper by Andor et al. in 2016.[3] The paper also describes a more sophisticated POS tagger that uses global normalization and beam search to significantly increase accuracy (compared to the POS tagger we built earlier in the chapter).

---

2 Andor, Daniel, et al. "Globally Normalized Transition-Based Neural Networks." *arXiv preprint arXiv*:1603.06042 (2016).

3 Ibid.

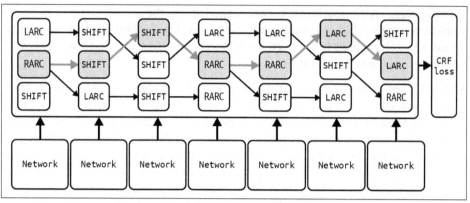

Figure 9-12. Coupling training and beam search can make global normalization in SyntaxNet tractable

A Case for Stateful Deep Learning Models

While we've explored several tricks to adapt feed-forward networks to sequence analysis, we've yet to truly find an elegant solution to sequence analysis. In the POS tagger example, we made the explicit assumption that we can ignore long-term dependencies. We were able to overcome some of the limitations of this assumption by introducing the concepts of beam searching and global normalization, but even still, the problem space was constrained to situations in which there was a one-to-one mapping between elements in the input sequence to elements in the output sequence. For example, even in the dependency parsing model, we had to reformulate the problem to discover a one-to-one mapping between a sequence of input configurations while constructing the parse tree and arc-standard actions.

Sometimes, however, the task is far more complicated than finding a one-to-one mapping between input and output sequences. For example, we might want to develop a model that can consume an entire input sequence at once and then conclude if the sentiment of the entire input was positive or negative. We'll build a simple model to perform this task later in the chapter. We may want an algorithm that consumes a complex input (such as an image) and generate a sentence, one word at a time, describing the input. We may event want to translate sentences from one language to another (e.g., from English to French). In all of these instances, there's no obvious mapping between input tokens and output tokens. Instead, the process is more like the situation in Figure 9-13.

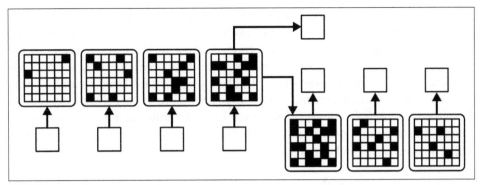

Figure 9-13. The ideal model for sequence analysis can store information in memory over long periods of time, leading to a coherent "thought" vector that it can use to generate an answer

The idea is simple. We want our model to maintain some sort of memory over the span of reading the input sequence. As it reads the input, the model should be able to modify this memory bank, taking into account the information that it observes. By the time it has reached the end of the input sequence, the internal memory contains a "thought" that represents the key pieces of information, that is, the meaning, of the original input. We should then, as shown in Figure 9-13, be able to use this thought vector to either produce a label for the original sequence or produce an appropriate output sequence (translation, description, abstractive summary, etc.).

The concept here isn't something we've explored in any of the previous chapters. Feed-forward networks are inherently "stateless." After it's been trained, the feed-forward network is a static structure. It isn't able to maintain memories between inputs, or change how it processes an input based on inputs it has seen in the past. To execute this strategy, we'll need to reconsider how we construct neural networks to create deep learning models that are "stateful." To do this, we'll have to return to how we think about networks on an individual neuron level. In the next section, we'll explore how *recurrent connections* (as opposed to the feed-forward connections we have studied this far) enable models to maintain state as we describe a class of models known as *recurrent neural networks* (RNNs).

Recurrent Neural Networks

RNNs were first introduced in the 1980s, but have regained popularity recently due to several intellectual and hardware breakthroughs that have made them tractable to train. RNNs are different from feed-forward networks because they leverage a special type of neural layer, known as recurrent layers, that enable the network to maintain state between uses of the network.

Figure 9-14 illustrates the neural architecture of a recurrent layer. All of the neurons have both (1) incoming connections emanating from all of the neurons of the previous layer and (2) outgoing connections leading to all of the neurons to the subsequent layer. We notice here, however, that these aren't the only connections that neurons of a recurrent layer have. Unlike a feed-forward layer, recurrent layers also have recurrent connections, which propagate information between neurons of the same layer. A fully connected recurrent layer has information flow from every neuron to every other neuron in its layer (including itself). Thus a recurrent layer with r neurons has a total of r^2 recurrent connections.

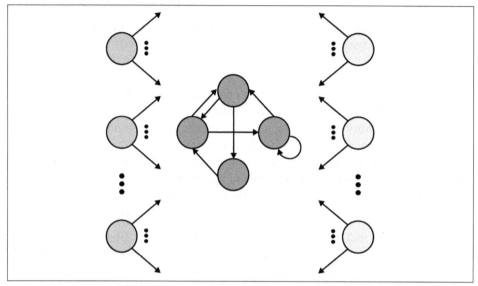

Figure 9-14. A recurrent layer contains recurrent connections, that is to say, connections between neurons that are located in the same layer

To better understand how RNNs work, let's explore how one functions after it's been appropriately trained. Every time we want to process a new sequence, we create a fresh instance of our model. We can reason about networks that contain recurrent layers by dividing the lifetime of the network instance into discrete time steps. At each time step, we feed the model the next element of the input. Feed-forward connections represent information flow from one neuron to another where the data being transferred is the computed neuronal activation from the current time step. Recurrent connections, however, represent information flow where the data is the stored neuronal activation from the *previous* time step. Thus, the activations of the neurons in a recurrent network represent the accumulating state of the network instance. The initial activations of neurons in the recurrent layer are parameters of our model, and we determine the optimal values for them just like we determine the optimal values for the weights of each connection during the process of training.

It turns out that, given a fixed lifetime (say t time steps) of an RNN instance, we can actually express the instance as a feed-forward network (albeit irregularly structured). This clever transformation, illustrated in Figure 9-15, is often referred to as "unrolling" the RNN through time. Let's consider the example RNN in the figure. We'd like to map a sequence of two inputs (each dimension 1) to a single output (also of dimension 1). We perform the transformation by taking the neurons of the single recurrent layer and replicating them it t times, once for each time step. We similarly replicate the neurons of the input and output layers. We redraw the feed-forward connections within each time replica just as they were in the original network. Then we draw the recurrent connections as feed-forward connections from each time replica to the next (since the recurrent connections carry the neuronal activation from the previous time step).

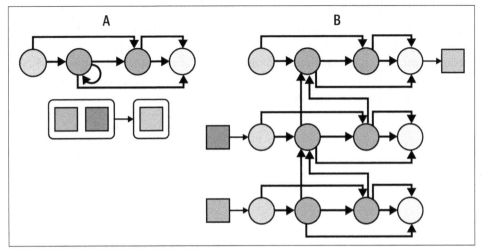

Figure 9-15. We can run an RNN through time to express it as a feed-forward network that we can train using backpropagation

We can also now train the RNN by computing the gradient based on the unrolled version. This means that all of the backpropagation techniques that we used for feed-forward networks also apply to training RNNs. We do run into one issue, however. After every batch of training examples we use, we need to modify the weights based on the error derivatives we calculate. In our unrolled network, we have sets of connections that all correspond to the same connection in the original RNN. The error derivatives calculated for these unrolled connections, however, are not guaranteed to be (and, in practice, probably won't be) equal. We can circumvent this issue by averaging or summing the error derivatives over all the connections that belong to the same set. This allows us to utilize an error derivative that considers all of the dynamics acting on the weight of a connection as we attempt to force the network to construct an accurate output.

The Challenges with Vanishing Gradients

Our motivation for using a stateful network model hinges on this idea of capturing long-term dependencies in the input sequence. It seems reasonable that an RNN with a large memory bank (i.e., a significantly sized recurrent layer) would be able to summarize these dependencies. In fact, from a theoretical perspective, Kilian and Siegelmann demonstrated in 1996 that the RNN is a universal functional representation.[4] In other words, with enough neurons and the right parameter settings, an RNN can be used to represent any functional mapping between input and output sequences.

The theory is promising, but it doesn't necessarily translate to practice. While it is nice to know that it is *possible* for an RNN to represent any arbitrary function, it is more useful to know whether it is *practical* to teach the RNN a realistic functional mapping from scratch by applying gradient descent algorithms. If it turns out to be impractical, we'll be in hot water, so it will be useful for us to be rigorous in exploring this question. Let's start our investigation by considering the simplest possible RNN, shown in Figure 9-16, with a single input neuron, a single output neuron, and a fully connected recurrent layer with one neuron.

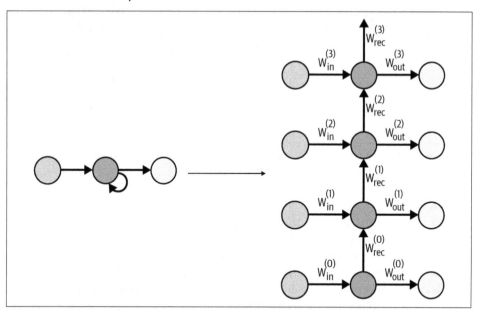

Figure 9-16. A single neuron, fully connected recurrent layer (both compressed and unrolled) for the sake of investigating gradient-based learning algorithms

---

4 Kilian, Joe, and Hava T. Siegelmann. "The dynamic universality of sigmoidal neural networks." *Information and computation* 128.1 (1996): 48-56.

Let's start off simple. Given nonlinearity f, we can express the activation $h^{(t)}$ of the hidden neuron of the recurrent layer at time step t as follows, where $i^{(t)}$ is the incoming logit from the input neuron at time step t:

$$h^{(t)} = f\left(w_{in}^{(t)}i^{(t)} + w_{rec}^{(t-1)}h^{(t-1)}\right)$$

Let's try to compute how the activation of the hidden neuron changes in response to changes to the input logit from k time steps in the past. In analyzing this component of the backpropagation gradient expressions, we can start to quantify how much "memory" is retained from past inputs. We start by taking the partial derivative and apply the chain rule:

$$\frac{\partial h^{(t)}}{\partial i^{(t-k)}} = f'\left(w_{in}^{(t)}i^{(t)} + w_{rec}^{(t-1)}h^{(t-1)}\right)\frac{\partial}{\partial i^{(t-k)}}\left(w_{in}^{(t)}i^{(t)} + w_{rec}^{(t-1)}h^{(t-1)}\right)$$

Because the values of the input and recurrent weights are independent of the input logit at time step $t - k$, we can further simplify this expression:

$$\frac{\partial h^{(t)}}{\partial i^{(t-k)}} = f'\left(w_{in}^{(t)}i^{(t)} + w_{rec}^{(t-1)}h^{(t-1)}\right)w_{rec}^{(t-1)}\frac{\partial h^{(t-1)}}{\partial i^{(t-k)}}$$

Because we care about the magnitude of this derivative, we can take the absolute value of both sides. We also know that for all common nonlinearities (the tanh, logistic, and ReLU nonlinearities), the maximum value of $|f'|$ is at most 1. This leads to the following recursive inequality:

$$\left|\frac{\partial h^{(t)}}{\partial i^{(t-k)}}\right| \leq \left|w_{rec}^{(t-1)}\right| \cdot \left|\frac{\partial h^{(t-1)}}{\partial i^{(t-k)}}\right|$$

We can continue to expand this inequality recursively until we reach the base case, at step $t - k$:

$$\left|\frac{\partial h^{(t)}}{\partial i^{(t-k)}}\right| \leq \left|w_{rec}^{(t-1)}\right| \cdot \dots \cdot \left|w_{rec}^{(t-k)}\right| \cdot \left|\frac{\partial h^{(t-k)}}{\partial i^{(t-k)}}\right|$$

We can evaluate this partial derivative similarly to how we proceeded previously:

$$h^{(t-k)} = f\left(w_{in}^{(t-k)}i^{(t-k)} + w_{rec}^{(t-k-1)}h^{(t-k-1)}\right)$$

$$\frac{\partial h^{(t-k)}}{\partial i^{(t-k)}} = f'\left(w_{in}^{(t-k)}i^{(t-k)} + w_{rec}^{(t-k-1)}h^{(t-k-1)}\right)\frac{\partial}{\partial i^{(t-k)}}\left(w_{in}^{(t-k)}i^{(t-k)}\right.$$
$$\left. + w_{rec}^{(t-k-1)}h^{(t-k-1)}\right)$$

In this expression, the hidden activation at time $t - k - 1$ is independent of the value of the input at $t - k$. Thus we can rewrite this expression as:

$$\frac{\partial h^{(t-k)}}{\partial i^{(t-k)}} = f'\left(w_{in}^{(t-k)}i^{(t-k)} + w_{rec}^{(t-k-1)}h^{(t-k-1)}\right)w_{in}^{(t-k)}$$

Finally, taking the absolute value on both sides and again applying the observation about the maximum value of $|f'|$, we can write:

$$\left|\frac{\partial h^{(t-k)}}{\partial i^{(t-k)}}\right| \leq \left|w_{in}^{(t-k)}\right|$$

This results in the final inequality (which we can simplify because we constrain the connections at different time steps to have equal value):

$$\left|\frac{\partial h^{(t)}}{\partial i^{(t-k)}}\right| \leq \left|w_{rec}^{(t-1)}\right| \cdot ... \cdot \left|w_{rec}^{(t-k)}\right| \cdot \left|w_{in}^{(t-k)}\right| = \left|w_{rec}\right|^k \cdot w_{in}$$

This relationship places a strong upper bound on how much a change in the input at time $t - k$ can impact the hidden state at time t. Because the weights of our model are initialized to small values at the beginning of training, the value of this derivative approaches zero as k increases. In other words, the gradient quickly diminishes when it's computed with respect to inputs several time steps into the past, severely limiting our model's ability to learn long-term dependencies. This issue is commonly referred to as the problem of *vanishing gradients*, and it severely impacts the learning capabilities of vanilla RNNs. In order to address this limitation, we will spend the next section exploring an extraordinarily influential twist on recurrent layers known as long short-term memory.

Long Short-Term Memory Units

To combat the problem of vanishing gradients, Sepp Hochreiter and Jürgen Schmidhuber introduced the *long short-term memory* (LSTM) architecture. The basic principle behind the architecture was that the network would be designed for the purpose of reliably transmitting important information many time steps into the future. The design considerations resulted in the architecture shown in Figure 9-17.

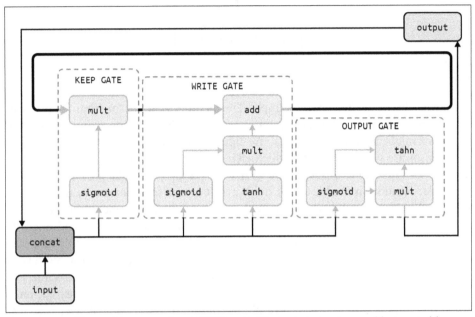

Figure 9-17. The architecture of an LSTM unit, illustrated at a tensor (designated by arrows) and operation (designated by the inner blocks) level

For the purposes of this discussion, we'll take a step back from the individual neuron level and start talking about the network as collection tensors and operations on tensors. As the figure indicates, the LSTM unit is composed of several key components. One of the core components of the LSTM architecture is the *memory cell*, a tensor represented by the bolded loop in the center of the figure. The memory cell holds critical information that it has learned over time, and the network is designed to effectively maintain useful information in the memory cell over many time steps. At every time step, the LSTM unit modifies the memory cell with new information with three different phases. First, the unit must determine how much of the previous memory to keep. This is determined by the *keep gate*, shown in detail in Figure 9-18.

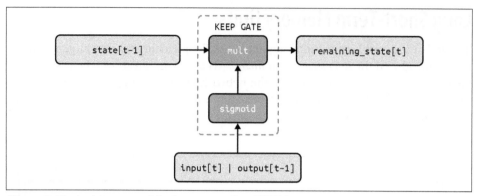

Figure 9-18. Architecture of the keep gate of an LSTM unit

The basic idea of the keep gate is simple. The memory state tensor from the previous time step is rich with information, but some of that information may be stale (and therefore might need to be erased). We figure out which elements in the memory state tensor are still relevant and which elements are irrelevant by trying to compute a bit tensor (a tensor of zeros and ones) that we multiply with the previous state. If a particular location in the bit tensor holds a 1, it means that location in the memory cell is still relevant and ought to be kept. If that particular location instead holds a 0, it means that the location in the memory cell is no longer relevant and ought to be eased. We approximate this bit tensor by concatenating the input of this time step and the LSTM unit's output from the previous time step and applying a sigmoid layer to the resulting tensor. A sigmoidal neuron, as you may recall, outputs a value that is either very close to 0 or very close to 1 most of the time (the only exception is when the input is close to 0). As a result, the output of the sigmoidal layer is a close approximation of a bit tensor, and we can use this to complete the keep gate.

Once we've figured out what information to keep in the old state and what to erase, we're ready to think about what information we'd like to write into the memory state. This part of the LSTM unit is known as the *write gate*, and it's depicted in Figure 9-19. This is broken down into two major parts. The first component is figuring out what information we'd like to write into the state. This is computed by the tanh layer to create an intermediate tensor. The second component is figuring out which components of this computed tensor we actually want to include into the new state and which we want to toss before writing. We do this by approximating a bit vector of 0's and 1's using the same strategy (a sigmoidal layer) as we used in the keep gate. We multiply the bit vector with our intermediate tensor and then add the result to create the new state vector for the LSTM.

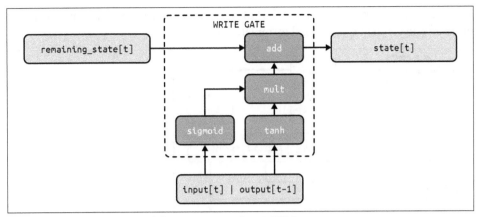

Figure 9-19. Architecture of the write gate of an LSTM unit

At every time step, we'd like the LSTM unit to provide an output. While we could treat the state vector as the output directly, the LSTM unit is engineered to provide more flexibility by emitting an output tensor that is an "interpretation" or external "communication" of what the state vector represents. The architecture of the output gate is shown in Figure 9-20. We use a nearly identical structure as the write gate: (1) the tanh layer creates an intermediate tensor from the state vector, (2) the sigmoid layer produces a bit tensor mask using the current input and previous output, and (3) the intermediate tensor is multiplied with the bit tensor to produce the final output.

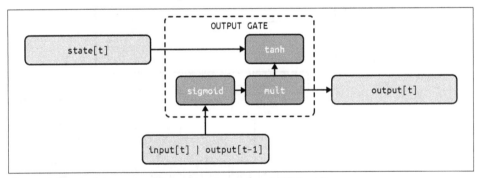

Figure 9-20. Architecture of the output gate of an LSTM unit

So why is this better than using a raw RNN unit? The key observation is how information propagates through the network when we unroll the LSTM unit through time. The unrolled architecture is shown in Figure 9-21. At the top, we can observed the propagation of the state vector, whose interactions are primarily linear through time. The result is that the gradient that relates an input several time steps in the past to the current output does not attenuate as dramatically as in the vanilla RNN architecture. This means that the LSTM can learn long-term relationships much more effectively than our original formulation of the RNN.

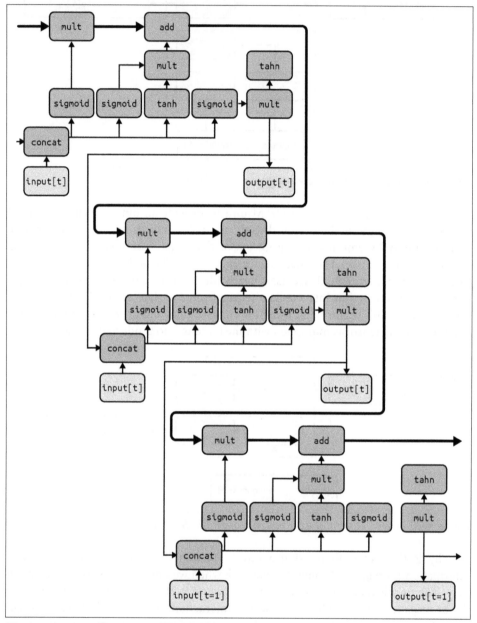

Figure 9-21. Unrolling an LSTM unit through time

Finally, we want to understand how easy it is to generate arbitrary architectures with LSTM units. How "composable" are LSTMs? Do we need to sacrifice flexibility to use LSTM units instead of a vanilla RNN? Just as we can we can stack RNN layers to create more expressive models with more capacity, we can stack LSTM units, where the input of the second unit is the output of the first unit, the input of the third unit is the output of the second, and so on. Figure 9-22 shows how this works with a multicellular architecture made of two LSTM units. This means that anywhere we use a vanilla RNN layer, we can easily substitute an LSTM unit.

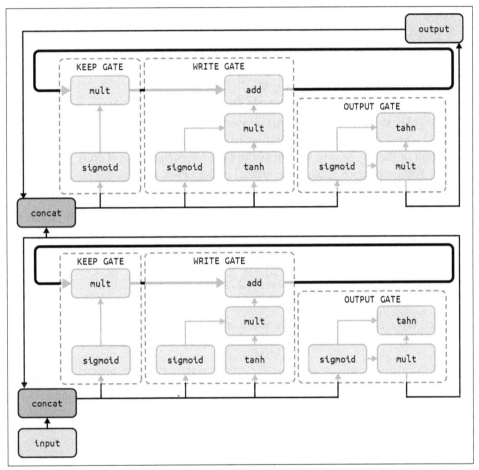

Figure 9-22. Composing LSTM units as one might stack recurrent layers in a neural network

Now that we have overcome the issue of vanishing gradients and understand the inner workings of LSTM units, we're ready to dive into the implementation of our first RNN models.

PyTorch Primitives for RNN Models

PyTorch provides seceral primitives that we can use out of the box in order to build RNN models. First, we have torch.nn.RNNCell objects that represent either an RNN layer or an LSTM unit:

```
import torch.nn as nn

cell_1 = nn.RNNCell(input_size = 10,
                    hidden_size = 20,
                    nonlinearity='tanh')

cell_2 = nn.LSTMCell(input_size = 10,
                     hidden_size = 20)

cell_3 = nn.GRUCell(input_size = 10,
                    hidden_size = 20)
```

The RNNCell abstraction represents a vanilla recurrent neuron layer, while the LSTMCell represents an implementation of the LSTM unit. PyTorch also includes a variation of the LSTM unit known as the *Gated Recurrent Unit* (GRU), proposed in 2014 by Yoshua Bengio's group. The critical initialization variable for all of these cells is the size of the hidden state vector or hidden_size.

In addition to the primitives, PyTorch provides multilayer RNN and LSTM classes for stacking layers. If we want to stack recurrent units or layers, we can use the following:

```
multi_layer_rnn = nn.RNN(input_size = 10,
                         hidden_size = 20,
                         num_layers = 2,
                         nonlinearity = 'tanh')

multi_layer_lstm = nn.LSTM(input_size = 10,
                           hidden_size = 20,
                           num_layers = 2)
```

We can also use the dropout parameter to apply dropout to the inputs and outputs of an LSTM with specified keep probability. If the dropout parameter is nonzero, the model introduces a dropout layer on the outputs of each LSTM layer except the last layer, with dropout probability equal to dropout:

```
multi_layer_rnn = nn.RNN(input_size = 10,
                         hidden_size = 20,
                         num_layers = 2,
                         nonlinearity = 'tanh',
                         batch_first = False,
                         dropout = 0.5)

multi_layer_lstm = nn.LSTM(input_size = 10,
                           hidden_size = 20,
                           num_layers = 2,
```

```
                    batch_first = False,
                    dropout = 0.5)
```

As shown here, the multilayer RNN and LSTM classes also provide a `batch_first` parameter. If `batch_first` equals `True`, then the input and output tensors are provided as (`batch`, `seq`, `feature`) instead of (`seq`, `batch`, `feature`). Note that this does not apply to hidden or cell states. The default value of `batch_first` is `False`. See the PyTorch documentation for details.

Finally, we instantiate an RNN by calling the PyTorch LSTM constructor:

```
input = torch.randn(5, 3, 10) # (time_steps, batch, input_size)
h_0 = torch.randn(2, 3, 20) # (n_layers, batch_size, hidden_size)
c_0 = torch.randn(2, 3, 20) # (n_layers, batch_size, hidden_size)

rnn = nn.LSTM(10, 20, 2) # (input_size, hidden_size, num_layers)
output_n, (hn, cn) = rnn(input, (h_0, c_0))
```

The result of calling `rnn` is a tensor representing the outputs of the RNN, `output_n`, along with the final state vectors for each layer. The first tensor, `hn`, contains the hidden state vectors for each layer that holds the outputs of the Output Gates at time, n. The second tensor, `cn`, contains the state vectors for the memory cells of each layer, which is the output of the write gates. Both `hn` and `cn` are of size (`n_layers`, `batch_size`, `hidden_size`).

Now that we have an understanding of the tools at our disposal in constructing RNNs in PyTorch, we'll build our first LSTM in the next section, focused on the task of sentiment analysis.

Implementing a Sentiment Analysis Model

In this section, we attempt to analyze the sentiment of movie reviews taken from the Large Movie Review Dataset. This dataset consists of 50,000 reviews from IMDb, each of which is labeled as having positive or negative sentiment. We use a simple LSTM model leveraging dropout to learn how to classify the sentiment of movie reviews. The LSTM model will consume the movie review one word at a time. Once it has consumed the entire review, we'll use its output as the basis of a binary classification to map the sentiment to be "positive" or "negative."

Let's start off by loading the dataset with the PyTorch library Torchtext, which comes preinstalled with Google Colab. If you're running on another machine, you can install Torchtext by running the following command:

```
$ pip install torchtext
```

Once we've installed the package, we can download the dataset and define a tokenizer. Torchtext provides many natural language processing (NLP) datasets and tokenizers through the `torchtext.datasets` and `torchtext.data.utils` submodules, respectively. We'll use the built-in IMDb dataset and standard `'basic_english'` tokenizer provided by PyTorch.

```
from torchtext.datasets import IMDB
from torchtext.data.utils import get_tokenizer

# Load dataset
train_iter = IMDB(split=('train'))

# Define tokenizer and build vocabulary
tokenizer = get_tokenizer('basic_english')
```

Until now, we've been using map-style datasets from PyTorch. Torchtext returns NLP datasets as iterable-style datasets, which are more appropriate for streaming data. Next, we need to create a vocabulary based on the training dataset and prune the vocabulary to include only the 30,000 most common words. Then, we need to pad each input sequence up to a length of 500 words, and process the labels.

```
from torchtext.vocab import build_vocab_from_iterator

def yield_tokens(data_iter):
    for _, text in data_iter:
        yield tokenizer(text)

# build vocab from iterator and add a list of any special tokens
text_vocab = build_vocab_from_iterator(yield_tokens(train_iter),
                                       specials=['<unk>', '<pad>'])
text_vocab.set_default_index(text_vocab['<unk>'])
```

As shown, Torchtext provides a function, `build_vocab_from_iterator`, to create a vocabulary. However, this function expects a list of tokens as input, where `next(train_iter)`would return a tuple (`label_string`, `review_string`). To satisfy this requirement, we define a function to yield tokens as the dataset is iterated. Finally, we add special tokens for unknown and padding, and set the default.

Next, we need to actually prune the vocabulary and pad the review sequences, as well as convert the label strings, `'neg'` or `'pos'`, to numbers. We accomplish this by defining a pipeline function for both the labels and review strings:

```
def text_pipeline(x, max_size=512):
    text = tokenizer(x)

    # reduce vocab size
    pruned_text = []
    for token in text:
      if text_vocab.get_stoi()[token] >= 30000:
        token = '<unk>'
      pruned_text.append(token)

    # pad sequence or truncate
    if len(pruned_text) <= max_size:
```

```
      pruned_text += ['<pad>'] * (max_size - len(pruned_text))
    else:
      pruned_text = pruned_text[0:max_size]
    return text_vocab(pruned_text)

  label_pipeline = lambda x: (0 if (x == 'neg') else 1)
```

The `text_pipeline` function converts the inputs to 500-dimensional vectors. Each vector corresponds to a movie review where the ith component of the vector corresponds to the index of the ith word of the review in our global dictionary of 30,000 words. To complete the data preparation, we create a special Python class designed to serve minibatches of a desired size from the underlying dataset.

We can use the built-in `DataLoader` class from PyTorch to sample the dataset in batches. Before we do so, we need to define a function, `collate_batch`, that will tell the `DataLoader` how to preprocess each batch:

```
def collate_batch(batch):
  label_list, text_list = [], []
  for label, review in batch:
    label_list.append(label_pipeline(label))
    text_list.append(text_pipeline(review))
  return (torch.tensor(label_list, dtype=torch.long),
          torch.tensor(text_list, dtype=torch.int32))
```

The `collate_batch` function simply runs the labels and review strings through each respective pipeline and returns the batch as a tuple of tensors (`labels_batch`, `reviews_batch`). Once the `collate_fn` is defined, we simply load the dataset using the IMDb constructor, and configure the dataloaders using the `DataLoader` constructor:

```
from torch.utils.data import DataLoader

train_iter, val_iter = IMDB(split=('train','test'))
trainloader = DataLoader(train_iter,
                         batch_size = 4,
                         shuffle=False,
                         collate_fn=collate_batch)
valloader = DataLoader(val_iter,
                       batch_size = 4,
                       shuffle=False,
                       collate_fn=collate_batch)
```

We use the `torchtext.datasets.IMDB` Python class to serve both the training and validation sets we'll use while training our sentiment analysis model.

Now that the data is ready to go, we'll begin to construct the sentiment analysis model, step by step. First, we'll want to map each word in the input review to a word vector. To do this, we'll utilize an embedding layer, which, as you may recall from

Chapter 8, is a simple lookup table that stores an embedding vector that corresponds to each word.

Unlike in previous examples, where we treated the learning of the word embeddings as a separate problem (i.e., by building a Skip-Gram model), we'll learn the word embeddings jointly with the sentiment analysis problem by treating the embedding matrix as a matrix of parameters in the full problem. We accomplish this by using the PyTorch primitives for managing embeddings (remember that input represents one full minibatch at a time, not just one movie review vector):

```
import torch.nn as nn

embedding = nn.Embedding(
                    num_embeddings=30000,
                    embedding_dim=512,
                    padding_idx=text_vocab.get_stoi()['<pad>'])
```

We then take the result of the embedding layer and build an LSTM with dropout using the primitives we saw in the previous section. The implementation of the LSTM can be achieved as follows:

```
class TextClassifier(nn.Module):
  def __init__(self):
    super(TextClassifier,self).__init__()
    self.layer_1 = nn.Embedding(
                    num_embeddings=30000,
                    embedding_dim=512,
                    padding_idx=1)
    self.layer_2 = nn.LSTMCell(input_size=512, hidden_size=512)
    self.layer_3 = nn.Dropout(p=0.5)
    self.layer_4 = nn.Sequential(
                    nn.Linear(512, 2),
                    nn.Sigmoid(),
                    nn.BatchNorm1d(2))

  def forward(self, x):
    x = self.layer_1(x)
    x = x.permute(1,0,2)
    h = torch.rand(x.shape[1], 512)
    c = torch.rand(x.shape[1], 512)
    for t in range(x.shape[0]):
      h, c = self.layer_2(x[t], (h,c))
      h = self.layer_3(h)
    return self.layer_4(h)
```

We top it all off using a batch-normalized hidden layer, identical to the ones we've used time and time again in previous examples. Stringing all of these components together, we can build the model by calling TextClassifier:

```
model = TextClassifier()
```

We omit the other boilerplate involved in setting up summary statistics, saving intermediate snapshots, and creating the session because it's identical to the other models we've built in this book (see the GitHub repository (*https://github.com/dark sigma/Fundamentals-of-Deep-Learning-Book*)). We can then run and visualize the performance of our model using TensorBoard (Figure 9-23).

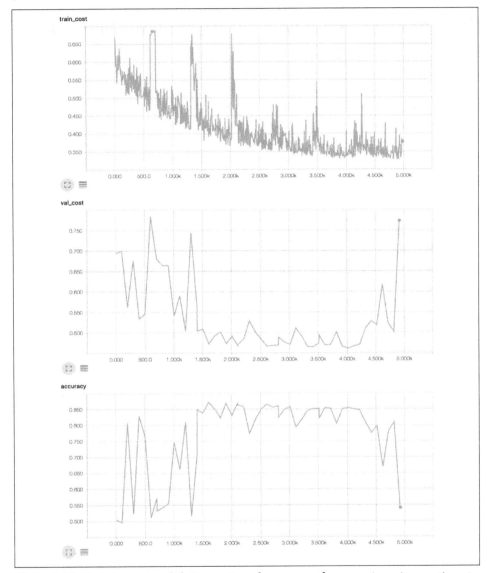

Figure 9-23. Training cost, validation cost, and accuracy of our movie review sentiment model

At the beginning of training, the model struggles slightly with stability, and toward the end of the training, the model clearly starts to overfit as training cost and validation cost significantly diverge. At its optimal performance, however, the model performs rather effectively and generalizes to approximately 86% accuracy on the test set. Congratulations! You've built your first RNN.

Solving seq2seq Tasks with Recurrent Neural Networks

Now that we've built a strong understanding of RNNs, we're ready to revisit the problem of seq2seq. We started off this chapter with an example of a seq2seq task: mapping a sequence of words in a sentence to a sequence of POS tags. Tackling this problem was tractable because we didn't need to take into account long-term dependencies to generate the appropriate tags. But there are several seq2seq problems, such as translating between languages or creating a summary for a video, where long-term dependencies are crucial to the success of the model. This is where RNNs come in.

The RNN approach to seq2seq looks a lot like the autoencoder we discussed in the previous chapter. The seq2seq model is composed of two separate networks. The first network is known as the *encoder* network. The encoder network is a recurrent network (usually one that uses LSTM units) that consumes the entire input sequence. The goal of the encoder network is to generate a condensed understanding of the input and summarize it into a singular thought represented by the final state of the encoder network. Then we use a *decoder* network, whose starting state is initialized with the final state of the encoder network, to produce the target output sequence token by token. At each step, the decoder network consumes its own output from the previous time step as the current time step's input. The entire process is visualized in Figure 9-24.

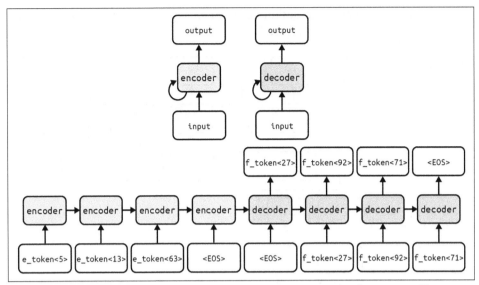

Figure 9-24. How we use an encoder/decoder recurrent network schema to tackle seq2seq problems

In this this setup, we are attempting to translate an English sentence into French. We tokenize the input sentence and use an embedding (similar to our approach in the sentiment analysis model we built in the previous section), one word at a time as an input to the encoder network. At the end of the sentence, we use a special "end-of-sequence" (EOS) token to indicate the end of the input sequence to the encoder network. Then we take the hidden state of the encoder network and use that as the initialization of the decoder network. The first input to the decoder network is the EOS token, and the output is interpreted as the first word of the predicted French translation. From that point onward, we use the output of the decoder network as the input to itself at the next time step. We continue until the decoder network emits an EOS token as its output, at which point we know that the network has completed producing the translation of the original English sentence. We'll dissect the practical, open source implementation of this network (with a couple of enhancements and tricks to improve accuracy) later in this chapter.

The seq2seq RNN architecture can also be reappropriated for the purpose of learning good embeddings of sequences. For example, Kiros et al. in 2015 invented the notion of a *skip-thought vector*,[5] which borrowed architectural characteristics from both the autoencoder framework and the Skip-Gram model discussed in Chapter 8. The skip-thought vector was generated by dividing a passage into a set of triplets consisting

---

5 Kiros, Ryan, et al. "Skip-Thought Vectors." *Advances in neural information processing systems*. 2015.

of consecutive sentences. The authors utilized a single encoder network and two decoder networks, as shown in Figure 9-25.

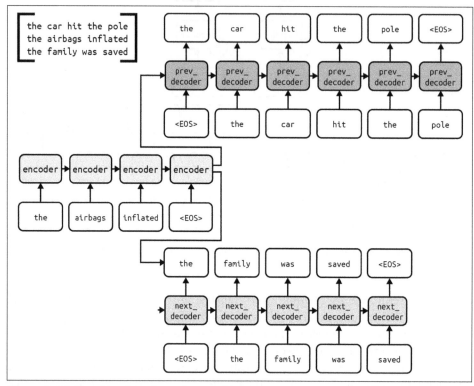

Figure 9-25. The skip-thought seq2seq architecture to generate embedding representations of entire sentences

The encoder network consumed the sentence for which we wanted to generate a condensed representation (which was stored in the final hidden state of the encoder network). Then came the decoding step. The first of the decoder networks would take that representation as the initialization of its own hidden state and attempt to reconstruct the sentence that appeared prior to the input sentence. The second decoder network would instead attempt the sentence that appeared immediately after the input sentence. The full system was trained end to end on these triplets, and once completed, could be used to generate seemingly cohesive passages of text in addition to improve performance on key sentence-level classification tasks.

Here's an example of story generation, excerpted from the original paper:

```
she grabbed my hand .
"come on . "
she fluttered her back in the air .
"i think we're at your place . I ca n't come get you . "
he locked himself back up
" no . she will . "
kyrian shook his head
```

Now that we've developed an understanding of how to leverage RNNs to tackle seq2seq problems, we're almost ready to try to build our own. Before we get there, however, we've got one more major challenge to tackle, and we'll address it head-on in the next section when we discuss the concept of attentions in seq2seq RNNs.

Augmenting Recurrent Networks with Attention

Let's think harder about the translation problem. If you've ever attempted to learn a foreign language, you'll know that there are several helpful steps when trying to complete a translation. First, it's helpful to read the full sentence to understand the concept you would like to convey. Then you write out the translation one word at a time, each word following logically from the word you wrote previously. But one important aspect of translation is that as you compose the new sentence, you often refer back to the original text, focusing on specific parts that are relevant to your current translation. At each step, you are paying attention to the most relevant parts of the original "input" so you can make the best decision about the next word to put on the page.

Recall our approach to seq2seq. By consuming the full input and summarizing it into a "thought" inside its hidden state, the encoder network effectively achieves the first part of the translation process. By using the previous output as its current input, the decoder network achieves the second part of the translation process. This phenomenon of *attention* has yet to be captured by our approach to seq2seq, and this is the final building block we'll need to engineer.

Currently, the sole input to the decoder network at a given time step t is its output at time step $t - 1$. One way to give the decoder network some vision into the original sentence is by giving the decoder access to all of the outputs from the encoder network (which we previously had completely ignored). These outputs are interesting to us because they represent how the encoder network's internal state evolves after seeing each new token. A proposed implementation of this strategy is shown in Figure 9-26. This attempt falls short because it fails to dynamically select the most relevant parts of the input to focus on.

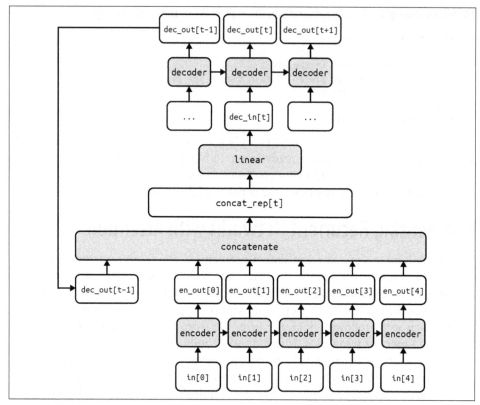

Figure 9-26. An attempt at engineering attentional abilities in a seq2seq architecture

This approach has a critical flaw, however. The problem here is that at every time step, the decoder considers all of the outputs of the encoder network in the exact same way. However, this is clearly not the case for a human during the translation process. We focus on different aspects of the original text when working on different parts of the translation. The key realization here is that it's not enough to merely give the decoder access to all the outputs. Instead, we must engineer a mechanism by which the decoder network can dynamically pay attention to a specific subset of the encoder's outputs.

We can fix this problem by changing the inputs to the concatenation operation, using the proposal in Bahdanau et al. 2015 as inspiration.[6] Instead of directly using the raw outputs from the encoder network, we perform a weighting operation on the encoder's outputs. We leverage the decoder network's state at time $t - 1$ as the basis for the weighting operation.

---

6 Bahdanau, Dzmitry, Kyunghyun Cho, and Yoshua Bengio. "Neural Machine Translation by Jointly Learning to Align and Translate." *arXiv preprint arXiv*:1409.0473 (2014).

The weighting operation is illustrated in Figure 9-27. First we create a scalar (a single number, not a tensor) relevance score for each of the encoder's outputs. The score is generated by computing the dot product between each encoder output and the decoder's state at time $t - 1$. We then normalize these scores using a softmax operation. Finally, we use these normalized scores to individually scale the encoder's outputs before plugging them into the concatenation operation. The key here is that the relative scores computed for each encoder output signify how important that particular encoder output is to the decision for the decoder at time step t. In fact, as we'll see later, we can visualize which parts of the input are most relevant to the translation at each time step by inspecting the output of the softmax.

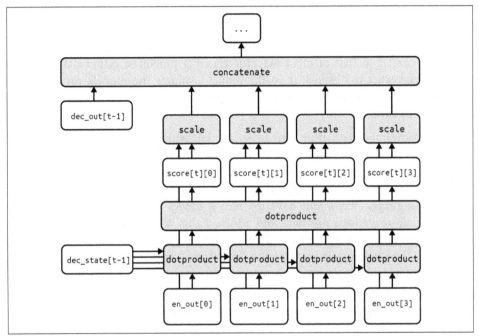

Figure 9-27. A modification to our original proposal that enables a dynamic attentional mechanism based on the hidden state of the decoder network in the previous time step

Armed with this strategy for engineering attention into seq2seq architectures, we're finally ready to get our hands dirty with an RNN model for translating English sentences into French. But before we jump in, it's worth noting that attentions are incredibly applicable in problems that extend beyond language translation. Attentions can be important in speech-to-text problems, where the algorithm learns to dynamically pay attention to corresponding parts of the audio while transcribing the audio into text. Similarly, attentions can be used to improve image captioning algorithms by helping the captioning algorithm focus on specific parts of the input image while writing out the caption. Anytime particular parts of the input are highly correlated to correctly producing corresponding segments of the output, attentions can dramatically improve performance.

Dissecting a Neural Translation Network

State-of-the-art neural translation networks use a number of different techniques and advancements that build on the basic seq2seq encoder-decoder architecture. Attention, as detailed in the previous section, is an important and critical architectural improvement. In this section, we will dissect a fully implemented neural machine translation system, complete with the data processing steps, building the model, training it, and eventually using it as a translation system to convert English phrases to French phrases.

The pipeline used in training and eventually using a neural machine translation system is similar to that of most machine learning pipelines: gather data, prepare the data, construct the model, train the model, evaluate the model's progress, and eventually use the trained model to predict or infer something useful. We review each of these steps here.

We first gather the data from the International Workshop on Spoken Language Translation (IWSLT2016) repository (*https://wit3.fbk.eu/2016-01*), which houses large corpora used in training translation systems. For our use case, we'll be using the English-to-French data. Note that if we want to be able to translate to or from different languages, we would have to train a model from scratch with the new data. We then preprocess our data into a format that is easily usable by our models during training and inference time. This will involve some amount of cleaning and tokenizing the sentences in each of the English and French phrases. What follows now is a set of techniques used in preparing the data, and later we will present the implementations of the techniques.

The first step is to parse sentences and phrases into formats that are more compatible with the model by *tokenization*. This is the process by which we discretize a particular English or French sentence into its constituent tokens. For instance, a simple word-level tokenizer will consume the sentence "I read." to produce the array ["I", "read", "."], or it would consume the French sentence "Je lis." to produce the array ["Je", "lis", "."].

A character-level tokenizer may break the sentence into individual characters or into pairs of characters like ["I", " ", "r", "e", "a", "d", "."] and ["I ", "re", "ad", "."], respectively. One kind of tokenization may work better than the other, and each has its pros and cons. For instance, a word-level tokenizer will ensure that the model produces words that are from some dictionary, but the size of the dictionary may be too large to efficiently choose from during decoding. This is in fact a known issue and something that we'll address in the coming discussions.

On the other hand, the decoder using a character-level tokenization may not produce intelligible outputs, but the total dictionary that the decoder must choose from is much smaller, as it is simply the set of all printable ASCII characters. In this tutorial, we use a word-level tokenization, but we encourage you to experiment with different tokenizations to observe the effects this has. It is worth noting that we must also add a special EOS character, to the end of all output sequences because we need to provide a definitive way for the decoder to indicate that it has reached the end of its decoding. We can't use regular punctuation because we cannot assume that we are translating full sentences. Note that we do not need EOS characters in our source sequences because we are feeding these in preformatted and do not need an EOS character for ourselves to denote the end of our source sequence.

The next optimization involves further modifying how we represent each source and target sequence, and we introduce a concept called *bucketing*. This is a method employed primarily in sequence-to-sequence tasks, especially machine translation, that helps the model efficiently handle sentences or phrases of different lengths. We first describe the naive method of feeding in training data and illustrate the shortcomings of this approach. Normally, when feeding in encoder and decoder tokens, the length of the source sequence and the target sequence is not always equal between pairs of examples. For example, the source sequence may have length X, and the target sequence may have length Y. It may seem that we need different seq2seq networks to accommodate each (X, Y) pair, yet this immediately seems wasteful and inefficient. Instead, we can do a little better if we *pad* each sequence up to a certain length, as shown in Figure 9-28, assuming we use a word-level tokenization and that we've appended EOS tokens to our target sequences.

I	read	.	<PAD>	<PAD>	<PAD>	<PAD>
Je	lis	.	<EOS>	<PAD>	<PAD>	<PAD>
See	you	in	a	little	while	.
A	tout	a	l'heure	<EOS>	<PAD>	<PAD>
			. . .			

Figure 9-28. Naive strategy for padding sequences

This step saves us the trouble of having to construct a different seq2seq model for each pair of source and target lengths. However, this introduces a different issue: if there were a very long sequence, it would mean that we would have to pad every other sequence *up to that length*. This would make a short sequence padded to the end take as much computational resources as a long one with few pad tokens, which is wasteful and could introduce a major performance hit to our model. We could consider breaking up every sentence in the corpus into phrases such that the length of each phrase does not exceed a certain maximum limit, but it's not clear how to break the corresponding translations. This is where bucketing helps us.

Bucketing is the idea that we can place encoder and decoder pairs into buckets of similar size, and only pad up to the maximum length of sequences in each respective bucket. For instance, we can denote a set of buckets, [(5, 10), (10, 15), (20, 25), (30, 40)], where each tuple in the list is the maximum length of the source sequence and target sequence, respectively. Borrowing the preceding example, we can place the pair of sequences (["I", "read", "."], ["Je", "lis", ".", "EOS"]) in the first bucket, as the source sequence is smaller than 5 tokens and the target sequence is smaller than 10 tokens. We would then place the (["See", "you", "in", "a", "little", "while"], ["A", "tout", "a", "l'heure", "EOS"]) in the second bucket, and so on. This technique allows us to compromise between the two extremes, where we need to pad only as much as necessary, as shown in Figure 9-29.

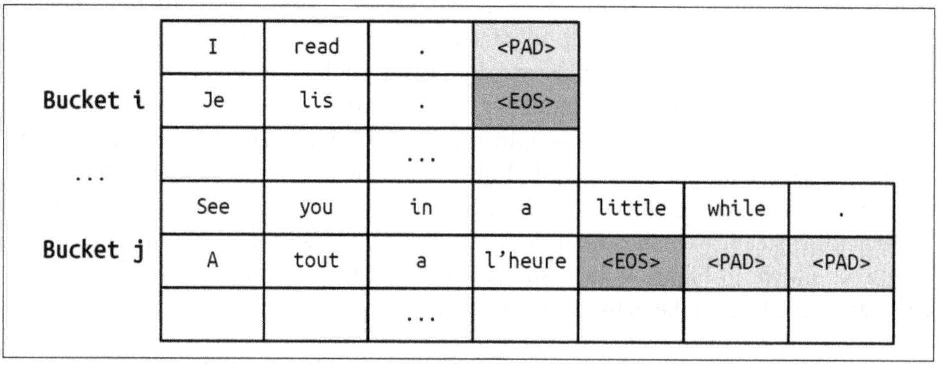

	I	read	.	<PAD>			
Bucket i	Je	lis	.	<EOS>			
...			...				
	See	you	in	a	little	while	.
Bucket j	A	tout	a	l'heure	<EOS>	<PAD>	<PAD>
			...				

Figure 9-29. Padding sequences with buckets

Using bucketing shows a considerable speedup during training and test time, and allows developers and frameworks to write very optimized code to leverage the fact that any sequence from a bucket will have the same size and pack the data together in ways that allow even further GPU efficiency.

With the sequences properly padded, we need to add one additional token to the target sequences: *a GO token*. This GO token will signal to the decoder that decoding needs to begin, at which point it will take over and begin decoding.

The last improvement we make in the data preparation side is to reverse the source sequences. Researchers found that doing so improved performance, and this has become a standard trick to try when training neural machine translation models. This is a bit of an engineering hack, but consider the fact that our fixed-size neural state can hold only so much information, and information encoded while processing the beginning of the sentence may be overwritten while encoding later parts of the sentence. In many language pairs, the beginning of sentences is harder to translate than the end of sentences, so this hack of reversing the sentence improves translation accuracy by giving the beginning of the sentence the last say on what final state is encoded. With these ideas in place, the final sequences look as they do in Figure 9-30.

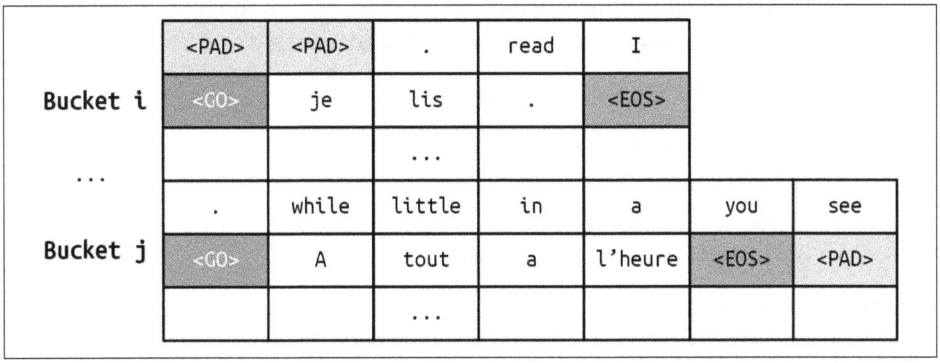

	\<PAD\>	\<PAD\>	.	read	I		
Bucket i	\<GO\>	je	lis	.	\<EOS\>		
			...				
...							
	.	while	little	in	a	you	see
Bucket j	\<GO\>	A	tout	a	l'heure	\<EOS\>	\<PAD\>
			...				

Figure 9-30. Final padding scheme with buckets, reversing the inputs, and adding the GO token

With these techniques described, we can now detail the implementation. First, we load the dataset, then we define our tokenizers and vocabularies. We do not define the word embeddings here, as we will train our model to compute them. PyTorch's Torchtext library supports IWSLT2016 in `torch.text.datasets`:

```
from torchtext.datasets import IWSLT2016

train_iter = IWSLT2016(split=('train'),
                       language_pair=('en','fr'))
```

The dataset constructor returns an iterable-style dataset that can retrieve English and French sentence pairs with `next(train_iter)`. We'll use this iterable-style dataset to create bucketed datasets for batching later in our code.

For now, let's also define our tokenizers and vocabularies for each language. PyTorch offers a `get_tokenizer` function that operates on common tokenizers. Here, we'll use the `spacy` tokenizer for each language. You may need to download the `spacy` language files first:

```
pip install -U spacy
python -m spacy download en_core_web_sm
python -m spacy download fr_core_news_sm
```

Once we have the language files, we can create the tokenizers as follows:

```
from torchtext.data.utils import get_tokenizer

tokenizer_en = get_tokenizer('spacy',language='en_core_web_sm')
tokenizer_fr = get_tokenizer('spacy',language='fr_core_news_sm')
```

Next, we will create our vocabularies for English and French using PyTorch's build_vocab_from_iterator function. This function takes tokens from an iterable-style dataset from a single language and creates a vocabulary. Since our dataset has both English and French sentences, we create a yield_tokens function to return only the English or French tokens, and pass this into build_vocab_from_iterator:

```python
def yield_tokens(data_iter, language):
    if language == 'en':
        for data_sample in data_iter:
            yield tokenizer_en(data_sample[0])
    else:
        for data_sample in data_iter:
            yield tokenizer_fr(data_sample[1])

UNK_IDX, PAD_IDX, GO_IDX, EOS_IDX = 0, 1, 2, 3
special_symbols = ['<unk>', '<pad>', '<go>', '<eos>']

# Create Vocabs
train_iter = IWSLT2016(root='.data', split=('train'),
                        language_pair=('en', 'fr'))

vocab_en = build_vocab_from_iterator(
                yield_tokens(train_iter, 'en'),
                min_freq=1,
                specials=special_symbols,
                special_first=True)

train_iter = IWSLT2016(root='.data', split=('train'),
                        language_pair=('en', 'fr'))
vocab_fr = build_vocab_from_iterator(
                yield_tokens(train_iter, 'fr'),
                min_freq=1,
                specials=special_symbols,
                special_first=True)
```

Notice that we need to reload the train_iter before building the French vocabulary to restart the iterable-style dataset. We also add in the special tokens and their indices.

Now that we have the dataset, tokenizers, and vocabularies, we need to create functions to preprocess the tokens and generate batches of bucketed data. First let's define a process_tokens function to apply the improvements we discussed earlier:

```python
def process_tokens(source, target, bucket_sizes):
  # find bucket_index
  for i in range(len(bucket_sizes)+2):
    # truncate if we exhauset list of buckets
    if i >= len(bucket_sizes):
      bucket = bucket_sizes[i-1]
      bucket_id = i-1
      if len(source) > bucket[0]:
        source = source[:bucket[0]]
```

```
    if len(target) > (bucket[1]-2):
        target = target[:bucket[1]-2]
    break

  bucket = bucket_sizes[i]
  if (len(source) < bucket[0]) and ((len(target)+1) < bucket[1]):
    bucket_id = i
    break

source += ((bucket_sizes[bucket_id][0] - len(source)) * ['<pad>'])
source = list(reversed(source))

target.insert(0,'<go>')
target.append('<eos>')
target += (bucket_sizes[bucket_id][1] - len(target)) * ['<pad>']

return vocab_en(source), vocab_fr(target), bucket_id
```

In this function, we pass in the variable size lists of source and target tokens, plus a list of bucket sizes. First, we decide on the smallest bucket size that will fit both the source and target token lists. Then, we process the source tokens by padding and reversing the sequence as described earlier. For the target tokens, we add a <go> token to the beginning and add an <eos> token to the end, then pad to the bucket size. When determining the smallest bucket size, we accounted for the two added tokens <go> and <eos>.

Now we have a function that takes lists of source and target tokens and prepares them appropriately. Next, we need to collect a single batch of data for our model and training loop. To do this, we will use the built-in PyTorch `Dataset` and `DataLoader` classes.

We are going to separate `Dataset` and `DataLoader` for each bucket size. This approach will enable us to use the built-in feature of the `DataLoader` for random batching and parallel processing.

First we create a `BucketedDataset` class by subclassing PyTorch's `Dataset` class. Since this will be a map-style dataset, we'll need to define the __getitem__ and __len__ methods for data access:

```
from torch.utils.data import Dataset

class BucketedDataset(Dataset):
  def __init__(self, bucketed_dataset, bucket_size):
    super(BucketedDataset, self).__init__()
    self.length = len(bucketed_dataset)
    self.input_len = bucket_size[0]
    self.target_len = bucket_size[1]
    self.bucketed_dataset = bucketed_dataset

  def __getitem__(self, index):
```

```
          return (torch.tensor(self.bucketed_dataset[index][0],
                                dtype=torch.float32),
                  torch.tensor(self.bucketed_dataset[index][1],
                               dtype=torch.float32))

  def __len__(self):
    return self.length

bucketed_datasets = []
for i, dataset in enumerate(datasets):
  bucketed_datasets.append(BucketedDataset(dataset,
                                           bucket_sizes[i]))
```

We create a list of `BucketedDataset` objects in `bucketed_datasets`, one for each bucket size. The `BucketedDataset` constructor also converts our vocabulary integers to PyTorch tensors so we can pass them into our model later.

Next we use the PyTorch's `DataLoader` class to create dataloaders for each dataset in `bucketed_datasets`. Since we created `Dataset` objects, we get the batching capabilities of the `DataLoader` class without writing any additional code:

```
from torch.utils.data import DataLoader

dataloaders = []
for dataset in bucketed_datasets:
  dataloaders.append(DataLoader(dataset,
                                batch_size=32,
                                shuffle=True))
```

The dataloaders list hold a dataloader for each bucket size, so when we run our training or test loops, we will select a bucket size (randomly for training) and use the corresponding dataloader to pull a batch of encoders and decoder inputs:

```
for epoch in range(n_epochs):
  # exhaust all dataloaders randomly
  # keep track of when we used up all values
  dataloader_sizes = []
  for dataloader in dataloaders:
    dataloader_sizes.append(len(dataloader))

  while np.array(dataloader_sizes).sum() != 0:
    bucket_id = torch.randint(0,len(bucket_sizes),(1,1)).item()
    if dataloader_sizes[bucket_id] == 0:
      continue
    source, target = next(iter(dataloaders[bucket_id]))
    dataloader_sizes[bucket_id] -= 1
    loss = train(encoder_inputs,
                 decoder_inputs,
                 target_weights,
                 bucket_id)
```

We measure the loss incurred during prediction time, as well as keep track of other running metrics:

```
loss += step_loss / steps_per_checkpoint current_step += 1
```

Lastly, every so often, as dictated by a global variable, we will carry out a number of tasks. First, we print statistics for the previous batch, such as the loss, the learning rate, and the perplexity. If we find that the loss is not decreasing, the model may have fallen into a local optima. To assist the model in escaping this, we anneal the learning rate so that it won't make large leaps in any particular direction. At this point, we also save a copy of the model and its weights and activations to disk.

This concludes the high-level details of training and using the models. We have largely abstracted away the fine details of the model itself. For more, see the book's repository (*https://github.com/darksigma/Fundamentals-of-Deep-Learning-Book*).

With this, we've successfully completed a full tour of the implementation details of a fairly sophisticated neural machine translation system. Production systems have additional tricks that are not as generalizable, and these systems are trained on huge compute servers to ensure that state-of-the-art performance is met.

For reference, this exact model was trained on eight NVIDIA Telsa M40 GPUs for four days. We show plots for the perplexity in Figures 9-31 and 9-32, and show the learning rate anneal over time as well. In Figure 9-31, we see that after 50,000 epochs, the perplexity decreases from about 6 to 4, which is a reasonable score for a neural machine translation system. In Figure 9-32, we observe that the learning rate almost smoothly declines to 0. This means that by the time we stopped training, the model was approaching a stable state.

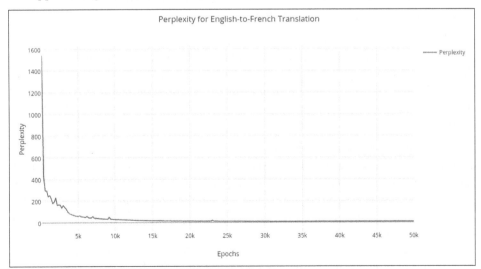

Figure 9-31. Plot of perplexity on training data over time

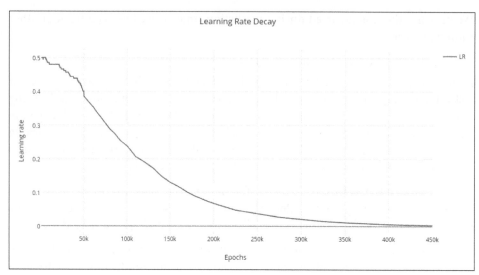

Figure 9-32. Plot of learning rate over time

To showcase the attentional model more explicitly, we can visualize the attention that the decoder LSTM computes while translating a sentence from English to French. In particular, we know that as the encoder LSTM is updating its cell state in order to compress the sentence into continuous vector representations, it also computes hidden states at every time step. We know that the decoder LSTM computes a convex sum over these hidden states, and we can think of this sum as the attention mechanism; when there is more weight on a particular hidden state, we can interpret that as the model is paying more attention to the token inputted at that time step. This is exactly what we visualize in Figure 9-33.

The English sentence to be translated is on the top row, and the resulting French translation is on the first column. The lighter a square is, the more attention the decoder paid to that particular column when decoding that row element. That is, the $(i, j)^{th}$ element in the attention map shows the amount of attention that was paid to the jth token in the English sentence when translating the ith token in the French sentence.

We can immediately see that the attention mechanism seems to be working quite well. Large amounts of attention are generally being placed in the right areas, even though there is slight noise in the model's prediction. It is possible that adding layers to the network would help produce crisper attention. One impressive aspect is that the phrase "the European Economic" is translated in reverse in French as the "zone économique européenne," and as such, the attention weights reflect this flip. These kinds of attention patterns may be even more interesting when translating from English to a different language that does not parse smoothly from left to right.

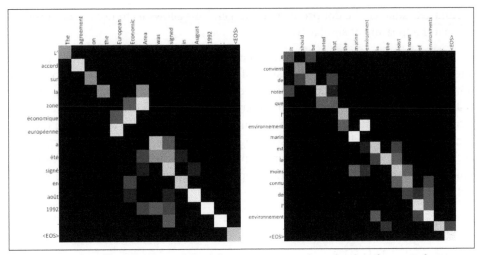

Figure 9-33. Visualizing the weights of the convex sum when the decoder attends over hidden states in the encoder

With one of the most fundamental architectures understood and implemented, we now move forward to study exciting new developments with RNNs and begin a foray into more sophisticated learning.

Self-Attention and Transformers

Earlier, we discussed a form of attention that was first presented in Bahdanau et al. in 2015. Specifically, we used a simple, feed-forward neural network to calculate the alignment score of each encoder hidden state with the decoder state at the current time step. In this section, we'll discuss a different form of attention called *scaled dot product attention,* its use in *self-attention,* and the *transformer,* a recent language modeling breakthrough. Transformer-based models have primarily replaced LSTM, and have been proven to be superior in quality for many sequence-to-sequence problems.

Dot product attention is really as simple as it sounds—this method calculates alignment scores as the dot product between each encoder hidden state s_t. These weights are used in the calculation of the context vector, which is a convex sum (via softmax) of the encoder hidden states. Why use the dot product to measure alignment? As we learned in Chapter 1, the dot product of two vectors can be expressed as a product of the norms of the two vectors and the cosine of the angle between them. As the angle between the two vectors goes to zero, the cosine goes to one. Also, recall from trigonometry that cosine has the range 1 to –1 when the input angle is between 0 degrees and 180 degrees, which is the only part of the domain of the angle we need to consider. The dot product has the nice property that, as the angle between two vectors gets smaller, the dot product gets larger. This allows us to use the dot product as a natural measure of similarity.

In 2017, Vaswani et al.[7] introduced a modification to the preexisting dot product attention framework via the inclusion of a scaling factor—the square root of the dimension of the hidden states. Vaswani et al. acknowledge the fact that, as hidden state representations get larger and larger in terms of dimension, we expect to see significantly more instances of high magnitude dot products. To understand the reasoning behind the inclusion of this scaling factor, assume, for the sake of argument, each index of h_i is drawn independently and identically distributed from a mean zero, unit variance random variable. Let's compute the expectation and variance of their dot product:

$$\mathbb{E}\left[s_t^T h_i\right] = \Sigma_{j=1}^k \mathbb{E}\left[s_{t,j} * h_{i,j}\right]$$
$$= \Sigma_{j=1}^k \mathbb{E}\left[s_{t,j}\right] \mathbb{E}\left[h_{i,j}\right]$$
$$= 0$$

$$Var\left(s_t^T h_i\right) = \Sigma_{j=1}^k Var\left(s_{t,j} * h_{i,j}\right)$$
$$= \Sigma_{j=1}^k \mathbb{E}\left[\left(s_{t,j}^2 * h_{i,j}^2\right)\right] - \mathbb{E}\left[s_{t,j} * h_{i,j}\right]^2$$
$$= \Sigma_{j=1}^k \mathbb{E}\left[s_{t,j}^2\right] \mathbb{E}\left[h_{i,j}^2\right]$$
$$= \Sigma_{j=1}^k 1$$
$$= k$$

Let's review the steps that got us to these conclusions regarding the expectation and variance. The first equality in the expectation is due to the linearity of expectation, since the dot product can be expressed as a sum of the product of each index. The second equality comes from the fact that the two random variables in each expectation are independent, so we can separate the expectation of the product into a product of expectations. The final step follows directly from the fact that each of these individual expectations are zero.

The first equality in the variance is due to the linearity of variance when the individual terms are all independent. The second equality is just the definition of variance. The third equality uses a result from our calculation of the expectation of the dot product (we can separate out the square of the expectation into the product of squares of expectations, where each individual expectation is zero). Additionally, the expectation of the product of squares can be split up into a product of expectations

---

7 Vaswani et. al. "Attention Is All You Need." *arXiv Preprint arXiv:1706.03762* 2017.

of squares, since the square of each random variable is independent of the squares of all other random variables. The second to last equality comes from the fact that the expectation of the square of each random variable is just the variance of the random variable (since the expectation of each random variable is zero). The final equality follows directly.

We see that the expectation of the dot product is zero, while its variance is k, the dimension of the hidden representation. Thus, as the dimension increases, the variance increases—this implies a higher probability of seeing high-magnitude dot products.

Unfortunately, with the presence of more high-magnitude dot products comes smaller gradients due to the softmax function. Although we won't derive it here, this makes a lot of intuitive sense—think back to the use of softmax in neural networks for classification problems. As the neural network gets more and more confident in a correct prediction (i.e., a high logit value for the true index), the gradient gets smaller and smaller. The scaling factor introduced by Vaswani et al. reduces the magnitude of dot products, leading to larger gradients and better learning.

Now that we've covered scaled dot product attention, we turn our attention to self-attention. In the previous sections, we saw attention through the context of machine translation where we are given a training set of sentences that are in English and French, and the goal is to be able to translate unseen English sentences to French. In this specific class of problems, there exists a direct supervision through the target French sentences. However, attention can also be used in a completely self-contained manner. The intuition is that, given a sentence in English, we may be able to perform more insightful sentiment analysis, more effective machine reading, and better understanding via learning relationships between tokens within sentences or paragraphs.

The transformer, our final topic for this section, utilizes both scaled dot product attention and self-attention. The transformer architecture (Vaswani et al. 2017) has both encoder and decoder architectures, where there exists self-attention within both the encoder and decoder, as well as standard attention between the encoder and decoder. The self-attention layers in the encoders and decoders allow each to attend to all positions prior to the current position in their respective architectures. The standard attention allows the decoder to attend to each encoder hidden state, as described earlier.

Summary

In this chapter, we've delved deep into the world of sequence analysis. We've analyzed how we might hack feed-forward networks to process sequences, developed a strong understanding of RNNs, and explored how attentional mechanisms can enable incredible applications ranging from language translation to audio transcription. Sequence analysis is a field that ranges problems not only in natural language, but also topics in finance, such as time-series analysis of returns of financial assets. Any field that involves longitudinal analyses, or analyses across time, could use the applications of sequence analysis described in this chapter. We advise you to really deepen your understanding of sequence analysis via implementation across different fields and by comparing the results of the techniques presented for natural language with the state-of-the-art in each field. There are also situations in which the techniques presented here may not be the most appropriate modeling choice, and we advise you to think deeply about why the modeling assumptions made here may not apply broadly. Sequence analysis is a powerful tool that has a place in almost all technical applications, not just natural language.

CHAPTER 10
Generative Models

Generative models attempt to understand the *latent*, or underlying, process that produces the data we see. For example, when breaking down images of digits in the MNIST dataset, we can interpret some attributes of the underlying process generating each image as the digit itself (a discrete variable ranging from zero through nine), the orientation or angle at which it will be drawn, the size of the resulting image, the thickness of the lines, and some noise component (all of which are continuous variables). So far, we've been concerned with *discriminative* models, either in the regression or classification setting. In the classification setting, discriminative models take as input an example such as an image from the MNIST dataset and attempt to determine the most likely digit category, from zero through nine, that the input belongs to. Generative models instead attempt to fully model the data distribution, and in the process may implicitly try to learn some of the features mentioned previously to generate images that look as if they were originally from the MNIST dataset. Note that generative modeling is a harder problem than discriminative modeling, as a discriminative model may, for example, need to learn only a few features well to distinguish between different digits in the MNIST dataset to a satisfactory degree. Generative models come in many varieties, and in this chapter, we provide a glimpse into a vast research landscape that has begun to blossom only in the past decade.

Generative Adversarial Networks

Generative Adversarial Networks, or GANs for short, are a form of generative model designed to produce realistic samples of entities, such as images, from noise. They were introduced by Goodfellow et al. in 2014.[1] For the remainder of this section, we will assume we are working with an image dataset such as MNIST or CIFAR-10. The original GAN architecture is broken down into two neural networks: the *discriminator* and the *generator.*

The generator takes in samples from some noise distribution, such as a multivariate Gaussian distribution, and outputs an image. The discriminator is tasked with predicting whether this image was produced by the generator or was sampled from the original dataset. As the generator gets better and better at producing images that look real, the discriminator has a harder time determining whether a given image was produced by the generator or sampled from the dataset. We can think of these two networks as participating in a game, competing against each other to develop. Each network evolves until the generator can eventually produce images that look as if they were drawn directly from the original dataset, and the discriminator cannot distinguish between the two sets of images, i.e., predicts that any image is from the dataset with probability $\frac{1}{2}$.

More rigorously, we define the data distribution to be $p_{\text{data}}(x)$. Although we can never really know the true data distribution, in practice we generally think of it as being approximated well enough by the dataset we have on hand ($p_{\text{data}}(x)$ is just a uniform distribution over all of the images present in the dataset and zero likelihood associated with all images that are not in the dataset).

We additionally define the distribution parametrized by the generator to be $p_g(x)$. The random variable x represents an entity such as an image, a collection of pixels that can each be thought of as their own random variables. The generator, which we also refer to as G, defines $p_g(x)$ by mapping samples from the noise distribution, which we will refer to as *p(z)*, to the data space, which consists of all possible images (not just those in the dataset). It is important to keep in mind that G itself is a deterministic function, but implicitly defines a distribution by acting on the noise distribution. Note that this distribution is implicit because we can generate samples from it only via *G(z),* rather than being an explicit distribution we can work with directly and query an image for its likelihood. Figure 10-1 shows the typical GAN architecture.

---

1 Goodfellow et al. "Generative Adversarial Networks." *arXiv Preprint arXiv*:1406.2661. 2014.

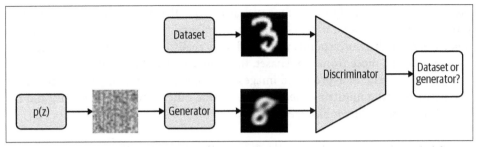

Figure 10-1. The discriminator determines whether any input image was sampled from the dataset or generator. The generator's goal is to trick the discriminator into believing its images were sampled from the dataset.

An optimal generator for a given dataset would also parametrize $p_{\text{data}}(x)$, as this would perfectly confuse even the best discriminator. In other words, if the generator parametrizes the exact same distribution as that of the dataset and it is equally likely to sample from either the generator or the dataset, then no discriminator would be able to tell where the query originated from, as both are always equally likely. We formalize this intuition in the next paragraph.

Thinking back to Chapter 2, given a generator that parametrizes the same distribution as the dataset, we have $p(x \mid y = \text{generator}) = p(x \mid y = \text{dataset})$, $\forall x$, where y is a Bernoulli random variable over the two options: generator or dataset. Note that we use $p_g(x)$ and $p(x \mid y = \text{generator})$ interchangeably, and $p_{\text{data}}(x)$ and $p(x \mid y = \text{dataset})$ interchangeably, since they mean the same thing. The latter option of each allows us to keep in mind we are working with conditional probabilities. Again, assuming that sampling from the generator and sampling from the dataset are equally likely, or $p(y = \text{generator}) = p(y = \text{dataset})$, we can use Bayes' Rule to obtain the equality: $p(y = \text{generator} \mid x) = p(y = \text{dataset} \mid x)$, $\forall x$. Since there are only two options, as y is a Bernoulli random variable, we are left with the perfectly confused discriminator alluded to earlier that predicts any image to be sampled from the dataset with probability $\frac{1}{2}$.

Knowing our end goal, we can now go about designing an objective function for training our generator and discriminator in tandem. In the original GAN paper, the objective presented was:

$$V(G, D) = \mathbb{E}_{x \sim p_{\text{data}}(x)}[\log D(x)] + \mathbb{E}_{z \sim p(z)}[\log (1 - D(G(z)))]$$

$G(z)$ represents the mapping from the noise distribution to the data space described earlier, and $D(x)$ represents the score assigned to the input image. $D(x)$ is interpreted as the probability that the input image was drawn from the dataset. Of course, the discriminator D would like to maximize this objective—this corresponds with assigning high probabilities to images drawn from the dataset rather than images produced by the generator G. G, on the other hand, would like to minimize this objective, since that corresponds with producing realistic images, or even images that look exactly like those from the dataset, that confuse D and cause it to return a high score for these generator-produced images. This idea of maximizing the objective for one network and minimizing the objective for the other is termed *minimax,* and the optimization procedure looks like this:

$$\min_G \max_D \mathbb{E}_{x \sim p_{\text{data}}(x)}[\log D(x)] + \mathbb{E}_{z \sim p(z)}[\log (1 - D(G(z)))]$$

The paper goes on to show that, for a fixed generator G, the optimal discriminator trained under this objective would output the following score:

$$\frac{p_{\text{data}}(x)}{p_{\text{data}}(x) + p_g(x)}$$

for a given image x. First, we consider why this should even describe the behavior of an optimal discriminator given a fixed generator. Before we get into the "why," it's important to keep in mind that D can be alternatively represented as $p_\theta(y = \text{dataset} \mid x)$, or the discriminator's belief that the image was drawn from the dataset. Here θ represents the parameters, or weights, of D. When we perform an update operation such as gradient descent, θ represents the set of weights that is being updated. It is important to keep in mind that this distribution is distinct from $p(y = \text{dataset} \mid x)$ mentioned earlier—the latter is the true probability that a given image was sampled from the dataset.

The optimal discriminator can never know the exact origin of the image unless it is impossible for the generator to have produced the image, i.e., $p_g(x) = 0$. We can quantify the uncertainty in the discriminator's prediction as a function of the image's likelihood under the data distribution, or $p_{\text{data}}(x)$, and the image's likelihood under the distribution defined by G, or $p_g(x)$. If the image's likelihood under the distribution defined by the generator is less than that of the data distribution, it makes sense that the optimal discriminator should be swayed accordingly and should score the image closer to one than zero.

 Note that a quick back-of-the-envelope check shows that this property is true for the score $\frac{p_{\text{data}}(x)}{p_{\text{data}}(x) + p_g(x)}$. But why is this the exact proportion by which the property is true? Let's take a more concrete look at the score $\frac{p_{\text{data}}(x)}{p_{\text{data}}(x) + p_g(x)}$ and determine why this is the optimal function of the two probabilities.

Taking some inspiration from our discussion regarding the perfectly confused discriminator, we can alternatively express the proposed optimal discriminator score in terms of conditional probabilities:

$$\frac{p(x \mid y = \text{dataset})}{p(x \mid y = \text{dataset}) + p(x \mid y = \text{generator})}$$

Additionally, making the same assumption regarding equal likelihood of sampling from the dataset versus sampling from the generator ($p(y = \text{dataset}) = p(y = \text{generator}) = 0.5$), we can get to a much more interpretable representation of the optimal score:

$$D^*(x) = \frac{p(x \mid y = \text{dataset})}{p(x \mid y = \text{dataset}) + p(x \mid y = \text{generator})}$$

$$= \frac{p(x \mid y = \text{dataset}) * p(y = \text{dataset})}{p(x \mid y = \text{dataset}) * p(y = \text{dataset}) + p(x \mid y = \text{generator}) * p(y = \text{generator})}$$

$$= \frac{p(x, y = \text{dataset})}{p(x)}$$

$$= p(y = \text{dataset} \mid x)$$

The denominator in the third equality is a result of having marginalized out y. The final result is just the conditional probability of having sampled from the dataset given the input image. It makes sense that the optimal discriminator, $p_{\theta^*}(y = \text{dataset} \mid x)$, should strive to match the true probability that the input image was drawn from the dataset, $p(y = \text{dataset} \mid x)$.

Now, we consider why the minimax objective defined earlier is maximized by $p(y = \text{dataset} \mid x)$, or the true conditional probability of having drawn from the dataset given an image x, under the assumption of a fixed generator. Let's take a closer look at the objective and try to reformulate it in a more informative manner that may provide us with some insight:

$$V(G, D) = \mathbb{E}_{x \sim p_{\text{data}}(x)}[\log D(x)] + \mathbb{E}_{z \sim p(z)}[\log (1 - D(G(z)))]$$

$$= \mathbb{E}_{x \sim p(x \mid y = \text{dataset})}[\log p_\theta(y = \text{dataset} \mid x)]$$
$$+ \mathbb{E}_{p_\phi(x \mid y = \text{generator})}[\log (1 - p_\theta(y = \text{dataset} \mid x))]$$

$$= \mathbb{E}_{x \sim p(x \mid y = \text{dataset})}[\log p_\theta(y = \text{dataset} \mid x)]$$
$$+ \mathbb{E}_{p_\phi(x \mid y = \text{generator})}[\log (p_\theta(y = \text{generator} \mid x))]$$

As usual, we have formulated the objective in terms of conditional probabilities. To get from the first equality to the second, we note that taking the expectation with respect to the noise distribution $p(z)$ and then applying a function such as G to each sample is equivalent to just taking the expectation with respect to the distribution over the data space defined by G's mapping. This is similar in spirit to a concept we discussed in Chapter 2, where random variables can be functions of other random variables. Also note the addition of the letter ϕ starting from the second line—this letter represents the parameters, or weights, of G.

Taking a closer look at the final expression, we start to see an awful lot of similarities between the objective and the concepts of entropy and cross entropy introduced in Chapter 2. It turns out that we can manipulate the objective slightly without affecting the best θ here to obtain a sum of the negatives of two cross-entropy terms:

$$\theta^* = \operatorname{argmin}_\theta V(G, D)$$

$$= \operatorname{argmin}_\theta \mathbb{E}_{x \,\sim\, p(x|y\,=\,\text{dataset})}\left[\log\, p_\theta(y = \text{dataset}\,|\,x)\right]$$
$$+ \mathbb{E}_{p_\phi(x|y\,=\,\text{generator})}\left[\log\,\left(p_\theta(y = \text{generator}\,|\,x)\right)\right]$$

$$= \operatorname{argmin}_\theta - H(p(x, y = \text{dataset}), p_\theta(x, y = \text{dataset}))$$
$$- H(p(x, y = \text{generator}), p_\theta(x, y = \text{generator}))$$

As discussed in Chapter 2, the cross entropy between two distributions is minimized when the two distributions are exactly the same—here we are doing the equivalent by simply maximizing the negative cross entropy instead. Thus, θ achieves the optimal set of weights θ^* when $p_\theta(x, y = \text{dataset}) = p(x, y = \text{dataset})$ and $p_\theta(x, y = \text{generator}) = p(x, y = \text{generator})$.

As our final step, we'd like to show that at θ^*, $p_{\theta^*}(y = \text{dataset}\,|\,x) = p(y = \text{dataset}\,|\,x)$ as promised. We already know that $p_{\theta^*}(x, y = \text{dataset}) = p(x, y = \text{dataset})$ from our prior work. Dividing by $p(x)$ on both sides leaves us with the desired result.

So far, we have assumed a fixed G, and shown various properties regarding the optimal D. Unfortunately, we can't assume a fixed G in practice, as we must train the generator as well as the discriminator. But now that we have shown some properties regarding the optimal D, we can begin to talk about the properties G must satisfy to achieve the global optimum—a generator that can perfectly confuse even the optimal discriminator. If we assume an optimal discriminator and plug in its score $\frac{p_{\text{data}}(x)}{p_{\text{data}}(x) + p_g(x)}$ to the objective $V(G,D)$, we obtain an objective that is solely dependent on the parameters, or weights, of G:

$$C(G) = \mathbb{E}_{x \,\sim\, p_{\text{data}}(x)}\left[\log \frac{p_{\text{data}}(x)}{p_{\text{data}}(x) + p_g(x)}\right] + \mathbb{E}_{x \,\sim\, p_g(x)}\left[\log\left(1 - \frac{p_{\text{data}}(x)}{p_{\text{data}}(x) + p_g(x)}\right)\right]$$

$$= \mathbb{E}_{x \,\sim\, p_{\text{data}}(x)}\left[\log \frac{p_{\text{data}}(x)}{p_{\text{data}}(x) + p_g(x)}\right] + \mathbb{E}_{x \,\sim\, p_g(x)}\left[\log \frac{p_g(x)}{p_{\text{data}}(x) + p_g(x)}\right]$$

$$= \mathbb{E}_{x \sim p(x \mid y = \text{dataset})} \left[\log \frac{p(x \mid y = \text{dataset})}{p(x \mid y = \text{dataset}) + p_\phi(x \mid y = \text{generator})} \right]$$
$$+ \mathbb{E}_{x \sim p_\phi(x \mid y = \text{generator})} \left[\log \frac{p_\phi(x \mid y = \text{generator})}{p(x \mid y = \text{dataset}) + p_\phi(x \mid y = \text{generator})} \right]$$

We can now minimize this objective by optimizing over the generator weights ϕ. We refer you to the original GAN paper for the rigorous derivation. However, as one might expect by now, it turns out that the optimal distribution G represents, or $p_{g^*}(x)$, is equal to $p_{\text{data}}(x)$, $\forall x$. This matches our original intuition regarding the perfectly confused discriminator and shows that the objective function proposed in the original GAN paper does indeed theoretically converge to this global optimum.

Now that we have an optimal generator and discriminator, how do we perform image generation? All we need to do is sample from our noise distribution $p(z)$ and run each sample through the generator. The generator, being optimal, should produce images that look as if they were drawn from the dataset itself. It may come as a surprise to you that the discriminator is no longer needed in this phase—but it has served its purpose. The discriminator played a key role in competing with the generator, each evolving until the latter could produce images that perfectly confused the discriminator.

Note that unlike the standard interpretation of generative modeling, z does not represent a set of latent variables from which the data is generated. z simply plays the role of being a random variable distributed as one of our standard distributions, such as a uniform distribution or a standard multivariate Gaussian distribution, which are easy to sample from. G, when fully trained and optimal, is a complex, differentiable function that transforms samples from $p(z)$ into samples from $p_{\text{data}}(x)$, which approximates $p(x)$. In the next section, we will see the parallels between $G(z)$ and the reparametrization trick, which also allows us to sample from a distribution by transforming samples (via a differentiable function) from a distribution that is easier to sample from.

Variational Autoencoders

In parallel to the introduction of GANs, Kingma and Welling introduced the *Variational Autoencoder*, or VAE for short, in their seminal paper, "Auto-Encoding Variational Bayes," from 2014.[2] The idea behind the VAE is more strongly rooted in probabilistic modeling than the aforementioned GAN. The VAE assumes there exists a set of unobserved latent variables, which we denote as z, that generate the data we see, which we denote as x. More formally, we say there exists a joint probability distribution $p(x,z)$ over the latent variables z and the observed data x that factors as

---

2 Kingma et al. "Auto-Encoding Variational Bayes." *arXiv Preprint arXiv*:1312.6114. 2014.

$p(x|z)p(z)$ (see Figure 10-2). Thinking back to Chapter 2, this factorization is quite intuitive. Given the predefined roles of z and x, the universe in which z takes on some value and x is generated from this setting of z makes much more sense than the other way around.

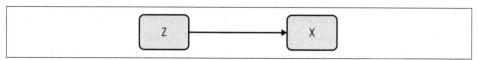

Figure 10-2. z represents the latent variables from which every instance of x is generated. The arrow pointing from z to x signifies this relationship.

x could represent any sort of continuous or discrete data, including images. We additionally know the domain of x due to our knowledge of the dataset. z, on the other hand, is much more elusive. We have no idea what z looks like, so we make some initial assumptions about it. For example, we may assume that it initially takes the form of a Gaussian distribution, i.e., $p(z)$ is Gaussian. Again, thinking back to Chapter 2, we say that $p(z)$, or our prior on z, is Gaussian.

Whenever we think about such a data-generation process, some natural probabilistic questions (should) come to mind. For example, what is the distribution $p(z|x)$, or the posterior of z having known x? As we observe data, our beliefs regarding the underlying parameters often change. Take the coin flip experiment from Chapter 2 as an example. We initially assumed a 50-50 chance of flipping heads, where the 50-50 can be thought of as our latent parameter α—the parameter dictating the data generation procedure of sequences of heads and tails. This is a little simplified—in reality, we initially have a distribution over α, the probability of flipping heads, which is our prior distribution. Of course, the domain of the prior is the range [0,1], where it is logical to design the prior $p(\alpha)$ such that $p(\alpha = 0.5)$ is larger than all other settings of α. As we observed sequences of flips, we updated our prior via Bayes' Theorem. In a similar manner, we initially assume $p(z)$ to be a Gaussian distribution with some mean and variance; but as we observe data, we recalculate our belief in the form of a posterior, $p(z|x)$ (see Figure 10-3).

Another question naturally comes to mind: what is the distribution $p(x|z)$, or the likelihood of the data x given a certain setting of the latent variables z? In the coin flip setting, $p(x|z)$ is easy to think about. Due to our complete knowledge of the experiment, we know the probability of any sequence is just the product of the probability of each flip, which is directly defined by z. In more intricate settings such as images, however, we can assume the relationship between the data x and the latent variables z is much more complicated than that. For example, when looking at images, it is clear that the value of a given pixel is quite affected by the values of its neighboring pixels and sometimes even by pixels much farther than one might think. The simple independence assumption we have for coin flips will not suffice for our purposes. This is just one reason why we can't simply use a method like Bayes'

Theorem to learn a posterior over *z*—it requires much more knowledge regarding the system than what is immediately available to us.

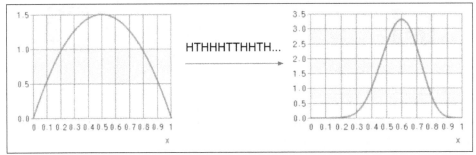

Figure 10-3. Here we have the coin flip experiment, where the prior is designed such that 0.5 has the highest likelihood. Once we see a series of heads and tails, the posterior shifts to the right due to there being more heads than tails.

In variational autoencoders, we encode these distributions as neural networks, which can be seen as complex, nonlinear functions that can accurately model the relationships between latent variables *z* and the observed data *x*. We denote the neural network that outputs a distribution over the data given a setting of the latent variables, also termed the *decoder*, as $p_\theta(x|z)$, where θ represents the weights of the neural network. In other words, the setting of θ, in addition to the predetermined architecture of the neural network, completely define the model's belief of the true distribution $p(x|z)$. We optimize θ to achieve a setting that is closest to that of the true distribution.

We additionally encode the posterior over *z*, or *p(z|x)*, as a neural network. We denote this neural network, termed the *encoder*, as $q_\phi(z|x)$. Similarly to the decoder, we optimize ϕ to achieve a setting that is closest to that of the true posterior.

Kingma and Welling made some key observations that made the variational autoencoder a practical means for generative modeling (Figure 10-4). The first was that the *evidence lower bound* (ELBO for short), which is a lower bound on the true log likelihood of the data $p(x)$, could be reformulated in a way that allowed for tractable optimization over the encoder and decoder parameters. The second was a reparametrization trick that enabled the computation of a low variance estimate of the gradient with respect to the parameters of the encoder, ϕ. Although this may sound like a lot of jargon right now, we will go into each of these key observations in much more detail and concretely motivate the encoder-decoder architecture.

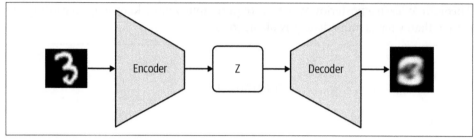

Figure 10-4. The overall VAE architecture presented in Kingma and Welling. Note that both z and the image after the decoder are both samples from the encoder distribution and decoder distribution, respectively.

Let's assume we have observed some data x, where each individual example can be denoted as $x^{(i)}$. Note that we are still under the assumption that there exist some set of latent variables z generating the data we've seen. We split our analysis over the observed data into one over each individual example $x^{(i)}$. We know there exists a true posterior over the latent variables $p(z \mid x^{(i)})$, but we have no idea what that true posterior is. We assume it can be approximated by some distribution over the latent variables $q_\phi(z \mid x^{(i)})$, where q is a family of distributions in which optimization is much easier but complex enough to accurately model the true posterior. An example would be a multilayer neural network, which, as we've already seen, can be efficiently optimized via gradient descent and can represent complex, nonlinear functions. Note that each example $x^{(i)}$ we've seen has some true probability of occurrence, which we can write as $p(x^{(i)})$. We instead work with $\log p(x^{(i)})$, since this allows us to do some convenient decomposition into terms we've encountered before and doesn't affect the verity of the optimization process:

$$\log p(x^{(i)}) = \log p(x^{(i)}, z) - \log p(z \mid x^{(i)})$$

$$= \log p(x^{(i)}, z) - \log p(z \mid x^{(i)}) + \log q_\phi(z \mid x^{(i)}) - \log q_\phi(z \mid x^{(i)})$$

$$= \mathbb{E}_{q_\phi(z \mid x^{(i)})}\left[\log p(x^{(i)}, z) - \log p(z \mid x^{(i)}) + \log q_\phi(z \mid x^{(i)}) - \log q_\phi(z \mid x^{(i)}) \right]$$

$$= \mathbb{E}_{q_\phi(z \mid x^{(i)})}\left[\log \frac{p(x^{(i)}, z)}{q_\phi(z \mid x^{(i)})} \right] + \mathbb{E}_{q_\phi(z \mid x^{(i)})}\left[\log \frac{q_\phi(z \mid x^{(i)})}{p(z \mid x^{(i)})} \right]$$

$$= \text{ELBO} + \text{KL}\left(q_\phi(z \mid x^{(i)}) \,\middle|\middle|\, p(z \mid x^{(i)})\right)$$

The first step is to express the marginal likelihood of the individual example $x^{(i)}$ as a function of the example itself and the latent factors z. As we learned earlier, the marginal likelihood can be broken down into a quotient of the joint distribution $p(z, x^{(i)})$ and the conditional distribution $p(z \mid x^{(i)})$. The log function allows us to separate this quotient into a difference between the logs of the two terms. In the second step, we use a little trick that allows us to conveniently insert the approximate posterior into the equality—adding and subtracting the same term shouldn't affect the equality. In the third step, we insert an expectation with respect to the approximate posterior. Why is this allowed? Well, a priori we know that $\log p(x^{(i)})$ is a constant. It is just the log of the probability of the example occurring under the true distribution, which is fixed. Thus, taking the expectation on both sides doesn't change anything about the left side of the equation, since the expectation of a constant is just the constant itself. On the right side, we have now gotten closer to expressing the log of the marginal likelihood in terms that we've seen before. In the second to last step, we combine logs back into quotients and use the linearity of expectation to arrive at a sum of two terms: (1) the KL divergence between the approximate posterior and the true posterior, and (2) the ELBO, or the evidence lower bound.

By now, you may have noticed that the form of the KL divergence is slightly different than what we encountered in Chapter 2. Recall the standard KL divergence presented earlier, where the true distribution was *p(x)* and its approximation was *q(x)*. The KL divergence we defined was the difference between the cross entropy of the two distributions and the entropy of the true distribution, which was expressed as follows:

$$\mathbb{E}_{p(x)}\left[\log \frac{p(x)}{q(x)} \right]$$

We can see that the KL divergence in this derivation is the exact opposite. The expectation is with respect to the approximate posterior rather than the true posterior, and the numerator and denominator are flipped. Essentially what we see is $\mathbb{E}_{q(x)}\left[\log \frac{q(x)}{p(x)} \right]$ instead of $\mathbb{E}_{p(x)}\left[\log \frac{p(x)}{q(x)} \right]$. We call this the *reverse KL divergence*, since the roles of the model and the truth have been switched, and is the quantity we attempt to minimize in VAEs. Although this does not have as clean a physical interpretation as the standard KL, note that the reverse KL divergence is *just a type of KL divergence* and retains all the properties we discussed in Chapter 2. Thus, optimizing the reverse KL divergence still achieves a unique global minimum of zero when $q(x) = p(x)$, $\forall x$, so it is a valid objective to be optimizing over as it reaches its unique minimum when the approximate posterior is exactly the same as the true posterior.

The reality, however, is that the true posterior $p(z|x^{(i)})$ is still unknown to us. As a result, we can't directly minimize any KL divergence with the true posterior. This is where the ELBO plays a key role. As we discussed earlier, $\log p(x^{(i)})$ is a constant. Thus, minimizing the reverse KL divergence is the same as maximizing the ELBO. The name evidence lower bound should make more sense now—as we maximize this term, it provides a better and better lower bound on the true log probability of the example. If we can develop a methodology for maximizing the ELBO efficiently, we should be well on our way to developing a generative model. Let's reformulate the ELBO into terms that might be easier to work with:

$$\mathbb{E}_{q_\phi(z|x^{(i)})}\left[\log \frac{p(x^{(i)}, z)}{q_\phi(z|x^{(i)})}\right] = \mathbb{E}_{q_\phi(z|x^{(i)})}\left[\log p(x^{(i)}, z) - \log q_\phi(z|x^{(i)})\right]$$

$$= \mathbb{E}_{q_\phi(z|x^{(i)})}\left[\log p(x^{(i)}|z) + \log p(z) - \log q_\phi(z|x^{(i)})\right]$$

$$= \mathbb{E}_{q_\phi(z|x^{(i)})}\left[\log p(x^{(i)}|z)\right] + \mathbb{E}_{q_\phi(z|x^{(i)})}\left[\log p(z) - \log q_\phi(z|x^{(i)})\right]$$

$$= \mathbb{E}_{q_\phi(z|x^{(i)})}\left[\log p(x^{(i)}|z)\right] - \mathbb{E}_{q_\phi(z|x^{(i)})}\left[\log \frac{q_\phi(z|x^{(i)})}{p(z)}\right]$$

$$= -KL(q_\phi(z|x^{(i)})||p(z)) + \mathbb{E}_{q_\phi(z|x^{(i)})}\left[\log p(x^{(i)}|z)\right]$$

At this point, we can start to see the beginnings of an architecture and an optimization procedure for maximizing the ELBO. For example, the first term is just the reverse KL divergence between the approximate posterior and the prior, which we already assumed to be a Gaussian distribution. We can use a neural network, or encoder, to represent the approximate posterior. The reverse KL divergence acts as a regularization term on the approximate posterior, since maximizing the negative of the reverse KL is the same as minimizing the reverse KL. Regularization prevents the approximate posterior from straying too far from the prior distribution. This is desirable since we have witnessed only a single example, and thus we don't want our belief over the latent variables to shift too much from our prior. The second term is the expected true log likelihood of the example given a setting of latent variables z, where z is sampled from the approximate posterior. Wanting to maximize this quantity with respect to ϕ is intuitively reasonable. This influences the approximate posterior to assign higher likelihoods to settings of z that, in turn, explain the input example $x^{(i)}$ as well as possible. The balancing act between regularization, which prevents overfitting, and maximum likelihood estimation, which on its own would reach an optimum where $q_\phi(z|x^{(i)})$ is just a point mass over the setting of z that best describes $x^{(i)}$, is a classic optimization procedure you've likely encountered in many data science and machine learning problems.

However, as noted earlier, we unfortunately don't have access to the true conditional distribution $p(x|z)$. Instead, we attempt to learn it using a second neural network—the decoder. We denote the parameters of the decoder as θ and let the decoder represent the distribution $p_\theta(x|z)$. In summary, we perform the following optimization procedure:

$$\phi^*, \theta^* = \text{argmax}_{\phi, \theta} - KL(q_\phi(z|x^{(i)})||p(z)) + \mathbb{E}_{q_\phi(z|x^{(i)})}\left[\log p_\theta(x^{(i)}|z)\right]$$

We've already discussed why this is a valid optimization procedure for the encoder parameters ϕ, assuming that $p_\theta(x|z) = p(x|z)$. Of course, this assumption is not satisfied at the beginning of training. However, as training progresses and θ becomes more and more optimal, we eventually arrive at the desired theoretical optimization. But the question still remains: why is this a valid optimization procedure for θ? If we assume the encoder represents the true posterior distribution, we'd want to maximize the likelihood of recovering the original example $x^{(i)}$ from our encoder samples z. Of course, just like the optimization of ϕ, our assumption about the approximate posterior is not satisfied at the beginning of training—but as training progresses and two networks improve jointly, we hope to eventually reach our goal.

This leads us into how to actually carry out the optimization. For θ, it turns out we can use standard minibatch gradient descent techniques directly:

$$\nabla_\theta - KL(q_\phi(z|x^{(i)})||p(z)) + \mathbb{E}_{q_\phi(z|x^{(i)})}\big[\log p_\theta(x^{(i)}|z)\big]$$

$$= \nabla_\theta - KL(q_\phi(z|x^{(i)})||p(z)) + \nabla_\theta\mathbb{E}_{q_\phi(z|x^{(i)})}\big[\log p_\theta(x^{(i)}|z)\big]$$

$$= \nabla_\theta\mathbb{E}_{q_\phi(z|x^{(i)})}\big[\log p_\theta(x^{(i)}|z)\big]$$

$$= \mathbb{E}_{q_\phi(z|x^{(i)})}\big[\nabla_\theta\log p_\theta(x^{(i)}|z)\big]$$

$$\approx \frac{1}{n}\Sigma_j^n{}_{=1}\nabla_\theta\log p_\theta(x^{(i)}|z=z_j)$$

The first equality arises from the fact that the gradient of a sum of terms is equal to the sum of the gradients of each of the terms. Since the first term is not a function of θ, its gradient with respect to θ is 0, leading us to the second equality. From there we have the standard minibatch gradient estimate derivation.

The optimization with respect to ϕ is not as simple. If we try to do the same for ϕ as we did for θ, we run into an unforeseen issue:

$$\nabla_\phi - KL(q_\phi(z|x^{(i)})||p(z)) + \mathbb{E}_{q_\phi(z|x^{(i)})}\big[\log p_\theta(x^{(i)}|z)\big]$$

$$= \nabla_\phi - KL(q_\phi(z|x^{(i)})||p(z)) + \nabla_\phi\mathbb{E}_{q_\phi(z|x^{(i)})}\big[\log p_\theta(x^{(i)}|z)\big]$$

$$= \nabla_\phi - KL(q_\phi(z|x^{(i)})||p(z)) + \nabla_\phi\int q_\phi(z|x^{(i)})\log p_\theta(x^{(i)}|z)dz$$

$$= \nabla_\phi - KL(q_\phi(z|x^{(i)})||p(z)) + \int \nabla_\phi q_\phi(z|x^{(i)})\log p_\theta(x^{(i)}|z)dz$$

In the last step, we can't express the second term as an expectation. This is because the gradient is with respect to the parameters of the distribution from which we are sampling. We can't simply switch the order of the expectation and gradient as we did for θ. To get around this, we make the following observation:

$$\nabla_\phi q_\phi\!\left(z\,\middle|\,x^{(i)}\right) = \nabla_\phi q_\phi\!\left(z\,\middle|\,x^{(i)}\right) * \frac{q_\phi\!\left(z\,\middle|\,x^{(i)}\right)}{q_\phi\!\left(z\,\middle|\,x^{(i)}\right)}$$

$$= q_\phi\!\left(z\,\middle|\,x^{(i)}\right) * \frac{\nabla_\phi q_\phi\!\left(z\,\middle|\,x^{(i)}\right)}{q_\phi\!\left(z\,\middle|\,x^{(i)}\right)}$$

$$= q_\phi\!\left(z\,\middle|\,x^{(i)}\right)\nabla_\phi \log q_\phi\!\left(z\,\middle|\,x^{(i)}\right)$$

With a bit of calculus and algebra, we have derived an equivalent form for the gradient. If we substitute this reformulation into the step we were stuck on:

$$= \nabla_\phi - KL(q_\phi\!\left(z\,\middle|\,x^{(i)}\right)||p(z)) + \int q_\phi\!\left(z\,\middle|\,x^{(i)}\right)\nabla_\phi \log q_\phi\!\left(z\,\middle|\,x^{(i)}\right) \log p_\theta\!\left(x^{(i)}\,\middle|\,z\right)dz$$

$$= \nabla_\phi - KL(q_\phi\!\left(z\,\middle|\,x^{(i)}\right)||p(z)) + \mathbb{E}_{q_\phi\!\left(z\,\middle|\,x^{(i)}\right)}\!\left[\nabla_\phi \log q_\phi\!\left(z\,\middle|\,x^{(i)}\right) \log p_\theta\!\left(x^{(i)}\,\middle|\,z\right)\right]$$

$$\approx \nabla_\phi - KL(q_\phi\!\left(z\,\middle|\,x^{(i)}\right)||p(z)) + \frac{1}{n}\Sigma_{j=1}^{n}\nabla_\phi \log q_\phi\!\left(z = z_j\,\middle|\,x^{(i)}\right) \log p_\theta\!\left(x^{(i)}\,\middle|\,z = z_j\right)$$

We can now use standard minibatch gradient estimation techniques to optimize our objective with respect to ϕ. The observation we made is a well-known technique in the machine learning community termed the *log trick*. We will see this technique used again later in the chapter on reinforcement learning when we introduce the policy gradient method.

Now that we have fully dissected the first observation that Kingma and Welling made, we now move to the second: the computation of a low variance estimate of the gradient with respect to ϕ. As we mentioned earlier, the log trick allows us to estimate this gradient. However, this estimate has been shown to be of high variance. This means that if we were to run trials where, in each trial, we draw a few samples z_j from the approximate posterior and estimate the gradient with respect to ϕ, we would expect to see vastly different estimates of the gradient across trials. Of course, this is undesirable, as we'd like trials for the same input example to be consistent with each other to have any confidence in our training procedure. We could try to ameliorate this by drawing many samples from the approximate posterior for each example, but this becomes computationally prohibitive for relatively little gain.

Kingma and Welling proposed an alternative method to the log trick for getting around the issue of taking the gradient with respect to the weights of the network parametrizing distribution from which we are sampling. This method is called the *reparametrization trick*, and it allows us to compute a low variance estimate of the gradient, as opposed to the log trick. Why this is the case is beyond the scope of this text, but we refer you to the vast amount of academic literature that exists on this and similar topics.

The reparametrization trick involves assuming the approximate posterior takes on some form, such as a multivariate Gaussian distribution, and then expressing this distribution as a function of another distribution that has no dependence on the weights of the encoder. Let's assume that $q_\phi(z|x^{(i)})$ takes on the form $N(z; \hat{\mu}_\phi, \hat{\sigma}^2_\phi I)$. This represents a multivariate Gaussian distribution where each component z_i is independent of all other components and $z_i \sim N(\mu_{\phi, i}, \sigma^2_{\phi, i})$, $\forall i$. We use ϕ in the subscript to explicitly show the approximate posterior's dependence on the parameters of the encoder through its mean and variance vectors, which are defined by the encoder. In its current form, we run into the issue of not being able to switch the order of the expectation and the gradient that we encountered earlier. Using the reparametrization trick, we can rewrite the sampling procedure as:

$$z \sim N(\hat{\mu}_\phi, \hat{\sigma}^2_\phi I) \Longleftrightarrow z = \hat{\mu}_\phi + \hat{\sigma}_\phi * \epsilon, \epsilon \sim N(0, I)$$

We highly encourage you to work out why the sampling procedure can be rewritten in this manner using the definition of the Gaussian distribution. It will be easier to consider the univariate case first, where X is a standard Gaussian random variable, and then show $Y = c*X$ is a Gaussian random variable with mean zero and variance c^2. Then, consider the general univariate case where X is any Gaussian random variable, and show $Y = X + c$ is a Gaussian random variable with mean $E[X] + c$ and variance $Var(X)$. Putting these steps together will get you to the reformulated sampling procedure described previously.

In summary, we have expressed the approximate posterior as a function of a distribution that is independent of ϕ, along with a mean vector and a standard deviation vector that are dependent on ϕ. We term the random variable ϵ an *auxiliary random variable*. Plugging this reformulation into our troublesome gradient expression from earlier:

$$\nabla_\phi \mathbb{E}_{q_\phi(z|x^{(i)})}\left[\log p_\theta(x^{(i)}|z)\right]$$

$$= \nabla_\phi \mathbb{E}_{\epsilon \sim N(0, I)}\left[\log p_\theta(x^{(i)}|g_\phi(\epsilon))\right]$$

$$= \mathbb{E}_{\epsilon \sim N(0, I)}\left[\nabla_\phi \log p_\theta(x^{(i)}|g_\phi(\epsilon))\right]$$

$$\approx \frac{1}{n}\Sigma^n_{j=1} \nabla_\phi \log p_\theta(x^{(i)}|g_\phi(\epsilon_j))$$

Where $g_\phi(\epsilon) = \hat{\mu}_\phi + \hat{\sigma}_\phi * \epsilon$. We rewrote z as $g_\phi(\epsilon)$ to explicitly show that the dependence on the encoder parameters is now only through the deterministic function applied to the sampling distribution, rather than the sampling distribution itself. This allows us to switch the order of the expectation and the gradient seamlessly, thereby lending it to standard minibatch gradient estimation techniques.

How does this change manifest itself in the encoder architecture? Earlier, when using the log trick, we could directly parametrize the approximate posterior via the encoder. Now, we instead have the encoder, for each example $x^{(i)}$, output a vector of means $\widehat{\mu}_\phi$, a vector of standard deviations $\widehat{\sigma}_\phi$, and sample ϵ from a standard Gaussian distribution that is completely separate from the encoder-decoder VAE architecture. Note that the reparametrization technique comes with its own restrictions—we must assume a form for the approximate posterior, in this case a Gaussian, that allows us to define a differentiable function such as g_ϕ. However, there's no guarantee the true posterior is Gaussian—it is most likely a complex distribution that cannot be represented as functions of our standard distributions. This is a trade-off we must make to achieve a low variance gradient estimate for tractable optimization (Figure 10-5).

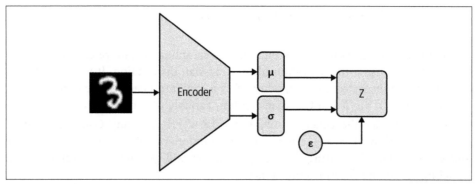

Figure 10-5. What the encoder looks like after the inclusion of reparametrization. It returns a mean and standard deviation vector, which we can combine with ϵ to generate the setting of z. The purpose of the circle versus rectangles is to show that the only sampling is happening for ϵ, completely independent of the encoder architecture. The mean and standard deviation vectors are produced deterministically from the input image. In addition, z is deterministic once we know the value of ϵ.

Note that the training procedure for a VAE is quite simple—the beast was in the motivation and mathematics behind the architecture and optimization. All we need to do is:

1. Sample an example $x^{(i)}$ from the dataset.

2. Run $x^{(i)}$ through the encoder network to generate a vector of means $\widehat{\mu}_\phi$ and a vector of standard deviations $\widehat{\sigma}_\phi$.

3. Sample ϵ and calculate the result of $g_\phi(\epsilon)$.

4. Run the result through the decoder network, which now represents the distribution $p_\theta\big(x\,\big|\,z = g_\phi(\epsilon)\big)$.

5. Query this distribution with our initial example $x^{(i)}$ and take the log of the resulting likelihood. This will be our *decoder loss*. If you took multiple samples of ϵ in step 3, run the above procedure for each sample, and average to get the decoder loss.

6. Sum the decoder loss with $-KL\big(q_\phi\big(z\,\big|\,x^{(i)}\big)\,\big|\big|\,p(z)\big)$, the *encoder loss*, to get a final loss. Use the negative of the final loss in the next step since we want to maximize it instead of minimize it.

7. Perform classical SGD/minibatch gradient descent to update ϕ and θ.

Now that we have covered how to train a VAE, how do we utilize it as a generative model once it is trained? Note that we initially defined the generative process as $p(x|z)p(z)$, where we start with some setting of the latent variables z sampled from the prior distribution and map z to an instance x in the data space via the conditional likelihood. We've already learned this generative process in the form of $p_\theta(x|z)$, or the decoder, and assumed the prior distribution $p(z)$ to be a multivariate standard Gaussian at the beginning. To generate samples from a VAE, we sample z_i from the prior distribution $p(z)$, pass this sample through the decoder so it now represents the distribution $p_\theta(x|z = z_i)$, and finally sample x_i from $p_\theta(x|z = z_i)$. Note that we no longer need the approximate posterior at this step—however, it played a key role in the training of the decoder and is still useful in understanding how our latent variable distribution shifts after witnessing an example from the dataset.

Implementing a VAE

In this section, we will build a VAE from scratch in PyTorch. We will additionally provide some example training and testing code on the famous MNIST digits dataset.

Before we begin, here is a list of the packages you will need to reproduce this section on your own:

```
import torch
from torch.distributions.multivariate_normal \
    import MultivariateNormal
import torch.nn as nn
from torchvision import datasets, transforms
from torchvision.utils import save_image
import torch.optim as optim
```

Let's start with the encoder. As we discussed in the previous section, the encoder is a neural network that outputs a vector of means and a vector of standard deviations. Each index represents a univariate Gaussian, and the entire vector represents a multivariate Gaussian where each component is independent from the others. Though we are working with image data, for the sake of simplicity we convert each image into a vector by flattening it at the start. This allows us to apply standard, fully connected layers on the input. Since each image in the MNIST dataset is of size 28 × 28, each resulting representation is a 784-dimensional vector. We also need to decide on the number of components, or latent variables, we will use to represent the latent space. We can treat the number of components as a hyperparameter—if we notice that the decoder log likelihoods of input examples are consistently low even after a significant amount of training, this may indicate an approximate posterior that is not expressive enough. Increasing the number of components and retraining in this case is advisable.

Here is example code for an encoder:

```
# Encoder layers (Gaussian MLP)
D_in, H, D_out = 784, 200, 20
input_layer = nn.Linear(D_in, H)
hidden_layer_mean = nn.Linear(H, D_out)
hidden_layer_var = nn.Linear(H, D_out)
```

For the sake of simplicity, we leave out nonlinearities between the layers for now. Our encoder consists of two levels of layers. The first level operates on the input, embedding the vector into a lower dimensional representation. The second level operates on the 200-d representation and consists of two independent layers: one for determining the means of each of the univariate Gaussian components, and one for determining the standard deviations of each of the univariate Gaussian components. Here, we use 20 components. As we stated earlier, we assume $q_\phi\left(z\middle|x^{(i)}\right)$ takes the form of a multivariate Gaussian, where each component is independent of the others. Note that attempting to learn a full covariance matrix is computationally prohibitive (amongst other concerns), as its size grows quadratically with the number of components.

Here is example code for a decoder:

```
# Decoder layers (Bernoulli MLP for MNIST data)
recon_layer = nn.Linear(D_out, H)
recon_output = nn.Linear(H, D_in)
```

Again, we leave out the nonlinearities for the sake of simplicity. The decoder operates on the sampled z, which we know is a 20-d vector. The rest of the decoder architecture is symmetrical to the encoder, and outputs a distribution over the input data. Although not in the code just yet, there is a final sigmoid layer that will be applied to the output of the recon_output layer which, recall, squashes each input dimension into the range (0,1). Since we are working with the discrete MNIST dataset where each pixel is represented as either a zero or a one, the output of the final sigmoid layer is used to represent a Bernoulli distribution for each pixel. Recall the Bernoulli distribution from Chapter 2, represented as *Ber(p)*, where *p* is the probability of returning a one and 1 − *p* is the the probability of returning a zero.

More formally, we have that the decoder likelihood distribution $p_\theta(x|z)$ can be rewritten as a product over each pixel:

$$p_\theta(x|z) = \Pi_{j=1}^{784} p_\theta(x_j|z)$$

where $p(x_j|z) = Ber(\text{decoder}(z)_j)$

Note that decoder(z) represents the 784-d vector after applying the sigmoid layer. For a given pixel $x_j^{(i)}$ in the input example $x^{(i)}$, we'd like its corresponding probability p to be close to one if $x_j^{(i)} = 1$, and its corresponding probability p to be close to zero if $x_j^{(i)} = 0$. As you may recall from the previous section, we work with $\log p_\theta(x|z)$, which reduces to $\Sigma_{j=1}^{784} \log p_\theta(x_j|z)$.

Now, we can put the encoder and decoder together into a single VAE architecture:

```
class VAE(nn.Module):
  def __init__(self, D_in, H, D_out):
    super(VAE, self).__init__()
    self.D_in, self.H, self.D_out = D_in, H, D_out

    # Encoder layers (Gaussian MLP)
    self.input_layer = nn.Linear(D_in, H)
    self.hidden_layer_mean = nn.Linear(H, D_out)
    self.hidden_layer_var = nn.Linear(H, D_out)

    # Decoder layers (Bernoulli MLP for MNIST data)
    self.recon_layer = nn.Linear(D_out, H)
    self.recon_output = nn.Linear(H, D_in)
    self.tanh = nn.Tanh()
    self.sigmoid = nn.Sigmoid()

  def encode(self, inp):
    h_vec = self.input_layer(inp)
    h_vec = self.sigmoid(h_vec)
    means = self.hidden_layer_mean(h_vec)
    log_vars = self.hidden_layer_var(h_vec)
    return means, log_vars

  def decode(self, means, log_vars):
    # Reparametrization trick
    std_devs = torch.pow(2,log_vars)**0.5
    aux = MultivariateNormal(torch.zeros(self.D_out), \
    torch.eye(self.D_out)).sample()
    sample = means + aux * std_devs

    # Reconstruction
    h_vec = self.recon_layer(sample)
    h_vec = self.tanh(h_vec)
    output = self.sigmoid(self.recon_output(h_vec))
```

```
        return output

    def forward(self, inp):
      means, log_vars = self.encode(inp)
      output = self.decode(means, log_vars)
      return output, means, log_vars

    def reconstruct(self, sample):
      h_vec = self.recon_layer(sample)
      h_vec = self.tanh(h_vec)
      output = self.sigmoid(self.recon_output(h_vec))
      return output
```

The call to encode is followed by the call to decode in the forward function. Note that decode uses only a single sample from the approximate posterior, as we found that a single sample is sufficient for the MNIST dataset, but this can be easily modified to work for multiple samples. To calculate the reverse KL, the forward function returns the results of the encode call in addition to the decoder likelihood distribution.

Here is example code for computing the loss:

```
    def compute_loss(inp, recon_inp, means, log_vars):
      # Calculate reverse KL divergence
      # (formula provided in Kingma and Welling)
      kl_loss = -0.5 * torch.sum(1 + log_vars
                            - means ** 2 - torch.pow(2,log_vars))

      # Calculate BCE loss
      loss = nn.BCELoss(reduction="sum")
      recon_loss = loss(recon_inp, inp)
      return kl_loss + recon_loss
```

We recommend you take a look at the PyTorch documentation for nn.BCELoss and verify that it is indeed computing the negative log likelihood of the input example $x^{(i)}$: $-\Sigma_{j=1}^{784} \log p_\theta\left(x_j^{(i)} \middle| z\right)$. We also recommend you verify that the kl_loss term is the reverse KL divergence between two Gaussian distributions as derived in Kingma and Welling. Returning the sum of the negative log likelihood and the reverse KL divergence as a final loss term gets us to the end of step 6 from the previous section. Finally, for some training code:

```
    D_in, H, D_out = 784, 500, 20
    vae = VAE(D_in, H, D_out)
    vae.to("cpu")

    def train():
      vae.train()
      optimizer = optim.Adam(vae.parameters(), lr=1e-3)

      train_loader = torch.utils.data.DataLoader(
          datasets.MNIST('../data',
                        train=True,
```

```
                download=True,
                transform=transforms.ToTensor()),
                batch_size=100,
                shuffle=True)

    epochs = 10
    for epoch in range(epochs):
        for batch_idx, (data, _) in enumerate(train_loader):
            optimizer.zero_grad()
            data = data.view((100,784))
            output, means, log_vars = vae(data)
            loss = compute_loss(data, output, means, log_vars)
            loss.backward()
            optimizer.step()
            if (batch_idx * len(data)) % 10000 == 0:
                print(
                    'Train Epoch: {} [{}/{} ({:.0f}%)]\tLoss: {:.6f}' \
                    .format(
                    epoch, batch_idx * len(data), len(train_loader.dataset),
                    100. * batch_idx / len(train_loader), loss.item()))
        torch.save(vae.state_dict(), "vae.%d" % epoch)
```

Here, we train the VAE for 10 epochs, saving the state of the VAE at the end of each epoch. Note that we set some hyperparameters fixed here, such as the learning rate of the optimizer and the number of latent variables. We recommend writing some validation code, in addition to the training code presented here, to select the best hyperparameter settings.

Finally, how can we test the generative capabilities of our fully trained VAE? We know that the generative process can be written as $p(z)p(x|z)$, where we first draw a sample z_j from our prior, run the sample through the decoder so the decoder's likelihood distribution now represents $p_\theta(x | z = z_j)$, and sample x_j from this distribution. Here is the code that puts this logic into action:

```
    def test():
        dist = MultivariateNormal(torch.zeros(D_out), torch.eye(D_out))
        vae = VAE(D_in, H, D_out)
        vae.load_state_dict(torch.load("vae.%d" % 9))
        vae.eval()
        outputs = []

        for i in range(100):
            sample = dist.sample()
            outputs.append(vae.reconstruct(sample).view((1,1,28,28)))
        outputs = torch.stack(outputs).view(100,1,28,28)
        save_image(outputs, "prior_reconstruct_100.png", nrow=10)
```

The for loop generates 100 samples from the approximate posterior, and for each of those samples, a sample from the corresponding decoder likelihood distribution over

the input data. The last couple of lines of code allow us to save the samples in a 10 ×
10 grid, depicted in Figure 10-6.

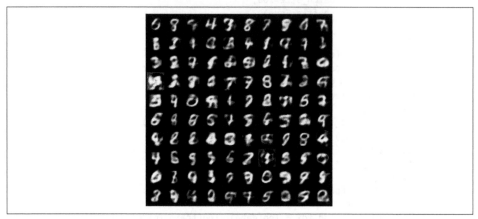

Figure 10-6. 100 samples from a VAE trained on the MNIST dataset for 10 epochs.

Though the images are a bit blurry, we can make out digits in most of the samples.
With more complex architectures such as RNNs, hyperparameter tuning, and longer
training times, we will surely see even better results. In the next section, we introduce a slightly different take on generative models that has recently been achieving
popularity.

Score-Based Generative Models

In this section, we approach generative modeling through a slightly different lens
than what we have encountered so far. In an optimally trained GAN, we first sample
from some noise distribution $p(z)$ and run this sample z_i through a generator G,
which deterministically transforms z_i into a sample x_i from the true data distribution
(where we approximate the true data distribution $p(x)$ using our dataset, $p_{data}(x)$).
Though G itself is a deterministic function, $G(z)$ is a random variable distributed as
the true data distribution. In summary, we have implicitly defined a distribution over
our domain via the generator's action on samples from $p(z)$, and a way of sampling
from the true data distribution via a simpler distribution $p(z)$, such as a multivariate
Gaussian distribution.

VAEs are more explicit in their probabilistic modeling. We define z to be a set of latent variables that generate the data we see, x. We explicitly learn a conditional distribution over the data $p_\theta(x|z)$ via the decoder, which we can sample from. In an optimally trained VAE, $p_\theta(x|z) = p(x|z)$, is the true conditional likelihood of the data. To generate data using an optimally trained VAE, we first sample a setting of the latent variables from $p(z)$ and run this sample z_i through the decoder, which now parametrizes the distribution $p(x|z = z_i)$. This is an explicit probability distribution we can now sample from.

Note that although GANs and VAEs themselves are quite distinct, both of their architectures and actions involve an additional distribution $p(z)$ (whether that is a noise distribution in GANs or a prior over latent variables in VAEs). Is there a way of sampling from the true data distribution without the additional distribution? Score-based generative models attempt to do just that.

One method of sampling from a probability distribution is an iterative process called *Langevin dynamics*. This process is actually an instance of a class of algorithms referred to as *Markov Chain Monte Carlo (MCMC)* algorithms. Motivating MCMC algorithms and proving why they sample from probability distributions in an unbiased manner are beyond the scope of this section, but we refer you to the vast amount of academic literature that exists on this topic.

Langevin dynamics follows the process defined as follows:

$$x^{(i+1)} = x^{(i)} + \eta \nabla_x \log p\left(x^{(i)}\right) + \sqrt{2\eta}\epsilon, \epsilon \sim N(0, I)$$

$x^{(i)}$ here represents a sample from $p(x)$, and this dynamics equation shows us how to generate the next sample $x^{(i+1)}$ given our current sample.

Note that if we were to remove the Gaussian noise component at the end of the dynamics equation, we would just be following the gradient to a maximum of $p(x)$, i.e., performing gradient ascent with some step-size η. The intuition behind this dynamics equation is that the addition of the noise component prevents us from simply reaching the maximum x and instead allows us to explore regions with high probability, thereby exploring regions of low probability less (Figure 10-7). Again, why this produces samples from $p(x)$ in an unbiased manner is beyond the scope of this text, but we highly encourage you to learn more from the academic literature.

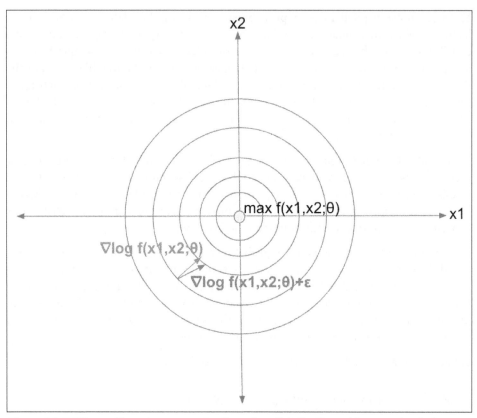

Figure 10-7. We use f here to represent a Gaussian distribution with mean (and also maximum) at the origin. Each of the contours represents locations with equal likelihood. As we can see from the diagram, the gradient points directly toward the maximum, but adding a bit of noise allows us to explore and sample from high-density regions without converging to the maximum.

Although we use the gradient of the log probability instead of the gradient of the probability, the value(s) of x that maximizes $\log p(x)$ is the same as the value(s) of x that maximizes *p(x)* due to the log's concaveness. More generally, the log's concaveness also preserves the ordering relationships between all possible values of x, i.e., if $p(x_1) \geq p(x_2)$, then $\log p(x_1) \geq \log p(x_2)$, and vice versa. For that reason, as we saw in "Implementing a VAE" on page 259, these sorts of optimization processes tend to not be affected meaningfully by the inclusion of the log.

However, the main issue with Langevin dynamics, as we've encountered before with other generative models, is that we don't know *p(x)*, let alone the gradient of its log! But there may be a way to model $\nabla_x \log p(x)$, which we call *p(x)*'s *score function*, directly. This would allow us to simply plug the score directly into the Langevin dynamics equation and draw samples from $p(x)$ as if we knew $p(x)$ all along. This is the idea of score-based generative modeling.

For a moment, let's forget the problem of sampling from an unknown distribution $p(x)$ and instead consider the problem of learning $p(x)$. From now until the end of this section, we will consider only the problems of learning and sampling from continuous probability distributions. In the same vein of explicitly learning approximate probability distributions like in VAEs, we can try to approximate $p(x)$ with a learned version $p_\theta(x)$, where θ represents the parameters of the learned model. What we envision is a learned function, such as a neural network, that takes as input an example x and outputs a likelihood $p_\theta(x)$. However, there is no way to ensure that $\int p_\theta(x) dx = 1$, which is a necessary condition of any probability distribution.

Instead, we settle for learning what we call an unnormalized probability distribution $q_\theta(x)$. This is a function that takes an example x and outputs an unnormalized likelihood. We can, in theory, represent the normalized probability distribution $p_\theta(x)$ via $\frac{q_\theta(x)}{Z(\theta)}$, where $Z(\theta) = \int q_\theta(x) dx$. Unfortunately, this integral is generally intractable and has no closed form solution. Of course, there are exceptions to the rule. For example, $Z(\theta) = \sigma * \sqrt{2\pi}$ for a univariate Gaussian distribution, where $\theta = (\mu, \sigma)$ are the mean and standard deviation of the Gaussian. But if we'd like to model more expressive distributions via a neural network, for example, it is almost always impossible to tractably calculate $Z(\theta)$, which we will also refer to as the *partition function*.

How can we go about learning such an unnormalized probability distribution? Researchers have presented many approaches for learning $q_\theta(x)$ throughout the history of machine learning and inference, but one particular method starts to bridge the gap between learning an unnormalized probability distribution and sampling from its normalized version via a process like Langevin dynamics. *Score matching*, or the idea of learning $q_\theta(x)$ via minimizing the difference between the score function of $q_\theta(x)$ and the score function of the true distribution $p(x)$, was first proposed by Hyvarinen in 2005.

Here, we show that minimizing the difference as stated is equivalent to minimizing the difference between the score function of $p_\theta(x)$ and the score function of $p(x)$:

$$\nabla_x \log q_\theta(x) = \nabla_x \log (p_\theta(x) * Z(\theta))$$
$$= \nabla_x \log p_\theta(x) + \nabla_x \log Z(\theta)$$
$$= \nabla_x \log p_\theta(x)$$

It turns out that the score function of $q_\theta(x)$ is the same as the score function of $p_\theta(x)$, $\forall x$. This is because the log first separates the product of $q_\theta(x)$ and the partition function into a sum of logs, and finally the gradient with respect to x eliminates the log of the partition function, since this term is solely dependent on the weights θ and is not a function of x itself. Thus, the optimal θ that minimizes the proposed difference is equivalent to the optimal θ that minimizes the difference in scores between $p_\theta(x)$ and $p(x)$. The following is the optimization procedure, which we call *explicit score matching*:

$$J(\theta) = \mathbb{E}_{p(x)}\left[\frac{1}{2}||\nabla_x \log q_\theta(x) - \nabla_x \log p(x)||_2^2\right]$$

$$\theta^* = \operatorname{argmin}_\theta J(\theta)$$

The reason for the leading $\frac{1}{2}$ is to simplify the resulting gradient (cancels out with the 2 that will be pulled down from the square of the norm). Note that we have completely removed the dependence on the partition function in our analysis, and we now have a way to (1) learn an unnormalized distribution $q_\theta(x)$, and (2) calculate the score of $p_\theta(x^{(i)})$ via our neural network. For item 1, in the case where we find a setting θ that results in $J(\theta) = 0$, $p_\theta(x)$ and $p(x)$ are the same for all x since their gradients are the same for all x. Of course, in general, two functions that have the same gradients everywhere can still be different functions by being off from each other by a nonzero constant. However, in our case, these two functions cannot be off by a nonzero constant since they are both probability distributions that must sum to one. Thus, we have a valid optimization procedure for learning an unnormalized distribution that, when normalized, should approximate the true distribution well.

To perform item 2, in theory all we would need to do is first run our example $x^{(i)}$ through our neural network to get $q_\theta(x^{(i)})$, take the log of $q_\theta(x^{(i)})$, and backpropagate this result through our network all the way back to the input. We've already shown that the resultant score is equivalent to the score of $p_\theta(x^{(i)})$. Going forward, we will refer to the score function of $p_\theta(x)$ (and $q_\theta(x)$) as $\Psi_\theta(x)$, and the score function of $p(x)$ as $\Psi(x)$. Using our new notation, we rewrite the explicit score matching objective as:

$$\theta^* = \operatorname{argmin}_\theta \mathbb{E}_{p(x)}\left[\frac{1}{2}||\Psi_\theta(x) - \Psi(x)||_2^2\right]$$

Although we have gotten around the issue of the partition function, we still have no idea what $\Psi(x)$ is. Hyvarinen, in 2005, in addition to proposing the notion of explicit score matching, proved an amazing property regarding explicit score matching (satisfied under certain weak regularity conditions):

$$\mathbb{E}_{p(x)}\left[\frac{1}{2}||\Psi_\theta(x) - \Psi(x)||_2^2\right] = \mathbb{E}_{p(x)}\left[\frac{1}{2}||\Psi_\theta(x)||_2^2 + \Sigma_{i=1}^d \nabla_{x_i}\Psi_{\theta,i}(x) + c\right]$$

Where $\Psi_{\theta,i}(x) = \nabla_{x_i} \log p_\theta(x)$—the score function is just a length d vector (assuming x is of d dimensions), where each index i corresponds with the partial derivative of the log probability with respect to x_i. c is a constant that has no dependence on θ, so it can simply be ignored during optimization. This is a method the community has come to know as *implicit score matching*.

Note that the equivalent expression has no dependence on the true probability distribution, and thus we can directly optimize θ, using it as we would any other objective. Once we learn the optimal θ, all we need to do to perform generative modeling is:

1. Follow the methodology presented earlier for calculating the score of $p_\theta(x^{(i)})$: run the example through our learned network, take the log of the result, and backpropagate all the way to the input.

2. Sample ϵ from $N(0,I)$.

3. Plug in the results of steps 1 and 2 into the Langevin dynamics equation to obtain the next sample, $x^{(i+1)}$.

4. Repeat steps 1 through 3 with $x^{(i+1)}$.

This procedure allows us to draw samples from $p_\theta(x)$, which, as shown earlier, should approximate $p(x)$ well once the network has been trained.

Can we do better than implicit score matching? For one, implicit score matching requires us to calculate second-order gradients, as can be seen from the $\sum_{i=1}^{d} \nabla_{x_i} \Psi_{\theta,i}(x)$ term in the implicit score matching objective. This can be quite computationally expensive depending on the size of x. In a framework such as PyTorch, this would require first calculating the first-order gradient through standard means such as backpropagation and then looping through each x_i manually to compute its second-order gradient. In the next section, we will cover *denoising autoencoders* and *denoising score matching*, which modify the objective and allow us to get around these complexity issues.

Denoising Autoencoders and Score Matching

Before explaining the connection between denoising autoencoders and score matching, we first motivate the denoising autoencoder architecture. In Chapter 9, we learned about autoencoders through the lens of representation learning. We used autoencoders to compress high-dimensional data, such as images, into low-dimensional representations that preserved the information, or useful features, necessary to reconstruct the original data. We additionally showed, through our experiments on MNIST, that we were able to reconstruct the data quite well and we generally saw, for instances of a given digit, clustering of its low-dimensional representations. This implies that if we were to train a standard classifier on these low-dimensional representations, with the label being their original digit categories, we'd expect to see great accuracy.

However, depending on the data we try to compress, it turns out that, at times, our compressions aren't able to capture useful features. In other words, when we use our trained autoencoder on real-world images outside of our sample that may be slightly corrupted, rotated, shifted, or captured under various light settings, our ability to classify these images using their low-dimensional representations takes a large dip.

Ideally, we would like our learned representations to be invariant to such noise. In 2008, Vincent proposed denoising autoencoders as a method for combating the issues we see with standard autoencoders. Denoising autoencoders first corrupt the original input data with noise, run the corrupted input through a standard autoencoder, and finally attempt to reconstruct the original input (Figure 10-8). The original paper used a corruption scheme that randomly zeroed out some portion of the input, but acknowledged that a variety of corruption schemes could be used instead. Intuitively, the representations learned from such a procedure should be much more robust to the challenges presented by real-world images. Indeed, the experiments on MNIST by Vincent in 2008 showed that, under various data augmentations such as rotation and background noise, the denoising autoencoder performed significantly better than the standard autoencoder in terms of classification accuracy.

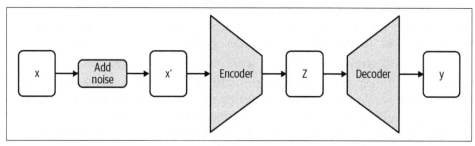

Figure 10-8. The denoising autoencoder architecture is the same as that of the standard autoencoder, except instead of minimizing the reconstruction error between y and the input x', we minimize the reconstruction error between y and the original x.

Following Vincent 2011, which first noticed the connection between denoising AEs and score matching, we instead define the corruption scheme to be the addition of Gaussian noise to the original data. Formally, we have that $p(x)$ represents the true distribution of the data, $p_{data}(x)$ represents the distribution of the data using our training set, and $p_\sigma(x'|x)$ represents the conditional distribution of the corrupted data given the original data. In particular:

$$p_\sigma(x'|x) = N(x'; x, \sigma^2 I)$$

Where the mean of the distribution is the original data and the subscript σ represents the standard deviation of the Gaussian noise applied to the original data. Note that x' and x are defined over the same domain (all possible images, for example). We can now calculate the distribution over the corrupted data:

$$p_\sigma(x') = \Sigma_x p_\sigma(x'|x)p(x)$$
$$\approx \Sigma_x p_\sigma(x'|x)p_{data}(x)$$
$$= \frac{1}{n}\Sigma_{i=1}^n p_\sigma\left(x'|x = x^{(i)}\right)$$

which is the empirical average over the conditional probabilities using each data point from our dataset as the reference. This follows naturally from letting the true distribution be approximated by the distribution defined by the dataset (same as how this was defined in "Generative Adversarial Networks" on page 244).

In 2011, Vincent explored the possibility of using $p_\sigma(x')$ as the reference instead of $p(x)$ as we do in explicit score matching. The reasoning for this is that $p_\sigma(x')$ can be viewed as a continuous approximation to the true distribution $p(x)$. The approximation defined by $p_{data}(x)$ is unbiased, but is unfortunately discontinuous everywhere x is not present in the dataset due to being a uniform distribution over all images in the dataset, with a likelihood of zero everywhere else. Of course, as σ gets larger, $p_\sigma(x')$ is seen as a less and less faithful approximation to $p(x)$, so we'd like to work with small σ's.

Vincent 2011 first proposed explicit score matching using $p_\sigma(x')$ as the reference:

$$J(\theta) = \mathbb{E}_{p_\sigma(x')}\left[\frac{1}{2}||\nabla_{x'} \log p_\theta(x') - \nabla_{x'} \log p_\sigma(x')||_2^2\right]$$
$$\theta^* = \text{argmin}_\theta J(\theta)$$

Note that the same reasoning for why this is a valid optimization procedure for $p_\theta(x)$ is the same as in the previous section—the only difference here is the reference distribution we are trying to match. Vincent 2011 actually goes an extra step and shows that this optimization procedure is equivalent to:

$$J_{\text{DSM}}(\theta) = \mathbb{E}_{p_\sigma(x, x')}\left[\frac{1}{2}||\nabla_{x'} \log p_\theta(x') - \nabla_{x'} \log p_\sigma(x'|x)||_2^2\right]$$
$$\theta^*_{\text{DSM}} = \text{argmin}_\theta J_{\text{DSM}}(\theta)$$

Although we won't show the proof here and refer you to Vincent 2011 for the full details, it does utilize the log trick we described in "Implementing a VAE" on page

259. We refer to optimizing this objective as *denoising score matching*, or *DSM* for short, and as we will show soon, it serves as the connection to denoising AEs.

We know that $p_\sigma(x'|x) = N(x'; x, \sigma^2 I)$, and now compute the gradient of its log:

$$\nabla_{x'} \log p_\sigma(x'|x) = \nabla_{x'} \log \left(\frac{1}{\sqrt{(2\pi)^d |\sigma^2 I|}} e^{\frac{-(x'-x)^T(x'-x)}{2\sigma^2}} \right)$$

$$= \nabla_{x'} \log \frac{1}{\sqrt{(2\pi)^d |\sigma^2 I|}} + \nabla_{x'} \log e^{\frac{-(x'-x)^T(x'-x)}{2\sigma^2}}$$

$$= -\frac{1}{2\sigma^2} \nabla_{x'} (x'-x)^T (x'-x)$$

$$= -\frac{1}{2\sigma^2} \left(\nabla_{x'} x'^T x' - 2\nabla_{x'} x'^T x + \nabla_{x'} x^T x \right)$$

$$= \frac{1}{\sigma^2} (x - x')$$

Let's break down the math. The first equality is simply the definition of a Gaussian distribution with mean x and variance $\sigma^2 I$. The second equality is a result of the log breaking up the product into a sum of logs, and the gradient of a sum being the sum of gradients. In the third equality, we see the first term has been removed since it is not a function of *x'*, and thus its gradient is zero. Additionally, the log of *e* raised to any power is just the power itself, since log as used here has base *e*. Finally, we expand out the dot product of *x'* – *x* with itself and apply the gradient to each individual term of the resulting sum. Note that we can simply rewrite $-x'^T x - x^T x'$ as $-2x'^T x$ since the two terms are transposes of each other and result in the same scalar. We refer you to an amazing text called *The Matrix Cookbook* by KB Petersen and Michael Syskind Pedersen, which can serve as a guide to evaluating these gradients (plus more) and arrive at the final equality. The intuition for the gradient of $x'^T x'$ is that it is the analog of the derivative of the square of a variable from single-variable calculus.

For the final step, we will show that optimizing the objective for denoising score matching is equivalent to optimizing the objective for denoising AEs. To recap, a denoising AE has the same architecture as that of a standard AE—the only difference is in the input data and the training objective. The training objective of the denoising AE looks like:

$$J_{\text{DAE}}(\theta) = \mathbb{E}_{p_\sigma(x, x')} [||\text{decode}(\text{encode}(x')) - x||_2^2]$$

$$\theta^\star_{\text{DAE}} = \text{argmin}_\theta J_{\text{DAE}}(\theta)$$

Note that the parameters, or weights, of both decode() and encode() are encompassed by θ. To summarize, we must show that θ^*_{DAE} and θ^*_{DSM} defined earlier are equivalent for some form of the unnormalized likelihood. Once again, following Vincent 2011, we define the denoising autoencoder as an encoder consisting of a single fully connected layer followed by a sigmoid layer and a decoder consisting solely of a single fully connected layer. Additionally, we add the constraint that the two fully connected layers are weight-tied so that they are transposes of each other. The training objective can now be specified as, where $\theta = (W, b, c)$:

$$J_{\text{DAE}}(\theta) = \mathbb{E}_{p_\sigma(x, x')}\left[||W^T(Wx' + b) + c - x||_2^2\right]$$

$$= 2\sigma^4 * \mathbb{E}_{p_\sigma(x, x')}\left[\frac{1}{2\sigma^4}||W^T(Wx' + b) + c - x||_2^2\right]$$

$$= 2\sigma^4 * \mathbb{E}_{p_\sigma(x, x')}\left[\frac{1}{2}||\frac{1}{\sigma^2}\left(W^T(Wx' + b) + c - x'\right) - \frac{1}{\sigma^2}(x - x')||_2^2\right]$$

You may notice that our algebraic manipulation has led to the appearance of $\nabla_{x'} \log p_\sigma(x'|x)$. All we need to do now is find a form for the unnormalized likelihood whose gradient with respect to x' is $\frac{1}{\sigma^2}\left(W^T(Wx' + b) + c - x'\right)$.

As it turns out, if we define the unnormalized likelihood $q_\theta(x')$ to be $-\frac{1}{\sigma^2}\left(c^T x - \frac{1}{2}||x||_2^2 + \Sigma_{j=1}^d \text{softplus}\left(W_j^T x + b_j\right)\right)$ and plug in this expression to the denoising score matching objective, we are left with an objective that is just $\frac{1}{2\sigma^4}J_{\text{DAE}}(\theta)$. We refer you to Vincent 2011 to see why this is the case.

Optimizing this new objective with respect to θ is no different from optimizing a denoising autoencoder. This is because σ is a positive constant and has no dependence on θ, thus only scaling the magnitude of the resulting gradient rather than affecting its direction. In summary, we have found that training a denoising AE is the same as optimizing the denoising score matching objective, where the unnormalized likelihood takes the form specified in the previous paragraph. More simply, the weights of a trained denoising AE would be the same as those of an unnormalized likelihood specified by $-\frac{1}{\sigma^2}\left(c^T x - \frac{1}{2}||x||_2^2 + \Sigma_{j=1}^d \text{softplus}\left(W_j^T x + b_j\right)\right)$ and trained via denoising score matching.

All we would need to do to perform generative modeling using a denoising AE is:

1. Fully train the denoising AE by minimizing $J_{\text{DAE}}(\theta)$.

2. For a given $x^{(i)}$, calculate its score by evaluating $\frac{1}{\sigma^2}\left(\text{decode}\left(\text{encode}\left(x^{(i)}\right)\right) - x^{(i)}\right)$.

3. Sample ϵ from $N(0,I)$.

4. Plug in the results of 2 and 3 into the Langevin dynamics equation to obtain the next sample $x^{(i+1)}$.

5. Repeat steps 2 through 4 with $x^{(i+1)}$.

Though we've gotten around the issue of needing to calculate second-order gradients by using this method, there is still the issue of being able to sample only from the noisy approximation of *p(x)*. More recent work builds off of concepts from both implicit score matching and denoising score matching to achieve even stronger and more realistic generative capabilities. We highly recommend you explore the literature further, as most of the prerequisite material has been covered in these sections.

Summary

In summary, we have learned a great deal about generative models. We covered the motivation and mathematics behind GANs, VAEs, and a few forms of score matching, and even implemented a VAE from scratch. We also learned about the similarities and differences between these methods. For example, a GAN implicitly models a complex distribution that we can sample from via its generator, while a VAE explicitly learns distributions but is slightly more restrictive in the complexity of distributions it can model. Implicit score matching, similarly to GANs, allowed us to sample from complex distributions via Langevin dynamics (without the use of an additional noise distribution *p(z)*), but having to compute second-order gradients led us to the development of the denoising score matching and its connection with pre-existing denoising AEs. Additionally, VAEs took on the strongest probabilistic modeling approach of the three by defining a set of latent variables and explicitly learning an approximate posterior, given an input example, and a likelihood function, given a setting of latent variables. In contrast, for GANs, the additional variable *z*'s purpose is solely as an intermediate for sampling. Although all of these models tackle generative modeling from distinct perspectives and motivations, they have all produced strong results and have laid a solid groundwork for current and future research.

## CHAPTER 11

Methods in Interpretability

Overview

The field of interpretability is broad and can be uniquely applied to a variety of tasks. Simply put, interpretability defines a model's ability to "explain" its decision making to a third party. There are many modern architectures that do not have this capability just by construction. A neural network, for example, is a prime example of one of these modern architectures. The term "opaque" is often used to describe neural networks, both in media and in literature. This is because, without post hoc techniques to explain the final classification or regression result of a neural network, the data transformations occurring within the trained model are unclear and difficult for the end user to interpret. All we know is that we fed in an example and out popped a result. Although we can examine the learned weights of a neural network, the composition of all of these weights is an extremely complex function. This makes it difficult to tell what part of the input ended up contributing the most to the final result.

A variety of post hoc methodologies have been designed to explain the output of a neural network—*saliency mapping* is a prime example. Saliency mapping measures the gradient of the output of a trained model with respect to the input. By the definition of the gradient, the input positions with the highest magnitude gradients would affect the output value, or class in the case of classification, the most when their values are changed slightly. Saliency mapping thus interprets the set of positions (and their respective values) with the highest magnitude gradients as the part of the input that contributes the most to the final result.

However, this is not the be-all and end-all of interpretability. One issue with saliency mapping is that it can be a bit noisy, especially when we consider the gradient at the individual pixel level for tasks like image classification. Additionally, if the input is categorical in nature rather than continuous, e.g., one-hot encodings for sentences, the gradient with respect to the input isn't interpretable in itself since the input space is discontinuous.

Further, as mentioned earlier, the task at hand is often key for determining what makes sense as a valid method of interpretability. We will expound on this more in the sections to come.

Oftentimes, interpretability comes at the expense of performance. Building interpretability into a model often adds some bias (the bias in bias-variance trade-off) by making simplifying model assumptions, e.g., in vanilla linear regression, where we assume a linear relationship between the features and the target variable. These simplifying assumptions, however, are what make the relationship between the input features and the target variable much clearer in a vanilla linear regression as opposed to a complex, neural architecture.

This all begs the question: why do we care about interpretability in the first place? In a world that is becoming increasingly dominated by technology, complex algorithms, and machine learning, the ability to explain decision making is imperative. Especially in fields such as medicine, where patient's lives are on the line, or in finance, where peoples' financial livelihoods are at stake, the ability to explain a model's decision making is a key step toward widespread adoption. In the next section, we will cover some classical models that have strong notions of interpretability built into their design.

Decision Trees and Tree-Based Algorithms

Most classical data science and machine learning methodologies have some built-in form of interpretability. Tree-based algorithms are a clear example of this. Decision trees are designed to classify an input based on a series of conditional statements, where each node in the tree is associated with a conditional statement. To understand how a trained tree-based model is making a decision, all we must do for any given input is follow the correct branch at each node in the tree (Figure 11-1).

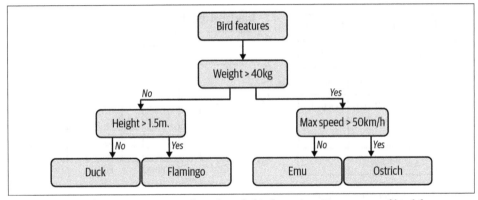

Figure 11-1. A decision tree trained to classify bird species. Given a set of bird features, follow the right "Yes" or "No" branch at each node to reach a final classification.

More complex tree-based algorithms, such as the random forest algorithm, which is composed of an ensemble of large decision trees, are also interpretable. For example, in the case of classification, random forest algorithms function by running a given input through each decision tree and then taking the majority output class amongst the decision trees as the final output (or an average in the case of regression). By the algorithm's construction, we know exactly how random forest came to a final conclusion regarding the input.

In addition to interpretability at the individual example level, decision trees and their more complex ensembles have built-in metrics for feature importance at the global level. For example, when a decision tree is being trained, it must determine which feature to split on and the threshold(s) of that feature at which to split. In the classification regime, one methodology to do this is to calculate the information gain by splitting on a proposed feature at a proposed threshold. To frame our thinking, let's think of the possible training labels as the domain of a discrete probability distribution, where the probability of each label is the frequency with which that label appears in the training dataset (Figure 11-2).

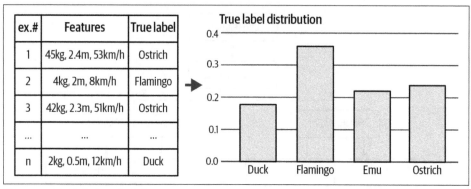

Figure 11-2. Label probabilities.

Thinking back to Chapter 2, a metric that summarizes the uncertainty within a probability distribution is the entropy of the distribution. When given a proposed feature and associated threshold(s) to split on, we can split the training data population into at least two separate groups based on which branch we would follow for each input example. Each subgroup now has its own distribution over the possible labels, and we take the difference between the training dataset's entropy and the weighted sum of each subgroup's entropy to calculate the information gain, where the weight is proportional to the number of elements in each subgroup. The feature and associated threshold(s) with the highest information gain at each branching point are the optimal split.

Why does this work? Although we won't do a rigorous proof here, consider the problem where we have a molecular dataset with a binary label, for example, indicating whether each compound is toxic or not, and we'd like to build a classifier to predict compound toxicity. Also assume that one of the features associated with each compound is a binary feature of whether the molecule contains a phenol functional group or not. The phenol functional group is both quite toxic and is a common cause of toxicity in compounds, so splitting on this feature would lead to two well-separated subgroups.

The positive subgroup, which contains compounds with phenol functional groups, is likely to have few false positives due to the phenol's level of toxicity. The negative subgroup, which contains compounds without phenol functional groups, is likely to have few false negatives due to phenol being a common cause of toxicity. Thus, each subgroup's associated entropy is quite low since the true label distribution over compounds in each subgroup is quite concentrated over a single label. The sum of their weighted entropies removed from the entire dataset's associated entropy demonstrates a significant information gain (Figure 11-3).

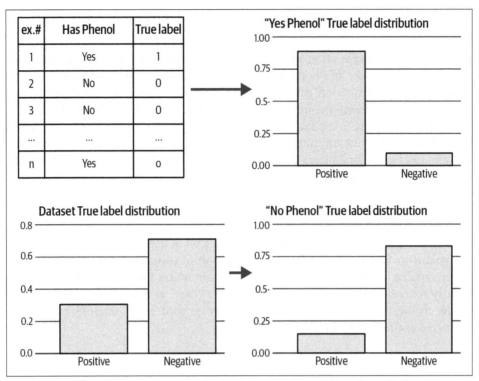

ex.#	Has Phenol	True label
1	Yes	1
2	No	0
3	No	0
...	...	...
n	Yes	0

Figure 11-3. The original dataset can be broken down into 30% toxic and 70% nontoxic, where a true label of 1 indicates toxicity and 0 otherwise. Breaking up the n examples into two subgroups based on containing phenol greatly concentrates the true probability over a single label in each subgroup.

This checks out well with our a priori knowledge of the phenol group—due to both its widespread nature in toxic compounds and its level of toxicity, we would have expected it to be a great feature for toxicity classification. The way we select features and their splits in decision trees is actually the same way we approach *greedy algorithms* in the more general algorithmic framework. Greedy algorithms select the most optimal local action at each decision point, and depending on the properties of the problem, the composition of these locally optimal actions leads to the global optimum. Decision trees similarly select the feature and split that locally lead to the largest gain in some metric at each decision point. For example, we just used information gain for toxicity classification, and although we showed the result of just one split, assuming splitting on the phenol trait leads to the highest information gain, we perform this same greedy procedure at each junction of every level in the tree. However, it turns out that the problem of finding the globally optimal decision tree for a dataset is NP-complete, which for the purposes of this text means that it is computationally very difficult. The best we can do to approach the problem in a tractable manner is the greedy approach, although it does not provably lead to the global optimum.

For each feature we split on in a tree, there exists an associated information gain with that feature. The order of importance of each feature is simply a list of the features sorted by their information gain. If we have a random forest rather than a single decision tree, we average the information gain for each feature across all of the trees in the forest and sort using the mean. Note that there is no extra work required in calculating the information gain, since we use information gain to train the individual decision trees in the first place. Thus, we have both example-level interpretability and a global understanding of feature importance for free in tree-based algorithms.

Linear Regression

A quick background on linear regression: given a set of features and a target variable, our goal is to find the "best" linear combination of features that approximates the target variable. Implicit in this model is the assumption that the input features are linearly related to the target variable. We define "best" as the set of coefficients that results in the linear combination with the lowest root mean squared error when compared against the ground truth:

$$y = \beta \cdot x + \epsilon, \epsilon \sim N(0, \sigma^2)$$

Where β represents the vector of coefficients. Our built-in, global notion of feature importance follows directly from this. The features that correspond with the coefficients with the highest magnitude are, globally, the most important features in the regression.

How about an example-level notion of feature importance? Recall that to get a prediction for a given example, we take the dot product between the example and the learned coefficients. Logically, the feature associated with the feature-coefficient product that contributes the most, in magnitude, to the final result is the feature that is most important for prediction. Without much effort, we have both an example-level and global-level notion of interpretability more or less built into linear regression.

However, linear regression has some unaddressed issues when considering feature importance. For example, when there exist significant correlations between the features in a multivariate regression, it is often difficult for the model to disentangle the effects of these correlated features on the output. In "SHAP" on page 292, we will describe Shapley values, which were designed to measure the marginal, unbiased impact of a given feature on the output in such cases.

Methods for Evaluating Feature Importance

For models where feature importance isn't built in, researchers have developed a variety of methods over the years to evaluate it. In this section, we will discuss a few that are used in the industry, in addition to their benefits and shortcomings.

Permutation Feature Importance

The idea behind permutation feature importance is quite simple: assume we have a trained neural model f and a set of features U that f has been trained on. We'd like to understand the impact that an individual feature s has on the predictions of f. One way to do this is to randomly rearrange the values that s takes on in the dataset amongst all of the examples and measure the resulting decrease in predictive accuracy. If the feature s did not add much predictive accuracy in the first place, we should see that the predictive accuracy of f decreases minimally when using the permuted samples. Inversely, if feature s was predictive of the output in the first place, we should see a large drop in predictive accuracy upon permuting the values of s in the dataset. In essence, if the feature s was originally strongly correlated with the true labels, randomizing the values of s would break this strong correlation and nullify its effectiveness at predicting the true label.

Unfortunately, as with all interpretability methods, this one is not perfect. Imagine the scenario in which our target is ice cream sales in a given region and two features in U are the readings of two temperature sensors within a one-mile radius of each other. We'd expect that each of these features is independently quite predictive of ice cream sales due to the seasonality of our target. However, if we were to perform the permutation methodology presented previously on this dataset, we'd counterintuitively get a low feature importance for both of these features. Why is this the case? Although each of these features is strongly predictive of the target, they are also strongly correlated due to the close proximity of the two temperature sensors. Additionally, permuting only one of these features at a time to compute its importance means that the other is kept intact, preserving most of the predictive information contained within the two features. Thus, we'd see little change in the predictive performance of f for both features, leading us to believe that the weather is not predictive of ice cream sales.

The moral of the story here is that we must always keep in mind correlations between features in our dataset. It is good data science and machine learning practice to understand the relationships between the features themselves before running these features through any sort of predictive modeling algorithm, simple or complex. One way to do this is to plot each of the z-scored features against each other to get a visual idea of feature correlation.

Partial Dependence Plots

Partial dependence plots, or PDPs for short, measure the marginal impact that a subset of features included in the model has on the output. As previously discussed, measuring this marginal impact in an unbiased manner is difficult for complex neural models. In the case of regression, we can represent the trained neural network (or any other complex, uninterpretable model) as a function f that takes as input a set of features U and outputs a value in the reals. Imagine that, as a user of this model, you are looking for an interpretability method that can measure the marginal impact of any subset of features S on the output of f. That is, if we are given an arbitrary setting of feature set S, we would like to calculate the expected output of the function f conditioned on this setting. The expectation of f is taken over $U \setminus S$, the rest of the features in U (conditioned on the known setting of S). Intuitively, we have marginalized out the feature subset $U \setminus S$ and have the output of a new function f' that takes as input only the feature set S. If we carry out this process for enough settings of S, we can learn the patterns of how f' changes as the feature set S changes.

For example, assume the output is the number of vehicles on the road in a given region and our feature set S consists of a single feature: precipitation levels in that region. The features that make up $U \setminus S$ could be variables like time of day, geographical location, population density, etc. By running the above process for a range of precipitation levels, we can estimate the number of vehicles we'd expect to see on the road at each level and observe the trend as precipitation levels get higher or lower. Plotting this trend is what gives us a PDP.

A couple of important notes: the first is that we do not plan on actually learning f', but rather estimating it using our trained model f. Learning f' itself would require retraining for every potential subset S to be explained, which is exponential in the number of features and thus intractable. The second is that it is currently unclear how we would go about computing the expectation of f taken over $U \setminus S$. As we will soon see, the PDP methodology addresses this second point. Before diving into the weeds, here is a simple yet concrete mathematical formulation of the process we have just described:

$$f\hat{a}(S) = \mathbb{E}_{U \setminus S | S}[f(U \setminus S, S)]$$

As stated, the conditional expectation is a bit tricky to estimate. So far in the text, we have approximated expectations in an unbiased manner via empirical averages. To estimate a conditional expectation, however, we are further constrained by the fact that we must take only the average over samples that contain the exact setting of S in question. Unfortunately, the only samples we have from the underlying distribution over U are contained within the dataset we are provided with. And in the common case that the features of U are continuous, the likelihood that we see the exact setting

---

of S in question even once in the dataset is exceedingly low. To get around this, PDP makes an independence assumption that allows us to use the entire dataset directly to estimate this expectation:

$$f\hat{a}(S) = \mathbb{E}_{U \setminus S | S}[f(U \setminus S, S)] = \mathbb{E}_{U \setminus S}[f(U \setminus S, S)] \approx \frac{1}{n}\Sigma_{i=1}^{n} f\left((U \setminus S)^i, S\right)$$

Where n is the number of samples in the dataset. PDP assumes that the features in S are independent from the features in $U \setminus S$. This assumption allows us to use all of the training samples indiscriminately for computing the expectation since, under this assumption, the sampling of $U \setminus S$ is independent from the setting of S anyway. We now have a concrete method for estimating the marginal impact of any arbitrary subset of features S on the output of f.

If there are significant correlations between the features in S and those in $U \setminus S$, then our generated PDP is likely not reflective of the true marginal effect of S on the output due to bias in our sampling assumption. Essentially, we would be taking the average over many samples that are very unlikely to occur, which means that we (1) can't expect f to generate meaningful outputs on these samples, and (2) are taking the average over the outputs for samples that do not accurately reflect the relationships in the underlying distribution over U.

The second concern is likely pretty clear, but to illustrate the first, imagine that you have trained a neural network to completion on the MNIST dataset. Now, I find an image of a dog online and run this image through the network. By chance, it turns out that the network returns a 9 with high confidence—should we trust these results? Since the input image is completely out of the distribution of images that the model expects to see, we can't trust the model to generalize to this extent. Although our situation with PDP is a bit less extreme, it is analogous—we have essentially created these unlikely, out-of-distribution "franken-samples" and are expecting f to produce meaningful outputs on these samples. The independence assumption that PDP makes is an inherent limitation of the method, again since the only samples we have are those from the dataset. Additionally, PDPs are often used to analyze the impact of small subsets of features (≤ 2), since humans can interpret only up to three dimensions visually. Regardless, PDPs can be an effective method for visualizing trends between subsets of input features and the output of a complex model.

Extractive Rationalization

Extractive rationalization, or the selection of concise portions of the input that retain most, or all, of the relevant information necessary to predict a property, is a built-in form of interpretability at the example level. In this section, we will review the methodology of the paper "Rationalizing Neural Predictions,"[1] which attempts to do this in the natural language space. In this paper, the task at hand is property prediction: given a textual review, predict some properties regarding the text. The paper specifically worked with a beer review dataset, where each review consisted of some text along with an appearance score, a smell score, and a palate score.

The high-performing but uninterpretable method would be to train a classic property predictor using a recurrent architecture, followed by a vanilla regression neural network that takes as input the final embedding produced by the recurrent architecture, as shown in Figure 11-4.

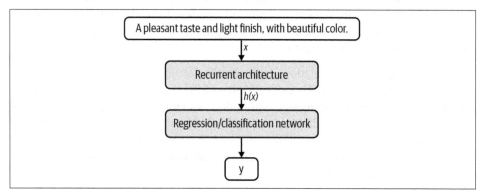

Figure 11-4. Depicted is the classical property predictor, where x is an encoding of the original sentence, h(x) is the hidden state produced by the recurrent architecture after reaching the end of x, and y is the result of a standard feed-forward neural architecture.

The goal of this paper is to additionally generate rationales, or selected, concise portions of the input text that are most relevant to the property being predicted, while limiting the hit to performance. This is why this method of rationalization is referred to as "extractive"—it works by extracting relevant portions of the input. You might be wondering why there is an emphasis on conciseness. If there were no limit or penalty on the conciseness of the rationale produced by the model, there would be no reason for the model to just return the entire input, which is a trivial solution. Of course, all of the information necessary for predicting the output is within the rationale if the rationale is the entire input.

How do we modify the structure of the proposed property predictor to also produce rationales as a built-in mechanism? This paper proposed a two-network approach, where the first network is termed the generator and the second network is termed the encoder. The generator is an RNN responsible for selecting the rationale, while the encoder is an RNN responsible for predicting the property given solely the rationale,

---

1 Lei et al. "Rationalizing Neural Predictions." *arXiv Preprint arXiv*:1606.04155. 2016.

not the entire input. The logic behind this is that, given the right objective function, the generator will have to learn to select meaningful portions of the input text to be able to accurately predict the ground truth rating. The generator parameterizes a distribution over all possible binary masks that can be applied to the input, where a 1 indicates that the word should be included in the rationale, and a 0 indicates otherwise. Figure 11-5 shows the proposed two-step architecture, where the encoder is just the single-step property predictor diagrammed earlier, and z represents a binary mask sampled from the generator.

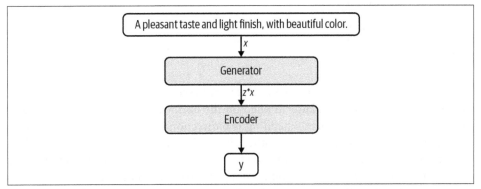

Figure 11-5. The generator parametrizes a distribution over masks z given input x, which we sample from to get the input to the encoder. The encoder follows the same structure as that of the classical property predictor depicted earlier.

More formally, we represent the input text x as a vector, where x_i represents the token at position i. The generator parameterizes the distribution $p(z|x)$, where z is a vector consisting of individual Bernoulli random variables z_i, which each take on the value 1 if x_i is to be included in the rationale, and 0 otherwise. Note that z is the same length as x, which changes depending on x. How exactly do we represent this distribution? A first step is to make a reasonable conditional independence assumption, which is that all z_i are mutually independent of each other conditioned on x: $p(z|x) = \prod_{i=1}^{n} p(z_i | z_1, ..., z_{i-1}, x) = \prod_{i=1}^{n} p(z_i | x)$. This is a very reasonable assumption because all of the information regarding whether x_i should be in the rationale or not should be contained within x itself (the token x_i and its surrounding context). Converting this to neural net speak, we can implement this by applying a fully connected layer followed by a sigmoid activation to each final hidden state h_i of the generator independently to get the probability of z_i taking on value 1, as we will see soon.

Before going into the specifics of the objective function, we'll describe the architectures of the generator and the encoder in more detail. The generator and encoder are both recurrent architectures, where the recurrent unit could be an LSTM or a GRU. As stated in the previous paragraph, the generator produces a hidden unit h_i for each token x_i. The final embedding for a token consists of two intermediate embeddings: the first intermediate embedding is the result of a forward pass through the tokens, while the second intermediate embedding is the result of a backward pass through the tokens. More formally, we have:

$$\overrightarrow{h}_i = \overrightarrow{f}\left(\overrightarrow{h}_{i-1}, x_i\right)$$

$$\overleftarrow{h}_i = \overleftarrow{f}\left(\overleftarrow{h}_{i+1}, x_i\right)$$

$$h_i = \text{concat}\left(\overrightarrow{h}_i, \overleftarrow{h}_i\right)$$

Where $\overrightarrow{f}$ and $\overleftarrow{f}$ correspond to two independent recurrent units, the former trained on the forward pass and the latter trained on the backward pass. From this formulation, we can see that the final embedding is bidirectional, incorporating information from the entire context of a token rather than information in solely one direction. The paper then applies a single, fully connected layer and sigmoid to each embedding to generate an independent Bernoulli random variable for each token:

$$p(z_i|x) = \sigma(w_z \cdot h_i + b_z)$$

The encoder is also a recurrent architecture, but is designed to be a regressive architecture due to its purpose of predicting the rating associated with the text. For this reason, the encoder can be designed the same way we design the vanilla property predictor alluded to earlier in the section.

So, what is the right objective function for training the two networks in tandem? In addition to any constraints we may want to have on the rationales the generator produces, we must also ensure that the predictor is accurate. If the predictor were not accurate, there would be no reason for the generator to produce meaningful rationales. Putting this all together into a mathematical formulation, we have the following objective function:

$$\theta^*, \phi^* = \text{argmin}_{\theta, \phi} L(\theta, \phi)$$

$$L(\theta, \phi) = \sum_{(x, y) \in D} \mathbb{E}_{z \sim gen_\theta(x)}[\text{cost}(x, y, z)]$$

$$\text{cost}(x, y, z) = \lambda_1 * |z| + \lambda_2 * \sum_t \left|z_t - z_{t-1}\right| + ||enc_\phi(x, z) - y||_2^2$$

Where λ_1 and λ_2 are hyperparameters we can tune during validation. The cost function used in the paper additionally contains a continuity penalty, which is higher when the rationale is interspersed throughout the text rather than one contiguous block. We want to minimize the sum of the expected cost for each training example, where the rationales are drawn according to the generator distribution. Calculating the expected cost exactly is computationally prohibitive due to the number of configurations of z growing exponentially with the length of x, so we'd instead like to be able to approximate the gradient of the expected cost via some empirical, sampled estimate.

This is feasible for the gradient of the cost function with respect to the parameters of the encoder, but when we try to do this for the generator, we run into a similar issue as we did when we first tried optimizing the VAE encoder:

$$\nabla_\theta \mathbb{E}_{z \sim gen_\theta(x)}[\text{cost}(x, y, z)] = \Sigma_z \text{cost}(x, y, z) * \nabla_\theta p_\theta(z \mid x)$$

Note that the cost function is only indirectly a function of θ via sampling from the generator, and thus can be treated as a constant. We can't re-express this as an expectation since the gradient is with respect to the distribution from which we are sampling from. This paper uses the log trick, which we also introduced in the section on VAEs, to resolve this issue:

$$\sum_z \text{cost}(x, y, z) * \nabla_\theta p_\theta(z \mid x)$$
$$= \sum_z \text{cost}(x, y, z) * p_\theta(z \mid x) * \nabla_\theta \log p_\theta(z \mid x)$$
$$= \mathbb{E}_{z \sim gen_\theta(x)}[\text{cost}(x, y, z) * \nabla_\theta \log p_\theta(z \mid x)]$$

The gradient of the cost function with respect to the parameters of the encoder is just:

$$\nabla_\phi \mathbb{E}_{z \sim gen_\theta(x)}[\text{cost}(x, y, z)]$$
$$= \sum_z p_\theta(z \mid x) * \nabla_\phi \text{cost}(x, y, z)$$
$$= \mathbb{E}_{z \sim gen_\theta(x)}[\nabla_\phi \text{cost}(x, y, z)]$$

Which resembles the standard empirical estimate of the expected gradient when performing SGD or minibatch gradient descent.

How do we go about training these two networks in tandem? It might be easier to consider a single training example for starters. We first select a training example at random from the dataset, where a training example consists of a text review and an associated rating, and feed the text review to the generator. The generator, which now represents a probability distribution over all possible binary masks given the input text review, can be sampled from by sampling each z_i independently due to our conditional independence claim from earlier. Each sampled binary mask represents a possible rationale, which we then feed to the encoder for prediction. After obtaining the result of the encoder for each rationale, we have all the information we need to calculate the cost function for each rationale. This will suffice for updating the weights of the encoder, but to update the weights of the generator we will also need to keep track of the log likelihood of the rationale, or log $p_\theta\left(z^k \mid x\right)$ for each sampled z^k.

Now that we have a mechanism for training, how do we translate this to validating and testing our model? During the validation and testing phases, instead of sampling binary masks from the generator, we select the most likely binary mask according to the generator probability distribution. To select the most likely binary mask, all we need to do is select the most likely z_i for each x_i in our input test review x, again due to our conditional independence assumption from earlier. This is a very reasonable approach to testing, since this is how we would determine the intended rationale when using this model in the real world.

You may have noticed some parallels to the concept of attention. After all, the generated binary mask can be thought of as a vector of weights we use to multiply the feature vectors that make up the input text review, where these weights are either 0 or 1, rather than some continuous weighting scheme implemented in standard attention. Indeed, the authors of this paper mention that their approach can be viewed as a form of "hard" attention, where we completely mask out or input tokens of the input according to a probability distribution rather than computing a weighted average of the feature vectors in the input. You might be wondering why hard attention makes more sense in this case rather than the "soft" attention schemes presented in the previous section. In this case, hard attention schemes make more sense because fractional weights on words in a sentence are hard to interpret as a measure of importance, while selecting a strict subset of words in the text as the explanation for a rating is much more interpretable.

LIME

LIME, or Local Interpretable Model-agnostic Explanations,[2] is an interpretability technique that is applied to a trained model rather than a built-in feature of the model itself. LIME is a per-example interpretability method, meaning that it generates a simple, local explanation of the underlying model's potentially complex behavior. It is also model agnostic, meaning that the structure of the underlying model itself does not matter when applying LIME.

---

2 Ribeiro et al. "Why Should I Trust You? Explaining the Predictions of Any Classifier." *arXiv Preprint arXiv*:1602.04938. 2016.

Before describing the methodology of LIME, the authors take some time to delineate a few characteristics they believe to be necessary components of any explainer. The first is that it should be interpretable, meaning that the explainer should provide a "qualitative relationship between input variables and response" that is easy for the user to understand. Even if the features used in the original model are uninterpretable, the explainer must use features that a human can interpret. For example, in an application of natural language processing, even if the underlying model utilizes a complex word embedding for any given word, the explainer must use features that a human can understand, such as the original words themselves.

The second characteristic is local fidelity, which means that the explainer must behave similarly to the underlying model within some vicinity of the chosen example. We might ask, why local and not global fidelity? Global fidelity, however, as the paper notes, is quite difficult to achieve and would require drastic advances in the field—much of the field of interpretability would be solved if global fidelity could be achieved. Thus, we settle for local fidelity.

The third is for the explainer to be model agnostic, which, as we explained earlier, means that the structure of the underlying model itself should not matter. The underlying model can range from a linear regression model to a complex convolutional neural architecture, and the explainer should still be able to satisfy the other three characteristics. Being model agnostic allows for flexibility in the structure of the underlying model, which is desirable as this doesn't necessitate changes in the structure of the explainer.

The fourth and final characteristic is global perspective, which is to select explanations for a subset of examples that is representative of the model's behavior. This helps build user trust in the model.

Now we will take some time to develop the methodology of LIME. As stated, the features of the original model may not be interpretable to a human (and usually aren't for most complex models), so the features used by the explainer will be different from those used by the underlying model. The features used by the explainer could be individual words in an NLP task, or functional groups in a chemical property prediction task—units, or interpretable components, that the end user can understand easily. Thus, any example when converted to the feature space of the explainer becomes a binary vector, where each index is associated with a distinct interpretable component (such as a functional group). A one at any index i indicates the presence of the associated interpretable component in the original example, and a zero indicates a lack of that component in the original example. Following the notation used in the referenced paper, we denote $x \in \mathbb{R}^d$ to be the original feature representation of the example to be explained and $x\hat{a} \in \{0, 1\}^{d'}$ to be the representation acted upon by the explainer, where d' is the number of interpretable components.

Further, the paper defines G to be a class of potentially interpretable models, such as linear regression or random forest, and an explainer to be an instance $g \in G$. g acts on an instance x' and returns a value in the range of the underlying model. We denote the underlying model to be f, which acts on an instance x and is a function from $\mathbb{R}^d \to \mathbb{R}$ in the case of regression or a function from $\mathbb{R}^d$ to the range $[0,1]$ in the case of classification, where f returns a probability distribution. Additionally, the paper defines a proximity measure, or kernel, $\pi_x(z)$ around the instance x. This function can be defined in a multitude of ways—most implementations of LIME use an exponential kernel that attains a maximum value at x and decreases exponentially as one gets farther and farther from x.

At a high level, LIME attempts to find the explanation g^* that minimizes a loss function that looks like:

$$g^* = \text{argmin}_{g \in G} L(f, g, x) + \omega(g)$$

Where $L(f,g,x)$ is a measure of the unfaithfulness of g in modeling f around the instance in question x, and $\omega(g)$ is a measure of the complexity of g. Thus, minimizing their sum results in an optimal explainer g^* that has the desired characteristics of local fidelity and interpretability described earlier.

How do we measure the unfaithfulness of a potential explainer? The paper's methodology is to sample an instance z' from the vicinity of x', convert z' back to an example z in the original feature space, and compute the difference between $f(z)$ and $g(z')$. The difference represents the loss for that sample—if $g(z')$ is far from $f(z)$, then it is not faithful to the model's predictions at that point. We can then weight this loss using the kernel $\pi_x(z)$, which increasingly discounts the loss as the sample z gets further and further from the original example x. Putting this together, the loss function looks like:

$$L(f, g, x) = \Sigma_{z, z\hat{a}} \pi_x(z) * \left(f(z) - g(z\hat{a}) \right)^2$$

How do we achieve the samples z' used in this loss function? The paper samples from the vicinity of x' by selecting a subset of the x' nonzero components, where each subset is chosen uniformly at random, and setting all other indices of the sample to zero (Figure 11-6).

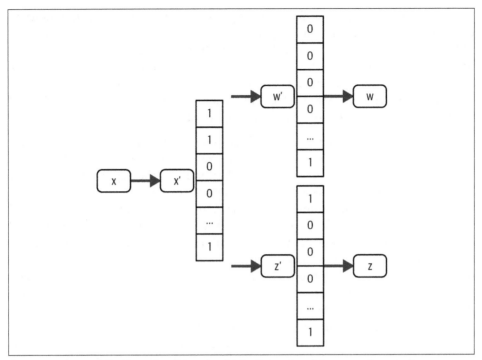

Figure 11-6. x can be thought of as some high-dimensional input such as an image, while each index of x' is associated with some interpretable feature, where a 1 denotes the existence of that feature in x. The sampling procedure selects some subset of nonzero indices in x' to keep nonzero in each of w' and z', which are then mapped back to the original input space.

LIME then maps these samples z' back to samples z from the original feature space so we can measure the fidelity of the explainer via $f(z) - g(z')$.

LIME also takes into account the complexity of the explainer via $\omega(g)$, which enforces the interpretability aspect of viable explainers. In the specific case where G represents the class of linear models, the paper uses a version of ω that places a hard limit on the number of nonzero weights in g:

$$\omega(g) = \infty * 1\left[\left|\left|w_g\right|\right|_0 > K\right]$$

Where $\omega(g)$ represents g's weight vector, the L0 norm counts the number of nonzero elements in $\omega(g)$, and *1[*]* is the indicator function, which evaluates to 1 if the condition within the function is satisfied, and 0 otherwise. The result is that $\omega(g)$ attains a value of infinity when $\omega(g)$ has more than K nonzero elements, and is 0 otherwise. This ensures that the chosen $\omega(g)$ will have at most K nonzero elements, since one can always do better than any proposed $\omega(g)$ that has more than K nonzero elements by simply zeroing out weights until there are at most K nonzero weights. This regularization approach is likely different from regularization approaches you have encountered in the past, such as the L1 or L2 norm on the weight vector. In fact, to optimize the objective function defined in the paper, the authors utilize an algorithm they term K-LASSO, which involves first selecting K features via LASSO and then performing standard least squares optimization.

After performing LIME, we are left with an optimal explainer g, which is a linear model with at most K nonzero weights in this case. Now we must check if g satisfies the goals that the authors set out from the beginning of the paper. First, g must be interpretable. Since we chose a relatively simple class of explainer models G, which were linear models in this example, all we need to explain the behavior of the model around the chosen example x are the values of the (at most) K nonzero weights of g. The interpretable components associated with the nonzero weights are considered to be most important for prediction in that locality. In terms of local fidelity, our optimization procedure helps to ensure local fidelity by minimizing the least squares loss between the explainer's predictions and the model's predictions. However, there do exist limitations; for example, the paper notes that if the underlying model is highly nonlinear even within a short vicinity of the example we are explaining, our linear explainer won't be able to do the model's local behavior justice. With regards to being model agnostic, note that methodology of LIME does not concern itself with the underlying model's structure. All LIME needs to function are predictions $f(z)$ from the underlying model. And finally, to achieve a global perspective, we can select examples that are representative of the model's behavior and display their explanations to the user.

SHAP

SHAP, or Shapley Additive Explanations,[3] are similarly a per-prediction interpretability method for complex models. The paper that introduces the methodology of SHAP first provides a framework that the authors feel unifies a variety of interpretability methods in the field. This framework is termed *additive feature attribution*, where all instances of this framework utilize a linear explanation model that acts on binary variables:

$$g(x') = \phi_0 + \Sigma_{i=1}^{M} \phi_i x_i'$$

---

3 Lundberg et al. "A Unified Approach to Interpreting Model Predictions." *arXiv Preprint arXiv*:1705.07874. 2017.

Where M is the number of binary variables. For example, LIME, when using a class of linear explainer models, follows this framework exactly, since each example to be explained is first converted to a binary vector over interpretable components. It turns out that, in the additive feature attribution framework, there exists a unique solution in this class that has three desirable properties: local accuracy, missingness, and consistency. Before discussing the unique solution, we will describe the three properties in more detail.

The first is *local accuracy*, which states that the explainer model must match the underlying model exactly at the example being interpreted. This is understandable as a desirable property, since it is reasonable that at least the example being interpreted should be explained perfectly. It's important to note that not all interpretability frameworks necessarily follow this property. For example, the explainer that is generated by LIME, as presented in its original paper and described in the previous section, need not be locally accurate in the way that the authors of SHAP define local accuracy. This will be discussed further near the end of this section. Mathematically, local accuracy in SHAP is defined as:

$$f(x) = g(x\hat{a}) = \phi_0 + \Sigma_{i=1}^{M} \phi_i x_i'$$

Note that x' is a simplified feature vector, where each feature in x' is a binary variable that represents the presence or absence of a complex feature in the original input space. The second desirable property is *missingness*, which states that if x' contains features equal to zero, the weights associated with those features in the explainer model should also be zero. This is also understandable as a desirable property, since there would be no influence of a feature with value of zero on the output under a linear explainer g, and thus no need to assign a nonzero weight to that feature in the explainer.

And finally, the third desirable property is *consistency*. This property states that if the underlying model changes such that a feature in the explainer space either increases or keeps its contribution constant, regardless of the values of the other features in the explainer space when compared to the original model, the explainer weight associated with that feature should be larger for the changed underlying model as compared to the original. That was a mouthful, so we represent it more precisely in mathematical notation:

If $f'(h_x(z')) - f'(h_x(z' \setminus \{i\})) \geq f(h_x(z')) - f(h_x(z' \setminus \{i\}))$, $\forall z'$, then $\phi_i(f', x) \geq \phi_i(f, x)$

Where h is the function that maps inputs from the interpretable space back to the original input space. Why is consistency a desirable property? For the new model, the delta between the existence of the corresponding, more complex feature in the input space and its absence is greater than or equal to the delta for the old model, regardless of all other feature settings. Thus, it makes sense that we should attribute at least as large a weight to it in the explainer for the new model as compared to the old model, since its existence is clearly more important for the new model.

As mentioned, for each underlying model f there exists a unique g within the additive attribution framework that also satisfies all three properties listed. Although we won't show this here, this result is one that follows from earlier results in cooperative game theory, where the learned weights are called Shapley values. Shapley values were originally defined to quantify per-example feature importance in multivariate linear regression models where individual features have significant correlations. This is an important problem, especially in the setting of significant correlations due to ambiguity between which features are the most predictive. It could be the case that a feature A is correlated with the target y, but when factoring in feature B it turns out that feature A provides only negligible additional value (i.e., predictions don't change significantly, test statistics remain relatively constant, etc.). On the other hand, feature B may provide significant predictive power both in the individual case and in the case where feature A is included.

Determining the relative importance of feature A and B in a vanilla multivariate regression that includes both features is difficult due to their non-negligible correlation. Shapley values tease out these relationships and compute the true marginal impact of a given feature, as we will soon see. Here is the formula for Shapley values, where i represents the feature in question:

$$\phi_i = \Sigma_{S \in F \setminus \{i\}} \frac{|S|! * (|F| - |S| - 1)!}{|F|!} * \left[f_{S \cup \{i\}}(x_{S \cup \{i\}}) - f_S(x_S) \right]$$

We will now break down this formula. Intuitively, the Shapley value for an individual feature is computed by first taking the difference between the predictions for a model trained over a subset of features S plus the feature in question i included, and predictions for a model trained over the same subset of features S but with feature i withheld. The final Shapley value is a weighted sum of these differences over all possible subsets of features S.

To find these differences, we can first train a multivariate linear regression model f_S that only uses some subset of features S, and then train a second multivariate linear regression model $f_{S \cup \{i\}}$ that uses the subset of features $S \cup \{i\}$. Let the example we are explaining be denoted as x, and x_A denote the portion of x that corresponds to some feature subset A. The difference $f_{S \cup \{i\}}(x_{S \cup \{i\}}) - f_S(x_S)$ represents how much the prediction changes when we include the feature i. Additionally, note that the formula is a sum over all possible feature subsets, which means that if the computed Shapley value for feature i is high, the difference between including feature i and not including feature i was likely substantial for a majority of possible feature subsets. This result signifies that feature i generally adds significant predictive power regardless of the features in S, which is captured by the high Shapley value. In the example provided earlier, we'd find that feature B has a higher Shapley value than feature A.

Additionally, the intuition behind the weighting scheme is that it achieves a more unbiased result for feature importance, since subsets of a given size occur either more or less frequently than subsets of a different size in the set of all subsets. The number of subsets of a given size is computed using the choose function, a concept from counting and probability. When this is inverted and used as a weighting scheme, the result of a subset whose size occurs more frequently in the set of all possible subsets is weighted less than, for example, a feature subset consisting of only a single feature other than the feature in question. As stated earlier, we won't prove why this is unbiased in full, but we hope that this makes the intuition clearer.

You may notice that computing exact Shapley regression values for any reasonable number of features is intractable. This would involve training a regression model on all possible subsets of features, where the number of subsets of features (and thus models to train) grows exponentially with the number of features. We instead resort to approximation via sampling to help. Given an example x to explain and a regression model f_S trained on some subset of features S, we can compute $f_{S \setminus \{i\}}$ by taking an expectation of f_S with respect to the distribution of feature i conditioned on x's setting of features $S \setminus \{i\}$:

$$f_{S \setminus \{i\}} = \mathbb{E}_{p(x_i | x_{S \setminus \{i\}})}[f_S(x_{S \setminus \{i\}}, x_i)]$$

Where the bold represents that $x_{S \setminus \{i\}}$ is being treated as a known entity taken from x, the example being explained, while x_i is being treated as an unknown, i.e., is a random variable rather than taking on the value provided by x. As has been a common theme throughout this book, we can approximate expectations like the preceding one in an unbiased manner by sampling and averaging:

$$\mathbb{E}_{p(x_i | x_{S \setminus \{i\}})}[f_S(x_{S \setminus \{i\}}, x_i)]$$
$$= \mathbb{E}_{p(x_i)}[f_S(x_{S \setminus \{i\}}, x_i)]$$
$$\approx \frac{1}{n} \sum_{j=1}^{n} f_S(x_{S \setminus \{i\}}, x_i^{(j)})$$

You may have noticed the parallels between the procedure we just described and the estimation procedure described in "Partial Dependence Plots" on page 282. In fact, these are doing the exact same thing—notice that we again assume independence between feature subset $S \setminus \{i\}$ and feature i, which allows us to use all samples of feature i from the dataset indiscriminately.

The authors propose SHAP values in the general case, where SHAP values are given by the formula:

$$\phi_i(f, x) = \Sigma_{z' \subseteq x'} \frac{|z'|! * (M - |z'| - 1)!}{M!} [f(h_x(z')) - f(h_x(z' \setminus \{i\}))]$$

Where z' is a subset of the nonzero components of x'. Additionally, $z' \setminus \{i\}$ represents setting feature i in the interpretable space equal to zero. Note that if feature i is already zero in the input x', then the formula outputs zero as well since $f(h_x(z')) = f(h_x(z' \setminus \{i\}))$, $\forall z' \subseteq x'$. This quick check shows that the formula indeed satisfies the property of missingness. The vector consisting of SHAP values for each feature in x' completely defines the optimal explainer model g in the additive attribution framework, where optimal signifies that g satisfies all three properties defined earlier: local accuracy, consistency, and missingness. Right off the bat, we can see the parallels between the proposed SHAP values and the Shapley values from multivariate regression. Additionally, we can use the same sampling procedure to estimate SHAP values.

As discussed, LIME is in the additive attribution framework. In the original LIME paper, the optimal explainer model g was selected via a specialized optimization procedure that first selected k features to have a nonzero contribution and then performed standard least squares optimization to achieve the final weights of g. Due to these heuristics, including the choice of kernel $\pi_x(z)$, there is no guarantee that the explainer selected using the procedure presented in the original LIME paper will satisfy the SHAP criteria of local accuracy, missingness, and consistency.

However, the optimization procedure presented in the LIME paper does achieve an explainer that satisfies the criteria for explainer models proposed in LIME; recall the concepts of being interpretable, having local fidelity, being model agnostic, and achieving global perspective from the previous section. We point this out specifically to show that different groups of knowledgeable individuals don't necessarily have the exact same idea of what it means for an explainer to be interpretable, and that interpretability as a concept has evolved over time.

It turns out that in LIME, there exists an exact form to the proximity measure $\pi_x(z)$, ω, and loss function L such that when minimized, results in an optimal explainer g that satisfies all three SHAP criteria for interpretability:

$$\omega(g) = 0$$

$$\pi_{x'}(z') = \frac{M - 1}{(M \text{ choose } |z'|) * |z'| * (M - |z'|)}$$

$$L(f, g, \pi) = \sum_{z' \in Z} \left(f(h_x(z')) - g(z')\right)^2 * \pi_{x'}(z')$$

We can optimize this loss function using a weighted least squares optimization to obtain the unique optimal g. Note that the kernel here is distinct in interpretation from the kernel choices presented in the original LIME paper. Instead of the kernel decreasing in value as the samples get farther from the example being explained, the SHAP kernel is symmetric. This can be verified by examining the output of the kernel when $|z'| = k$ and when $|z'| = M - k$. In fact, from just looking at the formula, we can see that the value of the kernel isn't even dependent on x'.

In conclusion, SHAP values unify several existing interpretability methods by first defining the additive attribution framework, which is shared amongst these methods, and second by proving the existence of a unique optimal explainer within this framework that satisfies three desirable properties.

Summary

Although interpretability often comes in a variety of forms, they are all designed with the end goal of being able to explain model behavior. We learned that not every model is interpretable by construction, and even those that are might only be superficially so. For example, although vanilla linear regression seems to be quite interpretable by design, correlations between features can muddle this initially clear picture. Additionally, we learned about interpretability methods that are built into the model itself, such as extractive rationalization, and post hoc interpretability methods such as LIME and SHAP. The right form of interpretability will often depend on the domain—for example, using gradient-based methods for image classification may make sense, but not so much in language problems. The soft attention scheme discussed in previous chapters may not be as desirable for sentiment analysis as, say, the hard selection methodology presented in our section on extractive rationalization. And finally, we learned about how interpretability does not carry the exact same meaning across the board, even in research—note our discussion on the differences between the optimal explainers generated by LIME and SHAP. We hope that this chapter served as a fruitful foray into the vast landscape of interpretability research.

## CHAPTER 12

Memory Augmented Neural Networks

Mostafa Samir

So far we've seen how effective an RNN can be at solving a complex problem like machine translation. However, we're still far from reaching its full potential! In Chapter 9 we mentioned that it's theoretically proven that the RNN architecture is a universal functional representer; a more precise statement of the same result is that RNNs are *Turing complete*. This simply means that given proper wiring and adequate parameters, an RNN can learn to solve any computable problem, which is basically any problem that can be solved by a computer algorithm or, equivalently, a Turing machine.

Neural Turing Machines

Though theoretically possible, it's extremely difficult to achieve that kind of universality in practice. This difficulty stems from the fact that we're looking at an immensely huge search space of possible wirings and parameter values of RNNs, a space so vastly large for gradient descent to find an appropriate solution for any arbitrary problem. However, in this chapter we'll start exploring some approaches at the edge of research that will allow us to start tapping into that potential.

Let's think for a while about a very simple reading comprehension question like the following:

```
Mary travelled to the hallway. She grabbed the milk glass there.
Then she travelled to the office, where she found an apple
and grabbed it.

How many objects is Mary carrying?
```

The answer is so trivial: it's two. But what actually happened in our brains that allowed us to come up with the answer so trivially? If we thought about how we could solve that comprehension question using a simple computer program, our approach would probably go like this:

1. allocate a memory location for a *counter*
2. initialize *counter* to 0
3. for each *word* in *passage*
   3.1. if *word* is **'grabbed'**
        3.1.1. increment *counter*
4. return *counter* value

It turns out that our brains tackle the same task in a similar way to that simple computer program. Once we start reading, we start allocating memory (just as our computer program) and store the pieces of information we receive. We start by storing that location of Mary, which after the first sentence is the hallway. In the second sentence we store the objects Mary is carrying, and by now it's only a glass of milk. Once we see the third sentence, our brain modifies the first memory location to point to the office. By the end of the fourth sentence, the second memory location is modified to include both the milk and the apple. When we finally encounter the question, our brains quickly query the second memory location and count the information there, which turns out to be two. In neuroscience and cognitive psychology, such a system of transient storing and manipulation of information is called a *working memory*, and it's the main inspiration behind the line of research we'll be discussing in the rest of this chapter.

In 2014, Graves et al. from Google DeepMind started this line of work in a paper called "Neural Turing Machines" (*https://arxiv.org/abs/1410.5401*) in which they introduced a new neural architecture with the same name, a *Neural Turing Machine* (NTM), that consists of a controller neural network (usually an RNN) with an external memory that resembles the brain's working memory. For the close resemblance between the working memory model and the computer model we just saw, Figure 12-1 shows that the same resemblance holds for the NTM architecture, with the external memory in place of the RAM, the read/write heads in place of the read/write buses, and the controller network in place of the CPU, except for the fact that the controller learns its program, unlike the CPU, which is fed its program. Figure 12-1 has a single read head and a single write head, but an NTM can have several in practice.

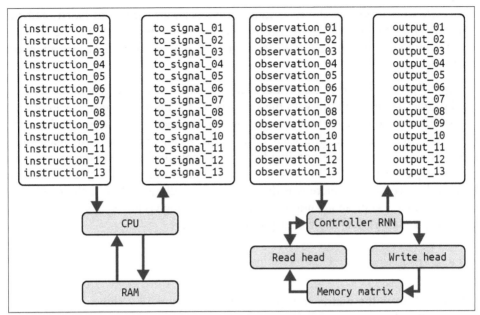

instruction_01	to_signal_01	observation_01	output_01
instruction_02	to_signal_02	observation_02	output_02
instruction_03	to_signal_03	observation_03	output_03
instruction_04	to_signal_04	observation_04	output_04
instruction_05	to_signal_05	observation_05	output_05
instruction_06	to_signal_06	observation_06	output_06
instruction_07	to_signal_07	observation_07	output_07
instruction_08	to_signal_08	observation_08	output_08
instruction_09	to_signal_09	observation_09	output_09
instruction_10	to_signal_10	observation_10	output_10
instruction_11	to_signal_11	observation_11	output_11
instruction_12	to_signal_12	observation_12	output_12
instruction_13	to_signal_13	observation_13	output_13

Figure 12-1. Comparing the architecture of a modern-day computer, which is fed its program (left) to an NTM that learns its program (right)

If we thought about NTMs in light of our earlier discussion of RNN's Turing completeness, we'll find that augmenting the RNN with an external memory for transient storage prunes a large portion out of that search space, as we now don't care about exploring RNNs that can both process and store the information; we're just looking for the RNNs that can process the information stored outside of them. This pruning of the search space allows us to start tapping into some of the RNN potentials that were locked away before augmenting it with a memory, evident by the variety of tasks that the NTM could learn: from copying input sequences after seeing them, to emulating N-gram models, to performing a priority sort on data. We'll even see by the end of the chapter how an extension to the NTM can learn to do reading comprehension tasks like the one we saw earlier, with nothing more than a gradient-based search.

Attention-Based Memory Access

To be able to train an NTM with a gradient-based search method, we need to make sure that the whole architecture is differentiable so that we can compute the gradient of some output loss with respect to the model's parameters that process the input. This property is called *end-to-end-differentiable*, with one end being the inputs and the other the outputs. If we attempted to access the NTM's memory in the same way a digital computer accesses its RAM, via discrete values of addresses, the discreteness of the addresses would introduce discontinuities in gradients of the output, and hence we would lose the ability to train the model with a gradient-based method. We need a continuous way to access the memory while being able to "focus" on a specific location in it. This kind of continuous focusing can be achieved via attention methods.

Instead of generating a discrete memory address, we let each head generate a normalized softmax attention vector with the same size as the number of memory locations. With this attention vector, we'll be accessing all the memory locations at the same time in a blurry manner, with each value in the vector telling us how much we're going to focus on the corresponding location, or how likely we're going to access it. For example, to read a vector at a time step t out of our $N \times W$ NTM's memory matrix denoted by M_t (where N is the number of locations and W is the size of the location), we generate an attention vector, or a weighting vector w_t of size N, and our read vector can be calculated via the product:

$$\mathbf{r}_t = M_t^\top w_t$$

where $\top$ denotes the matrix transpose operation. Figure 12-2 shows how with the weights attending to a specific location, we can retrieve a read vector that approximately contains the same information as the content of that memory location.

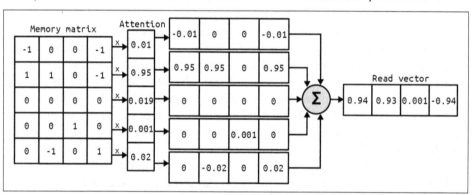

Figure 12-2. A demonstration of how a blurry attention-based reading can retrieve a vector containing approximately the same information as in the focused-on location

A similar attention weighting method is used for the write head: a weighting vector w_t is generated and used for erasing specific information from the memory, as specified by the controller in an erase vector e_t that has W values between 0 and 1 specifying what to erase and what to keep. Then we use the same weighting for writing to the erased memory matrix some new information, also specified by the controller in a write vector v_t containing W values:

$$M_t = M_{t-1} \circ \left(E - w_t e_t^\top \right) + w_t v_t^\top$$

where E is a matrix of ones and $\circ$ is element-wise multiplication. Similar to the reading case, the weighting w_t tells us where to focus our erasing (the first term of the equation) and writing operations (the second term).

NTM Memory Addressing Mechanisms

Now that we understand how NTMs access their memories in a continuous manner via attention weighting, we're left with how these weightings are generated and what forms of memory addressing mechanisms they represent. We can understand that by exploring what NTMs are expected to do with their memories, and based on the model they are mimicking (the Turning machine), we expect them to be able to access a location by the value it contains, and to be able to go forward or backward from a given location.

The first mode of behavior can be achieved with an access mechanism that we'll call *content-based addressing*. In this form of addressing, the controller emits the value that it's looking for, which we'll call a key k_t, then it measures its similarity to the information stored in each location and focuses the attention on the most similar one. This kind of weighting can be calculated via:

$$C(M,k,\beta) = \frac{\exp\left(\beta \mathscr{D}(M, k)\right)}{\Sigma_{i=0}^N \exp\left(\beta \mathscr{D}(M[i], k)\right)}$$

where D is some similarity measure, like the cosine similarity. The equation is nothing more than a normalized softmax distribution over the similarity scores. There is, however, an extra parameter β that is used to attenuate the attention weights if needed. We call that the *key strength*. The main idea behind that parameter is that for some tasks, the key emitted by the controller may not be close to any of the information in the memory, which would result in seemingly uniform attention weights. Figure 12-3 shows how the key strength allows the controller to learn how to attenuate such uniform attention to be more focused on a single location that is the most probable; the controller then learns what value of the strength to emit with each possible key it emits.

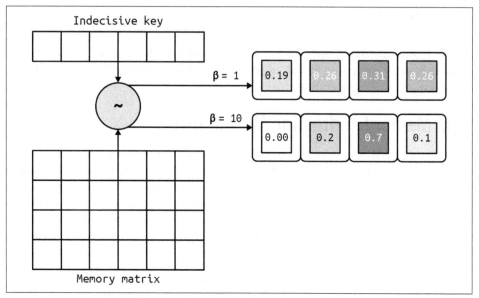

Figure 12-3. An indecisive key with unit strength results in a nearly uniform attention vector; increasing the strength for keys like that focuses the attention on the most probable location

To move forward and backward in the memory, we first need to know where we are we standing now, and such information is located in the access weighting from the last time step w_{t-1}. So to preserve the information about our current location with the new content-based weighting w_t^c we just got, we interpolate between the two weighting using a scalar g_t that lies between 0 and 1:

$$w_t^g = g_t w_t^c + (1 - g_t) w_{t-1}$$

We call g_t the *interpolation gate*, and it's also emitted by the controller to control the kind of information we want to use in the current time step. When the gate's value is close to 1, we favor the addressing given by content lookup. However, when it's close to 0, we tend to pass the information about our current location through and ignore the content-based addressing. The controller learns to use this gate so that, for example, it could set it to 0 when iteration through consecutive locations is desired and information about the current location is crucial. The type of information the controller chooses to gate through is denoted by the *gated weighting* w_t^g.

To start moving around the memory we need a way to take our current gated weighting and shift the focus from one location to another. This can be done by convoluting the gated weighting with a *shift weighting* s_t, also emitted by the controller. This shift weighting is a normalized softmax attention vector of size $n + 1$, where n is an even integer specifying the number of possible shifts around the focused-on location in the gated weighting; for example, if it has a size of 3, then there are two possible shifts around a location: one forward and one backward. Figure 12-4 shows how a shift weighting can move around the focused-on location in gated weighting. The shifting occurs by convoluting the gated weighting by the shift weighting in pretty much the same way we convoluted images with feature maps back in Chapter 7. The only exception is how we handle the case when the shift weightings go outside the gated weighting. Instead of using padding like we did before, we use a rotational convolution operator where overflown weights get applied to the values at the other end of the gated weighting, as shown in the middle panel of Figure 12-4. This operation can be expressed element-wise as:

$$\widetilde{w}_t[i] = \Sigma_{j=0}^{|s_t|} w_t^g\left[\left(i + \frac{|s_t|-1}{2} - j\right) \bmod N\right]s_t[j]$$

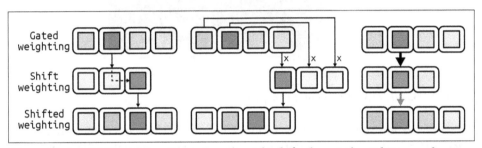

Figure 12-4. A shift weighting focused on the right shifts the gated weighting one location to the right (left). Rotational convolution on a left-focused shift weighting, shifting the gated weighting to the left (middle). A nonsharp centered shift weighting keeps the gated weighting intact but disperses it (right).

With the introduction of the shifting operation, our heads' weightings can now move around the memory freely forward and backward. However, a problem occurs if at any time the shift weighting is not sharp enough. Because of the nature of the convolution operation, a nonsharp shift weighting (as in the right panel of Figure 12-4) disperses the original gated weightings around its surroundings and results in a less-focused shifted weighting. To overcome that blurring effect, we run the shifted weightings through one last operation: a sharpening operation. The controller emits one last scalar $\gamma_t \geq 1$ that sharpens the shifted weightings via:

$$w_t = \frac{\widetilde{w}_t^{\gamma t}}{\Sigma_{i=0}^{N} \widetilde{w}_t[i]^{\gamma t}}$$

Starting from interpolation down to the final weighting vector out of sharpening, this process constitutes the second addressing mechanism of NTMs: the *location-based mechanism*. Using a combination of both addressing mechanisms, an NTM is able to utilize its memory to learn to solve various tasks. One of these tasks that would allow us to get a deeper look into the NTM in action is the copy task shown in Figure 12-5. In this task, we present the model with a sequence of random binary vectors that terminate with a special end symbol. We then request the same input sequence to be copied to the output.

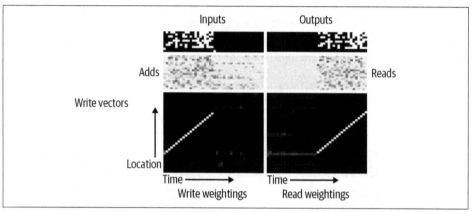

Figure 12-5. An NTM trained on the copy task[1]

The visualization shows how at the input time, the NTM starts writing the inputs step-by-step into consecutive locations in the memory. In the output time, the NTM goes back at the first written vector and iterates through the next locations to read and return the previously written input sequence. The original NTM paper contains several other visualizations of NTMs trained on different problems that are worth checking. These visualizations demonstrate the architecture's ability to utilize the addressing mechanisms to adapt to and learn to solve various tasks.

We'll suffice with our current understanding of NTMs and skip its implementation. Instead, we will spend the rest of the chapter exploring the drawbacks of NTMs and how the novel architecture of the differentiable neural computer (DNC) was able to overcome these drawbacks. We'll conclude our discussion by implementing that novel architecture on simple reading comprehension tasks like the one we saw earlier.

---

1 Source: Graves et al. "Neural Turing Machines." (2014) (*https://arxiv.org/abs/1410.5401*)

Differentiable Neural Computers

Despite the power of NTMs, they have a few limitations regarding their memory mechanisms. The first of these limitations is that NTMs have no way to ensure that no interference or overlap between written data would occur. This is due to the nature of the "differentiable" writing operation in which we write new data everywhere in the memory to some extent specified by the attention. Usually, the attention mechanisms learn to focus the write weightings strongly on a single memory location, and the NTM converges to a mostly interference-free behavior, but that's not guaranteed.

However, even when the NTM converges to an interference-free behavior, once a memory location has been written to, there's no way to reuse that location again, even when the data stored in it becomes irrelevant. The inability to free and reuse memory locations is the second limitation of the NTM architecture. This results in new data being written to new locations that are likely to be contiguous, as we saw with the copy task. This contiguous writing fashion is the only way for an NTM to record any temporal information about the data being written: consecutive data is stored in consecutive locations. If the write head jumped to another place in the memory while writing some consecutive data, a read head won't be able to recover the temporal link between the data written before and after the jump: this constitutes the third limitation of NTMs.

In October 2016, Graves et al. from DeepMind published in *Nature* a paper titled, "Hybrid Computing Using a Neural Network with Dynamic External Memory," (*http://go.nature.com/2peM8m2*) in which they introduced a new memory-augmented neural architecture called *differentiable neural computer* (DNC) that improves on NTMs and addresses the limitations we just discussed. Similar to NTMs, DNCs consists of a controller that interacts with an external memory. The memory consists of N words of size W, making up an $N \times W$ matrix we'll be calling M. The controller takes in an input vector of size X and the R vectors of size W read from memory in the previous step, where R is the number of read heads. The controller then processes them through a neural network and returns two pieces of information:

- An *interface vector* that contains all the necessary information to query the memory (i.e., write and read from it)
- A *pre-output* vector of size Y

The external memory then takes in the interface vector, performs the necessary writing through a single write head, then reads R new vectors from the memory. It returns the newly read vectors to the controller to be added with the pre-output vector, producing the final output vector of size Y.

Figure 12-6 summarizes the operation of the DNC that we just described. We can see that unlike NTMs, DNCs keep other data structures alongside the memory itself to keep track of the state of the memory. As we'll shortly see, with these data structures and some clever new attention mechanisms, DNCs are able to successfully overcome NTM's limitations.

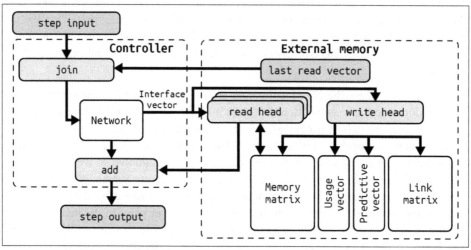

Figure 12-6. An overview of DNC's architecture and operation

To make the whole architecture differentiable, DNCs access the memory through weight vectors of size N whose elements determine how much the heads focus on each memory location. There are R weightings for the read heads $w_t^{r,1}, \cdots, w_t^{r,R}$ where t denotes the time step. On the other hand, there's one write weighting w_t^w for the single write head. Once we obtain these weightings, we can modify the memory matrix and get updated via:

$$M_t = M_{t-1} \circ \left(E - w_t^w e_t^\top \right) + w_t^w v_t^\top$$

and e_t, v_t are the *erase* and *write* vectors we saw earlier with NTMs, coming from the controller through the interface vector as instructions about what to erase from and write to the memory.

As soon as we get the updated memory matrix M_t, we can read out the new read vectors $r_t^1, r_t^2, \cdots, r_t^R$ using the following equation for each read weighting:

$$r_t^i = M_t^\top w_t^{r,i}$$

Up until now, it seems that there's nothing different from how NTMs write to and read from memory. However, the differences will start to show up when we discuss the attention mechanisms DNCs use to obtain their access weightings. While they both share the content-based addressing mechanism $C(M, k, \beta)$ defined earlier, DNCs use more sophisticated mechanisms to attend more efficiently to the memory.

Interference-Free Writing in DNCs

The first limitation we discussed for NTMs was their inability to ensure an interference-free writing behavior. An intuitive way to address this issue is to design the architecture to focus strongly on a single, free memory location and not wait for NTM to learn to do so. To keep track of which locations are free and which are busy, we need to introduce a new data structure that can hold this kind of information. We'll call it the *usage vector*.

The usage vector u_t is a vector of size N, where each element holds a value between 0 and 1 that represents how much of the corresponding memory location is used; with 0 indicating a completely free location, and 1 indicating a completely used one.

The usage vector initially contains zeros $u_0 = \mathbf{0}$ and gets updated with the usage information across the steps. Using this information, it's clear that the location to which the weights should attend most strongly is the one with the least usage value. To obtain such weighting, we need to first sort the usage vector and obtain the list of location indices in ascending order of the usage; we call such a list a *free list* and denote it by ϕ_t. Using that free list, we can construct an intermediate weighting called the *allocation weighting* a_t that would determine which memory location should be allocated for new data. We calculate a_t using:

$$a_t[\phi_t[j]] = (1 - u_t[\phi_t[j]])\Pi_{i=1}^{j-1}u_t[\phi_t[i]] \quad \text{where } j \in 1, \cdots, N$$

This equation may look incomprehensible at first glance. A good way to understand it is to work through it with a numerical example, for example, when $u_t = [1, 0.7, 0.2, 0.4]$. We'll leave the details for you to go through. In the end, you should arrive at the allocation weighting being $a_t = [0, 0.024, 0.8, 0.12]$. As we go through the calculations, we'll begin to understand how this formula works: the $1 - u_t[\phi_t[j]]$ makes the location weight proportional to how free it is. By noticing that the product $\Pi_{i=1}^{j-1}u_t[\phi_t[j]]$ gets smaller and smaller as we iterate through the free list (because we keep multiplying small values between 0 and 1), we can see that this product decreases the location weight even more as we go from the least used location to the most used one, which finally results in the least used location having the largest weight, while the most used one gets the smallest weight. So we're able to guarantee the ability to focus on a single location by design without the the need to hope for the model to learn it on its own from scratch; this means more reliability as well as faster training time.

With the allocation weighting a_t and lookup weighting c_t^w we get from the content-based addressing mechanism $c_t^w = \mathscr{C}(M_{t-1}, k_t^w, \beta_t^w)$, where k_t^w, β_t^w are the lookup key and the lookup strength we receive through the interface vector, we can now construct our final write weighting:

$$ w_t^w = g_t^w \big[g_t^a a_t + (1 - g_t^a) c_t^w \big] $$

where g_t^w and g_t^a are values between 0 and 1 and are called the write and allocation gates, which we also get from the controller through the interface vector. These gates control the writing operation, with g_t^w determining if any writing is going to happen in the first place, and g_t^a specifying whether we'll write to a new location using the allocation weighting or modify an existing value specified by the lookup weighting.

DNC Memory Reuse

What if while we calculate the allocation weighting we find that all locations are used, or in other words, $u_t = 1$? This means that the allocation weightings will turn out all zeros and no new data can be allocated to memory. This raises the need for the ability to free and reuse the memory.

In order to know which locations can be freed and which cannot, we construct a *retention vector* ψ_t of size N that specifies how much of each location should be retained and not get freed. Each element of this vector takes a value between 0 and 1, with 0 indicating that the corresponding location can be freed, and 1 indicating that it should be retained. This vector is calculated using:

$$ \psi_t = \Pi_{i=1}^{R} \big(1 - f_t^i w_{t-1}^{r,i} \big) $$

This equation is basically saying that the degree to which a memory location should be freed is proportional to how much is read from it in the last time steps by the various read heads (represented by the values of the read weightings $w_{t-1}^{r,i}$). However, continuously freeing a memory location once its data is read is not generally preferable as we might still need the data afterward. We let the controller decide when to free and when to retain a location after reading by emitting a set of R free gates $f_t^1, \cdots, f_t^R$ that have a value between 0 and 1. This determines how much freeing should be done based on the fact that the location was just read from. The controller will then learn how to use these gates to achieve the behavior it desires.

Once the retention vector is obtained, we can use it to update the usage vector to reflect any freeing or retention made via:

$$\mathbf{u}_t = \left(\mathbf{u}_{t-1} + \mathbf{w}_{t-1}^w - \mathbf{u}_{t-1} \circ \mathbf{w}_{t-1}^w\right) \circ \psi_t$$

This equation can be read as follows: a location will be used if it has been retained (its value in $\psi_t \approx 1$) and either it's already in use or has just been written to (indicated by its value in $\mathbf{u}_{t-1} + \mathbf{w}_{t-1}^w$). Subtracting the element-wise product $\mathbf{u}_{t-1} \circ \mathbf{w}_{t-1}^w$ brings the whole expression back between 0 and 1 to be a valid usage value in case the addition between the previous usage got the write weighting past 1.

By doing this usage update step before calculating the allocation, we can introduce some free memory for possible new data. We're also able to use and reuse a limited amount of memory efficiently and overcome the second limitation of NTMs.

Temporal Linking of DNC Writes

With the dynamic memory management mechanisms that DNCs use, each time a memory location is requested for allocation, we're going to get the most unused location, and there'll be no positional relation between that location and the location of the previous write. With this type of memory access, NTM's way of preserving temporal relation with contiguity is not suitable. We'll need to keep an explicit record of the order of the written data.

This explicit recording is achieved in DNCs via two additional data structures alongside the memory matrix and the usage vector. The first is called a *precedence vector* $\mathbf{p}_t$, an N-sized vector considered to be a probability distribution over the memory locations, with each value indicating how likely the corresponding location was the last one written to. The precedence is initially set to $\mathbf{p}_0 = \mathbf{0}$ and gets updated in the following steps via:

$$\mathbf{p}_t = \left(1 - \Sigma_{i=1}^N \mathbf{w}_t^w[i]\right)\mathbf{p}_{t-1} + \mathbf{w}_t^w$$

Updating is done by first resetting the previous values of the precedence with a reset factor that is proportionate to how much writing was just made to the memory (indicated by the summation of the write weighting's components). Then the value of write weighting is added to the reset value so that a location with a large write weighting (that is the most recent location written to) would also get a large value in the precedence vector.

The second data structure we need to record temporal information is the *link matrix* $\mathbf{L}_t$. The link matrix is an $N \times N$ matrix in which the element $\mathbf{L}_t[i, j]$ has a value between 0,1, indicating how likely it is that location i was written after location j. This matrix is also initialized to zeros, and the diagonal elements are kept at zero throughout the time $L_t[i, i] = 0$, as it's meaningless to track if a location was written after itself when the previous data has already been overwritten and lost. However, each other element in the matrix is updated using:

$$L_t[i, j] = \left(1 - w_t^w[i] - w_t^w[j]\right)L_{t-1}[i, j] + w_t^w[i]p_{t-1}[j]$$

The equation follows the same pattern we saw with other update rules: first the link element is reset by a factor proportional to how much writing had been done on locations i, j. Then the link is updated by the correlation (represented here by multiplication) between the write weighting at location i and the previous precedence value of location j. This eliminates NTM's third limitation; now we can keep track of temporal information no matter how the write head hops around the memory.

Understanding the DNC Read Head

Once the write head has finished updating the memory matrix and the associated data structures, the read head is now ready to work. Its operation is simple: it needs to be able to look up values in the memory and be able to iterate forward and backward in temporal ordering between data. The lookup ability can simply be achieved with content-based addressing: for each read head i, we calculate an intermediate weighting $c_t^{r, i} = \mathscr{C}\left(M_t, k_t^{r, i}, \beta_t^{r, i}\right)$, where $k_t^{r, 1}, \cdots, k_t^{r, R}$ and $\beta_t^{r, 1}, \cdots, \beta_t^{r, R}$ are two sets of R read keys and strengths received from the controller in the interface vector.

To achieve forward and backward iterations, we need to make the weightings go a step ahead or back from the location they recently read from. We can achieve that for the forward iteration by multiplying the link matrix by the last read weightings. This shifts the weights from the last read location to the location of the last write specified by the link matrix and constructs an intermediate forward weighting for each read head i: $f_t^i = L_t w_{t-1}^{r, i}$. Similarly, we construct an intermediate backward weighting by multiplying the transpose of the link matrix by the last read weightings $b_t^i = L_{t-1}^\top w_{t-1}^{r, i}$.

We can now construct the new read weightings for each read using the following rule:

$$w_t^{r, i} = \pi_t^i[1]b_t^i + \pi_t^i[2]c_t^i + \pi_t^i[3]f_t^i$$

where $\pi_t^1, \cdots, \pi_t^R$ are called the *read modes*. Each of these are a softmax distribution over three elements that come from the controller on the interface vector. Its three values determine the emphasis the read head should put on each read mechanism:

---

backward, lookup, and forward, respectively. The controller learns to use these modes to instruct the memory on how data should be read.

The DNC Controller Network

Now that we've figured out the internal workings of the external memory in the DNC architecture, we're left with understanding how the controller that coordinates all the memory operations work. The controller's operation is simple: in its heart there's a neural network (recurrent or feed-forward) that takes in the input step along with the read-vectors from the last step and outputs a vector whose size depends on the architecture we chose for the network. Let's denote that vector by $N(\chi_t)$, where N denotes whatever function is computed by the neural network, and χ_t denotes the concatenation of the input step and the last read vectors $\chi_t = \left[x_t; r_{t-1}^1; \cdots; r_{t-1}^R \right]$. This concatenation of the last read vectors serves a similar purpose as the hidden state in a regular LSTM: to condition the output on the past.

From that vector emitted from the neural network, we need two pieces of information. The first one is the interface vector ζ_t. As we saw, the interface vector holds all the information for the memory to carry out its operation. We can look at the ζ_t vector as a concatenation of the individual elements we encountered before, as depicted in Figure 12-7.

$$\zeta_t = \big[\underbrace{k_t^{r,1}; \ldots; k_t^{r,R}}_{\text{each of size } W}; \overbrace{\beta_t^{r,1}; \ldots; \beta_t^{r,R}}^{\text{each of size } 1}; k_t^w; \beta_t^w; \underbrace{e_t; v_t}_{\text{size } W}; \overbrace{f_t^1; \ldots; f_t^R}^{\text{each of size } 1}; g_t^a; g_t^w; \underbrace{\pi_t^1; \ldots; \pi_t^R}_{\text{each of size } 3}\big]$$

Figure 12-7. The interface vector decomposed to its individual components

By summing up the sizes along the components, we can consider the ζ_t vector as one big vector of size $R \times W + 3W + 5R + 3$. So in order to obtain that vector from the network output, we construct a learnable $|\mathcal{N}| \times (R \times W + 3W + 5R + 3)$ weights matrix W_ζ, where $|\mathcal{N}|$ is the size of the network's output, such that:

$$\zeta_t = W_\zeta \mathcal{N}(\chi_t)$$

Before passing that ζ_t vector to the memory, we need to make sure that each component has a valid value. For example, all the gates as well as the erase vector must have values between 0 and 1, so we pass them through a sigmoid function to ensure that requirement:

$$e_t = \sigma(e_t), f_t^i = \sigma\big(f_t^i\big), g_t^a = \sigma(g_t^a), g_t^w = \sigma(g_t^w) \text{ where } \sigma(z) = \frac{1}{1 + e^{-z}}$$

Also, all the lookup strengths need to have a value larger than or equal to 1, so we pass them through a *oneplus* function first:

$$\beta_t^{r,i} = \text{oneplus}\left(\beta_t^{r,i}\right), \beta_t^{w} = \text{oneplus}\left(\beta_t^{w}\right) \text{ where } \text{oneplus}(z) = 1 + \log\left(1 + e^z\right)$$

And finally, the read modes must have a valid softmax distribution:

$$\pi_t^i = \text{softmax}\left(\pi_t^i\right) \text{ where } \text{softmax}(z) = \frac{e^z}{\sum_j e^{z_j}}$$

By these transformations, the interface vector is now ready to be passed to the memory; and while it guides the memory in its operations, we'll be needing a second piece of information from the neural network, the *pre-output* vector v_t. This is a vector of the same size of the final output vector, but it's not the final output vector. By using another learnable $|\mathcal{N}| \times Y$ weights matrix W_y, we can obtain the pre-output via:

$$v_t = W_y \mathcal{N}(\chi_t)$$

This pre-output vector gives us the ability to condition our final output not just on the network output, but also on the recently read vectors r_t from memory. Via a third learnable $(R \times W) \times Y$ weights matrix W_r, we can get the final output as:

$$y_t = v_t + W_r\left[r_t^1; \cdots; r_t^R\right]$$

Given that the controller knows nothing about the memory except for the word size W, an already learned controller can be scaled to a larger memory with more locations without any need for retraining. Also, the fact that we didn't specify any particular structure for the neural network or any particular loss function makes DNC a universal architecture that can be applied to a variety of tasks and learning problems.

Visualizing the DNC in Action

One way to see DNC's operation in action is to train it on a simple task that would allow us to look at the weightings and the parameters' values and visualize them in an interpretable way. For this simple task, we'll use the copy problem we already saw with NTMs, but in a slightly modified form.

Instead of trying to copy a single sequence of binary vectors, our task here will be to copy a series of such sequences. In Figure 12-8, (a) shows the single sequence input. After processing such single sequence input and copying the same sequence to the output, the DNC would have finished its program, and its memory would be reset in a way that will not allow us to see how it can dynamically manage it. Instead we'll treat a series of such sequences, shown in Figure 12-8 (b), as a single input.

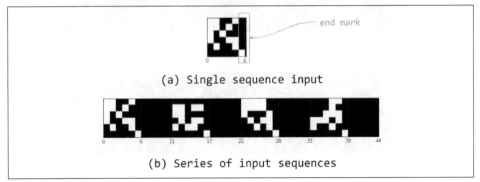

(a) Single sequence input

(b) Series of input sequences

Figure 12-8. Single sequence input versus a series of input sequences

Figure 12-9 shows a visualization of the DNC operation after being trained on a series of length 4 where each sequence contains five binary vectors and an end mark. The DNC used here has only 10 memory locations, so there's no way it can store all 20 vectors in the input. A feed-forward controller is used to ensure that nothing would be stored in a recurrent state, and only one read head is used to make the visualization more clear. These constraints should force the DNC to learn how to deallocate and reuse memory to successfully copy the whole input, and indeed it does.

We can see in that visualization how the DNC is writing each vector of the five in a sequence into a single memory location. As soon as the end mark is seen, the read head starts reading from these locations in the exact same order of writing. We can see how both the allocation and free gates alternate in activation between writing and reading phases of each sequence in the series. From the usage vector chart at the bottom, we can also see how after a memory location is written to, its usage becomes exactly 1, and how it drops to 0 just after reading from that location, indicating that it was freed and can be reused again.

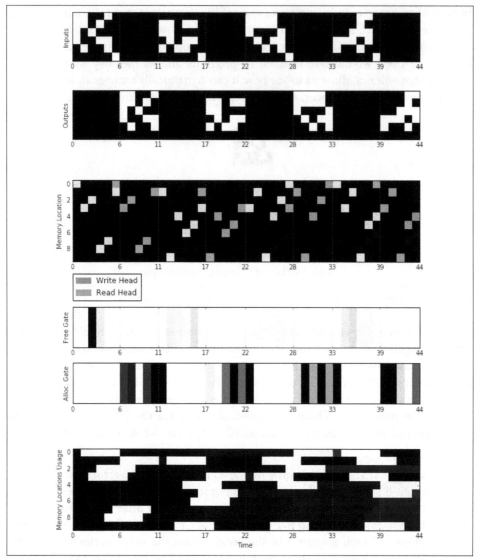

Figure 12-9. Visualization of the DNC operation on the copy problem

This visualization is part of the open source implementation of the DNC architecture by Mostafa Samir (*https://oreil.ly/TtKJ8*). In the next section we'll learn the important tips and tricks that will allow us to implement a simpler version of DNC on the reading comprehension tasks.

Implementing the DNC in PyTorch

Implementing the DNC architecture is essentially a direct application of the math we just discussed. So with the full implementation in the code repository associated with the book, we'll just be focusing on the tricky parts and introduce some new PyTorch practice while we're at it.

The main part of the implementation resides in the *mem_ops.py* file where all of the attention and access mechanisms are implemented. This file is then imported to be used with the controller. Two operations that might be a little tricky to implement are the link matrix update and the allocation weighting calculation. Both of these operations can be naively implemented with for loops, but using for loops in creating a computational graph is generally not a good idea. Let's take the link matrix update operation first and see how it looks with a loop-based implementation:

```
def Lt(L, wwt, p, N):

    L_t = torch.zeros((N,N), dtype=torch.float32)
    for i in range(N):
        for j in range(N):
            if i == j:
                continue
            mask = torch.zeros((N,N), dtype=torch.float32)
            mask[i,j] = 1.0

            link_t = (1 - wwt[i] - wwt[j]) * L[i,j] + \
                        wwt[i] * p[j]
            L_t += mask * link_t
    return L_t
```

After that computational graph is fully defined, it's then fed with concrete values and executed. With that in mind, we can see, as depicted in Figure 12-10, how in most of the iterations of the for loop, a new set of nodes representing the loop body gets added in the computational graph. So for N memory locations, we end up with $N^2 - N$ identical copies of the same nodes, each for each iteration, each taking up a chunk of our RAM and needing its own time to be processed before the next can be. When N is a small number, say 5, we get 20 identical copies, which is not so bad. However, if we want to use a larger memory, like with $N = 256$, we get 65,280 identical copies of the nodes, which is catastrophic for both the memory usage and the execution time.

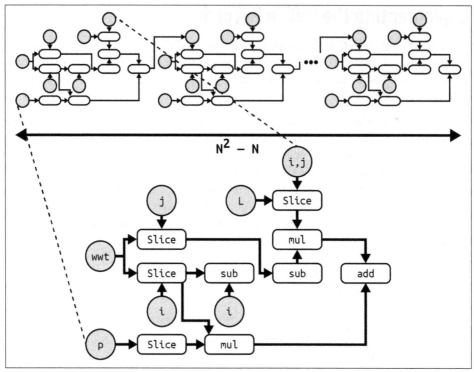

Figure 12-10. The computational graph of the link matrix update operation built with the for loop implementation

One possible way to overcome such an issue is *vectorization*. In vectorization, we take an array operation that is originally defined in terms of individual elements and rewrite it as an operation on the whole array at once. For the link matrix update, we can rewrite the operation as:

$$L_t = \left[\left(1 - w_t^w \oplus w_t^w \right) \circ L_{t-1} + w_t^w p_{t-1} \right] \circ \left(1 - I \right)$$

Where I is the identity matrix, and the product $w_t^w p_{t-1}$ is an outer product. To achieve this vectorization, we define a new operator, the pairwise-addition of vectors, denoted by $\oplus$. This new operator is simply defined as:

$$u \oplus v = \begin{pmatrix} u_1 + v_1 & \cdots & u_1 + v_n \\ \vdots & \ddots & \vdots \\ u_n + v_1 & \cdots & u_n + v_n \end{pmatrix}$$

This operator adds a little bit to the memory requirements of the implementation, but not as much as the case in the loop-based implementation. With this vectorized reformulation of the update rule, we rewrite a more memory- and time-efficient implementation:

```
def Lt(L, wwt, p, N):
    """
    returns the updated link matrix given the previous one along
    with the updated write weightings and the previous precedence
    vector
    """
    def pairwise_add(v):
        """
        returns the matrix of pairs - adding the elements of v to
        themselves
        """
        n = v.shape[0]
        # a NxN matrix of duplicates of u along the columns
        V = v.repeat(1,n)
        return V + V

    # expand dimensions of wwt and p to make matmul behave as outer
    # product
    wwt = torch.unsqueeze(wwt, 1)
    p = torch.unsqueeze(p, 0)

    I = torch.eye(N, dtype=torch.float32)
    return (((1 - pairwise_add(wwt)) * L +
            torch.matmul(wwt, p)) * (1 - I))
```

A similar process could be made for the allocation weightings rule. Instead of having a single rule for each element in the weighting vector, we can decompose it into a few operations that work on the whole vector at once:

1. While sorting the usage vector to get the free list, we also grab the sorted usage vector itself.

2. We calculate the cumulative product vector of the sorted usage. Each element of that vector is the same as the product term in our original element-wise rule.

3. We multiply the cumulative product vector by (1 – the sorted usage vector). The resulting vector is the allocation weighting but in the sorted order, not the original order of the memory location.

4. For each element of that out-of-order allocation weighting, we take its value and put it in the corresponding index in the free list. The resulting vector is now the correct allocation weighting that we want.

Figure 12-11 summarizes this process with a numerical example.

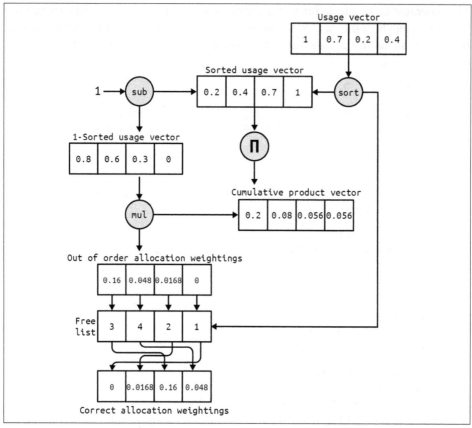

Figure 12-11. The vectorized process of calculating the allocation weightings

It may seem that we still need loops for the sorting operation in step 1 and for reordering the weights in step 4, but fortunately PyTorch provides symbolic operations that would allow us to carry out these operations without the need for a Python loop.

For sorting we'll be using `torch.topk`. This operation takes a tensor and a number k, and returns both the sorted top k values in descending order and the indices of these values. To get the sorted usage vector in ascending order, we need to get the top N values of the negative of the usage vector. We can bring back the sorted values to their original signs by multiplying the resulting vector by -1:

```
sorted_ut, free_list = torch.topk(-1*ut, N)
sorted_ut *= -1
```

For reordering the allocation weights, we first create an empty tensor array of size N to be the container of the weights in their correct order, and then put the values in their correct places using the instance method `scatter(indices, values)`. This method takes in its second argument a tensor, and scatters the values along its first dimension across the array, with the first argument being a list of indices of the locations to which we want to scatter the corresponding values. In our case here, the first argument is the free list, and the second is the out-of-order allocation weightings. Once we get the array with the weights in the correct places, we use another instance method, pack(), to wrap up the whole array into a Tensor object:

```
empty_at = torch.empty(N)
a_t = empty_at.scatter(0, free_list, out_of_location_at)
```

The last part of the implementation that requires looping is the controller loop itself —the loop that goes over each step of the input sequence to process it. Because vectorization works only when operations are defined element-wise, the controller's loop can't be vectorized. Fortunately, PyTorch still provides us with a method to escape Python's for loops and their massive performance hit; this method is the *symbolic loop*. A symbolic loop works like most of our symbolic operations: instead of unrolling the actual loop into the graph, it defines a node that would be executed as a loop when the graph is executed.

We'll leave the symbolic loop implementation in PyTorch up to the reader. More information on how you can use symbolic loops in PyTorch can be found in the torch.fx documentation (*https://oreil.ly/qtgBt*).

The TensorFlow implementation of our symbolic loop can be found in the *train_babi.py* file in the code repository.

Teaching a DNC to Read and Comprehend

Earlier in the chapter, when we were talking about neural n-grams, we said that it's not of the complexity of an AI that can answer questions after reading a story. Now we have reached the point where we can build such a system because this is exactly what DNCs do when applied on the bAbI dataset.

The bAbI dataset is a synthetic dataset consisting of 20 sets of stories, questions on those stories, and their answers. Each set represents a specific and unique task of reasoning and inference from text. In the version we'll use, each task contains 10,000 questions for training and 1,000 questions for testing. For example, the following story (from which the passage we saw earlier was adapted) is from the *lists-and-sets* task where the answers to the questions are lists/sets of objects mentioned in the story:

```
1 Mary took the milk there.
2 Mary went to the office.
3 What is Mary carrying?    milk 1
4 Mary took the apple there.
5 Sandra journeyed to the bedroom.
6 What is Mary carrying?    milk,apple 1 4
```

This is taken directly from the dataset, and as you can see, a story is organized into numbered sentences that start from 1. Each question ends with a question mark, and the words that directly follow the question mark are the answers. If an answer consists of more than one word, the words are separated by commas. The numbers that follow the answers are supervisory signals that point to the sentences that contain the answers' words.

To make the tasks more challenging, we'll discard these supervisory signals and let the system learn to read the text and figure out the answer on its own. Following the DNC paper, we'll preprocess our dataset by removing all the numbers and punctuation except for "?" and ",", bringing all the words to lowercase, and replacing the answer words with dashes "-" in the input sequence. After this we get 159 unique words and marks (lexicons) across all the tasks, so we'll encode each lexicon as a one-hot vector of size 159, no embeddings, just the plain words directly. Finally, we combine all of the 200,000 training questions to train the model jointly on them, and we keep each task's test questions separate to test the trained model afterward on each task individually. This whole process is implemented in the *preprocess.py* file in the code repository.

To train the model, we randomly sample a story from the encoded training data, pass it through the DNC with an LSTM controller, and get the corresponding output sequence. We then measure the loss between the output sequence and the desired sequence using the softmax cross-entropy loss, but only on the steps that contain answers. All the other steps are ignored by weighting the loss with a weights vector that has 1 at the answer's steps and 0 elsewhere. This process is implemented in the *train_babi.py* file.

After the model is trained, we test its performance on the remaining test questions. Our metric will be the percentage of questions the model failed to answer in each task. An answer to a question is the word with the largest softmax value in the output, or the most probable word. A question is considered to be answered correctly if all of its answer's words are the correct words. If the model failed to answer more than 5% of a task's questions, we consider that the model failed on that task. The testing procedure is found in the *test_babi.py* file.

After training the model for about 500,000 iterations (caution—it takes a long time!), we can see that it's performing pretty well on most of the tasks. At the same time, it's performing badly on more difficult tasks like *pathfinding*, where the task is to answer questions about how to get from one place to another. The following report compares our model's results to the mean values reported in the original DNC paper:

Task	Result	Paper's Mean
single supporting fact	0.00%	9.0±12.6%
two supporting facts	11.88%	39.2±20.5%
three supporting facts	27.80%	39.6±16.4%
two arg relations	1.40%	0.4±0.7%
three arg relations	1.70%	1.5±1.0%
yes no questions	0.50%	6.9±7.5%
counting	4.90%	9.8±7.0%
lists sets	2.10%	5.5±5.9%
simple negation	0.80%	7.7±8.3%
indefinite knowledge	1.70%	9.6±11.4%
basic coreference	0.10%	3.3±5.7%
conjunction	0.00%	5.0±6.3%
compound coreference	0.40%	3.1±3.6%
time reasoning	11.80%	11.0±7.5%
basic deduction	45.44%	27.2±20.1%
basic induction	56.43%	53.6±1.9%
positional reasoning	39.02%	32.4±8.0%
size reasoning	8.68%	4.2±1.8%
path finding	98.21%	64.6±37.4%
agents motivations	2.71%	0.0±0.1%
Mean Err.	15.78%	16.7±7.6%
Failed (err. > 5%)	8	11.2±5.4

Summary

In this chapter, we've explored the cutting edge of deep learning research with NTMs and DNCs, culminating with the implementation of a model that can solve an involved reading comprehension task.

In the final chapter of this book, we'll begin to explore a very different space of problems known as reinforcement learning. We'll build an intuition for this new class of tasks and develop an algorithmic foundation to tackle these problems using the deep learning tools we've developed thus far.

## CHAPTER 13

Deep Reinforcement Learning

Nicholas Locascio

In this chapter, we'll discuss reinforcement learning, which is a branch of machine learning that deals with learning via interaction and feedback. Reinforcement learning is essential to building agents that can not only perceive and interpret the world, but also take action and interact with it. We will discuss how to incorporate deep neural networks into the framework of reinforcement learning and discuss recent advances and improvements in this field.

Deep Reinforcement Learning Masters Atari Games

The application of deep neural networks to reinforcement learning had a major breakthrough in 2014, when the London startup DeepMind astonished the machine learning community by unveiling a deep neural network that could learn to play Atari games with superhuman skill. This network, termed a *deep Q-network* (DQN) was the first large-scale successful application of reinforcement learning with deep neural networks. DQN was so remarkable because the same architecture, without any changes, was capable of learning 49 different Atari games, despite each game having different rules, goals, and game-play structure. To accomplish this feat, Deep-Mind brought together many traditional ideas in reinforcement learning while also developing a few novel techniques that proved key to DQN's success. Later in this chapter, we will implement DQN, as described in the *Nature* paper, "Human-Level Control Through Deep Reinforcement Learning."[1] But first, let's take a dive into reinforcement learning (Figure 13-1).

---

1 Mnih, Volodymyr, et al. "Human-Level Control Through Deep Reinforcement Learning." *Nature* 518.7540 (2015): 529-533.

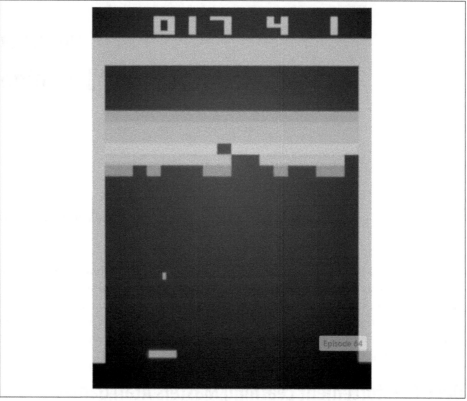

Figure 13-1. A deep reinforcement learning agent playing Breakout[2]

What Is Reinforcement Learning?

Reinforcement learning, at its essentials, is learning by interacting with an environment. This learning process involves an *agent*, an *environment*, and a *reward signal*. The agent chooses to take an action in the environment, for which the agent is rewarded accordingly. The way in which an actor chooses actions is called a *policy*. The agent wants to increase the reward it receives, and so must learn an optimal policy for interacting with the environment (Figure 13-2).

Reinforcement learning is different from the other types of learning that we have covered thus far. In traditional supervised learning, we are given data and labels, and are tasked with predicting labels given data. In unsupervised learning, we are given just data and are tasked with discovering underlying structure in this data. In

---

2 This image is from the OpenAI Gym DQN agent that we build in this chapter: Brockman, Greg, et al. "OpenAI Gym." *arXiv preprint arXiv*:1606.01540 (2016). *https://gym.openai.com*

reinforcement learning, we are given neither data nor labels. Our learning signal is derived from the rewards given to the agent by the environment.

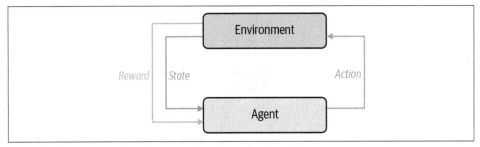

Figure 13-2. Reinforcement learning setup

Reinforcement learning is exciting to many in the AI community because it is a general-purpose framework for creating intelligent agents. Given an environment and some rewards, the agent learns to interact with that environment to maximize its total reward. This type of learning is more in line with how humans develop. Yes, we can build a pretty good model to classify dogs from cats with extremely high accuracy by training on thousands of images. But you won't find this approach used in any elementary schools. Humans interact with their environment to learn representations of the world that they can use to make decisions.

Furthermore, reinforcement learning applications are at the forefront of many cutting-edge technologies, including self-driving cars, robotic motor control, game playing, air-conditioning control, ad placement optimization, and stock market trading strategies.

As an illustrative exercise, we'll be tackling a simple reinforcement learning and control problem called pole balancing. In this problem, there is a cart with a pole that is connected by a hinge, so the pole can swing around the cart. There is an agent that can control the cart, moving it left or right. There is an environment, which rewards the agent when the pole is pointed upward, and penalizes the agent when the pole falls over (Figure 13-3).

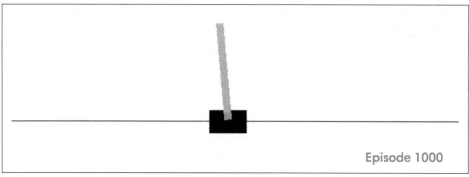

Figure 13-3. A simple reinforcement learning agent: balancing a pole[3]

Markov Decision Processes

Our pole-balancing example has a few important elements, which we formalize as a *Markov decision process* (MDP). These elements are:

State
> The cart has a range of possible places on the x-plane where it can be. Similarly, the pole has a range of possible angles.

Action
> The agent can take action by moving the cart either left or right.

State transition
> When the agent acts, the environment changes: the cart moves and the pole changes angle and velocity.

Reward
> If an agent balances the pole well, it receives a positive reward. If the pole falls, the agent receives a negative reward.

An MDP is defined as the following:

- S, a finite set of possible states
- A, a finite set of actions
- $P(r, s' \mid s, a)$, a state transition function
- R, reward function

MDPs offer a mathematical framework for modeling decision making in a given environment. Figure 13-4 shows an example, with circles representing the states of

---

3 This image is from our OpenAI Gym Policy Gradient agent that we build in this chapter.

the environment, diamonds representing actions that can be taken, and the edges from diamonds to circles representing the transition from one state to the next. The numbers along these edges represent the probability of taking a certain action, and the numbers at the end of the arrows represent the reward given to the agent for making the given transition.

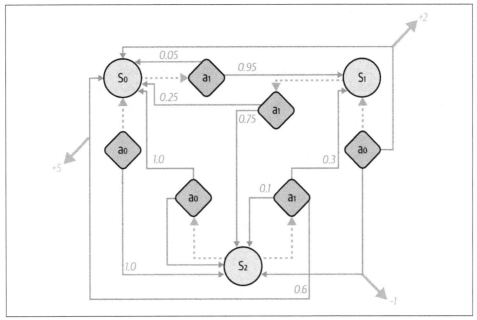

Figure 13-4. Example of an MDP

As an agent takes action in an MDP framework, it forms an *episode*. An episode consists of series of tuples of states, actions, and rewards. Episodes run until the environment reaches a terminal state, like the "Game Over" screen in Atari games, or when the pole hits the ground in our pole-cart example. The following equation shows the variables in an episode:

$$(s_0, a_0, r_0), (s_1, a_1, r_1), ...(s_n, a_n, r_n)$$

In pole-cart, our environment state can be a tuple of the position of the cart and the angle of the pole, like so: $(x_{cart}, \theta_{pole})$.

Policy

MDP's aim is to find an optimal policy for our agent. *Policies* are how our agent acts based on its current state. Formally, policies can be represented as a function π that chooses the action a that the agent will take in state s.

The objective of our MDP is to find a policy to maximize the expected future return:

$$\max_\pi \ E[R_0 + R_1 + \ ... \ R_t | \pi]$$

In this objective, R represents the *future return* of each episode. Let's define exactly what future return means.

Future Return

Future return is how we consider the rewards of the future. Choosing the best action requires consideration of not only the immediate effects of that action, but also the long-term consequences. Sometimes the best action actually has a negative immediate effect, but a better long-term result. For example, a mountain-climbing agent that is rewarded by its altitude may actually have to climb downhill to reach a better path to the mountain's peak.

Therefore, we want our agents to optimize for *future return*. To do that, the agent must consider the future consequences of its actions. For example, in a game of Pong, the agent receives a reward when the ball passes into the opponent's goal. However, the actions responsible for this reward (the inputs that position the racquet to strike a scoring hit) happen many time steps before the reward is received. The reward for each of those actions is delayed.

We can incorporate delayed rewards into our overall reward signal by constructing a *return* for each time step that takes into account future rewards as well as immediate rewards. A naive approach for calculating *future return* for a time step may be a simple sum like so:

$$R_t = \Sigma_{k\,=\,0}^{T} r_{t+k}$$

We can calculate all returns, R, where $R = \{R_0, R_1, ...R_i, ...R_n\}$, with the following code:

```
def calculate_naive_returns(rewards):
""" Calculates a list of naive returns given a
    list of rewards."""
    total_returns = np.zeros(len(rewards))
    total_return = 0.0
    for t in range(len(rewards), 0):
        total_return = total_return + reward
        total_returns[t] = total_return
    return total_returns
```

This naive approach successfully incorporates future rewards so the agent can learn an optimal global policy. This approach values future rewards equally to immediate rewards. However, this equal consideration of all rewards is problematic. With infinite time steps, this expression can diverge to infinity, so we must find a way to bind it. Furthermore, with equal consideration at each time step, the agent can optimize for a future reward, and we would learn a policy that lacks any sense of urgency or time sensitivity in pursuing its rewards.

Instead, we should value future rewards slightly less in order to force our agents to learn to get rewards quickly. We accomplish this with a strategy called *discounted future return*.

Discounted Future Return

To implement discounted future return, we scale the reward of a current state by the discount factor, γ, to the power of the current time step. In this way, we penalize agents that take many actions before receiving positive reward. Discounted rewards bias our agent to prefer receiving the reward in the immediate future, which is advantageous to learning a good policy. We can express the reward as follows:

$$R_t = \Sigma_{k=0}^{T} \gamma^t r_{t+k+1}$$

The discount factor, γ, represents the level of discounting we want to achieve, and can be between 0 and 1. High γ means little discounting, low γ provides much discounting. A typical γ hyperparameter setting is between 0.99 and 0.97.

We can implement discounted return like so:

```
def discount_rewards(rewards, gamma=0.98):
    discounted_returns = [0 for _ in rewards]
    discounted_returns[-1] = rewards[-1]
    for t in range(len(rewards)-2, -1, -1): # iterate backwards
        discounted_returns[t] = rewards[t] +
            discounted_returns[t+1]*gamma
    return discounted_returns
```

Explore Versus Exploit

Reinforcement learning is fundamentally a trial-and-error process. In such a framework, an agent afraid to make mistakes can prove to be highly problematic. Consider the following scenario. A mouse is placed in the maze shown in Figure 13-5. Our agent must control the mouse to maximize reward. If the mouse gets the water, it receives a reward of +1; if the mouse reaches a poison container (red), it receives a reward of -10; if the mouse gets the cheese, it receives a reward of +100. Upon receiving reward, the episode is over. The optimal policy involves the mouse successfully navigating to the cheese and eating it.

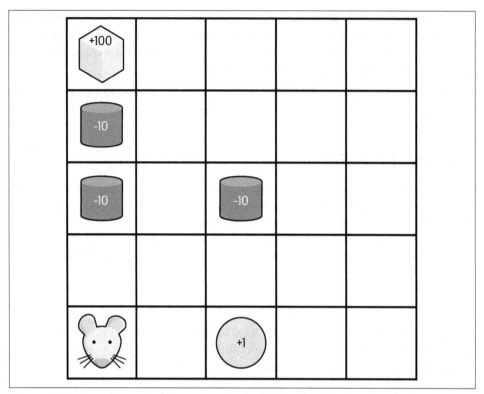

Figure 13-5. A predicament that many mice find themselves in

In the first episode, the mouse takes the left route, steps on a trap, and receives a -10 reward. In the second episode, the mouse avoids the left path, since it resulted in such a negative reward, and drinks the water immediately to its right for a +1 reward. After two episodes, it would seem that the mouse has found a good policy. It continues to follow its learned policy on subsequent episodes and achieves the moderate +1 reward reliably. Since our agent utilizes a greedy strategy—always choosing the model's best action—it is stuck in a policy that is a *local maximum*.

To prevent such a situation, it may be useful for the agent to deviate from the model's recommendation and take a suboptimal action in order to *explore* more of the environment. So instead of taking the immediate right turn to *exploit* the environment to get water and the reliable +1 reward, our agent may choose to take a left turn and venture into more treacherous areas in search of a more optimal policy. Too much exploration, and our agent fails to optimize any reward. Not enough exploration can result in our agent getting stuck in a local minimum. This balance of *explore versus exploit* is crucial to learning a successful policy.

ϵ-Greedy

One strategy for balancing the explore-exploit dilemma is called ϵ-*greedy*. ϵ-greedy is a simple strategy that involves making a choice at each step to either take the agent's top recommended action or take a random action. The probability that the agent takes a random action is the value known as ϵ.

We can implement ϵ-greedy like so:

```python
def epsilon_greedy_action(action_distribution,
                          epsilon=1e-1):
    action_distribution = action_distribution.detach().numpy()
    if random.random() < epsilon:
        return np.argmax(np.random.random(
            action_distribution.shape))
    else:
        return np.argmax(action_distribution)
```

Annealed ϵ-Greedy

When training a reinforcement learning model, oftentimes we want to do more exploring in the beginning since our model knows little of the world. Later, once our model has seen much of the environment and learned a good policy, we want our agent to trust itself more to further optimize its policy. To accomplish this, we cast aside the idea of a fixed ϵ, and instead anneal it over time, having it start low and increase by a factor after each training episode. Typical settings for annealed ϵ-greedy scenarios include annealing from 0.99 to 0.1 over 10,000 scenarios. We can implement annealing like so:

```python
def epsilon_greedy_action_annealed(action_distribution,
                                   percentage,
                                   epsilon_start=1.0,
                                   epsilon_end=1e-2):
    action_distribution = action_distribution.detach().numpy()
    annealed_epsilon = (epsilon_start*(1.0-percentage) +
                        epsilon_end*percentage)
    if random.random() < annealed_epsilon:
        return np.argmax(np.random.random(
            action_distribution.shape))
    else:
        return np.argmax(action_distribution)
```

Policy Versus Value Learning

So far we've defined the setup of reinforcement learning, discussed discounted future return, and looked at the trade-offs of explore versus exploit. What we haven't talked about is how we're actually going to teach an agent to maximize its reward. Approaches to this fall into two broad categories: *policy learning* and *value learning*. In policy learning, we are directly learning a policy that maximizes reward. In value learning, we are learning the value of every state + action pair. If you were trying to learn to ride a bike, a policy learning approach would be to think about how pushing on the right pedal while you were falling to the left would course-correct you. If you were trying to learn to ride a bike with a value learning approach, you would assign a score to different bike orientations and actions you can take in those positions. We'll be covering both in this chapter, so let's start with policy learning.

In typical supervised learning, we can use stochastic gradient descent to update our parameters to minimize the loss computed from our network's output and the true label. We are optimizing the expression:

$$\arg\ \min_\theta \Sigma_i \log p(y_i \mid x_i; \theta)$$

In reinforcement learning, we don't have a true label, only reward signals. However, we can still use SGD to optimize our weights using something called *policy gradients*.[4] We can use the actions the agent takes, and the returns associated with those actions, to encourage our model weights to take good actions that lead to high reward, and to avoid bad ones that lead to low reward. The expression we optimize for is:

$$\arg\ \min_\theta \ - \Sigma_i R_i \log p(y_i \mid x_i; \theta)$$

where y_i is the action taken by the agent at time step t and where R_i is our discounted future return. A In this way, we scale our loss by the value of our return, so if the model chose an action that led to negative return, this would lead to greater loss. Furthermore, if the model is confident in that bad decision, it would get penalized even more, since we are taking into account the log probability of the model choosing that action. With our loss function defined, we can apply SGD to minimize our loss and learn a good policy.

---

4 Sutton, Richard S., et al. "Policy Gradient Methods for Reinforcement Learning with Function Approximation." NIPS. Vol. 99. 1999.

Pole-Cart with Policy Gradients

We're going to implement a policy-gradient agent to solve pole-cart, a classic reinforcement learning problem. We will be using an environment from the OpenAI Gym created just for this task.

OpenAI Gym

The OpenAI Gym is a Python toolkit for developing reinforcement agents. OpenAI Gym provides an easy-to-use interface for interacting with a variety of environments. It contains over one hundred open source implementations of common reinforcement learning environments. OpenAI Gym speeds up development of reinforcement learning agents by handling everything on the environment simulation side, allowing researchers to focus on their agent and learning algorithms. Another benefit of OpenAI Gym is that researchers can fairly compare and evaluate their results with others because they can all use the same standardized environment for a task. We'll be using the pole-cart environment from OpenAI Gym to create an agent that can easily interact with this environment.

Creating an Agent

To create an agent that can interact with an OpenAI environment, we'll define a class PGAgent, which will contain our model architecture, model weights, and hyperparameters:

```
from torch import optim
class PGAgent(object):
    def __init__(self, state_size, num_actions,
                 hidden_size,
                 learning_rate=1e-3,
                 explore_exploit_setting= \
                 'epsilon_greedy_annealed_1.0->0.001'):
        self.state_size = state_size
        self.num_actions = num_actions
        self.hidden_size = hidden_size
        self.learning_rate = learning_rate
        self.explore_exploit_setting = \
                      explore_exploit_setting
        self.build_model()


    def build_model(self):
      self.model = torch.nn.Sequential(
        nn.Linear(self.state_size, self.hidden_size),
        nn.Linear(self.hidden_size, self.hidden_size),
        nn.Linear(self.hidden_size, self.num_actions),
        nn.Softmax(dim=0))
```

```python
    def train(self, state, action_input, reward_input):
        state = torch.tensor(state).float()
        action_input = torch.tensor(action_input).long()
        reward_input = torch.tensor(reward_input).float()
        self.output = self.model(state)
        # Select the logits related to the action taken
        logits_for_actions = self.output.gather(1,
                                           action_input.view(-1,1))

        self.loss = -torch.mean(
            torch.log(logits_for_actions) * reward_input)
        self.loss.backward()
        self.optimizer = optim.Adam(self.model.parameters())
        self.optimizer.step()
        self.optimizer.zero_grad()
        return self.loss.item()



    def sample_action_from_distribution(self,
                                        action_distribution,
                                        epsilon_percentage):
        # Choose an action based on the action probability
        # distribution and an explore vs exploit
        if self.explore_exploit_setting == 'greedy':
            action = epsilon_greedy_action(action_distribution,
                                           0.00)
        elif self.explore_exploit_setting == 'epsilon_greedy_0.05':
            action = epsilon_greedy_action(action_distribution,
                                           0.05)
        elif self.explore_exploit_setting == 'epsilon_greedy_0.25':
            action = epsilon_greedy_action(action_distribution,
                                           0.25)
        elif self.explore_exploit_setting == 'epsilon_greedy_0.50':
            action = epsilon_greedy_action(action_distribution,
                                           0.50)
        elif self.explore_exploit_setting == 'epsilon_greedy_0.90':
            action = epsilon_greedy_action(action_distribution,
                                           0.90)
        elif self.explore_exploit_setting == \
          'epsilon_greedy_annealed_1.0->0.001':
            action = epsilon_greedy_action_annealed(
                action_distribution,
                epsilon_percentage, 1.0,0.001)
        elif self.explore_exploit_setting == \
          'epsilon_greedy_annealed_0.5->0.001':
            action = epsilon_greedy_action_annealed(
                action_distribution,
                epsilon_percentage, 0.5, 0.001)
        elif self.explore_exploit_setting == \
          'epsilon_greedy_annealed_0.25->0.001':
            action = epsilon_greedy_action_annealed(
```

```
                        action_distribution,
                        epsilon_percentage, 0.25, 0.001)
            return action

    def predict_action(self, state, epsilon_percentage):
        action_distribution = self.model(
                              torch.from_numpy(state).float())
        action = self.sample_action_from_distribution(
            action_distribution, epsilon_percentage)
        return action
```

Building the Model and Optimizer

Let's break down some important functions. In `build_model()`, we define our model architecture as a three-layer neural network. The model returns a layer of three nodes, each representing the model's action probability distribution. In `build_train ing()`, we implement our policy gradient optimizer. We express our objective loss as we talked about, scaling the model's prediction probability for an action with the return received for taking that action, and summing these all up to form a minibatch. With our objective defined, we can use `torch.optim.AdamOptimizer`, which will adjust our weights according to the gradient to minimize our loss.

Sampling Actions

We define the `predict_action` function, which samples an action based on the model's action probability distribution output. We support the various sampling strategies that we talked about to balance explore versus exploit, including greedy, ϵ greedy, and ϵ greedy annealing.

Keeping Track of History

We'll be aggregating our gradients from multiple episode runs, so it will be useful to keep track of state, action, and reward tuples. To this end, we implement an episode history and memory:

```
class EpisodeHistory(object):

    def __init__(self):
        self.states = []
        self.actions = []
        self.rewards = []
        self.state_primes = []
        self.discounted_returns = []

    def add_to_history(self, state, action, reward,
      state_prime):
        self.states.append(state)
        self.actions.append(action)
```

```
        self.rewards.append(reward)
        self.state_primes.append(state_prime)


class Memory(object):

    def __init__(self):
        self.states = []
        self.actions = []
        self.rewards = []
        self.state_primes = []
        self.discounted_returns = []

    def reset_memory(self):
        self.states = []
        self.actions = []
        self.rewards = []
        self.state_primes = []
        self.discounted_returns = []

    def add_episode(self, episode):
        self.states += episode.states
        self.actions += episode.actions
        self.rewards += episode.rewards
        self.discounted_returns += episode.discounted_returns
```

Policy Gradient Main Function

Let's put this all together in our main function, which will create an OpenAI Gym environment for CartPole, make an instance of our agent, and have our agent interact with and train on the CartPole environment:

```
# Configure Settings
#total_episodes = 5000
total_episodes = 16
total_steps_max = 10000
epsilon_stop = 3000
train_frequency = 8
max_episode_length = 500
render_start = -1
should_render = False

explore_exploit_setting = 'epsilon_greedy_annealed_1.0->0.001'

env = gym.make('CartPole-v0')
state_size = env.observation_space.shape[0]   # 4 for
                                              # CartPole-v0
num_actions = env.action_space.n  # 2 for CartPole-v0

solved = False
agent = PGAgent(state_size=state_size,
            num_actions=num_actions,
```

```
                hidden_size=16,
                explore_exploit_setting= \
                  explore_exploit_setting)


episode_rewards = []
batch_losses = []

global_memory = Memory()
steps = 0
for i in range(total_episodes):
  state = env.reset()
  episode_reward = 0.0
  episode_history = EpisodeHistory()
  epsilon_percentage = float(min(i/float(epsilon_stop), 1.0))

  for j in range(max_episode_length):
      action = agent.predict_action(state, epsilon_percentage)
      state_prime, reward, terminal, _ = env.step(action)

      episode_history.add_to_history(
          state, action, reward, state_prime)
      state = state_prime
      episode_reward += reward
      steps += 1

      if j == (max_episode_length - 1):
          terminal = True

      if terminal:
          episode_history.discounted_returns = \
            discount_rewards(episode_history.rewards)
          global_memory.add_episode(episode_history)

          # every 8th episode train the NN
          # train on all actions from episodes in memory,
          # then reset memory
          if np.mod(i, train_frequency) == 0:
            reward_input = global_memory.discounted_returns
            action_input = global_memory.actions
            state = global_memory.states

            # train step
            batch_loss = agent.train(state, action_input,
                                     reward_input)
              # print(f'Batch loss: {batch_loss}')
              # batch_losses.append(batch_loss)
            global_memory.reset_memory()

          episode_rewards.append(episode_reward)

          if i % 10 == 0:
```

```
        mean_rewards = torch.mean(torch.tensor(
                                    episode_rewards[:-10]))
        if mean_rewards > 10.0:
            solved = True
        else:
            solved = False
        print(f'Solved: {solved} Mean Reward: {mean_rewards}')
    break # stop playing if terminal

print(f'Episode[{i}]: {len(episode_history.actions)} \
    actions {episode_reward} reward')
```

This code will train a CartPole agent to successfully and consistently balance the pole.

PGAgent Performance on Pole-Cart

Figure 13-6 is a chart of the average reward of our agent at each step of training. We try out 8 different sampling methods, and achieve best results with ε greedy annealing from 1.0 to 0.001.

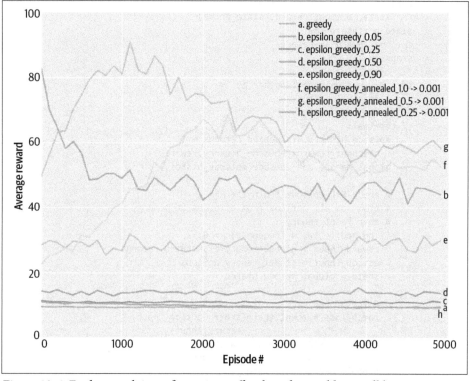

Figure 13-6. Explore-exploit configurations affect how fast and how well learning occurs

Notice how, across the board, standard ϵ greedy does very poorly. Let's talk about why this might be. With a high ϵ set to 0.9, we are taking a random action 90% of the time. Even if the model learns to execute the perfect actions, we'll still be using these only 10% of the time. On the other end, with a low ϵ of 0.05, we are taking what our model believes to be optimal actions the vast majority of the time. This performance is a bit better, but gets stuck in a local reward minimum because it lacks the ability to explore other strategies. So neither ϵ greedy of 0.05 nor 0.9 gives us great results. The former places too much emphasis on exploration, and the latter, too little. This is why ϵ annealing is such a powerful sampling strategy. It allows the model to explore early and exploit late, which is crucial to learning good policies.

Trust-Region Policy Optimization

Trust-region policy optimization, or *TRPO* for short, is a framework that ensures policy improvement while preventing the policy from shifting too much during each training step. TRPO has been empirically shown to outperform many of its fellow policy gradient and policy iteration methods, allowing researchers to effectively learn complex, nonlinear policies (often parametrized by large neural networks) that weren't previously possible through gradient-based methods. In this section, we will motivate TRPO and describe its objective in more detail.

The idea of preventing the policy from shifting too much during each training step is not a new one—most regularized optimization procedures do this indirectly by penalizing the norm of the parameters, for example, globally ensuring the norm of the parameters doesn't get too high. Of course, in cases where regularized optimization can also be formulated as constrained optimization (where there are explicit bounds on the norm of the parameter vector), such as L2-regularized linear regression, we have a direct equivalence to the idea of preventing the policy from shifting too much during each training step. The per-step change in the norm of the parameters is bounded by the range of the constraint, since all possible parameter values must fall in this range. For those interested, I would recommend looking further into the equivalence between Tikhonov and Ivanov regularization in linear regression.

Preventing the policy from shifting too much during each training step has the standard effect of regularized optimization: it promotes stability in training, which is ideal in preventing overfitting to new data. How do we define a shift in the policy? Policies are simply discrete probability distributions over the action space given a state, $\pi_\theta(a \mid s)$, for which we can use notions of dissimilarity, introduced in Chapter 2. The original TRPO paper introduced a bound on the average KL divergence (over all possible states) between the current policy and the new policy.

Now that we've introduced the constraint portion of TRPO's constrained optimization, we will motivate and define the objective function.

Let's recap and introduce some terminology:

$$\eta(\pi) = \mathbb{E}_{s_0, a_0, s_1, a_1, \dots}\left[\Sigma_{t=0}^{\infty}\gamma^t r(s_t)\right]$$

$$Q_\pi(s_t, a_t) = \mathbb{E}_{s_{t+1}, a_{t+1}, \dots}\left[\Sigma_{l=0}^{\infty}\gamma^l r(s_{t+l})\right]$$

$$V_\pi(s_t) = \mathbb{E}_{a_t, s_{t+1}, a_{t+1}\dots}\left[\Sigma_{l=0}^{\infty}\gamma^l r(s_{t+l})\right]$$

$$A_\pi(s, a) = Q_\pi(s, a) - V_\pi(s)$$

$$\rho_\pi(s) = \Sigma_{i=0}^{\infty}\gamma^i P(s_t = s)$$

The first term is $\eta(\pi)$, which represents the *expected discounted reward*. We saw the finite-time horizon version of the term inside the expectation earlier when we discussed future discounted reward. Instead of looking at a single trajectory here, we take the expectation over all possible trajectories as defined by our policy π. As usual, we can estimate this expectation via an empirical average by sampling trajectories using π. The second term, which will be discussed in more detail in "Q-Learning and Deep Q-Networks" on page 347, is the *Q-function* $Q_\pi(s_t, a_t)$, which looks very similar to the previous term but is instead defined as the expected discounted return from time t, given we are in some state s_t and perform a defined action a_t in that state. We again calculate the expectation using our policy π. Note that the time t doesn't actually matter all too much since we only consider an infinite time horizon and the expected discounted return from t rather than from the beginning of the trajectory.

The third term is $V_\pi(s_t)$, or the *value function* at a particular state at time t. The value function can actually be more concisely written as $V_\pi(s_t) = \mathbb{E}_{a_t}[Q_\pi(s_t, a_t)]$, or the expectation of the Q-function with respect to $\pi(a_t | s_t)$. In essence, the Q-function supposes that we take a defined action a_t in state s_t, while the value function leaves a_t as a variable. Thus, to get the value function, all we need to do is take the expectation of the Q-function with respect to the distribution over a_t knowing the current state s_t. The result is the weighted average of the Q-function, where the weights are $\pi(a_t | s_t)$. In essence, this term captures the average future discounted return we'd expect to see starting in some state s_t.

The fourth term is $A_\pi(s, a)$, or the *advantage function*. Note that we have dropped the time t by now for the reasons mentioned earlier. The intuition for the advantage function is that it quantifies, under a fixed policy π, the benefit of letting trajectories play out after taking a particular action a in the current state s, over simply letting trajectories play out from the current state s completely unconstrained. Even more concisely, it defines how much better, or worse, in the long run it is to initially take action a in state s compared to the average.

The final term, or the *unnormalized discounted visitation frequency*, reintroduces the time term t. This term is a function of the probability of being in state s at each time t from the start to infinity. This term will be important in our definition of the objective function. The original TRPO paper chose to optimize the model parameters by maximizing this objective function:

$$L_{\theta_{old}}(\theta) = \Sigma_s \rho_{\theta_{old}}(s) \Sigma_a \pi_\theta(a \mid s) A_{\theta_{old}}(s, a)$$

$$\theta_{new} = \text{argmax}_\theta L_{\theta_{old}}(\theta)$$

Although we won't fully show the derivation behind this objective as it is quite mathematically involved and beyond the scope of this text, we provide some intuition. Let's first examine this term: $\Sigma_a \pi_\theta(a \mid s) A_{\theta_{old}}(s, a)$, assuming a fixed state s. For the sake of argument, let's replace θ with θ_{old} as our proposed policy's parameters, which also represents our current policy's parameters:

$$\Sigma_a \pi_{\theta_{old}}(a \mid s) A_{\pi_{\theta_{old}}}(s, a) = \mathbb{E}_{a \sim \pi_{\theta_{old}}(a \mid s)} \left[A_{\pi_{\theta_{old}}}(s, a) \right]$$

$$= \mathbb{E}_{a \sim \pi_{\theta_{old}}(a \mid s)} \left[Q_{\pi_{\theta_{old}}}(s, a) \right] - \mathbb{E}_{a \sim \pi_{\theta_{old}}(a \mid s)} \left[V_{\pi_{\theta_{old}}}(s) \right]$$

$$= \mathbb{E}_{a \sim \pi_{\theta_{old}}(a \mid s)} \left[Q_{\pi_{\theta_{old}}}(s, a) \right] - V_{\pi_{\theta_{old}}}(s)$$

$$= V_{\pi_{\theta_{old}}}(s) - V_{\pi_{\theta_{old}}}(s)$$

$$= 0$$

What have we shown here? Earlier, we talked about how $A_{\pi_{\theta_{old}}}(s, a)$ defines how much better or worse it is, under the current policy, to take action a in state s compared to what we expect to see starting from state s unconstrained. Here, we showed that if we average each of these advantages weighted by the current policy's distribution, we are left with zero average advantage over the current policy—this makes a lot of intuitive sense, since the proposed policy and the current policy are the exact same. We don't expect to see any performance gain by replacing the current policy with itself.

Now, if we replace θ with a different proposed policy's parameters θ_{alt}, the above derivation leads us to:

$$\mathbb{E}_{a \sim \pi_{\theta_{alt}}(a \mid s)} \left[Q_{\pi_{\theta_{old}}}(s, a) \right] - V_{\pi_{\theta_{old}}}(s)$$

This is as far as simplification will take us, since the actions in the first term are no longer distributed as the current policy and we can't make the simplification that led us to the penultimate step. If we evaluate this expression and we receive a positive result, we can interpret the result as representing a positive average advantage from following the proposed policy compared to following the current policy, directly translating to a performance gain for this specific state s by replacing the current policy with the proposed policy.

 Note that we have only been considering a specific state s. But even if we see a performance gain for some state, it might be the case that that state only rarely shows up. This leads us to the inclusion of the term $\Sigma_s \rho_{\theta_{old}}(s)$, which quantifies how often we see a given state. We can actually rewrite this as an expectation even though this is an unnormalized distribution—all we'd need to do is factor out the normalizing constant, which is also a constant from the perspective of θ since the normalizing constant is solely a function of θ_{old}.

Keep in mind that $\Sigma_s \rho_{\theta_{old}}(s)$ is evaluated using the current policy rather than the proposed policy; this is because, as noted in the paper, the complex dependency this introduces on θ when optimizing the alternative objective (which uses $\Sigma_s \rho_\theta(s)$) with respect to θ makes the optimization process difficult. Additionally, the paper proves that the first-order gradient matches that of the alternative objective anyway, allowing us to make this substitution without introducing a biased gradient estimate. We won't show this here, however, as it is beyond the scope of the text.

Putting everything together, we have the following constrained optimization objective:

$$\theta^* = \text{argmax}_\theta \Sigma_s \rho_{\theta_{old}}(s) \Sigma_a \pi_\theta(a \mid s) A_{\theta_{old}}(s, a)$$

$$s.t.\, \text{Avg. KL}(\theta_{old}, \theta) \leq \delta$$

where the average KL divergence denotes the expected KL divergence between policies over all states. This is what we call the *trust region,* and it represents the parameter settings that lie close enough to the current parameter setting, mitigate training instability, and mitigate overfitting. How do we go about optimizing this objective? The inner summation looks like an expectation with respect to $\pi_\theta(a, s)$, but all we have is our current setting of parameter values θ_{old}. In the standard setting, or *on-policy* setting, we are sampling from the same policy we are optimizing, so we can use classic policy gradient optimization for this. However, TRPO can be modified to work in the *off-policy* setting as well, where the policy we are sampling from is different from the policy we are optimizing. Generally, the reason for this distinction is that we may have a behavior policy, the policy we are sampling from that may be more exploratory in nature, while we learn the target policy, which is to be optimized. In the off-policy setting, since we are sampling actions from a different distribution $q(a|s)$ (the behavior policy) from $\pi_\theta(a|s)$ (the target policy), we instead use the following constrained optimization objective:

$$\theta^* = \operatorname{argmax}_\theta \Sigma_s \rho_{\theta_{old}}(s) \Sigma_a \frac{\pi_\theta(a|s)}{q(a|s)} A_{\theta_{old}}(s, a)$$

$$s.t.\, \text{Avg. KL}(\theta_{old}, \theta) \le \delta$$

The addition of $q(a|s)$ accounts for the fact that we are sampling from a separate behavior policy. We can think about this more concretely in terms of expectations:

$$\Sigma_a \pi_\theta(a|s) A_{\theta_{old}}(s, a) = \Sigma_a \frac{q(a|s)}{q(a|s)} \pi_\theta(a|s) A_{\theta_{old}}(s, a)$$

$$= \Sigma_a q(a|s) \frac{\pi_\theta(a|s)}{q(a|s)} A_{\theta_{old}}(s, a)$$

$$= \mathbb{E}_{q(a|s)} \left[\frac{\pi_\theta(a|s)}{q(a|s)} A_{\theta_{old}}(s, a) \right]$$

Note that the left side of the first equality can be written as an expectation of the advantage with respect to the target policy. In a few algebraic manipulations, we were able to convert our original objective into an equivalent objective, but with an expectation that is taken with respect to the behavior policy. This is ideal because we are sampling from the behavior policy and can thus use standard minibatch gradient descent techniques to optimize this objective (adding in the constraint on the KL divergence makes this a bit more complicated than just standard gradient descent). And finally, we have already seen methods for sampling from the unnormalized probability distribution $\rho_{old}(s)$ for the outer expectation, amongst others that exist in academic literature.

Proximal Policy Optimization

One issue with TRPO is that its optimization is relatively complicated due to the inclusion of the average KL divergence term and involves second-order optimization to perform. *Proximal policy optimization*, or *PPO* for short, is an algorithm that tries to retain the benefits of TRPO without the complicated optimization. PPO proposes the following objective instead:

$$J(\theta) = \mathbb{E} \left[\min \left(\frac{\pi_\theta(a|s)}{\pi_{\theta_{old}}(a|s)} A_{\theta_{old}}(s, a), \text{clip}\left(\frac{\pi_\theta(a|s)}{\pi_{\theta_{old}}(a|s)}, 1 - \epsilon, 1 + \epsilon \right) A_{\theta_{old}}(s, a) \right) \right]$$

$$\theta^* = \text{argmax}_\theta J(\theta)$$

Note that we no longer have a complex constraint, but rather an extra term built into the optimization objective. The clip function represents an upper limit and a lower limit on the ratio between the target policy and the behavior policy, where any ratio above or below these limits is set equal to the corresponding limit. Note the inclusion of the minimum between the original and the clipped, which prevents us from making extreme updates and keeps us from overfitting.

As stated in the paper introducing PPO, it's important to notice that the objective for TRPO and PPO have the same gradient at $\theta = \theta_{old}$. This is the case in at least the on-policy setting, where we have a single policy from which we are sampling and optimizing (i.e., no distinction between the behavior and target policy). Let's take a closer look at why this is the case. To do this, we first need to reformulate TRPO's constrained optimization objective as an equivalent regularized optimization objective (recall from early in the previous section), which we can do according to the theory. The objective looks like:

$$J^{TRPO}(\theta) = \mathbb{E}\left[\frac{\pi_\theta(a\,|\,s)}{\pi_{\theta_{old}}(a\,|\,s)} A(s, a) - \beta * \text{KL}(\pi_{\theta_{old}}(a\,|\,s)\,||\,\pi_\theta(a\,|\,s))\right]$$

Notice that we can separate the expression within the expectation into a difference of expectations due to the linearity of expectation. If we first consider the second expectation, or the KL term, we'll notice that this term is minimized at $\theta = \theta_{old}$, since the reference distribution is parametrized using θ_{old}. Thus, the gradient at this setting is zero, since we have already reached the global minimum. We are left with only the gradient of the first expectation:

$$\nabla_\theta \mathbb{E}\left[\frac{\pi_\theta(a\,|\,s)}{\pi_{\theta_{old}}(a\,|\,s)} A(s, a)\right]$$

Looking to the objective for PPO, we notice that at $\theta = \theta_{old}$, the ratio between the two policies is one, eliminating the need for the clip term. Thus, we are left with a minimum over two equivalent terms, which simplifies to the expectation over a single term. The gradient comes out to exactly what we just saw for the TRPO objective:

$$\nabla_\theta \mathbb{E}\left[\frac{\pi_\theta(a\,|\,s)}{\pi_{\theta_{old}}(a\,|\,s)} A(s, a)\right]$$

We have shown that PPO has the same gradient as TRPO in the select on-policy setting, and is additionally much easier to optimize in practice. PPO has also shown strong empirical results on a variety of tasks, and has become widely used in the field of deep RL.

Q-Learning and Deep Q-Networks

Q-learning is in the category of reinforcement learning called value learning. Instead of directly learning a policy, we will be learning the value of states and actions. Q-learning involves learning a function, a *Q-function*, which represents the quality of a state, action pair. The Q-function, defined *Q(s, a)*, is a function that calculates the maximum discounted future return when action *a* is performed in state *s*.

The Q-value represents our expected long-term rewards, given we are at a state, and take an action, and then take every subsequent action perfectly (to maximize expected future reward). This can be expressed formally as:

$$Q^*(s_t, a_t) = max_\pi E\left[\Sigma_{i=t}^{T} \gamma^i r^i\right]$$

A question you may be asking is, how can we know Q-values? It is difficult, even for humans, to know how good an action is, because you need to know how you are going to act in the future. Our expected future returns depend on what our long-term strategy is going to be. This seems to be a bit of a chicken-and-egg problem. In order to value a state, action pair, you need to know all the perfect subsequent actions. And in order to know the best actions, you need to have accurate values for a state and action.

The Bellman Equation

We solve this dilemma by defining our Q-values as a function of future Q-values. This relation is called the *Bellman equation*, and it states that the maximum future reward for taking action is the current reward plus the next step's *max* future reward from taking the next action *a'*:

$$Q^*(s_t, a_t) = E\left[r_t + \gamma \max_{a'} Q^*(s_{t+1}, a')\right]$$

This recursive definition allows us to relate between Q-values.

And since we can now relate between Q-values past and future, this equation conveniently defines an update rule. Namely, we can update past Q-values to be based on future Q-values. This is powerful because there exists a Q-value we know is correct: the Q-value of the very last action before the episode is over. For this last state, we know exactly that the next action led to the next reward, so we can perfectly set the Q-values for that state. We can use the update rule, then, to propagate that Q-value to the previous time step:

$$\widehat{Q_j} \rightarrow \widehat{Q_{j+1}} \rightarrow \widehat{Q_{j+2}} \rightarrow ... \rightarrow Q^*$$

This updating of the Q-value is known as *value iteration.*

Our first Q-value starts out completely wrong, but this is perfectly acceptable. With each iteration, we can update our Q-value via the correct one from the future. After one iteration, the last Q-value is accurate, since it is just the reward from the last state and action before episode termination. Then we perform our Q-value update, which sets the second-to-last Q-value. In our next iteration, we can guarantee that the last two Q-values are correct, and so on and so forth. Through value iteration, we will be guaranteed convergence on the ultimate optimal Q-value.

Issues with Value Iteration

Value iteration produces a mapping between state and action pairs with corresponding Q-values, and we are constructing a table of these mappings, or a *Q-table.* Let's briefly talk about the size of this Q-table. Value iteration is an exhaustive process that requires a full traversal of the entire space of state, action pairs. In a game like Breakout, with 100 bricks that can be either present or not, with 50 positions for the paddle to be in, and 250 positions for the ball to be in, and 3 actions, we have already constructed a space that is far, far larger than the sum of all computational capacity of humanity. Furthermore, in stochastic environments, the space of our Q-table would be even larger, and possibly infinite. With such a large space, it will be intractable for us to find all of the Q-values for every state, action pair. Clearly this approach is not going to work. How else are we going to do Q-learning?

Approximating the Q-Function

The size of our Q-table makes the naive approach intractable for any nontoy problem. However, what if we relax our requirement for an optimal Q-function? If instead, we learn approximations of the Q-function, we can use a model to estimate our Q-function. Instead of having to experience every state, action pair to update our Q-table, we can learn a function that approximates this table, and even generalizes outside of its own experience. This means we won't have to perform an exhaustive search through all possible Q-values to learn a Q-function.

Deep Q-Network

This was the main motivation behind DeepMind's work on deep Q-network (DQN). DQN uses a deep neural network that takes an image (the state) in to estimate the Q-value for all possible actions.

Training DQN

We would like to train our network to approximate the Q-function. We express this Q-function approximation as a function of our model's parameters, like this:

$$\widehat{Q_\theta}(s, a \mid \theta) \sim Q^*(s, a)$$

Remember, Q-learning is a value-learning algorithm. We are not learning a policy directly, but rather we are learning the values of each state, action pair, regardless if they are good or not. We have expressed our model's Q-function approximation as Qtheta, and we would like this to be close to the future expected reward. Using the Bellman equation from earlier, we can express this future expected reward as:

$$R_t^* = \left(r_t + \gamma \max_{a'} \widehat{Q}(s_{t+1}, a' \mid \theta) \right)$$

Our objective is to minimize the difference between our Q's approximation, and the next Q value:

$$\min_\theta \Sigma_{e \in E} \Sigma_{t=0}^T \widehat{Q}(s_t, a_t \mid \theta) - R_t^*$$

Expanding this expression gives us our full objective:

$$\min_\theta \Sigma_{e \in E} \Sigma_{t=0}^T \widehat{Q}(s_t, a_t \mid \theta) - \left(r_t + \gamma \max_{a'} \widehat{Q}(s_{t+1}, a' \mid \theta) \right)$$

This objective is fully differentiable as a function of our model parameters, and we can find gradients to use in stochastic gradient descent to minimize this loss.

Learning Stability

One issue you may have noticed is that we are defining our loss function based on the difference of our model's predicted Q-value of this step and the predicted Q-value of the next step. In this way, our loss is doubly dependent on our model parameters. With each parameter update, the Q-values are constantly shifting, and we are using shifting Q-values to do further updates. This high correlation of updates can lead to feedback loops and instability in our learning, where our parameters may oscillate and make the loss diverge.

We can employ a couple of simple engineering hacks to remedy this correlation problem: namely, target Q-network and experience replay.

Target Q-Network

Instead of updating a single network frequently with respect to itself, we can reduce this codependence by introducing a second network, called the *target network*. Our loss function features to instances of the Q-function, $\widehat{Q}(s_t, a_t | \theta)$ and $\widehat{Q}(s_{t+1}, a' | \theta)$. We are going to have the first Q be represented as our prediction network, and our second Q will be produced by the target Q-network. The target Q-network is a copy of our prediction network that lags in its parameter updates. We update the target Q-network to equal the prediction network only every few batches. This provides much needed stability to our Q-values, and we can now properly learn a good Q-function.

Experience Replay

There is yet another source of irksome instability to our learning: the high correlations of recent experiences. If we train our DQN with batches drawn from recent experience, these action, state pairs are all going to be related to one another. This is harmful because we want our batch gradients to be representative of the entire gradient, and if our data is not representative of the data distribution, our batch gradient will not be an accurate estimate of the true gradient.

So, we have to break up this correlation of data in our batches. We can do this using something called *experience replay*. In experience replay, we store all of the agent's experiences as a table, and to construct a batch, we randomly sample from these experiences. We store these experiences in a table as (s_i, a_i, r_i, s_{i+1}) tuples. From these four values, we can compute our loss function, and thus our gradient to optimize our network.

This experience replay table is more of a queue than a table. The experiences an agent sees early in training may not be representative of the experiences a trained agent finds itself in later, so it is useful to remove old experiences from our table.

From Q-Function to Policy

Q-learning is a value learning paradigm, not a policy learning algorithm. This means we are not directly learning a policy for acting in our environment. But can't we construct a policy from what our Q-function tells us? If we have learned a good Q-function approximation, this means we know the value of every action for every state. We could then trivially construct an optimal policy in the following way: look at our Q-function for all actions in our current state, choose the action with the max Q-value, enter a new state, and repeat. If our Q-function is optimal, our policy derived from it will be optimal. With this in mind, we can express the optimal policy as follows:

$$\pi(s; \theta) = \text{arg max}_{a'} \widehat{Q^*}(s, a'; \theta)$$

We can also use the sampling techniques we discussed earlier to make a stochastic policy that sometime deviates from the Q-function recommendations to vary the amount of exploration our agent does.

DQN and the Markov Assumption

DQN is still a Markov decision process that relies on the *Markov assumption*, which assumes that the next state s_{i+1} depends only on the current state s_i and action a_i, and not on any previous states or actions. This assumption doesn't hold true for many environments where the game's state cannot be summed up in a single frame. For example, in Pong, the ball's velocity (an important factor in successful game play) is not captured in any single game frame. The Markov assumption makes modeling decision processes much simpler and reliable, but often at a loss of modeling power.

DQN's Solution to the Markov Assumption

DQN solves this problem by utilizing *state history*. Instead of processing one game frame as the game's state, DQN considers the past four game frames as the game's current state. This allows DQN to utilize time-dependent information. This is a bit of an engineering hack, and we will discuss better ways of dealing with sequences of states at the end of this chapter.

Playing Breakout with DQN

Let's pull all of what we learned together and actually go about implementing DQN to play Breakout. We start out by defining our DQNAgent:

```
# DQNAgent

class DQNAgent(object):

    def __init__(self, num_actions,
                 learning_rate=1e-3, history_length=4,
                 screen_height=84, screen_width=84,
                 gamma=0.99):
        self.num_actions = num_actions
        self.learning_rate = learning_rate
        self.history_length = history_length
        self.screen_height = screen_height
        self.screen_width = screen_width
        self.gamma = gamma

        self.build_prediction_network()
        self.build_target_network()
        #self.build_training()
```

```python
def build_prediction_network(self):
    self.model_predict = nn.Sequential(
      nn.Conv2d(4, 32, kernel_size=8 , stride=4),
      nn.Conv2d(32, 64, kernel_size=4, stride=2),
      nn.Conv2d(64, 64, kernel_size=3, stride=1),
      nn.Flatten(),
      nn.Linear(3136, 512),
      nn.Linear(512, self.num_actions)
      )

def build_target_network(self):
    self.model_target = nn.Sequential(
      nn.Conv2d(4, 32, kernel_size=8 , stride=4),
      nn.Conv2d(32, 64, kernel_size=4, stride=2),
      nn.Conv2d(64, 64, kernel_size=3, stride=1),
      nn.Flatten(),
      nn.Linear(3136, 512),
      nn.Linear(512, self.num_actions)
      )

def sample_and_train_pred(self, replay_table, batch_size):

    s_t, action, reward, s_t_plus_1, terminal = \
            replay_table.sample_batch(batch_size)

    # given state_t, find q_t (predict_model) and
    #   q_t+1 (target_model)
    # do it in batches
    # Find q_t_plus_1
    input_t = torch.from_numpy(s_t_plus_1).float()
    model_t = self.model_target.float()
    q_t_plus_1 = model_t(input_t)

    terminal = torch.tensor(terminal).float()
    max_q_t_plus_1, _ = torch.max(q_t_plus_1, dim=1)
    reward = torch.from_numpy(reward).float()
    target_q_t = (1. - terminal) * self.gamma * \
            max_q_t_plus_1 + reward

    # Find q_t, and q_of_action
    input_p = torch.from_numpy(s_t).float()
    model_p = self.model_predict.float()
    q_t = model_p(input_p)
    action = torch.from_numpy(action)
    action_one_hot = nn.functional.one_hot(action,
                                    self.num_actions)
    q_of_action = torch.sum(q_t * action_one_hot)

    # Compute loss
    self.delta = (target_q_t - q_of_action)
    self.loss = torch.mean(self.delta)
```

```python
        # Update predict_model gradients (only)
        self.optimizer = optim.Adam(self.model_predict.parameters(),
                                    lr = self.learning_rate)
        self.loss.backward()
        self.optimizer.step()

        return q_t

    def predict_action(self, state, epsilon_percentage):
        input_p = torch.from_numpy(state).float().unsqueeze(dim=0)
        model_p = self.model_predict.float()
        action_distribution = model_p(input_p)
        # sample from action distribution
        action = epsilon_greedy_action_annealed(
                                    action_distribution.detach(),
                                    epsilon_percentage)
        return action

    def process_state_into_stacked_frames(self,
                                          frame,
                                          past_frames,
                                          past_state=None):
        full_state = np.zeros((self.history_length,
                               self.screen_width,
                               self.screen_height))

        if past_state is not None:
            for i in range(len(past_state)-1):
                full_state[i, :, :] = past_state[i+1, :, :]
            full_state[-1, :, :] = self.preprocess_frame(frame,
                                            (self.screen_width,
                                             self.screen_height)
                                            )
        else:
            all_frames = past_frames + [frame]
            for i, frame_f in enumerate(all_frames):
                full_state[i, :, :] = self.preprocess_frame(frame_f,
                                            (self.screen_width,
                                             self.screen_height)
                                            )
        return full_state

    def to_grayscale(self, x):
        return np.dot(x[...,:3], [0.299, 0.587, 0.114])

    def preprocess_frame(self, im, shape):
        cropped = im[16:201,:] # (185, 160, 3)
        grayscaled = self.to_grayscale(cropped) # (185, 160)
        # resize to (84,84)
        resized = np.array(Image.fromarray(grayscaled).resize(shape))
        mean, std = 40.45, 64.15
```

```
frame = (resized-mean)/std
return frame
```

There is a lot going on in this class, so let's break it down in the following sections.

Building Our Architecture

We build our two Q-networks: the prediction network and the target Q-network. Notice how they have the same architecture definition, since they are the same network, with the target Q just having delayed parameter updates. Since we are learning to play Breakout from pure pixel input, our game state is an array of pixels. We pass this image through three convolution layers, and then two fully connected layers to produce our Q-values for each of our potential actions.

Stacking Frames

You may notice that our state input is actually of size [None, self.history_length, self.screen_height, self.screen_width]. Remember, in order to model and capture time-dependent state variables like speed, DQN uses not just one image, but a group of consecutive images, also known as a *history*. Each of these consecutive images is treated as a separate channel. We construct these stacked frames with the helper function process_state_into_stacked_frames(self, frame, past_frames, past_state=None).

Setting Up Training Operations

Our loss function is derived from our objective expression from earlier in this chapter:

$$\min_\theta \Sigma_{e \in E} \Sigma_{t=0}^{T} \widehat{Q}(s_t, a_t | \theta) - \left(r_t + \gamma \max_{a'} \widehat{Q}(s_{t+1}, a' | \theta) \right)$$

We want our prediction network to equal our target network, plus the return at the current time step. We can express this in pure PyTorch code as the difference between the output of our prediction network and the output of our target network. We use this gradient to update and train our prediction network, using AdamOptimizer.

Updating Our Target Q-Network

To ensure a stable learning environment, we update our target Q-network only once every four batches. Our update rule for the target Q-network is pretty simple: we just set its weights equal to the prediction network. We do this in the function update_target_q_network(self). The optimizer_predict.step() function sets the target Q-network's weights equal to those of the prediction network.

Implementing Experience Replay

We've discussed how experience replay can help de-correlate our gradient batch updates to improve the quality of our Q-learning and subsequent derived policy. Let's walk though a simple implementation of experience replay. We expose a method `add_episode(self, episode)`, which takes an entire episode (an `EpisodeHistory` object) and adds it to the ExperienceReplayTable. It then checks if the table is full and removes the oldest experiences from the table.

When it comes time to sample from this table, we can call `sample_batch(self, batch_size)` to randomly construct a batch from our table of experiences:

```python
class ExperienceReplayTable(object):

    def __init__(self, table_size=50000):
        self.states = []
        self.actions = []
        self.rewards = []
        self.state_primes = []
        self.terminals = []

        self.table_size = table_size

    def add_episode(self, episode):
        self.states += episode.states
        self.actions += episode.actions
        self.rewards += episode.rewards
        self.state_primes += episode.state_primes
        self.terminals += episode.terminals

        self.purge_old_experiences()

    def purge_old_experiences(self):
        while len(self.states) > self.table_size:
            self.states.pop(0)
            self.actions.pop(0)
            self.rewards.pop(0)
            self.state_primes.pop(0)

    def sample_batch(self, batch_size):
        s_t, action, reward, s_t_plus_1, terminal = [], [], [],
                                                     [], []
        rands = np.arange(len(self.states))
        np.random.shuffle(rands)
        rands = rands[:batch_size]

        for r_i in rands:
            s_t.append(self.states[r_i])
            action.append(self.actions[r_i])
            reward.append(self.rewards[r_i])
            s_t_plus_1.append(self.state_primes[r_i])
```

```
        terminal.append(self.terminals[r_i])
    return (np.array(s_t), np.array(action), np.array(reward),
        np.array(s_t_plus_1), np.array(terminal))
```

DQN Main Loop

Let's put this all together in our main function, which will create an OpenAI Gym environment for Breakout, make an instance of our DQNAgent, and have our agent interact with and train to play Breakout successfully:

```
learn_start = 4
total_episodes = 32
epsilon_stop = 32
train_frequency = 2
target_frequency = 4
batch_size = 4
max_episode_length = 1000
env = gym.make('Breakout-v4')
num_actions = env.action_space.n
solved = False

agent = DQNAgent(num_actions=num_actions,
                 learning_rate=1e-4,
                 history_length=4,
                 gamma=0.98)


episode_rewards = []
q_t_list = []
batch_losses = []
past_frames_last_time = None

replay_table = ExperienceReplayTable()
global_step_counter = 0

for i in range(total_episodes):
    # Get initial frame -> state
    frame = env.reset() # np.array of shape (210, 160, 3)
    # past_frames is a list of past 3 frames (np.arrays)
    past_frames = [copy.deepcopy(frame) for _ in range(
                                        agent.history_length-1)]
    state = agent.process_state_into_stacked_frames(
        frame, past_frames, past_state=None) # state is (4,84,84)

    # initialize episode history (s_t, a, r, s_t+1, terminal)
    episode_reward = 0.0
    episode_history = EpisodeHistory()
    epsilon_percentage = float(min(i/float(epsilon_stop), 1.0))

    for j in range(max_episode_length):
        # predict action or choose random action at first
        if global_step_counter < learn_start:
```

```
      action = np.argmax(np.random.random((agent.num_actions)))
    else:
      action = agent.predict_action(state, epsilon_percentage)

    # take action, get next frame (-> next state), reward,
    # and terminal
    reward = 0
    frame_prime, reward, terminal, _ = env.step(action)
    if terminal == True:
      reward -= 1

    # get next state from next frame and past frames
    state_prime = agent.process_state_into_stacked_frames(
                                        frame_prime,
                                        past_frames,
                                        past_state=state)
    # Update past_frames with frame_prime for next time
    past_frames.append(frame_prime)
    past_frames = past_frames[len(past_frames)- \
                      agent.history_length:]
    past_frames_last_time = past_frames

    # Add to episode history (state, action, reward,
    #  state_prime, terminal)
    episode_history.add_to_history(
            state, action, reward, state_prime, terminal)
    state = state_prime
    episode_reward += reward
    global_step_counter += 1

    #  Do not train predict_model until we have enough
    #   episodes in episode history
    if global_step_counter > learn_start:
      if global_step_counter % train_frequency == 0:
        if(len(replay_table.actions) != 0):
          q_t = agent.sample_and_train_pred(replay_table,
                                          batch_size)

          q_t_list.append(q_t)

          if global_step_counter % target_frequency == 0:
            agent.model_target.load_state_dict(
                agent.model_predict.state_dict())

    # If terminal or max episodes reached,
    #   add episode_history to replay table
    if j == (max_episode_length - 1):
        terminal = True

    if terminal:
        replay_table.add_episode(episode_history)
        episode_rewards.append(episode_reward)
        break
```

```
print(f'Episode[{i}]: {len(episode_history.actions)} \
        actions {episode_reward} reward')
```

DQNAgent Results on Breakout

We train our DQNAgent for one thousand episodes to see the learning curve. To obtain superhuman results on Atari, typical training time runs up to several days. However, we can see a general upward trend in reward pretty quickly, as shown in Figure 13-7.

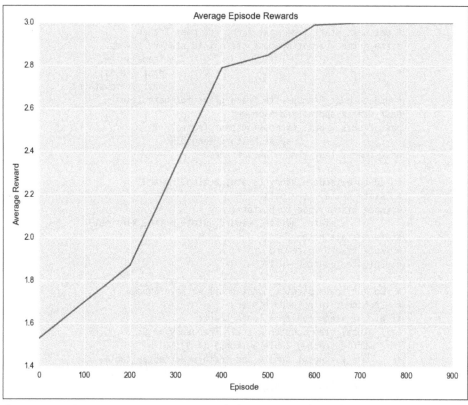

Figure 13-7. Our DQNAgent gets increasingly better at Breakout during training as it learns a good value function and also acts less stochastically due to ε-greedy annealing

Improving and Moving Beyond DQN

DQN did a pretty good job back in 2013 in solving Atari tasks, but had some serious shortcomings. DQN's many weaknesses include that it takes very long to train, doesn't work well on certain types of games, and requires retraining for every new game. Much of the deep reinforcement learning research of the past few years has been in addressing these various weaknesses.

Deep Recurrent Q-Networks

Remember the Markov assumption? The one that states that the next state relies only on the previous state and the action taken by the agent? DQN's solution to the Markov assumption problem, stacking four consecutive frames as separate channels, sidesteps this issue and is a bit of an ad hoc engineering hack. Why 4 frames and not 10? This imposed frames history hyperparameter limits the model's generality. How do we deal with arbitrary sequences of related data? That's right: we can use what we learned back in Chapter 8 on RNNs to model sequences with *deep recurrent Q-networks* (DRQNs).

DRQN uses a recurrent layer to transfer a latent knowledge of state from one time step to the next. In this way, the model itself can learn how many frames are informative to include in its state and can even learn to throw away noninformative ones or remember things from long ago.

DRQN has even been extended to include neural attention mechanism, as shown in Sorokin et al.'s 2015 paper, "Deep Attention Recurrent Q-Network" (DAQRN).[5] Since DRQN is dealing with sequences of data, it can attend to certain parts of the sequence. This ability to attend to certain parts of the image both improves performance and provides model interpretability by producing a rationale for the action taken.

DRQN has shown to be better than DQN at playing first-person shooter (FPS) games like DOOM (*https://oreil.ly/KKZC7*), as well as improving performance on certain Atari games with long time dependencies, like Seaquest (*https://oreil.ly/uevTS*).

Asynchronous Advantage Actor-Critic Agent

Asynchronous advantage actor-critic (A3C) is a new approach to deep reinforcement learning introduced in the 2016 DeepMind paper, "Asynchronous Methods for Deep Reinforcement Learning."[6] Let's discuss what it is and why it improves upon DQN.

A3C is *asynchronous*, which means we can parallelize our agent across many threads, which means orders of magnitude faster training by speeding up our environment simulation. A3C runs many environments at once to gather experiences. Beyond the speed increase, this approach presents another significant advantage in that it further decorrelates the experiences in our batches, because the batch is being filled with the experiences of numerous agents in different scenarios simultaneously.

---

5 Sorokin, Ivan, et al. "Deep Attention Recurrent Q-Network." *arXiv preprint arXiv*:1512.01693 (2015).

6 Mnih, Volodymyr, et al. "Asynchronous Methods for Deep Reinforcement Learning." *International Conference on Machine Learning*. 2016.

A3C uses an *actor-critic* method.[7] Actor-critic methods involve learning both a value function $V(s_t)$ (the critic) and also a policy $\pi(s_t)$ (the actor). Early in this chapter, we delineated two different approaches to reinforcement learning: value learning and policy learning. A3C combines the strengths of each, using the critic's value function to improve the actor's policy.

A3C uses an *advantage* function instead of a pure discounted future return. When doing policy learning, we want to penalize the agent when it chooses an action that leads to a bad reward. A3C aims to achieve this same goal, but uses advantage instead of reward as its criterion. Advantage represents the difference between the model's prediction of the quality of the action taken versus the actual quality of the action taken. We can express advantage as:

$$A_t = Q^*(s_t, a_t) - V(s_t).$$

A3C has a value function, V(t), but it does not express a Q-function. Instead, A3C estimates the advantage by using the discounted future reward as an approximation for the Q-function:

$$A_t = R_t - V(s_t)$$

These three techniques proved key to A3C's takeover of most deep reinforcement learning benchmarks. A3C agents can learn to play Atari Breakout in less than 12 hours, whereas DQN agents may take 3 to 4 days.

UNsupervised REinforcement and Auxiliary Learning

UNREAL is an improvement on A3C introduced in "Reinforcement learning with unsupervised auxiliary tasks" by Jaderberg et al.,[8] who, you guessed it, are from DeepMind.

UNREAL addresses the problem of reward sparsity. Reinforcement learning is so difficult because our agent just receives rewards, and it is hard to determine exactly why rewards increase or decrease, which makes learning difficult. Additionally, in reinforcement learning, we must learn a good representation of the world as well as a good policy to achieve reward. Doing all of this with a weak learning signal like sparse rewards is quite a tall order.

---

7 Konda, Vijay R., and John N. Tsitsiklis. "Actor-Critic Algorithms." *NIPS*. Vol. 13. 1999.

8 Jaderberg, Max, et al. "Reinforcement Learning with Unsupervised Auxiliary Tasks." *arXiv preprint arXiv*:1611.05397 (2016).

UNREAL asks the question, what can we learn from the world without rewards? It aims to learn a useful world representation in an unsupervised matter. Specifically, UNREAL adds some additional unsupervised auxiliary tasks to its overall objective.

The first task involves the UNREAL agent learning about how its actions affect the environment. The agent is tasked with controlling pixel values on the screen by taking actions. To produce a set of pixel values in the next frame, the agent must take a specific action in this frame. In this way, the agent learns how its actions affect the world around it, enabling it to learn a representation of the world that takes into account its own actions.

The second task involves the UNREAL agent learning *reward prediction*. Given a sequence of states, the agent is tasked with predicting the value of the next reward received. The intuition behind this is that if an agent can predict the next reward, it probably has a pretty good model of the future state of the environment, which will be useful when constructing a policy.

As a result of these unsupervised auxiliary tasks, UNREAL is able to learn around 10 times faster than A3C in the Labyrynth game environment. UNREAL highlights the importance of learning good world representations and how unsupervised learning can aid in weak learning signal or low-resource learning problems like reinforcement learning.

Summary

In this chapter, we covered the fundamentals of reinforcement learning, including MDPs, maximum discounted future rewards, and explore versus exploit. We also covered various approaches to deep reinforcement learning, including policy gradients and deep Q-networks, and touched on some recent improvements on DQN and new developments in deep reinforcement learning.

Reinforcement learning is essential to building agents that can not only perceive and interpret the world, but also take action and interact with it. Deep reinforcement learning has made major advancements toward this goal, successfully producing agents capable of mastering Atari games, safely driving automobiles, trading stocks profitably, controlling robots, and more.

Index

broadcasting, 81
Broyden–Fletcher–Goldfarb–Shanno (BFGS) algorithm, 110
bucketing, 231
build_vocab_from_iterator function, 220

C

CBOW (Continuous Bag of Words model), 179
cell bodies, 46
Central Limit Theorem (CLT), 34
characteristic polynomial, 14
CIFAR-10 challenge, 141
classification, 20
classifiers, 20
closed under scalar multiplication and closed under addition, 9
CLT (Central Limit Theorem), 34
code, 160
code examples, obtaining and using, x
column space, 7-10
column vector, 6
column vector interpretation of matrix multiplication, 4
comments and questions, xi
complement, 18
Compose transform, 137
compressive embeddings, 160, 175
computer programs, 40
conda package management system, 77
conditional probability, 20-21
conjugate gradient descent, 109
consistency, 293
content-based addressing, 303
Continuous Bag of Words (CBOW) model, 179
continuous probability distributions, 32-36
convolutional filters, 152
convolutional neural networks (CNNs)
    applying to other domains, 154
    batch normalization, 137-139
    CIFAR-10 challenge, 141
    convolutional filters, 152
    feature selection, 118-120
    filters and feature maps, 122-127
    full architectural description of, 132-133
    full description of, 127-131
    group normalization, 139
    image preprocessing pipelines, 136
    inception of, 120
    max pooling, 131

MNIST classifier using, 134-135
    neurons in human vision, 117
    residual learning and skip connections, 147-149
    residual networks with superhuman vision, 149-152
    scaling problems, 121
    space required for, 133
    visualizing learning in, 143-146
convolutions, 124
copy.deepcopy method, 99
covariance, 27
critical point, 102
cross entropy, 31, 36
cross-entropy loss metric, 86

D

DAQRN (Deep Attention Recurrent Q-Network), 359
data matrix, 74
data structures and operations
    matrix arrays, 1
    matrix operations, 3-6
    matrix-vector multiplication, 7
    vector operations, 6
DataLoader class (PyTorch), 88-89, 221
Dataset class (PyTorch), 87-89
dataset normalization, 136
decision trees, 276-280
decoders, 161, 224, 251
Deep Attention Recurrent Q-Network (DAQRN), 359
deep learning
    approach to learning, x
    approach to problem solving, 68
    core concepts of, 1
    definition of term, 39
    prerequisites to learning, ix
    stateful deep learning models, 206
    success of, 45
deep Q-networks (DQNs) (see also Q-learning)
    building architecture, 354
    DQNAgent results on Breakout, 358
    experience replay, 350
    from Q-function to policy, 350
    implementing experience replay, 355
    learning stability, 349
    main loop, 356
    Markov assumption and, 351

neural networks (see also memory augmented
    neural networks)
    artificially intelligent machines, 39
    feed-forward neural networks, 48-51, 55-73,
        189
    linear neurons, 51
    linear perceptrons expressed as neurons, 47
    machine learning, 41-45
    neurons, 45-47
    scaling problems, 121
    sigmoid, tanh, and ReLU neurons, 51-52
    softmax output layers, 54
    traditional computer programs, 40
neural style algorithm, 152
neural translation networks, 230-239
Neural Turing Machines (NTMs)
    attention-based memory access, 301-303
    basics of, 299-301
    memory addressing mechanisms, 303-306
neurons
    artificial, 46
    biological, 45
    in human vision, 117
    linear neurons, 51
    linear perceptrons expressed as, 47
    sigmoid, tanh, and ReLU neurons, 51-52
nn module (PyTorch), 84-87, 134
nn.BCELoss, 262
noise-contrastive estimation (NCE), 180
nonidentifiability, 97
normalization
    batch normalization, 137-139
    dataset normalization, 136
    global normalization, 205
    group normalization, 139
    local normalization, 205
Normalize transform, 136
NTM (see Neural Turing Machines)
null space, 10-13
num_features argument, 138

O

off-policy setting, 344
on-policy setting, 344
one-hot vector representations, 178
oneplus function, 314
OpenAI Gym, 335
optimization
    critical challenges to, 104-106

definition of term, 44
learning rate adaptation, 111-115
momentum-based, 106-109
philosophy behind optimizer selection, 115
primary challenge in, 96
second-order methods, 109
opt_state_dict, 99
orthogonality, 6
out_channels argument, 131
overfitting
    preventing, 71-73
    problem of, 65-71

P

pack() method, 321
padding, 231
padding argument, 131
parameter vectors, 55
parameters() function, 86
Parsey McParseface, 202
part-of-speech (POS) tags
    implementing taggers, 192-196
    producing with neural n-grams, 190
partial dependence plots (PDPs), 282
partition function, 267
pathfinding, 322
PCA (see principal component analysis)
PDPs (partial dependence plots), 282
perceptrons
    definition of term, 43
    expressing linear as neurons, 47
permutation feature importance, 281
PGAgent class, 335
pole-cart problem
    agent creation, 335
    history, 337
    model and optimizer, 337
    OpenAI Gym, 335
    PGAgent performance, 340
    policy gradient main function, 338
    sampling actions, 337
policy, 326
policy gradients, 334
policy learning, 334
policy optimization
    proximal policy optimization, 345
    trust-region policy optimization , 341-345
population risk, 75
posterior, 18

(see also deep reinforcement learning)
RMSProp optimizer, 112
rotational invariance, 187
row vector, 6

S

About the Authors

Nithin Buduma is one of the first machine learning engineers at XY.ai, a startup based out of Harvard and Stanford working to help healthcare companies leverage their massive datasets.

Nikhil Buduma is the cofounder and chief scientist of Remedy, a San Francisco-based company that is building a new system for data-driven primary healthcare. At the age of 16, he managed a drug discovery laboratory at San Jose State University and developed novel low-cost screening methodologies for resource-constrained communities. By the age of 19, he was a two-time gold medalist at the International Biology Olympiad. He later attended MIT, where he focused on developing large-scale data systems to impact healthcare delivery, mental health, and medical research. At MIT, he cofounded Lean On Me, a national nonprofit organization that provides an anonymous text hotline to enable effective peer support on college campuses, and leverages data to effect positive mental health and wellness outcomes. Today, Nikhil spends his free time investing in hard technology and data companies through his venture fund, Q Venture Partners, and managing a data analytics team for the Milwaukee Brewers baseball team.

Joe Papa is the author of the *PyTorch Pocket Reference* (O'Reilly) and founder of PyTorch Academy and TeachMe.AI. He has over 25 years of experience in research and development and currently leads AI projects as Chief AI Engineer at Mobile Insights. He holds an MSEE and has led AI research teams with PyTorch at Booz Allen Hamilton and Perspecta Labs. Joe has mentored hundreds of data scientists and has taught more than 7,000 students across the world on Udemy, Packt, and O'Reilly Learning.

Colophon

The animal on the cover of *Fundamentals of Deep Learning* is a North Pacific crestfish (*Lophotus capellei*), also known as the unicornfish. It's part of the Lophotidae family and lives in the deep waters of the Atlantic and Pacific oceans. Because of their seclusion from researchers, little is known about this fish. Some have been caught, however, that are six feet in length.

Many of the animals on O'Reilly covers are endangered; all of them are important to the world. To learn more about how you can help, go to *animals.oreilly.com*.

The cover image is by Karen Montgomery, based on a black and white engraving from *Lydekker's Royal Natural History*. The cover fonts are Gilroy Semibold and Guardian Sans. The text font is Adobe Minion Pro; the heading font is Adobe Myriad Condensed; and the code font is Dalton Maag's Ubuntu Mono.

O'REILLY®

Learn from experts.
Become one yourself.

Books | Live online courses
Instant Answers | Virtual events
Videos | Interactive learning

Get started at oreilly.com.